UNESCO COLLECTION OF REPRESENTATIVE WORKS—JAPANESE SERIES

D0878446

JAPANESE STORIES

An Anthology

EDITED BY Ivan Morris

WITH TRANSLATIONS BY
Edward Seidensticker
George Saitō
Geoffrey Sargent
Ivan Morris

AND WOODCUTS BY
Masakazu Kuwata

CHARLES E. TUTTLE COMPANY
Rutland, Vermont — Tokyo, Japan

To. A.M.

Published by the Charles E. Tuttle Company, Inc.
of Rutland, Vermont and Tokyo, Japan
with editorial offices at
Suido 1-chome, 2-6, Bunkyo-ku, Tokyo

Copyright in Japan, 1962, by Charles E. Tuttle Co., Inc.
All Rights Reserved

Library of Congress Catalog Card No. 61-11971
International Standard Book No. 0-8048-1226-8

First edition, 1962
Twenty-first printing, 1992

Printed in Japan

TABLE OF CONTENTS

Introduction : 9

MORI ŌGAI : Under Reconstruction : 35

TOKUDA SHŪSEI : Order of the White Paulownia : 45

NAGAI KAFŪ : Hydrangea : 65

SHIGA NAOYA : Seibei's Gourds : 81

TANIZAKI JUNICHIRŌ : Tattoo : 90

KIKUCHI KAN : On the Conduct of Lord Tadanao : 101

SATOMI TON : The Camellia : 138

MURŌ SAISEI : Brother and Sister : 144

SATŌ HARUO : The House of a Spanish Dog : 162

AKUTAGAWA RYŪNOSUKÉ : "Autumn Mountain" : 173

OGAWA MIMEI : The Handstand : 185

HAYAMA YOSHIKI : Letter Found in a Cement-Barrel : 204

IBUSÉ MASUJI : The Charcoal Bus : 211

YOKOMITSU RIICHI : Machine : 223

KAWABATA YASUNARI : The Moon on the Water : 245

ITŌ EINOSUKÉ : Nightingale : 258

NAGAI TATSUO : Morning Mist : 302

NIWA FUMIO : The Hateful Age : 320

5

HAYASHI FUMIKO : Downtown : 349

HIRABAYASHI TAIKO : A Man's Life : 365

SAKAGUCHI ANGO : The Idiot : 383

INOUÉ YASUSHI : Shotgun : 416

NAKAJIMA TON : Tiger-Poet : 452

DAZAI OSAMU : The Courtesy Call : 464

MISHIMA YUKIO : The Priest and His Love : 481

    Selected Bibliography : 503

    Index of Authors : 510

    Index of Translators : 511

ACKNOWLEDGMENTS

ACKNOWLEDGMENTS are due to the *Japan Quarterly* for permission to use the translations of "Seibei's Gourds" (there called "The Artist"), "Autumn Mountain," "Tiger-Poet" ("The Wild Beast"), and "The Hateful Age"; to *Today's Japan* for "Under Reconstruction," "The Handstand" ("Wager in Midair"), and "The Courtesy Call" ("A Visitor"); to the *Paris Review* for "Tattoo" ("The Victim"); to *United Asia* for "The Moon on the Water"; to Grove Press for "Downtown" ("Tokyo"); and to Alfred A. Knopf, Inc., for permission to translate works by Tanizaki, Kawabata, and Mishima.

FACTUAL NOTES

1. Japanese names are given in the usual Japanese order, with the family name preceding the personal name. Well-known writers in Japan are often called by their personal names, especially after their deaths. Thus most people refer to Ogai and Sōseki, although their respective surnames were Mori and Natsumé.

2. Japanese vowels are pronounced as in Spanish or Italian, each being given approximately its full value. Consonants are much as in English, except that *g* is always hard. Macrons, used to indicate long *o*'s and *u*'s, have been omitted from such common place names as Tokyo and Kobe and from words like Shinto and Shogunate. Acute accents have occasionally been used in such words as Abé and saké that might otherwise be mispronounced.

3. The period names Meiji, Taishō, and Shōwa are frequently used in the Introduction and in the notes on the authors. These refer to the reigns of the three modern emperors and have much the same significance in a literary discussion as do Victorian, Edwardian, and the like in English. The periods are: Meiji, 1868–1912; Taishō, 1912–1926; Shōwa, 1926 to date.

4. A rough indication of money equivalents may be helpful since prices, wages, etc., are frequently mentioned in the stories. One hundred sen equal one yen. In terms of English and American currencies, since 1949 the value of 1,000 yen has remained stable at approximately $2.80 or £1. By referring to the date of a story, the reader can determine the approximate money equivalent from the following table, which is based on the price of rice, the main staple commodity; the second figure in each pair shows the value of one yen in terms of 1958 prices: 1912 = ¥615.00; 1930 = ¥456.00; 1940 = ¥286.00; 1944 = ¥232.00; 1946 = ¥42.00; 1949 = ¥1.70; 1954 = ¥1.08.

INTRODUCTION

BY Ivan Morris

CONTEMPORARY literature in Japan, despite its remote ancestry, may be regarded as a new literature, scarcely beyond its formative stage. The Meiji Restoration, which ended two and a half centuries of strictest seclusion, marked a departure in Japanese writing, as it did in politics, education, and so many other fields. For a general understanding of the modern Japanese novel or short story it is hardly necessary to go back more than a century. The Japanese language has undergone a continuous development since the earliest times and to this extent modern fiction derives stylistically from classical and medieval writing. Even here, however, the Restoration had an important effect by bringing the literary language closer to that of ordinary speech. The major influences can be found among works of foreign literature introduced into Japan after about 1860 and among certain important Japanese writers of the Meiji period.

This introduction cannot attempt to present a systematic history of modern Japanese literature, but it may be worthwhile to indicate a few general trends that can help the reader to view in context the twenty-five stories presented here. A note concerning each of the twenty-five authors and his place in modern Japanese writing has been placed before his story.

The historical approach has many dangers. Too much concentration on "social backgrounds," "literary influences," and "schools of writing" may lead us to read the stories, not as independent works, but as representatives of some particular period, and to regard their writers, not as unique individuals having their own views of life and their

9

characteristic methods of expression, but simply as members of certain literary schools with established outlooks or programs.

When, however, we are faced with a writing as remote from most Western readers as that of Japan, the historical approach can hardly be avoided. As Mr. Angus Wilson has said: "To read the literature of a civilization or age entirely or almost entirely unfamiliar emphasizes one's unconscious dependence on historical background. To begin with, the unfamiliar is likely immediately to present a number of specious qualities—the 'quaint', the 'charming', the 'horrific'—which are merely attempts to come to terms with a strange world on a surface level. Greater familiarity always destroys the immediate impressions."

* * *

In few countries is the dividing line that marks the beginning of the "modern" period so clear as in Japan. What historians term the Meiji Restoration was the result of interacting processes that had been continuing for a very long time. When these processes finally reached their culmination, the collapse of the old regime, which had given the country some two and a half centuries of peace and stability, occurred with remarkable speed. In 1867 the gradual stagnation and disintegration of the economic system, increasing pressure from foreign powers, and the revolt of four of the great clans combined with numerous other factors to bring about the downfall of the centralized feudal government that had been in the hands of a succession of military rulers belonging to the Tokugawa family. Political power was handed over in 1867 to the Emperor Meiji and his advisers. In the years that followed, every effort was made to abolish feudalism, especially in its political and economic aspects, and to turn Japan into a centralized nation-state on the European model. The political structure was completely reorganized and a capitalist economy rapidly developed with the impetus of a belated industrial revolution. In the effort to become "modern," countless old customs, habits, and heritages were scrapped in a wave of cultural iconoclasm which at one stage went so far that there were serious proposals to replace the Japanese language by English and the native religions by Christianity.

Following 1868 every effort was made to adopt the techniques and culture of the West. Japan, which for two hundred and fifty years had

to a large extent been isolated from the main stream of Western development, tried in the period of a few decades to absorb everything from the outside that would turn her into a modern nineteenth-century state; such a state might be able to deal with foreign nations on a basis of equality and, above all, to avoid the fate that had overtaken other materially backward Asian countries. By the last decade of the century the Meiji oligarchy had succeeded in forging a modern military establishment which enabled the country to defeat China in 1895 and, one decade later, to win the war against Russia, thus establishing Japan as one of the Great Powers.

The cumulative effect on the country's literature of all these immense changes can hardly be overestimated. Nonetheless, the destruction of the old and the adoption of the new was not immediately reflected in Japanese writing. The original aim of the oligarchy was to import the techniques of the West while preserving the Japanese "spirit" intact. Chimerical as this ideal eventually proved to be, it caused the emphasis to be placed at first on the material aspects of Westernization. There was a cultural lag of some fifteen years during which literature continued on its course, relatively unaffected by Western influences. This literature, it should be noted, had sunk to a remarkably low level. The prose fiction of the late Tokugawa period was in a groove of mediocrity, having largely lost the power and originality that animated the work of the great prose writers of the seventeenth and eighteenth centuries, such as Saikaku, Kiseki, and Akinari. Frivolous tales about courtesans, banal stories of licentiousness in the gay quarters, and prolix works of a didactic nature were the stock-in-trade of the early nineteenth-century prose writers with only two or three notable exceptions.

Had late Tokugawa literature been more vigorous and creative, it is possible that the literary impact of Western culture would have proved to be less overwhelming. As it was, the introduction of European culture resulted in a major break with the past that has no parallel in any of the important literatures of the West.

Until about 1860 the only foreign literary influences of importance had come from China. For over two centuries, contacts with Europe had by and large been limited to the small Dutch settlement off Nagasaki; and there the focus was on trade rather than culture. Translations of European literature began in the 1860's, but it was not until 1878 that the first complete novel from the West was translated into Japanese. As in the case of many of the early translations, the choice, Bulwer-Lytton's "Ernest Maltravers," strikes one as peculiar. Practical information was at least as important a criterion as literary value in introducing books from the West and one of the most successful of all the early importations was Samuel Smiles' utilitarian tract, "Self-Help." The novels of Disraeli, reflecting modern political processes, were also given a strange degree of attention.

In the 1880's the trickle of Western works grew into a stream and, by the end of the century, into a mighty torrent which is still continuing in the present day. Several of the most gifted writers of the Meiji period devoted much of their energies to the translation of one or more European authors; indeed, it was mainly through these translations that the reading public first became acquainted with the various aspects of modern fiction. In many cases Japanese writers then tried to produce the same type of novels in Japanese, with rather surprising results. One Japanese author, for example, under the impact of "Crime and Punishment," wrote a story about the life and tribulations of a man belonging to the untouchable *eta* class. For even in these early days of direct assimilation, European literary influence was rarely a matter of straightforward imitation. Naive interpretation, and often misunderstanding, of the models played a capital part in the process of absorbing Western literature. As a modern Japanese critic, Mr. Yoshida Kenichi, has pointed out, Tolstoy's "Resurrection" when first introduced into Japan was considered to be merely a romantic tale of unhappy love.

The main effect of the influx from the West was not so much to provide specific literary models as to encourage Japanese to break away from sterile traditions and to describe in a more or less realistic way the brave new world that they saw growing up about them. The year 1885 is generally regarded as a key date in the development of modern Japanese fiction. That year saw the publication of "The Essence of the Novel" *(Shōsetsu Shinzui)* by Tsubouchi Shōyō (1859–1935). Not only was this the first important critical work of the new era, but it was the first serious theoretical study of the novel in Japan. During the Tokugawa period, and indeed ever since the days of "The Tale of

Genji," scholars had looked down on prose fiction, which was widely regarded as being fit only for women, children, and the lesser breeds. Writers like Saikaku were largely ignored and critical attention was concentrated on *tanka* and other forms of classical poetry and, to a lesser extent, on dramatic works. As a rule, the only novelists who were accorded any respect were didactic writers like Bakin. One result of the introduction of Western literature was to enhance the position of prose fiction in Japan.

Like so many of the important literary figures of the Meiji period, Tsubouchi Shōyō devoted a considerable part of his time to translation. He was a specialist in English literature and among other things he translated the complete works of Shakespeare into Japanese. His acquaintance with the writing of the West brought home to him the low state of fiction in Japan. A considerable part of "The Essence of the Novel" is concerned with criticizing the current state of Japanese fiction in the light of literary lessons from Europe. Tsubouchi referred to the recent resurgence of the novel in Japan as a result of new printing methods and of increasing literacy. The standard, however, was low: "An endless number of the most diverse novels and romances is now being produced in our country and the bookshelves groan under their weight; yet they all consist of mere foolishness."*

Tsubouchi blamed this on the lack of discrimination among readers and on the failure of writers themselves to cut loose from the late Tokugawa tradition of tedious didacticism. In the typical spirit of the Meiji intellectual, Tsubouchi declared that the solution lay in "modernizing" Japanese literature. This involved, on the one hand, adopting the realistic approach of modern Western fiction. In particular, Japanese writers should strive for psychological realism whereby they might faithfully reproduce the actual complex workings of men and women. According to Tsubouchi, the novelist's task was not to apportion praise or blame, but to observe and describe the underlying passions that make human beings act as they do. Here we find an adumbration of the naturalist approach that was to play so important a part in subsequent Japanese literature. At the same time, however, Tsubouchi stressed the aesthetic purpose of the novel. The function of the writer was neither

* *Shōyō Senshū* ("Collected Works of Shōyō"), Tokyo, 1927. Vol. III, p. 3.

to teach nor to expound approved moral sentiments, but to produce works of artistic merit which would serve to elevate the public taste.

Banal as many of Tsubouchi's ideas may strike the present-day reader, their effect on Meiji literature was momentous. Indeed, the development of modern realistic fiction can be dated from the publication of "The Essence of the Novel." After 1885, fantastic tales of jejune romances began to give place to accounts of real people living in contemporary society. Tsubouchi tried to put his own theories into practice in a novel with the inauspicious title of "The Spirit of Present-day Students." His effort was singularly unsuccessful.

The first important work to reflect Tsubouchi's theories was "The Drifting Cloud" *(Ukigumo)*, a novel by Futabatei Shimei (1864–1909) that appeared between 1887 and 1889. This unfinished work deals realistically with a commonplace, rather lethargic young intellectual of the Meiji period. Futabatei's study of Russian literature, in particular of Turgenev, had convinced him of the need for realism both in subject and in style. He was the first important novelist to abandon the conventional literary language and to use ordinary colloquial forms in describing the inner struggles of the modern man. In this and many other ways "The Drifting Cloud" occupies a pioneer role in the development of modern Japanese fiction, although it will hardly strike most present-day readers as a literary masterpiece.

Another outstanding figure in Meiji literature was Mori Ōgai (1863–1922), the first of the twenty-five writers represented in the present anthology (see page 35). Whereas previous writers knew the West mainly through their readings, Ōgai became acquainted with Europe at first hand as an army doctor in Germany from 1884 to 1888. During these years he became familiar with current European literature and his voluminous translations and essays greatly affected the development of modern Japanese drama and poetry, as well as of the novel and the short story. In his literary criticism Ōgai was greatly influenced by the idealistic aestheticism which was current in Germany during the latter part of the nineteenth century and which was expressed by such philosophers as Karl von Hartmann. He returned from Europe at a time when German influence was steadily becoming stronger in Japan, as seen for example in the enactment of the Meiji Constitution (1889), based to an important extent on German principles of absolutism.

Ōgai criticized many of Tsubouchi's theories concerning realistic literature and in their place advanced a form of romanticism that laid stress on the emotional realization of the self. His first piece of fiction, which appeared in 1890, was the romantic account of a tragic love affair in Berlin between a young Japanese gentleman engaged in research work and a beautiful German ballet dancer named Alice. Evidently based on personal experience, "The Dancing Girl" *(Maihime)* was written in the first person and was described by Ōgai himself as an *Ich Roman*. "I have attempted," wrote Ōgai, "to portray a Japanese who was living in Berlin at the same time as I and who came to grips with the kind of situation described in the story." Then (as a typical afterthought of the Western-influenced Meiji writer) Ōgai added: "There are a good many European works of fiction with similar plots." "The Dancing Girl" is hardly a great work of literature, but it stands out as one of the earliest examples of the *shi-shōsetsu* ("I-novel" and "I-story"), the autobiographical, confessional type of writing that has occupied such an important role in modern Japanese literature.

It is one of the peculiarities of this literature that the writers who were most enthusiastically to adopt the *shi-shōsetsu* should have been the members of the naturalist school. The introduction into Japan of the writings of Zola and Maupassant had far-reaching effects in literary circles. It accelerated the movement away from traditionalism and, at about the time of the Russo-Japanese War (1904–05), produced a group of influential writers who proclaimed that the purpose of literature was to search for the truth and to describe it with the detached accuracy of a scientist. Literary embellishments and conventional sentiments had to be discarded in favor of a cold, objective presentation of life as it was actually lived by ordinary men and women. Factual detail was more important than style, form, or atmosphere; the modern writer must strive to achieve the unadorned directness of the policeman's statement or the clinical report.

From the outset, however, Japanese naturalism began to diverge from the movement in Europe that had inspired it. The publication in 1908 of "The Quilt" *(Futon),* a novel by Tayama Katai, one of the leading naturalists, served to establish the autobiographical approach as the standard for Japanese writers of the naturalist school. This novel deals in exhaustive detail with the events and emotions in the life of the author-hero and is one of the first in the long series of Japanese novels that unabashedly describe the experiences and emotions of the character known as *watakushi* ("I").

Many reasons have been suggested for this confessional aspect of Japanese naturalism. According to some critics, the late collapse of feudalism and the fact that important changes have always come from above rather than as a result of popular effort resulted in a peculiarly wide gulf between individual and social life, and made the Japanese far less interested in political and social questions than people in most modern Western countries. Strong authoritarian traditions gave rise to a widespread feeling of indifference or resignation to outside problems, and official censorship discouraged Meiji writers from voicing any criticism of current conditions. Writers who wished to present life strictly on the basis of facts concentrated on their direct personal experiences, tending to neglect the wider subjects that had been treated by Zola and the other naturalists of the West. Readers, for their part, were prone to be more interested in books that described the detailed experiences of a single individual, preferably the writer himself, rather than in novels giving a broad picture of society by means of a more objective handling of a variety of characters.

The main legacy of naturalism in Japan has been the belief of many writers that the only worthwhile and "sincere" form of literature is that which takes its material directly from the facts of the author's physical and spiritual life. This trend affected several writers who were in other respects strongly opposed to the naturalists. Among them was Shiga Naoya (see page 81), whose success in the genre encouraged many less talented authors to probe into their personal experiences for literary material.

The *shi-shōsetsu* tradition, though it has sometimes given rise to works of unusual sharpness and honesty, has had a number of baneful effects. In their efforts at faithful reproduction, many modern Japanese writers tended to forget the demands of fiction and of literary style. Furthermore, the confessional type of literature implies a rather dangerous form of conceit, based on the idea that there is something intrinsically interesting in an honest account of one's inner life. In the case of gifted authors this assumption has sometimes been justified. However, less talented and original writers have often been led to produce works of extraordinary dullness in which the fictional element is so attenuated that the term novel or short story seems hardly appropriate.

The great decade of modern Japanese writing was that which followed the end of the Russo-Japanese War. It was during these years that many of the most important writers did their best work, while others started their careers. (Among those included in the present collection are Mori Ōgai, Tokuda Shūsei, Nagai Kafū, Shiga Naoya, Tanizaki Junichirō, Satomi Ton, and Akutagawa Ryūnosuké.) Victory against a major foreign power led to an upsurge of national self-confidence and prosperity. At the same time the multifarious European cultural influences were coming to fruition. Although the literary scene was dominated by the naturalists, many of the important authors who were active during this period were vocally opposed to the naturalist approach and reflected this opposition in their writing.

Several of the "schools" of writing that Japanese critics spend so much time in classifying and sub-classifying (neo-romanticist, neo-idealist, neo-realist, etc.) arose in protest against the prevailing naturalism. The early careers of a surprisingly large number of important modern writers were marked by a conscious revolt against the gloom, aridity, and lack of style that marked the naturalists (see biographical notes on Mori Ōgai, Nagai Kafū, Shiga Naoya, Tanizaki Junichirō, Akutagawa Ryūnosuké, etc.). It is worthwhile to observe that it is frequently the works of these writers that are read and valued today, whereas much of the naturalist literature against which they were rebelling has passed into oblivion.

The proliferation in Japan of exclusive literary groups may require a few words of comment. The phenomenon of cliquishness is by no means limited to the world of literature; it exists in almost every sphere of Japanese life, including the academic world, politics, bureaucracy, and business, as well as music, painting, and all the traditional arts. The tendency of writers and others to band together in groups or societies derives directly from the pre-modern period, when the individual young artist had scant chance of recognition unless he could be identified with some established family or school that would give him its protection and encouragement. This relates to the feudal tradition of a close relationship between master and pupil, which even today plays an important part in literature and other fields.

Japan, of course, is not unique in having literary coteries, but there can be few countries where their existence and the resulting rivalries have had so much influence. The ramifications of the various schools and factions need not concern the general Western reader, but some of the more important groupings, such as the Shirakaba and the neo-perceptionists, are identified in the biographical notes. The personal nexus, reinforced by bonds of loyalty and obligation, often plays at least as important a part in the development of these cliques as does common adherence to a literary program. This also applies to the fields of politics and elsewhere.

The First World War was on the whole a material boon to Japan, and the outbreak of hostilities (in which Japan participated on the Allied side) possessed none of the disruptive significance that it did for English, French, or German literature. Far more important was the unrest subsequent to the end of the war. Inflation and economic dislocation produced considerable social turmoil, which combined with the repercussions of the Russian Revolution to stimulate left-wing and labor movements. A large part of the Japanese intelligentsia, including not a few writers, was affected by these developments and during the years following 1918 several of them participated directly or indirectly in the incipient trade-union, socialist, and communist activities.

The proletarian school of writing arose in 1920 (the year in which fierce riots broke out to protest soaring rice prices), and it attracted to its ranks a considerable number of vocal writers. Despite severe government represssion, which started at the time of the great earthquake in 1923 and became intensified after the passing of the draconian Peace Preservation Law in 1925, proletarian writers continued to be active during the 1920's and the early part of the 1930's, exerting an extremely important influence on Japanese literature between the wars.

Most of these proletarian writers took an active part in political and labor activities; indeed, their writing was often done in prison cells, where many of them spent a considerable portion of their lives.* The characteristic work of the proletarian school was concerned with the sufferings of the exploited urban workers and seamen (also to a lesser

---

* See, for example, the biographical note on Hayama Yoshiki. One of the best known proletarian writers, Kobayashi Takiji (1903–33) died while in the hands of the local police during one of his many periods under arrest.

extent of the peasantry) and with the supposed iniquities of the capital-
ists and of the repressive government that supported them. In many
cases the Union of Soviet Socialist Republics hovers in the background
as an adumbration of better days to come.

Despite the many differences in approach between the proletarians
and the naturalists, the two schools may be regarded as occupying
analogous positions in the development of modern Japanese literature.
In both cases literary style was considered to be secondary to content,
and emotions were rejected in favor of a "scientific" treatment of
reality. In both cases, also, this seemingly hardheaded, realistic approach
frequently masked a fundamentally sentimental outlook. Many writers
who did not actually belong to the proletarian school were influenced
by its teachings (see biographical notes on Ogawa Mimei and Hayashi
Fumiko). The concept that worthwhile modern literature must be
concerned with the harsh realities of working-class life was widely
held for many years.

As in the case of the naturalist writers, the prestige of the proletarians
served to provoke a reaction on the part of several young writers who set
out to reaffirm the primacy of literary values (e.g., Yokomitsu Riichi,
Kawabata Yasunari, and the so-called neo-perceptionists). Many of the
important men who started to write in the late Taishō and early Shōwa
periods were consciously rebelling against the influence of the "committed" left-wing authors. As a rule their work has survived far better
than that of the proletarians, which by its very nature was bound to
become hopelessly dated.

The militarist period, inaugurated by the Manchurian Incident in
1931, saw the progressive suppression of thought and speech as the
government regimented the country in the cause of right-wing nationalism and aggressive expansionism. During the 1930's a thoroughgoing police state grew up. Democracy and liberalism were rejected
as foreign creeds unsuited to Japanese conditions; individualism was
attacked as a manifestation of "egoism"; and all unorthodoxy was
burked as constituting "dangerous thoughts." Left-wing writers were
harshly persecuted and those with liberal views frequently preferred
to remain silent rather than to speak out their beliefs in the atmosphere
of intolerance and jingoism that prevailed. It is pleasing to record that
only a small number of reputable writers lent their talents to assisting

the government in its propaganda efforts. Fanatic nationalism reached its height during the four years of the Pacific War. Thought control became more thorough than ever, and this, combined with a severe paper shortage, resulted in a tragic blank so far as real literature was concerned.

Japan's defeat in 1945 led to Allied occupation and to the loss of national independence for the first time in the country's history. Paradoxically, its effect on many Japanese intellectuals was that of emancipation. Freedom of speech and thought was finally restored; unorthodoxy and radicalism received legal protection. No longer did the police have the power to suppress "suspicious" literary works or to arrest their authors for "thought crimes." Occupation censorship, being directed mainly at journalism and political writing, had relatively little effect on fiction.

The early postwar period was marked by a breakdown of the traditional values that had been systematically foisted on the country by the central government since the time of the Meiji Restoration. In their place the Occupation reformers attempted to instill a respect for the liberal democratic principles of the West. Democracy, however, was not something that could effectively be imposed from the outside like many of the more concrete Occupation reforms; despite the initial enthusiasm for *demokurashii,* especially among the youth, it was clear that considerable time would be needed before it became sufficiently implanted in people's minds to take the place of official state nationalism as a guiding and inspiring force. Meanwhile the country was faced with what is frequently described as a spiritual vacuum. The staggering wartime losses and the prostration of defeat resulted in a period of economic chaos and political confusion.

The years following 1945 saw an impetuous reaction to the many-sided suppressions of the militarist era. There was a release of pent-up intellectual energies and a general sense of license that inevitably affected the early postwar literature. One important aspect was freedom to treat the subject of sex. After years of caviling censorship, during which not only contemporary works but even some of the country's great classics were bowdlerized or suppressed, writers were once more free to describe emotions and events that the militarists had frowned on as being decadent. As an inevitable result there was an outpouring of pornographic works. Yet serious authors were now able to write naturally, without concern over captious censorship.

With the removal of restrictions, writers were free to criticize national military traditions, emperor worship, the family system—the entire structure, indeed, which nationalists had described as being "flawless like a golden chalice," but which appeared to have brought the country to ruin. The breakdown of constituted authority and of old social traditions induced in many young writers a mood of thoroughgoing skepticism, which frequently took the form of nihilism, hedonism, irresponsibility, and despair.

Shortly after the war there was a vogue (which continues until this day) for French existentialism, introduced to Japan through translations of Sartre and Camus. As so often happens in the case of Japanese importations, the content of existentialism was frequently oversimplified and misunderstood. Its main effect was to give certain writers a specious philosophical basis for their prevailing nihilistic mood.

A number of the *apuré* (après-guerre) writers lived in a state of desperate disorder of a type that Rimbaud had made familiar at an earlier stage of European development. Alcohol, drugs, sexual promiscuity, nihilism, and thoughts of suicide played a large part in their lives and in their writing. To express the complexities and confusions of the new rootless age these writers attempted to break away from such literary tradition as existed and to create new and freer forms of literature. Apart from Dazai Osamu, however, few of them succeeded in producing works of much literary value; and Dazai, with his personal, "confessional" approach, was in many ways less of an innovator than is often imagined.*

The year 1948, in which Dazai Osamu committed suicide, may be regarded as marking the end of the turbulent *apuré* period in Japanese writing. The steady improvement of economic conditions, political stabilization under a succession of conservative governments, and the official resumption of national independence in 1952 led to a more normal and tranquil atmosphere; this inevitably had its effect on literature, even though many of the iconoclastic *apuré* trends continued.

---

* See p. 464. Dazai started to write long before the war and, strictly speaking, cannot be regarded as an *apuré* writer. There is no doubt, however, that he was the literary hero of the *apuré* generation.

A remarkably large number of the important Meiji-period writers were still alive. Many of them had been obliged to remain silent during the years of militarist repression, but after the war they once more became active. Their earlier works were republished and many of them continued to write novels and stories. It is a tribute to the longevity and energy of Japanese authors that so many of those who first made their names some forty years ago should still be alive and engaged in new work. Of those included in the present collection Nagai Kafū, Shiga Naoya, Tanizaki Junichirō, Satomi Ton, Murō Saisei, Satō Haruo, and Ogawa Mimei were all flourishing at the end of 1958. Nagai Kafū died in 1959.

The present literary scene is one of immense activity. Publishers and literary magazines abound, and the number of novels and stories published every year is overwhelming. With books extremely cheap (an average novel costs the equivalent of 80 cents, and only 20 cents in a paper-backed edition) and with the reading public large and alert, sales are vastly in excess of those before the war. The material rewards for literary success, therefore, are considerable, and some of the most substantial incomes in Japan are at present earned by popular writers.

This situation is not without its dangers—dangers almost as great as those that beset the economically hard-pressed writers before the war. There is a considerable risk that "pure literature" (as it is rather primly termed in Japan) will still further lose audiences to commercial literature and to the so-called "middle novels," which occupy a place somewhere between the artistic and the popular. In order to earn money, many of the best writers produce serial novels for newspapers and magazines of large circulation. Sometimes an author will be working on two or more serial novels at the same time, as well as turning out articles on assorted subjects from birth control to Japanese-American relations, giving lecture tours, and dashing off occasional stories to satisfy the requests of the numerous literary and semi-literary magazines. One popular novelist recently became so confused by the number of different things he was writing simultaneously that he inadvertently changed the name of the main character in the middle of one of his serial novels—an error that was not caught up in proof and which caused considerable bewilderment to his readers.

For the successful Japanese writer "it never rains, it pours." To remain successful he cannot afford to be long out of the public eye, and the artistic energy necessary to produce serious work is often dissipated by commercial demands. Such conditions are, of course, not limited to Japan, but the lack of solid tradition in modern Japanese literature adds to the danger. Fortunately the risk of total commercialization is recognized and deliberately resisted by a number of the better authors.

Among those who oppose commercialism, though not for literary reasons, are the "committed" writers. In the present political scene this invariably means communist and near-communist writers. They are organized into two or three main groups; in these groups they energetically carry on the tradition of the prewar proletarian school and look on the writers of "pure literature" as escapists. The economic distress of the early postwar years, the discrediting of the old regime and all that it stood for, the moral vacuum left by defeat—these and other factors led many writers to join such groups. With improving material conditions the appeal of the extreme left has steadily diminished —its period of greatest influence was in 1949—and the "committed" writers have been increasingly out of touch with the mood of the country, which remains predominantly conservative. The complete freedom of thought and expression since 1945 has not, so far, led the contemporary "committed" writers to produce fiction of any higher quality than that of the prewar proletarian writers, and their calls for a literature of social protest have had very little effect on postwar fiction. Their voices are heard more in the political than in the literary field; they frequently emerge as vocal opponents of conservative policy or as apologists for left-wing causes.

The *shi-shōsetsu* tradition of semi-autobiographical "fiction" has survived into the postwar period, but it is no longer so widely followed as some decades ago. Most contemporary writers seem to be aware of the need for a wider approach than is usually manifested in the "I-novel" and the "I-story." Nevertheless, the confessional, diary type of writing, in which everything is seen through the eyes of one lone, sensitive individual, continues to be far more popular in Japan than in the West.

After 1945 the torrent of translations from foreign languages, which naturally subsided during the war, reached new heights. Novels, plays, short stories, and poems from almost every country in the world were translated and published for a public whose appetite had been whetted by the years of official xenophobia and isolation. The choice of books for translation was often indiscriminate, sometimes incomprehensible. Nevertheless, in the influx a large mass of worthwhile literature from the outside world has been made available.

To what extent, then, is current Japanese literature influenced by that of the West? In the first place, it should be emphasized that on the whole the influence is not nearly so direct as is often assumed by Western readers. Japan has now had some seventy years in which to absorb the literary traditions of the West. European and American literature have come to be taken for granted, and works from the outside no longer carry the aura of the exotic and the startling that they had in the early days of importation. Even more important, Japanese writers now have their own great literary figures—Natsumé Sōseki and Mori Ōgai, among others. They can look back with a sense of belonging to an indigenous, if recent, tradition. Although in many ways the Pacific War and its aftermath constituted a break with the past as great as or even greater than that provided by the Meiji Restoration, there was no rupture with native literary tradition such as occurred in the nineteenth century. Whereas the new Meiji writers tended to look entirely to the West for their models, the writers of the present day receive their influence both from the West and from their own writers of the past sixty years.

Even in the early days of importation, literary influence in Japan rarely produced slavish imitation of certain specific European or American models. It was usually a much more indirect and complex process. As the young postwar writer Mishima Yukio has pointed out, Japanese novelists have usually assimilated only those elements of foreign literature that are in some way close to the recipient. This is more than ever true today when the Japanese writer has such an immense selection of world literature at his disposal.

Although the most conspicuous influences have certainly come from Europe, it would be a mistake to discount the effect of Chinese and Japanese classical literature on certain modern writers. This classical influence is reflected in the imagery, the descriptions, the general mood, and sometimes the structural technique of many outstanding post-Meiji writers and their successors.* One of the most interesting aspects of writers like Nagai Kafū, Tanizaki Junichirō, and Kawabata Yasunari is precisely the way in which they succeeded in melding classical traditions with modern Western thought and technique.

However, the fact remains that the modern Japanese novel and story are essentially Western forms; in so far as literary influence has played a part, most Japanese prose writers are indebted to modern Western literature far more than to their own country's classical tradition. It is writers like Hugo, Poe, Whitman, Baudelaire, Dostoievsky, Tolstoy, Hardy, Zola, Huysmans, Maupassant, Wilde, and D. H. Lawrence that have exercised influence rather than Murasaki Shikibu, Saikaku, Bakin, and the other famous prose writers of earlier centuries. The remark made in 1910 by Natsumé Sōseki, one of the most important of the post-Meiji novelists, could well be uttered by the vast majority of modern Japanese prose writers: "What governs my mind at this moment, what will influence all my future work, is not, alas, the tradition of my ancestors, but, rather, thoughts brought over from across the sea, and by an alien race."† But if they were to make such a statement, few postwar writers would be inclined to include Sōseki's expression of regret.

Japan is, of course, not the only country in which imported literature has exerted an influence, but the historical conditions of the Meiji period made this influence of primary importance. As Mr. Mishima (who, among the younger writers, is particularly conscious of his own country's classical heritage) has said: "In most other countries there exists a strong literary tradition into which writers can assimilate whatever is imported. In Japan our literature does not rest on any such tradition. Although our talented writers have managed to utilize their abilities individually, there are very few of them who have managed to ground their works on secure tradition."

*   *   *

In Japan, as in most other countries, the story or tale has an extremely

* Among the writers included in the present collection Mori Ōgai, Nagai Kafū, Tanizaki Junichirō, and Satō Haruo frequently show classical Chinese or Japanese influence in their writing; the tradition has been carried on by Kawabata Yasunari, Nakajima Ton, and Mishima Yukio.

† Quoted by Miyata Shimpachirō in "Translated Literature in Japan," Japan Quarterly, Vol. IV, p. 169.

long and varied history. Among the earliest collections that have come down to us (leaving aside ancient mythological collections where the literary motive is secondary) are those from the Heian period in which brief prose passages serve to provide the background for 31-syllable classical poems or to link a series of such poems by means of rudimentary plots. "The Tales of Isé" (ninth century) is the best-known example; "The Tales of Yamato" (tenth century) belongs to the same tradition. "The Tales of Tsutsumi Chūnagon" (which includes the charming and original fragment "The Lady Who Loved Insects," beautifully translated by Arthur Waley) is a collection of ten stories with well-defined plots and considerable realism. The eleventh-century "Tales of Past and Present," consisting of more than one thousand stories taken from Indian, Chinese, and Japanese history and folklore, represents a considerable advance in construction (though certainly not in artistry) over the lyrical tales of the early Heian period. *Otogi-zōshi* is the generic term for collections of popular stories, mostly simple fairy tales, that were in circulation during the Muromachi period (c. 1300–1600).

In a more recent period the numerous collections of stories by Ihara Saikaku (1642–93) deal in a more or less realistic way with the lives of contemporary men and women, mostly members of the seventeenth-century townsman class. "Tales of the Moonlight and the Rain" (1776), a famous collection of nine ghost stories by Ueda Akinari, belongs to a tradition of supernatural tales that goes back to the eighth century. We should also take note of a common form that is to be found in much of Saikaku's work and elsewhere. This consists of a collection of stories having a common thread or theme; a typical example is Saikaku's "Reckonings That Carry Men Through the World" (*Seken Munesanyō*, 1693), which is a volume of twenty independent stories, all dealing with the torments that different groups of characters experience on the last day of the year, when all debts become due for payment.

Despite this ancient and diverse tradition, the modern Japanese story form in this century has owed remarkably little to the pre-Meiji collections of which examples have been given above. It is true that a number of the Meiji-period writers (including Higuchi Ichiyō, Ozaki Kōyō, Kōda Rohan, and Tayama Katai) recognized in Saikaku's stories the same vigorous realism that they had found in modern French literature. Saikaku's realism, however, served to confirm such writers in their already established literary approach, rather than to inspire them. When it actually came to writing stories, the main influences derived, not from Saikaku or the other pre-Meiji masters of realistic fiction, but from the recent literature of Europe and America.

The history of the modern story in Japan can be considered to date from the introduction of Maupassant's work in the 1890's. One of the earliest writers to attempt to produce in Japanese the type of story that was current in Europe was Mori Ōgai, who after his return from Germany in 1888 did so much to familiarize Japanese readers with Western literary forms.

Of the two masters of the late-nineteenth-century short story in Europe, Maupassant exerted considerably greater influence in Japan than Chekhov. The reason is not far to seek: the introduction of Maupassant's short stories coincided with the rise of naturalism in Japanese literature and, indeed, was one of the important influences on this movement. It was Maupassant's direct, realistic, and often harsh approach to his material that affected Japanese writers, rather than his mastery of the short-story form itself.

Although Maupassant, like Chekhov, regarded the short story as being a genre in itself and although he contributed so greatly to giving it the characteristic form with which we are now familiar, his early influence in Japan did not on the whole lead writers to make the clear differentiation between the novel and the short story that is accepted in the West. The line of demarcation in Japan between the two genres has always tended to be vague. This is reflected in the terminology. Both forms are known as *shōsetsu,* the word for "short story" being differentiated only by the prefix *tampen* ("short piece"). *Shōsetsu* is also used with the prefix *chūhen* ("middle piece") to describe an intermediate length of work having about 40,000 to 60,000 words; this roughly corresponds to what is sometimes known as "novelette," but the form is very much more popular in Japan than in the West. Thus there is a regular continuum from *tampen-shōsetsu* through *chūhen-shōsetsu* to *shōsetsu.* The only real differentiation is in the matter of length, which itself tends to be very indefinite. This is not simply a matter of terminology, but extends to the conception—or rather, lack of conception—of the short story as a distinct literary form. Very frequently we find the same piece of fiction being described alternatively as a "novel" and as a "short story."

One result of this vague differentiation is the absence from so many Japanese stories of certain stylistic qualities that we have come to regard as essential to the modern short story in the West. This is certainly not to suggest that the story is a narrow form with certain strictly defined rules or canons. Far from it. A genre that so greatly antedates the novel is bound to have enormous flexibility. The history of the story in the West goes back to the "Tales of the Magicians" and traces its complex descent through Aesop, Boccaccio, Chaucer, the Bible, and La Fontaine, to name only a few of the great landmarks. Any neat definition is both impossible and undesirable. As the well-known short-story writer Kay Boyle has said: "The only continuity it [the story] possesses is that it was isolated individuals, sometimes writing centuries apart, who spoke with freshness and vigor, in a short-winded rather than a long-winded form, of people, and ideas, and incidents, which seemed to the reader moving and true."

Since the time of Gogol, however, the story has developed in a certain manner that we may characterize as the "style of the modern Western short story." Its outstanding feature is an economy of means. This has involved a tendency to compression, to the dropping, as H. E. Bates puts it, of all inessential paraphernalia. The tendency has continued until the present day and has been given particular impetus by the short stories of Ernest Hemingway, whom H. E. Bates describes as the "man with an axe . . . [who] cut out a whole forest of verbosity."* Without economy there can be no short story in the modern sense of the term. This, of course, does not preclude the existence of short stories of considerable length. The tendency since the time of Tolstoy has certainly been in the direction of brevity, but the modern story may vary from a few hundred words to fifteen or even twenty thousand. What is essential is the close construction, the casting of all the material round a single central image, and the over-all compression that have become the marks of the successful modern short story in the West.

By these general standards a considerable proportion of *tampen-*

* H. E. Bates: "The Modern Short Story," pp. 168-69.

shōsetsu are not short stories at all; frequently they appear to be sketches, essays, or truncated novels. A large number of Japanese story writers are primarily novelists for whom stories tend to be what Elizabeth Bowen has called "side-issues from the crowded imagination." Since the novel and the modern short story are two totally different genres it is most unlikely that a writer will be equally at home in both, and this applies in Japan quite as much as in the West. The plethora of literary magazines in Japan has encouraged many writers to produce stories when their style was better suited to the novel. As a result, their work frequently lacks the stylistic compression that is the essence of the modern short story. This is not primarily a matter of word length (though it is worth noting that Japanese stories are as a rule far longer than their modern Western counterparts), but of failure to apply the indirect, suggestive, and dramatic methods which are indispensable for economy of style. In a country that has produced the most compressed forms of poetry in world literature it is remarkable that stories should so frequently be marked by a turgid verbosity which cries out for the ministration of a blue pencil.

Fortunately a number of good modern writers in Japan have treated the short story as an equal and separate genre of literature, not merely as an abbreviated novel or as a sketch. Of the authors represented in the present collection, the three who stand out in Japanese letters as short-story writers are Shiga Naoya, Akutagawa Ryūnosuké, and Nakajima Ton. The fact that these three writers are all masters of literary style is not irrelevant. Like the poem, the short story is undoubtedly a type of writing in which style or form is all-important. An indifferent-ly written or poorly constructed novel may succeed by the ingenuity of its plot, by the evocation of some unusual scene or atmosphere, or again by the vivid portrayal of a character; but a badly written short story is almost bound to fail, regardless of its content.

*　　　*　　　*

In the present collection twenty-five well-known modern Japanese writers were chosen and each of these writers represented by one story. The period covered by the stories is from 1910 to 1954; the stories appear in the order of the authors' years of birth. About one half of the stories were selected by the editor, the other half by Mr. Kawabata Yasunari and members of the Japanese National Commission for Unesco, for whose advice and cooperation I should here like to express my grateful thanks. The stories were divided among four translators, three of whom have English as their mother tongue and one Japanese.

Any selection implies a degree of criticism. Omission of certain distinguished writers from the present collection does not, however, suggest any adverse judgment. In several cases writers were omitted because it seemed impossible to represent their work adequately by means of a story. The most notable instance is that of the great novelist, Natsumé Soseki (1867–1916), whose name has appeared several times in the present introduction. Ozaki Kōyō (1867–1903), Kōda Rohan (1867–1947), Shimazaki Tōson (1872–1943), Arishima Takeo (1878–1923), Itō Sei (b. 1905), and many others would certainly have been included if it had been possible to find suitable stories.

The many-sided literary gifts of men like Nagai Kafū and Tanizaki Junichirō can certainly not be represented by a single story or even by a single novel. The most that can be hoped is to display some facet of their talents. Clearly this is more difficult in the case of writers whose forte was the novel and for whom the writing of a story was merely a side issue. From the point of view of most readers, however, a story provides a more satisfactory way of sampling the work of an unfamiliar writer than a selected passage or a synopsis of a novel, even though the novel itself may be a far more representative and interesting work than the story. Few modern novels are susceptible of effective extract and the summary of a novel can hardly be enjoyed as literature. Fortunately a number of modern novels, as well as many other short stories, have been translated into English; readers who wish to read further works by a particular author may find the fairly complete list at the end of the book helpful.

Even the best chosen story, of course, is unlikely to convey the real individuality of the writer, and when stories by twenty-five different writers are put together the effect is likely to be one of blurring and confusion. It is hoped, however, that if each story is read in conjunction with the corresponding note on the author, something of his distinctive personality will emerge. The notes are the work of the respective translators.

Readers who are acquainted with modern Japanese literature will undoubtedly be struck by the inclusion of works by certain writers

who have a far less important place in modern Japanese fiction than some others who (for lack of space) have not been represented at all. Two reasons account for this seeming anomaly. First, certain selections were made, not to represent the work of a particular writer, but because the story itself seemed to be worth including on its own literary merits. Secondly, it was felt that a collection of this type should attempt to carry a few works which, if not eminently successful as short stories, represented certain specific types of modern Japanese writing. Examples of this are the naturalist story, the proletarian story, the plotless, lyrical story, the political satire, the historical story, and the story of village life. The twenty-five selections represent almost every main type of modern Japanese story—with the exception, that is, of the most common form of all, namely, cheap-magazine stories written by popular writers *(taishū-sakka)* whose sole aim is to appeal to as large a public as possible.

There has been no deliberate effort to represent all the different aspects of modern Japanese life. The twenty-five stories do, however, give a remarkably wide picture of the various strata of society during the first half of the present century, and for many readers unfamiliar with Japan this may provide as much interest as their actual literary content. Not a single story has been chosen for its specifically Japanese or Oriental quality. While characteristic Japanese scenes, customs, and psychology emerge throughout the stories, the reader will find nothing in the way of quaintness or "Japonaiserie." Many of the stories do provide an insight into unfamiliar ways of life and thought. In social life as well as in literature it is often the very degree of Westernization in post-Meiji Japan that makes the specifically Japanese qualities stand out. To read the works of a wide range of modern Japanese writers is to rid oneself of many preconceptions and commonly accepted generalizations concerning Japan and her people. At the same time it brings home to us that, impressive as it has been, the break with the past marked by the years 1868 and 1945 was in some ways not nearly so complete as might be supposed.

The question of tradition and foreign influence may be briefly outlined as follows. The Meiji Restoration marked an almost complete break in some fields (e.g., official recognition of a social system in which the warrior class was supreme, official support for Confucianism) and a partial break in others (e.g., the bureaucratic structure, eating habits); but in some fields (e.g., Noh theater, family system in rural areas) there was considerable continuity.

In the case of literature there was hardly any break in the development of Noh or in Haiku poetry, for example, but an almost complete break in the novel and the story. It follows that when we read a collection of modern Japanese stories which attempt to give a realistic picture of contemporary life, we find two things. First, the actual form of the stories owes far more to modern Western influences than to pre-Meiji Japanese literature (here we have a case of the "almost complete break"). Secondly, much of what is reflected in the stories about modern Japanese life (e.g., the social position of women, the geisha system and its ramifications, the attitude to authority, the Buddhist sense of fatalism, the absence of any sense of sin regarding suicide) derives from pre-Meiji cultural traditions. For those who value the persistence of cultural diversity in the modern world this continuity is bound to be a cause for satisfaction.

Modern Japanese Stories

UNDER RECONSTRUCTION

BY Mori Ōgai

TRANSLATED BY Ivan Morris

Mori Ōgai (1862–1922) is considered by many Japanese critics to be the country's outstanding literary figure since the Meiji Restoration. Whether or not we accept this view, Ōgai's name comes logically at the head of any list of modern Japanese story writers.

Ōgai was the son of a doctor. After graduating from the medical department of Tokyo University, he became a surgeon in the imperial army. In 1884 he was sent to Germany to pursue his study of medicine. He remained there for four years, and was thus the first important Japanese writer to become well acquainted at first hand with Europe. Of the Western countries, Germany was to have the greatest influence on Ōgai's thinking and writing.

Ōgai was endowed with extraordinary energy and he succeeded in pursuing a very active literary career while at the same time carrying out his official army duties. Much of his early work consisted of translations of German poems and short stories. In 1890 he published his first piece of fiction. This was "The Dancing Girl," the romantic story of an unhappy love affair between a German dancer and a Japanese man. (There is an echo of this subject in "Under Reconstruction," translated here.) The story appears to have been closely based on personal experience, and Ōgai himself describes it as an Ich Roman. This is an early example of the "confessional" type of writing that was so enthusiastically espoused by the naturalists and the other practitioners of the "I-novel."

Having served in the army during both the Sino-Japanese and Russo-Japanese wars, Ōgai rose in 1907 to the rank of surgeon-general. He retired in 1916 and was appointed director of the Imperial Museum.

During all these years, and until his death in 1922, Ōgai continued his

35

voluminous and many-sided contributions to the literature of the Meiji and Taishō periods. Whatever doubts the Western reader may have about the encomiums that are bestowed on Ōgai by Japanese critics, there is no denying the important pioneer role that he played in the development of the modern literature of the country. His great linguistic ability, combined with an unusual literary gift, enabled him to produce translations of very high quality—and the importance of translations during the Meiji period can hardly be exaggerated. Ōgai is especially noted for his translations of Goethe, Schiller, Ibsen, and Hans Christian Andersen. His translations of Ibsen and Hauptmann had a great influence on the development of shingeki (modern theater), while his translation of a volume of European verse gave a strong impetus to modern Japanese poetry. A profound student of the Japanese classics and of Chinese literature, Ōgai developed a limpid, lucid style which enabled him to set a new standard for translated literature.

Apart from translation, Ōgai was instrumental in introducing the Western type of short story to Japan. He wrote plays in the Western style and at the same time took a very active interest in classical Kabuki. Not the least of Ōgai's contributions was that he helped to found the first systematic literary criticism in the Meiji period; in this he was greatly influenced by the aesthetic theories of Karl von Hartmann.

Together with Natsumé Sōseki, Ōgai was one of the first important writers of the Meiji period to rebel against the influence of the naturalists. Despite the "confessional" aspect of many of his early works and despite his interest in realistic psychological analysis and clinical detail, Ōgai vigorously opposed the naturalists, mainly because of their mechanical attitude to life and their disregard of aesthetic values. In 1909, at the height of the naturalist movement, Ōgai published his novel "Vita Sexualis," a sort of sexual autobiography, in which he attacked the naturalists on their own ground, insisting that the sex instinct, strong as it was, must be considered as only one aspect of human life and not necessarily the most important.

Ōgai's wealth of erudition, as well as his interest in the traditional samurai code of self-discipline, led him in his later years to concentrate on historical stories, novels, and biographies. These are frequently considered to be his finest works. They reveal his minute research into national history and traditions, and also the development of a very high artistic consciousness. By their nature, however, they are not designed to appeal to a large public; nor (as a rule) are they suitable for translation. Although the intellectual element in Ōgai's fiction prevented him from becoming a really popular writer, he was generally respected as the preeminent leader of the Meiji and Taishō world of letters.

The present story (Fushinchū in Japanese) was first published in 1910, when the author was forty-eight. Its background is Tokyo a few years after the victorious war against Russia when Japan herself was "under reconstruction." The Seiyōken Hotel, which continues to do a flourishing business in the Ueno district of Tokyo, represents in microcosm the results of the country's efforts at rapid Westernization, which so often tended to be clumsy and, for those familiar with the West, somewhat ludicrous. It is because Mori Ōgai knew Europe so well himself that he was able, as in this story, to describe the pseudo-Westernization of his own country with such penetration.

IT HAD just stopped raining when Councilor Watanabé got off the tram in front of the Kabuki playhouse. Carefully avoiding the puddles, he hurried through the Kobiki district in the direction of the Department of Communications. Surely that restaurant was somewhere around here, he thought as he strode along the canal; he remembered having noticed the signboard on one of these corners.

The streets were fairly empty. He passed a group of young men in Western clothes. They were talking noisily and looked as if they had all just left their office. Then a girl in a kimono and a gaily-colored sash hurried by, almost bumping into him. She was probably a waitress from some local teahouse, he thought. A rickshaw with its hood up passed him from behind.

Finally he caught sight of a small signboard with the inscription written horizontally in the Western style: "Seiyōken Hotel." The front of the building facing the canal was covered with scaffolding. The side entrance was on a small street. There were two oblique flights of stairs outside the restaurant, forming a sort of truncated triangle. At the head of each staircase was a glass door; after hesitating a moment, Watanabé entered the one on the left on which were written the characters for "Entrance."

Inside he found a wide passage. By the door was a pile of little cloths for wiping one's shoes and next to these a large Western doormat. Watanabé's shoes were muddy after the rain and he carefully cleaned them with both implements. Apparently in this restaurant one was supposed to observe the Western custom and wear one's shoes indoors.

There was no sign of life in the passage, but from the distance came a great sound of hammering and sawing. The place was under reconstruction, thought Watanabé.

He waited awhile, but as no one came to receive him, he walked to the end of the passage. Here he stopped, not knowing which way to turn. Suddenly he noticed a man with a napkin under his arm leaning against the wall a few yards away. He went up to him.

"I telephoned yesterday for a reservation."

The man sprang to attention. "Oh yes, sir. A table for two, I believe? It's on the second floor. Would you mind coming with me, sir."

The waiter followed him up another flight of stairs. The man had known immediately who he was, thought Watanabé. Customers must be few and far between with the repairs underway. As he mounted the stairs, the clatter and banging of the workmen became almost deafening.

"Quite a lively place," said Watanabé, looking back at the waiter.

"Oh no, sir. The men go home at five o'clock. You won't be disturbed while you're dining, sir."

When they reached the top of the stairs, the waiter hurried past Watanabé and opened a door to the left. It was a large room overlooking the canal. It seemed rather big for just two people. Round each of the three small tables in the room were squeezed as many chairs as could possibly be fitted. Under the window was a huge sofa and next to it a potted vine about three feet high and a dwarfed plant with large hothouse grapes.

The waiter walked across the room and opened another door. "This is your dining room, sir." Watanabé followed him. The room was small—just right, in fact, for a couple. In the middle a table was elaborately set with two covers and a large basket of azaleas and rhododendrons.

With a certain feeling of satisfaction, Watanabé returned to the large room. The waiter withdrew and Watanabé again found himself alone. Abruptly the sound of hammering stopped. He looked at his watch:

yes, it was exactly five o'clock. There was still half an hour till his appointment. Watanabé took a cigar from an open box on the table, pierced the end, and lit it.

Strangely enough, he did not have the slightest feeling of anticipation. It was as if it did not matter who was to join him in this room, as if he did not care in the slightest whose face it was that he would soon be seeing across that flower basket. He was surprised at his own coolness.

Puffing comfortably at his cigar, he walked over to the window and opened it. Directly below were stacked huge piles of timber. This was the main entrance. The water in the canal appeared completely stationary. On the other side he could see a row of wooden buildings. They looked like houses of assignation. Except for a woman with a child on her back, walking slowly back and forth outside one of the houses, there was no one in sight. At the far right, the massive red-brick structure of the Naval Museum imposingly blocked his view.

Watanabé sat down on the sofa and examined the room. The walls were decorated with an ill-assorted collection of pictures: nightingales on a plum tree, an illustration from a fairy tale, a hawk. The scrolls were small and narrow, and on the high walls they looked strangely short as if the bottom portions had been tucked under and concealed. Over the door was a large framed Buddhist text. And this is meant to be the land of art, thought Watanabé.

For a while he sat there smoking his cigar and simply enjoying a sensation of physical well-being. Then he heard the sound of voices in the passage and the door opened. It was she.

She wore a large Anne-Marie straw hat decorated with beads. Under her long gray coat he noticed a white embroidered batiste blouse. Her skirt was also gray. She carried a tiny umbrella with a tassel. Watanabé forced a smile to his face. Throwing his cigar in an ashtray, he got up from the sofa.

The German woman removed her veil and glanced back at the waiter, who had followed her into the room and who was now standing by the door. Then she turned her eyes to Watanabé. They were the large, brown eyes of a brunette. They were the eyes into which he had so often gazed in the past. Yet he did not remember those mauve shadows from their days in Berlin. . . .

"I'm sorry I kept you waiting," she said abruptly in German.

She transferred her umbrella to her left hand and stiffly extended the gloved fingers of her right hand. No doubt all this was for the benefit of the waiter, thought Watanabé as he courteously took the fingers in his hand.

"You can let me know when dinner is ready," he said, glancing at the door. The waiter bowed and left the room.

"How delightful to see you," he said in German.

The woman nonchalantly threw her umbrella on a chair and sat down on the sofa with a slight gasp of exhaustion. Putting her elbows on the table, she gazed silently at Watanabé. He drew up a chair next to the table and sat down.

"It's very quiet here, isn't it?" she said after a while.

"It's under reconstruction," said Watanabé. "They were making a terrible noise when I arrived."

"Oh, that explains it. The place does give one rather an unsettled feeling. Not that I'm a particularly calm sort of person at best."

"When did you arrive in Japan?"

"The day before yesterday. And then yesterday I happened to see you on the street."

"And why did you come?"

"Well, you see, I've been in Vladivostok since the end of last year."

"I suppose you've been singing in that hotel there, whatever it's called."

"Yes."

"You obviously weren't alone. Were you with a company?"

"No, I wasn't with a company. But I wasn't alone either. . . . I was with a man. In fact you know him." She hesitated a moment. "I've been with Kosinsky."

"Oh, that Pole. So I suppose you're called Kosinskaya now."

"Don't be silly! It's simply that I sing and Kosinsky accompanies me."

"Are you sure that's all?"

"You mean, do we have a good time together? Well, I can't say it never happens."

"That's hardly surprising. I suppose he's in Tokyo with you?"

"Yes, we're both at the Aikokusan Hotel."

"But he lets you come out alone."

"My dear friend, I only let him accompany me in singing, you know." She used the word *begleiten*. If he accompanied her on the piano, thought Watanabé, he accompanied her in other ways too.

"I told him that I'd seen you on the Ginza," she continued, "and he's very anxious to meet you."

"Allow me to deprive myself of that pleasure."

"Don't worry. He isn't short of money or anything."

"No, but he probably will be before long if he stays here," said Watanabé with a smile. "And where do you plan to go next?"

"I'm going to America. Everyone tells me that Japan is hopeless, so I'm not going to count on getting work here."

"You're quite right. America is a good place to go after Russia. Japan is still backward. . . . It's still under reconstruction, you see."

"Good heavens! If you aren't careful, I'll tell them in America that a Japanese gentleman admitted his country was backward. In fact, I'll say it was a Japanese government official. You are a government official, aren't you?"

"Yes, I'm in the government."

"And behaving yourself very correctly, no doubt?"

"Frighteningly so! I've become a real *Fürst,* you know. Tonight's the only exception."

"I'm very honored!" She slowly undid the buttons of her long gloves, took them off, and held out her right hand to Watanabé. It was a beautiful, dazzlingly white hand. He clasped it firmly, amazed at its coldness.Without removing her hand fromWatanabé's grasp, she looked steadily at him. Her large, brown eyes seemed with their dark shadows to have grown to twice their former size.

"Would you like me to kiss you?" she said.

Watanabé made a wry face. "We are in Japan," he said.

Without any warning, the door was flung open and the waiter appeared. "Dinner is served, sir."

"We are in Japan," repeatedWatanabé. He got up and led the woman into the little dining room. The waiter suddenly turned on the glaring overhead lights.

The woman sat down opposite Watanabé and glanced round the room. "They've given us a *chambre séparée,*" she said, laughing. "How exciting! She straightened her back and looked directly at Watanabé as if to see how he would react.

"I'm sure it's quite by chance," he said calmly.

Three waiters were in constant attendance on the two of them. One poured sherry, the other served slices of melon, and the third bustled about ineffectually.

"The place is alive with waiters," said Watanabé.

"Yes, and they seem to be a clumsy lot," she said, squaring her elbows as she started on her melon. "They're just as bad at my hotel."

"I expect you and Kosinsky find they get in your way. Always barging in without knocking. . . ."

"You're wrong about all that, you know. Well, the melon is good anyway."

"In America you'll be getting stacks of food to eat every morning as soon as you wake up."

The conversation drifted along lightly. Finally the waiters brought in fruit salad and poured champagne.

"Aren't you jealous—even a little?" the woman suddenly asked. All the time they had been eating and chatting away. She had remembered how they used to sit facing each other like this after the theater at the little restaurant above the Blühr Steps. Sometimes they had quarreled, but they had always made it up in the end. She had meant to sound as if she were joking; but despite herself, her voice was serious and she felt ashamed.

Watanabé lifted his champagne glass high above the flowers and said in a clear voice: "Kosinsky *soll leben!*"

The woman silently raised her glass. There was a frozen smile on her face. Under the table her hand trembled uncontrollably.

*   *   *

It was still only half past eight when a solitary, black car drove slowly along the Ginza through an ocean of flickering lights. In the back sat a woman, her face hidden by a veil.

ORDER OF THE
WHITE PAULOWNIA

BY Tokuda Shūsei

TRANSLATED BY Ivan Morris

*Tokuda Shūsei (1870–1943) is one of the representative
writers of the naturalist school, which exercised a preponderant influence on
Japanese literature during the period following the Russo-Japanese War
(1904–05).*

*Unlike most of the authors in this collection, Shūsei received no university
education. After leaving school, he obtained a job on a magazine; later he
worked in a newspaper office. He did not settle down to serious writing until
his thirties.*

*Shūsei's early work consisted chiefly of romantic stories and attracted
little attention. After some years, however, he turned to naturalism, and the
publication in 1908 of his first long novel, "The New Home" (Shinjotai),
immediately won him recognition. Thereafter he produced a voluminous body
of novels and, together with Tayama Katai, Shimazaki Tōson, and Masa-
muné Hakuchō, became established as one of the "four pillars" of Japanese
naturalism.*

*Tokuda Shūsei's terse, direct, unpoetic style was perfectly suited to the
objective and non-sentimental approach that he cultivated in his stories and
novels. Like the other naturalists, he was greatly under the influence of such
late-nineteenth-century French writers as Zola. The aim in his work was to
search out the truth and to provide a scientifically accurate description of it.
His novels are noted for their cold, sharp observation and for their picture of
general gloom and hopelessness. The characters are almost always middle- or
lower-class people of no particular distinction, and the usual settings are the
shabby houses and rooms in the industrial cities of Japan. Shūsei specialized in
portraying women who lived in economically depressed circumstances, and he*

took great pains to describe these women's struggles to manage their husbands, their domestic finances, and all their multifarious difficulties. A recurrent subject is the gloomy type of marriage that is kept intact, not by love or affection, but by inertia, convention, and economic pressure. "Mould" (Kabi, 1911) describes such a marriage from a man's point of view; "The Tough One" (Arakure, 1915) and "Order of the White Paulownia" look at it through the woman's eyes. Another frequent subject is the misery caused by inherited weaknesses. Like Zola, Shūsei was keenly interested in the progressive effects of heredity in families with physical or mental deficiencies.

The present story (Kunshō in Japanese) was first published in 1935, when the author was sixty-five. It is typical of Shūsei's later naturalistic works. Toward the end of his long career, Shūsei grew out of rigid naturalism into a more resigned attitude of acceptance, and his writing reflected a less harsh interpretation of life. It was as a leader of the strict naturalist approach, however, that he exerted his main influence and it was against this approach that so many outstanding Japanese writers of the present century rebelled.

SHE had no great expectations. All she hoped was that she would attain a degree of economic security befitting her modest station in life and, when she got married, an average amount of conjugal happiness. Unlike her younger sisters, who had all succeeded in finding jobs with good prospects, she was in the dismal position of having to get married in order to live. Worse still, the years were passing rapidly as she wavered and soon she would be too old to make a satisfactory marriage.

At the moment she was working as cashier in a cheap restaurant on the Ginza. The waitresses were all about the same age as her youngest sister, and they vividly brought home to Kanako the fact that she herself had already passed the prime of her youth. It had been different in the hosiery factory where she had worked before.

She often thought about that factory. It specialized in the manufacture of Japanese-style socks. Unfortunately the owner had started to run after women. As a result he had neglected his factory, and business had fallen off badly. Just then he had died. His widow was a clever woman. Rising to the occasion, she had taken charge of the management herself. Gradually the factory had been restored to its former prosperity and Kanako had again found it a pleasure to work there.

Everything had been all right until another factory girl, who was her best friend, had a terrible accident. She had been washing her long hair and as she stood near one of the machines a few strands were caught in the cogwheel. An instant later her hair was being pulled into the machine with a fearful swishing sound. Everyone rushed up to her and someone managed to stop the machine. But it was too late. Just like a piece of lawn that has been torn out of the earth, her hair had been dragged out by its roots and nothing was left but a bleeding scalp. It had of course been the girl's fault, yet Kanako could not help being tormented by the wretched fate of her friend. The awful groaning of the machinery now made her unbearably nervous and the factory, once so enjoyable, began to strike her as gloomy and oppressive. The owner was generally considered solicitous about her workers; but Kanako now regarded her as a monster and could not bear to look at her. Her friend had returned to her home in the country immediately after the accident. Kanako did not know the details, but she understood that the amount of compensation the girl received from the factory as a result of ruining her entire life had been nothing short of ridiculous. Yet even this, she was told, was more than the girl would have received from most other employers. Whatever the truth of the matter might be, Kanako had no longer felt like setting foot in the factory.

During the following year she lived at home and helped her mother with the housework. Kanako's mother was a fierce, dauntless woman who had been brought up in the hinterland and who, after many long years, had still not been softened by city ways. She was a stubborn old realist and when she was not preparing for the morrow she was making sure that not a grain of today's rice was being wasted. Even when Kanako sat down to do her sewing she felt her mother's eagle eyes on her and she could not relax for a moment.

In the end the atmosphere in the house became unbearable and Kanako went to Shitaya, where her elder sister ran a little teashop. There she was able to help in the kitchen and with the clothes and the bedding. When it came to waiting on customers in the shop, however, Kanako was too heavy and sluggish by nature to be of much use. Not that she did not try. The relative gaiety of her sister's life filled her with envy and she did her best to mix with the male customers. Yet she was not sufficiently self-confident about her looks or her manners. She tried copying the other waitresses by powdering her face and curling her hair, but it all struck her as rather pointless. As soon as she began to make herself amiable, she felt that she was in some way betraying her own nature.

"Your eyes are just like Madam's," the girls in the shop used to tell Kanako. "You've got a nice round face and lovely white skin like hers, too." She could not help smiling at these compliments; yet she was well aware that, much as she might resemble her sister in some ways, she had none of the elder girl's attraction. Never once was Kanako flattered into believing that she possessed any real charm. Her face was always slightly crooked as though she were about to cry; it reminded one of Chōjirō, the actor.

One of the waitresses in the teashop had formerly been a dancer and she told Kanako about the easy life in the dance halls. Kanako decided to take some lessons, but at her first visit to a dance hall she was thoroughly disillusioned. She could not bear the idea of being dragged round the floor in the arms of one man after another, all complete strangers.

Kanako was afraid that if she continued her present life she might succumb to temptation. She was therefore glad to accept the job as cashier in a Ginza restaurant that one of her sister's patrons, a wool draper, mentioned to her. Here at least she was safe. But it was no easy job to stand by the cash register all day and late into the night.

Meanwhile marriage plans were being discussed. A couple who came from the same village as Kanako's mother called separately on her parents with the suggestion that she should marry Sōichi, the husband's son by his first wife. Originally it had been intended that she should be the bride of Sōichi's stepbrother, Shinichi (who was the wife's son from her first marriage), and negotiations had gone on for some time between Kanako's parents and Shinichi's mother. Shinichi was a fairly pleasant young man. He often used to call at Kanako's house with a bundle of clothes for repair, and he would sit for hours discussing horses with her father, who was a great racing fan. Kanako came to know him quite well. Shinichi's position as a shopkeeper was entirely to her

taste and she grew used to the idea that in due course she would become his wife.

Then in the middle of it all Shinichi's stepfather, Wasao, had pro-
posed to Kanako's parents that she should marry instead his own son,
Sōichi, who was three years younger than the stepbrother. Her parents
made no objection. At first Kanako felt that she was somehow acting
wrongly toward Shinichi, but since he did not seem to care particularly,
she silently resigned herself to the new arrangement and exchanged
the traditional betrothal cups with Sōichi, about whom she knew next
to nothing.

*   *   *

Sōichi, who worked in a large clock factory where his father was
a foreman, had recently come back from military service in Manchuria.
Before entering the army, he had fallen in with a set of bad companions who were employed in the same factory under his father's
superintendence. Through their influence he had started gambling and
had also visited bars and brothels. It was with the aim of having his son
settle down that Wasao arranged for him to be married immediately
on his return from Manchuria. There was no pressing need for his wife's
son, Shinichi, to get married, and Wasao had therefore substituted
Sōichi as Kanako's bridegroom.

After the marriage the young couple moved into Wasao's house.
The father gave them the second story, which consisted of one six-mat
room and one three-mat room.* For himself, his wife, and their two
daughters he reserved the six-mat room and the four-mat room on
the ground floor. Despite this arrangement, Kanako soon found that
the crowded house prevented her from enjoying the happiness of married life to which she had so eagerly looked forward.

The younger of the two sisters, who had just turned sixteen, had
suffered from an attack of pleurisy and since her recovery had been
hanging about the house doing nothing. Yoshiko, the other sister, was
eighteen. She had recently started to learn sewing. After the marriage
she announced that it was too crowded for her to work downstairs and
installed her sewing machine in the three-mat room on the second
story. Kanako soon became accustomed to the whirring of the machine,

* All Japanese-style rooms are measured by the number of straw mats *(tatami)*. A
mat is about three by six feet.

but when Yoshiko took to spreading her bedding next to the room where she and Sōichi slept, she really found it intolerable. She felt that strange eyes were peeping into the happy world which they shared at night, and soon she became extremely reserved with her husband.

Yoshiko, on the other hand, felt as if Kanako were an elder sister who had been added to the family, and for a time she tried to make friends. It soon became clear, however, that they had little in common. Kanako, thanks to her mother's training, had an eminently practical approach, whereas Yoshiko thought of nothing but films and revues. The young girl was a great fan of Chōjirō, the film actor. Not long before, Chōjirō had made a personal appearance at the nearby Kinshi Hall. Yoshiko had pushed her way through the throng of girls and young wives who flocked from the neighborhood to admire him. When she saw that the actor was going to step into his car, she leaped out in front of the crowd and tried to approach him as he stood there in his formal crested kimono. With a frenzied look in her eyes she seized his hand and screamed out his nickname, "Chōsan." There was a stir among the onlookers and they broke into loud applause. Even Chōjirō, accustomed though he was to overenthusiastic fans, was taken aback by this, and he looked at the girl in blank amazement.

When Kanako heard the story, it gave her a strange feeling. She realized that such giddy behavior was fairly frequent among the younger generation, yet it seemed odd that she should be living in the same house with so uncontrolled a girl. Every time that Kanako looked at Yoshiko's freakish features, which she had obviously inherited from her mother, she felt amused and at the same time deeply sorry for her.

In order to show her friendliness, Yoshiko said that she would make a light dress for Kanako to wear in the early spring. From then on she began pestering Kanako about the exact sort of material and pattern that she wanted. It was all the more annoying in that Kanako did not have the remotest intention of wearing the dress. She would gladly have had an extra kimono to add to her wardrobe, but Western-style clothes were utterly out of character.

Kanako's main occupations were washing and sewing. As a rule she would spend the greater part of the day working in her room on the second floor without saying a word to anyone. The cooking was the responsibility of the mother and her daughters. Kanako would have liked occasionally to prepare a meal with a variety of dishes that she could enjoy with her husband. But the household stuck strictly to the rule of having only one kind of food with the rice each day. If there were potatoes, there would be nothing but potatoes for all three meals; if they had cod, there would be nothing but slices of cod. There was never the slightest effort to combine different dishes and Kanako could not help feeling depressed as she sat down with the family to their monotonous meals. To make things even more trying, they never had vegetable pickles. Whatever else she might have missed during her life, Kanako had always had plenty of pickles, and rice without pickles struck her as extremely insipid. Her parents' house was fairly near and she now began stopping by on her way back from the hairdresser's or the public bath. She would slip in by the back door and ask for some pickles, which she then mixed in a bowl with rice and tea and gulped down greedily. Yet the knowledge that she now belonged to another family made her ashamed of these visits and took away most of the pleasure.

Her husband liked Kanako's hair best when she did it up in the old-fashioned, matron style. At first she used to take great trouble in arranging it and would tie the chignon with a red band. Yet gradually she became imbued with the drab, gloomy atmosphere of the household. The mood that had buoyed her up during the early months of her marriage disappeared and she no longer took any pains with her coiffure. Why make her hair beautiful when everything else was so unlovely?

It was just at this time that Sōichi came home late one night thoroughly drunk. Earlier in the evening Kanako had sat downstairs with the younger sister and listened to records. Then she had heated the saké for her father-in-law to sip when he came back from the bathhouse. Wasao returned and said that he would wait for his son to join him at his saké as was their habit in the evenings. Time went by, but still the young man did not return. Wasao was reminded of his son's nocturnal outings in the past and the saké failed to produce its usual enlivening effect. He began to mumble some halfhearted apology on behalf of Sōichi. It made Kanako rather uncomfortable and she took the first opportunity to leave him and go upstairs.

Ten o'clock passed, then eleven, and still there was no sign of Sōichi.

Kanako became impatient. She emptied some old photographs out of a drawer and examined them. Then she began to rummage through some old magazines and storybooks which had been gathering dust in a cupboard. At that moment she became aware of a pungent smell of saké. Sōichi was back. Without a word he sprawled out on the floor like a refractory child and fell into a drunken sleep. This was Kanako's first experience of such behavior and she felt that in a flash she had been confronted with the true nature of men.

* * *

Some time after this incident the young couple moved into a little rented house not far from the parents' home. Wasao, who would normally have objected strongly to the change, was in no position to do so. For on a certain evening while Kanako was pouring saké for him he had made an objectionable suggestion that had utterly infuriated her.

His wife had gone out that evening to the local cinema. She had taken along the younger daughter, but Yoshiko had stayed behind. The elder girl's mental condition had been growing steadily worse and when the time came for the cherry blossoms she had lapsed into real lunacy. After the worst period had passed, they found that her nature had completely changed. The girl, who had formerly suffered from manic frenzy, now became extremely subdued. Occasionally she fell into fits of fearful depression, but most of the time she was reasonably calm. The genesis of Yoshiko's disorder appeared to lie in her obsession with her beloved Chōjirō. One night she had jumped out of bed, crying that Chōjirō was passing outside the window, and she had tried to rush into the street. Evidently she had been aroused by the sound of a group of factory girls walking by after a visit to the cinema; this had in some way stirred up images of the memorable occasion when she had seized Chōjirō by the hand. Wasao was well aware that his daughter's tendency to madness was shared by his wife, who loved him so frenziedly, and he felt that he was imprisoned by bonds of cause and effect from which he could never escape. He sighed deeply and took another sip of saké. Until that year Wasao had always observed the strictest economy. He never made any objections, however, when his wife used to dress up and go out shopping. She used to get terribly lonely when he left for work and sometimes she could not bear to stay in the house.

His wife really adored him. Even in front of the children she would nestle up amorously to her solemn-faced husband and cause him the liveliest embarrassment. The fact that she was a couple of years older than Wasao made her affection all the keener.

"You know, my girl," he said to Kanako, "I really love the old woman. So long as she's alive I won't do anything to cause her unnecessary worry. But when she's dead I'm going to find myself someone better. After all, what's the use of sweating away and making a pile if I can't get any pleasure out of it? The way things are now, I come straight home from work every day. I never set foot in a teahouse, I never go to the races or have any real fun. I just have a bottle or two of saké, get a little tipsy, turn out the lights, and go to bed. Sometimes I feel pretty fed up, I can tell you. There are lots of ways a man can enjoy himself in this world if he's got a little money. Why shouldn't I want to do the same things that Sōichi likes doing? Most men my age, when they've made a decent position for themselves, keep a mistress or two. Now don't get the idea that I'm waiting for the old woman to die. But sometimes I can't help feeling that it would be a good thing if she did die fairly soon. It's not simply that I want my freedom. Just think what would happen if I died first! It would be terrible for my poor wife, and the rest of the family would be in a pretty bad state, too."

Wasao muttered away affectedly. He drained his cup and handed it to Kanako.

"Here, have some saké" he said.

Kanako found it irritating enough to have to pour the saké; to be asked to drink it was doubly annoying.

"Me?" she laughed. "How absurd!"

"Too shy to drink, eh, my girl? That's rather sweet."

He pressed the cup on her, but when she again refused he gave up and resumed his rambling monologue. "That boy of mine's an awful fool," he said, "but I still love him the best, you know. Of course, my children are all the same and there's no real reason I should love one of them more than the others. But Sōichi is the living image of my dead wife. I suppose that's why I worry about him most of all. If only you could have a child by him, my girl, I could pass on my money with a free mind. The trouble is—well, I suppose it's something you should have been told about before you got married, but it was a terribly hard thing to mention at the time. Now that you're a wife you'll understand quite easily and you'll realize it's nothing so bad. The fact is that Sōichi led too wild a life before he went into the army and as a result he can't have any children. It's not too bad, is it? Still, it makes me rather sad that my family line is going to end when Sōichi dies. Now please don't think I'm using all this as an excuse. I'd hate you to think that. But suppose you were to have a child for Sōichi. You know what I mean, girl, don't you?"

Kanako had been listening carefully to what her father-in-law had to say, but suddenly her expression changed. She jumped to her feet and ran upstairs without paying the slightest attention to Wasao's apologies. A few moments later he heard her quietly leaving the house. He did not even try to stop her.

Thus Wasao's plans for a united family in which all the money would remain secure were abruptly shattered. The young couple rented a separate house and the family was split.

Kanako was happy about the change. She thought that at last she and her husband would be able to live a life of their own. She remembered the hosiery factory, which she had not thought about for a long time. When she had worked there, she had given part of her earnings to her mother, and this had been a great help for the household expenses. Why should she not help her husband by doing some work now? As soon as they were settled in the new house, she visited the proprietress of the factory and discussed the matter. It was agreed that she could very well work at home on mending socks which came out of the machine with tangled threads, tears, and other imperfections.

Kanako promptly set to work and to her satisfaction found that she was earning enough to pay for their rent and their rice. So long as Sōichi handed her his monthly pay envelope intact, they would have enough to pay a visit to the cinema a couple of times a month, to have a meal in the restaurant of one of the big department stores when they went shopping, and even to deposit something in the postal savings account.

"I'm not going to stop you two from living apart if that's what you've decided to do," Wasao had told them when they left, "but you'll

have to manage your own finances from now on. Of course if you get ill or something I'll try to help out, but you'd better not count on me too much."

Kanako determined not to ask him for money whatever happened, and she made her plans for their new budget accordingly. Everything would have been all right if Sōichi had given her his full pay as agreed. But he did so only the first month. Toward the end of the second month Sōichi took on someone else's work in the factory and Kanako was happily looking forward to the extra money that he would be earning. When pay day came, however, Kanako found that all her household plans had been in vain. Profiting from the fact that his father no longer was watching him, Sōichi had gone back to his old habit of gambling and had succeeded in losing over half his month's pay. He came home drunk and without a word threw his pay envelope on the floor. Kanako picked it up and emptied the contents.

"Is this all?" she said, holding up two notes.

Sōichi did not answer. He merely stood there, smoothing his unkempt hair.

When they had moved into their new house, Sōichi had taken out his tool box and busied himself with putting up shelves, installing the radio that he had brought from his father's place, and other odd jobs. Occasionally he had taken his wife to a shrine festival, and they had bought themselves something at a stall—a little potted tree or a cage of singing insects. Or again, he had locked up the house and taken her out to a film. Once they had been to see some Western-style dancing at the pleasure pavilion in Sumida Park and had been so captivated by the gaiety of the event that they had not returned home till quite late in the evening.

All this came to an end now that Sōichi had fallen in with his old gambling associates. A small group would get together during the lunch break and secretly play their game behind a pile of crates in one of the factory warehouses. In the evenings they would go to some house and gamble until late at night, and sometimes even until dawn. Most of them worked under Wasao. In theory, the foreman was supposed to prohibit gambling by his subordinates, but in fact Wasao usually turned a blind eye to what was going on. He had got into the habit of advancing money at interest to those who could not pay their gambling debts, and this obliged him to settle Sōichi's losses out of his own pocket when his son fell hopelessly in arrears. Wasao secretly fumed at the stupidity and shiftlessness of this son who, despite his utter lack of skill, had let himself become involved with experienced gamblers. But there was nothing that he could do. As a matter of fact, he himself was far from being ignorant about the game, and he would not have minded Sōichi's gambling if only the young man had been able to win a little money from time to time—money enough, for instance, to pay for an occasional visit to a brothel. But even on those rare occasions when Sōichi did manage to win, his fellow gamblers, who were well aware that his father had saved up a good sum of money over the years, were far too shrewd to let him leave while he was ahead.

Once Sōichi stayed away from home for two whole days. Kanako waited up till late at night, repairing socks that had come from the factory with imperfections. Now all their household expenses had to come out of her own earnings. The New Year's holidays were only a few days off, yet she did not even have enough money left over to buy herself a new collar for her kimono. Sōichi had started to run up debts. He had borrowed money left and right, thirty yen from one man, fifty from another, until his debts, including interest, amounted to some four hundred yen. Whatever happened, he would have to pay this sum before the end of the year. He had been cudgeling his brains about how he could extract the money from his father. The trouble was that Wasao had deliberately entrusted the responsibility for all such matters to his wife. Sōichi found it extremely difficult to approach his stepmother. Despite her good heart she had a very sharp tongue, and any request for money was bound to be met with shouts of "You stupid fool!" or "You good-for-nothing trash!" Sōichi did not relish the prospect.

As she sat sewing her socks, Kanako remembered what her husband had intimated a few days before. "If I don't pay back that money," he had said, "I can't possibly go on living." He was a rather weak-kneed fellow, to be sure, but Kanako could not help worrying lest in a moment of desperation he might have decided to take his life. Perhaps at that very moment he was lying on some railway line waiting for the train to run over him. Since an attack of appendicitis this autumn, he had become more uncontrolled than ever. "I shan't live long anyhow," he had blurted out, "so I might as well enjoy the short time that's left and do just what I feel like."

Kanako was half awake all night, listening for his footsteps at the door. Finally dawn broke and she heard the sound of shutters being opened in the nearby houses and of people going out to empty their buckets. Next to her house was a large yard where a construction company stored stones and rocks, and behind this a small house shared by an umbrella mender and an industrious Korean scrap peddler with a Japanese wife. Directly on the other side of the wall was a widower with two children. Until recently this man had been a traffic policeman and he had made a good reputation for himself. Now he was confined to bed with tuberculosis and had been obliged to leave the force.

Kanako noticed that the Korean scrap peddler used to change into a neat cotton kimono every evening as soon as he came home from work and that he would then take his children out to the public bath. It looked like a happy family. People say a lot of unflattering things about Koreans, thought Kanako, but Koreans can be much kinder than Japanese men. The scrap peddler's wife often used to speak to Kanako at the back door, and Kanako began to wonder whether this woman's marriage to a foreigner wasn't far happier than her own.

She also began to observe the other neighbors. The tubercular policeman received regular calls from the ward physician, and various members of the neighborhood committee would also come to see him. She heard that one of his children had died of tuberculosis that winter and that the father had caught the disease from him. The other two children were no doubt doomed to catch the illness themselves in due course.

In the next house lived a woman of about fifty. After working for twenty long years as a charwoman in an oil company, she had received a retirement allowance of one thousand yen. This piece of luck had completely unhinged her and during the following year she had spent the entire sum on visits to department stores and theaters. Now she scraped along by doing various odd jobs and by using the minute wages of her fifteen-year-old stepdaughter.

Kanako was accustomed to seeing all these people from morning till night, but it was only now that she began to think about them.

Their fates struck her as an ironic commentary on human existence. Life, it seemed to her, was a very gloomy business indeed.

Toward morning Kanako managed to doze off for a while. When she awoke, Sōichi had still not returned. It occurred to her that he might have gone to her sister's teashop, and asking one of the neighbors to look after the house, she set out for Shitaya. But he was not there.

"I'm fed up with him," she told her sister. "I want to leave him and work here with you."

Her sister laughed. "It's funny," she said. "You're the one who was always talking about marriage. But look, Kanako, surely the sensible thing would be to go and talk to his parents."

"I don't want to see those people."

"Well, in that case why don't I phone Wasao at the factory for you? He certainly ought to be told about his son's debts."

As a result of the telephone call, Wasao came directly from the factory in his overalls. It was evening when he reached the teashop in Shitaya. Hearing about the debts, he instantly surmised who had lent his son the money.

"Ah well," he said, "I should have kept Sōichi living with me. I'd have stopped him from this nonsense. I'm not saying that I won't settle for him, but I don't see how I'm going to hide it from the old woman. She'll make a terrible fuss when it comes to paying off those debts. I suppose you think I'm too easy on my wife—letting her control the money like that. But that's how I keep things peaceful and happy at home. Well, I'll manage somehow. Still, it's terrible to have this idiot son of mine fleeced of the money that I've sweated for all these years." He sat there sunk in thought and did not touch the whisky and the plate of cheese that they set before him.

With the help of his first wife's brother, Wasao started making discreet inquiries about his son's whereabouts. Perhaps there was some basis for Kanako's concern. It was just possible that Sōichi might have jumped under a passing train or thrown himself into the crater on Ōshima Island.* Tragic as this would be, it would not, Wasao told himself, be an unmitigated disaster: at least it would save him from having to worry about his feckless son.

* The crater of Mt. Mihara, a truncated volcano on Ōshima Island (some 60 miles southwest of Tokyo), is a popular place for suicides.

There was no news on the following day, but on the evening of the twenty-eighth, just at the beginning of the New Year's holidays, Kanako's parents sent word that Sōichi had returned. So after three days' absence his boy was safe and sound. Wasao hurried off to see him, bringing along the money that he had secretly put aside.

Sōichi was in the middle of supper when his father arrived. He had evidently been involved in a long bout of gambling. His face was unshaven, his cheeks were pale and emaciated; but there was a glitter in his sunken eyes.

"You're safe, my boy," said Wasao. "That's all I care about. I don't know what I'd have done if anything had happened to you. What do four or five hundred yen matter so long as you're all right?"

The tears streamed down his face as he seized his son's hands in his own.

*   *   *

One day the following summer Kanako appeared by herself at the back entrance of her sister's teashop. Since the crisis in December she had been there only twice, once to pay a New Year's call, once at the cherry-blossom season. On both occasions she had been accompanied by her husband. The sister had assumed that Kanako's married life had improved. In view of Sōichi's character this had surprised her somewhat, but at the same time she had felt greatly relieved.

Now a glance at Kanako's dejected face made her realize that her optimism had been unjustified. She put aside her cinema magazine and turned off the electric fan that had been cooling her plump body.

"What's wrong?" she said.

"Nothing . . . nothing really," answered Kanako, looking aside awkwardly. It soon turned out that she had come once again to speak to her sister about separating from Sōichi. Kanako's desire for a separation, however, was rather vague and as soon as she was confronted with her direct, efficient sister she felt that her resolution was ebbing.

After the December crisis Sōichi had made a show of controlling himself. He still did not turn over his full salary, but Kanako decided that she too should try to change her attitude, and she avoided speaking about money matters. Sōichi lost no time in taking advantage of this.

One day Sōichi announced that he was being granted a decoration of the eighth rank and a war medal, together with a small pension for his overseas service. He was as delighted as a child who has received a toy saber from his parents.

"I happened to see it in a copy of the Official Gazette at the milk bar," he told Kanako.

Kanako was overjoyed. "That's splendid," she said. "Really splendid. Don't forget to buy me a little souvenir, will you?"

"Hm," replied Sōichi dubiously. "I don't expect I'll have much money left over. You see, I've promised to stand all my friends a treat."

"What? Already?"

"Yes. But I'm waiting till they've given me the decoration."

A few days later Sōichi received the official notice. He went to the Military Affairs Section of the War Office and was handed a box containing the Order of the White Paulownia and the war medal. On his way home he took them round to show his acquaintances.

Two days later he invited seven of his friends for dinner. He ordered the food from a nearby restaurant and also provided a generous supply of saké. After everyone had had plenty to drink, they turned on the radio and listened to a program of popular songs. One of their group, who despite his rough appearance and raucous voice pretended to some artistic talent, was inspired to give a solo recital. Next a few of the guests sang folk songs. After a time someone complained loudly about the absence of a samisen accompaniment.

"Let's go somewhere and have a good time. What about it, Sōichi?" said one of his friends.

"Good idea," chimed in another of the guests. "Let's get some girls to play for us."

"No, better stay here," someone demurred. "The Order of the White Paulownia will start weeping if it sees us celebrating like that."

Meanwhile the saké was flowing freely and soon their supply was exhausted. Kanako was wondering whether she should go and buy some more when she noticed that a couple of the guests had stood up and were about to leave. Wasao got to his feet, stuffed his purse securely in his pocket, and hurried out. Just then Sōichi came up to her.

"Money," he whispered into her ear. "For God's sake, let me have some money!"

Kanako went to her drawer and took out the thirty-three yen that she had been planning to deposit in their postal savings account. Even

as she handed the sum over to her husband, she knew that she was throwing good money away on the spur of the moment, and afterwards she cursed herself for having been so spiritless.

Now as she sat in her sister's room with a bowl of sherbet in front of her, Kanako felt the hot tears welling up in her eyes.

"Of course he didn't come home that night," she said. "Three·yen and a few coppers—that's all he left me with. Then a couple of days ago he told me that on his next half holiday he was planning to go to the seaside. I haven't been away a single time all summer and I was sure that he would offer to take me along. But no, it turned out that he had arranged to go to Enoshima with some friend and that he couldn't take me. It's really more than I can stand. I even have to go to the cinema by myself now. And those thirty yen—I never dreamed he'd go and spend the whole lot."

Kanako pressed a handkerchief to her eyes.

"You're partly to blame yourself," said her sister impatiently. "You should do things in a more clear-cut way."

As usual, they telephoned the factory and in the evening Wasao appeared at the teashop. He was accompanied by his brother, who was the exact image of Sōichi. It was extremely hot, but Wasao did not touch the iced coffee that was placed before him. Instead he sat there wiping his forehead and complaining of his parasitic children.

"I'm not going to try to keep you from leaving him," he said after he had been told of Sōichi's latest behavior. "All the same, my girl, you were very foolish to give him such a large sum of money. I know how a woman feels in a case like that. She hands over the money before she knows what she's doing. But that's exactly the point I'd like to advise you about. You must be a little firmer, Kanako. You must take a strong attitude with Sōichi instead of just moping. The reason he behaves badly isn't that he dislikes you but that you're too easy with him. I wish you'd give him another chance. But I'm through with him myself and I really don't have the right to ask you."

The uncle, who until then had said nothing, announced his opinion. "I strongly believe that you should go back to your husband," he said.

At this, Kanako's sister took a firmer stand.

"Yes, Kanako," she said, "you really can't continue like this. Each time something goes wrong and you're unhappy, you slip into this sort of irresponsible talk about separation. After all, marriage is a very different thing from what you find in cinemas and novels."

"Yes, I know it is," said Kanako. "But I can't believe it's meant to be like ours. My husband has never shown me the slightest appreciation. Never once. And now I suppose he's got someone else on the side. What a fool I've been!"

"But really, Kanako, you should listen to what everyone's telling you. There'll always be the time later on to break up the marriage if it turns out to be completely hopeless."

In the end Kanako was won over by the uncle's firm attitude and she decided to try again.

* * *

A few days later a large photograph of Kanako and her husband arrived at the teashop. Sōichi was in uniform; the Order of the White Paulownia and the war medal were neatly pinned to his chest. Kanako had her hair in the old-fashioned style and was wearing a silk kimono with a splashed pattern. Behind them was a Shinto shrine sacred to the spirits of the war dead.

HYDRANGEA

BY Nagai Kafū

TRANSLATED BY Edward Seidensticker

    *Nagai Kafū was born in Tokyo in 1879 and died there in
1959. Although descended from a samurai family, he preferred to seek his
spiritual ancestors in the merchant class that made Edo culture. The changing
city was his great subject: nostalgia for the Edo (Tokyo) of the past; dislike
for the untidy, semi-Westernized Tokyo of the present; affection for the near-
outcasts, the geisha and (as in the story translated below) their hangers-on,
who have managed to preserve a little of Edo culture.*

    *His first important work appeared at about the turn of the century, strongly
under the influence of French naturalism. The influence of late-Edo fiction is
also to be detected, however, and with it a lyrical awareness of the moods of
the city that characterized his best work after that. It might be worth noting
that place names play an important part in this lyricism. Japanese literature
has always had a sort of symbolic vocabulary of place names, and a name like
Honjō in "Hydrangea" brings memories of plebeian Edo.*

    *Kafū was in the United States from 1903 to 1907 and in France for a few
months in 1907. The chief products of the years abroad were two volumes of
short stories and sketches, written under the somewhat contradictory influences
of Maupassant and Musset. The major works of the years after his return were
filled on the one hand with rather querulous irritation at Meiji Tokyo, and on
the other with longing for France and affection for the disappearing remains of
Edo. Probably the best of them is "The River Sumida," which, as will be
seen from the Bibliography, is available in English translation. By now Kafū,
like so many other writers of his time was reacting against naturalist trends.*

    *The First World War brought rapid changes to Tokyo, and a growing note
of saaness and loneliness to Kafū's writing. Perhaps concluding that the last*

of Edo was gone, he fell silent from about 1921. When the silence was broken, a decade or so later, it was with novels and short stories which marked a return to his earliest manner, half French and half Edo. The subjects were now barmaids and prostitutes, unlovely successors to the Meiji geisha. Kafū's inability to hide his dislike for his characters rather marred the works of these years.

From about 1937, nostalgia came back again—nostalgia now for the Meiji Tokyo that was once so distasteful. A number of works denied publication during the war appeared after the surrender. They were for the most part expressions of an old man's loneliness, the more intense because the old man had seen so much happen to the most changeable of the world's great cities. "A Strange Tale from East of the River" is usually considered to be the masterpiece of his late years. About half of it has been translated into English.

The present story (Ajisai in Japanese) was first published in 1931, when the author was fifty-two.

WALKING through Komagomé one day, I stepped inside a temple gate and came upon him quite by chance: a samisen player, Tsurusawa Sōkichi by name, from whom I had once taken lessons. That must have been twenty years before. Tsurukidayū was still alive, I remembered, and appearing occasionally on the variety stage.

"An odd place to meet you," I said. "I see you've managed to keep well."

"Very well, thank you, sir. I've often thought how kind you were in the old days, and I've been meaning to stop by."

"Is it true that you've given up the samisen?"

"Yes, sir. I saw that the end was in sight, and decided to quit while I could."

"Good. And what are you doing now?"

"Oh, I have a shabby little geisha house out on the edge of Yotsuya."

"That's much better than trying to make your way as a musician. People don't get ahead by talent these days. Very farsighted of you."

"It's good of you to say so. There were all sorts of reasons. At first I hardly knew what to do next, but now I can see that I was right to make the change."

"You're visiting someone's grave?"

"Yes, sir. And is this your family temple?"

"Oh, no. No, it's just that I'm getting old, and things are expensive —and worthless when you've paid the price. I get bored, and sometimes I go round looking for graves."

"I see. Your companions have all gone on, have they?"

"You sound like a poet, Sōkichi. Do I remember that you wrote haiku?"

"No, sir. The hike from bottle to bed is about all I'm good for."

We had walked round the main hall to the cemetery. The old flower woman was waiting, incense in hand, for Sōkichi. She had sprinkled a tombstone with ritual water and changed the flowers in the bamboo pail. The stone, which carried a woman's posthumous name, was not particularly old.

"Your mother's grave?" I asked casually.

"No, sir." Sōkichi took a rosary from his kimono sleeve. "I wouldn't tell most people, but since it's you, sir—a geisha I was once fond of is buried here."

"You must be getting old yourself, Sōkichi."

"I am indeed, sir. I'm a doddering old man. But you mustn't laugh at me." Sōkichi knelt down, rattled his beads, and muttered a passage from a sutra. "The truth is," he said as he got to his feet, "that I put this stone up without telling my wife."

"It sounds like an interesting story."

"I can't deny that it is, sir. I haven't put up stones for my own mother and father, after all these years. And to put one up at my age for a woman who didn't even ask me—I'm almost shocked at myself. It cost me a good twenty yen, too. Ten for the stone, five to the temple, a little here and a little there."

"What house was she in?"

"The Fusahana in Yoshi-chō. Her name was Kosono."

"I think I've heard of her."

"Most unlikely, sir. She wasn't a geisha you'd have been likely to call. Her house wasn't good, she had no talent. You can guess what sort she was from the fact that even I was a little ashamed to be seen out with her. A person with an eye for it can tell at a glance how good a geisha is, after all."

Across the street there was an old-style noodle shop, its garden as thick with shrubs as a nursery. We followed the flagstones to a little veranda-enclosed cottage. There I heard Sōkichi's story.

*   *   *

It must be fourteen or fifteen years ago now [Sōkichi began]. I was just thirty. It wasn't at Yoshi-chō that I first met her. She was in Shitaya, and she called herself Kimika. I used to see her sometimes after I'd been to your house and had a little to drink. You may remember, sir. I had a geisha in Shimbashi named Maruji. She was well along in years, and I was young and hot-blooded, not one to be satisfied with her and her big-sister ways. She just wasn't the sort you gave up everything for. Well, I was living with her, and sometimes when I had a little extra money, thanks to you or some other gentleman, I would sneak out and buy myself a cheap geisha where I could find one. I had the one regular geisha, you see, and I went round looking for others. You know how it is: there's a special flavor, somehow, in having an occasional drink in a cheap stall. You see, sir?

That's how it was when I first had Kimika, at a little inn just down the hill from the Yushima Shrine. I couldn't pick and choose, after all, when I came at ten and had to be home at twelve. Anyone would do provided she came in a hurry.

I'd be looking at my watch. Sometimes I'd undress while I was waiting, and have a cigarette, and go at her the minute she came in the door. It was pretty much that way with her. I waited awhile, and the one who finally came in was better than I'd expected. I still remember everything. She had on a kimono with a small pattern, dyed over, I'd say. The stiffening at the neck and sleeves had buckled, and the neck band on the under-kimono was dirty. One of the unlucky ones who had to go out any hour of the day or night, you knew right away—sold body and soul to her house. Her chignon was held up in front by wires, and that only made it more obvious how thin her hair was. But her eyelashes were long, her eyes were big and round, and her face was thin and white, and somehow a little sad. Her long neck, her sloping shoulders, in a kimono twice as loose at the throat as an ordinary woman would wear it—a fragile, delicate thing, sir, if anyone ever was. She said very little, she was always looking at the floor, she didn't seem quite used to the work. A shy, retiring girl, you'd have said yourself. I began to feel sorry for her. She didn't have the look of a person who could stay in the business long.

Well, that was the beginning of my mistake. You can't tell about people by their looks, sir, but there haven't been many you could tell less about than her.

"That doesn't sound like you. You let her get the better of you?"

I believe you could say that I did. I don't think she meant to deceive me, but she was not one you could shake off. She almost made a murderer of me. It gives me a good fright even now to think how near I came. I was saved because someone else murdered her first. My name was not involved, but the murder of the geisha in Yoshi-chō did get into the papers. You may have seen it, sir. She had me help her move from Shitaya to Yoshi-chō so that she could get rid of the man she had at the time, a wandering Shinnai singer named Shimezō.

I didn't know then how much she liked men, how quick she was to move from one to another. She was like a hydrangea, sir, that will change color half a dozen times in a day.

Well, when the business was finished, I had nothing to talk to her about and I was in a hurry to go. But she turned those melancholy eyes on me from under her tangled hair and asked me to call her again. She hung on my sleeve and pleaded with me, and there was nothing I could do. It's the ones who have little to say at the table that turn to you when you have them in bed.

I had been seeing her for about a month. I suppose we had met seven or eight times altogether. We knew each other thoroughly, we had told each other everything, and yet there was still a certain restraint between us. Neither wanted to put the other off, neither wanted to bore the other. For lovers, it was the best time of all. Though I hadn't asked her, Kimika had told me all about herself, from when she was very young. Finally she told me how she had become friendly with the Shinnai singer Shimezō. He drank too much, she said, and he liked to gamble, and she hardly knew where it would end. She wanted to break with him. She wondered if she should go back to the country for a while.

My infatuation was growing, and I couldn't tell her to go. "Don't be silly," I said. "Stay in Tokyo. Why not let me take care of you?"

I couldn't help myself, sir. I was no amateur, and I knew well enough how a geisha went about changing houses. She would do better to let me arrange things for her than to go through a broker and pay a fee for a low-grade house. I decided to have her run away to the country. She was to pretend she was going out to visit a shrine. If she had debts, I would arrange to have the master of her house settle for her earnings.

Her home was in Kisarazu and her father was a janitor or something of the sort in a school or the town office. I don't really remember. In any case he was apparently a decent enough person. I first had her go home and write a letter to the house saying that she was ill and would not be back for several days. Then I called her to Tokyo, so that I could see her every day until matters were settled. I wanted most of all to be able to see her, and I had not the slightest intention of using her. I gave her spending money and bought her a return ticket when she left, and after I called her back I rented a second floor from a person I knew in Honjō and bought her what clothes and bedding she had to have—she had left everything at the geisha house.

It all took considerable arranging. Because I was being kept at Maruji's, I couldn't spend my nights away. I had to sneak out at odd hours, and I began to neglect lessons and to lose pupils. There were warnings from my old teacher. My relations with the world narrowed, and I was pressed for money. But the infatuation only grew deeper—that is the way with infatuations. I began to think that I did not want to send her out again as a geisha. It had been decided, true enough, that she would move, and yet I wanted to keep her even a day longer as an ordinary woman. I strained my credit to the breaking. I was sure that, if she were to find out, she would insist on moving to a new house immediately. To forestall the possibility, I pretended that I had all the money in the world. One day I would bring her a length of Akashi crepe, since it happened to be summer, the next I would bring a bottle of perfume. Thinking that it must depress her to be shut up in that second floor all day long, I would take her to the movies in parts of town where we were not likely to be seen, and on the way back we would go to some restaurant for dinner.

Not knowing the real facts, she was deliriously happy. "If only I could go on like this!" she would say, almost in tears. I could no longer be satisfied with seeing her just in the daytime. I would tell Maruji that my mother was ill, or I would say that the weather was warm and a rich patron had invited me to his country villa. After three days or so I would put on a sober face and come back to Shimbashi.

But secrets will out. The world is a small place, sir. The family of the old woman who cooked for Maruji had a house a few doors away from the place I had taken for Kimika. I hadn't the faintest idea that my dirty linen was out in public, and I only made matters worse when I tried to give a sweet answer: "Leave you now? You must be joking. Surely we've gone beyond any talk of separating."

"Sōkichi. There's a limit to making a fool of a person." Maruji gave the straw mat a sharp rap with her pipe. "I'm a geisha too. If you're so much in love with her, go ahead and marry her. I won't complain and I won't interfere. You must excuse me for saying so, but I'm not as hard up for a man as all that. I may have my bad times, but Maruji of Shimbashi is fairly well known and she's not one to be stepped on. I'll send you away all done up in ribbons, Sōkichi, so just sign a statement that there won't be trouble afterwards. And here is a last little token of my esteem."

I counted it later, and there were five hundred-yen notes. Even if he is a broken-down musician, a man doesn't take separation money from a woman. I wanted to push it back and take a kick at that arrogant profile as I turned to stalk from the room. But a thought came to me: this would be enough to settle Kimika's debts. My hand trembling, tears of chagrin in my eyes, I wrote out the statement. I finally gave up playing the samisen because I could not forget the ignominy of that moment. I would not have been subjected to it if I had not been a samisen player.

But as I left Maruji's with the five hundred yen in my pocket, the shame and the chagrin disappeared. I was quite beside myself at the thought of how pleased Kimika would be. The streetcar was intolerably slow. I took a cab to that house by the filled-in Honjō canal. Though it was a summer night, the breeze from the river was cool; and though it was not yet midnight, the strand and the back streets were quiet, and Kimika's windows upstairs and the glass doors downstairs were behind shutters. I knocked and someone switched on the light.

"What? All alone?" It was the woman downstairs.

"You seem to have a bond with wandering musicians," I said. "You break with Shinnai and now it's the fat Gidayū samisen. But don't worry. Stay with me a little longer, and I'll go to the maestro and somehow persuade him to take me back."

But as I wandered the uptown pleasure districts, I caught a bad cold and had to go to bed. We had at last come to the end. I wept, but there was nothing I could do but let her go. She arranged through her broker to become Kosono at the Fusahana in Yoshi-chō, and again put on the bright robes. She said that her debt covered on y the clothes she had to have immediately, and that she was to get sixty percent of her earnings; but when, out of bed, I went to see her, I found that the arrangements were far different: a debt of seven hundred yen, earnings to be evenly divided between her and the house. Her answer was vague when I asked where the money had gone. In my heart I knew that the time had come to give her up. There was no hope of making myself over, I knew, if I went on playing with a woman like her.

Yet I held back. An apology had come from the woman in Shimbashi, but I had my perverse pride. I might have fallen in the world, but I was no kept man. After shaming me as much as a man can be shamed, she had her gall, coming at me now with this sort of pretense. She cared all that much for me, did she? Then she oughtn't to mind if I had a flirtation or two on the side. I wanted no more of her and her big-sister ways. I would show her! I would somehow redeem Kimika and make her an ordinary woman again. Yet at other times I could not understand myself. What could have made me lose myself over such a cheap, fickle, untalented, useless woman?

She was just nineteen. She had begun seeing men when she was no more than thirteen or fourteen, and after leaving home and making the rounds of the provincial teahouses, she had emerged at Shitaya toward the end of her seventeenth year. Suited by nature for the trade she had chosen, she was fairly much in demand, and had decent enough customers; but she was not one to worry about the future. Quite without ambition, she cared nothing about the appearance she made. She simply let the days and months go by—something, you felt, was wanting in her. Yet that very fact made her seem genuine and unpretentious, and somehow sad. I could not see my way toward leaving her. It was, in a word, a ruinous match. I knew how worthless she was.

As I lived with her, however, I too became insensitive to the jeers of the world and my duties to the world. I too came to care less than nothing about work and appearances. Absently, half in a dream, half immobile, I would lie in bed the whole day, not washing my face and not eating. I thought how pleasant it would be if the two of us could become beggars together.

After Kimi moved to Yoshi-chō, memories of the slovenly life we had lived together became a nostalgic dream, and my one pleasure in the world was waiting for the day or two a month when she would stop by, as she had promised, on her way to or from the shrine. Since I had made the gesture of giving her up, I was able to approach my old teacher through an intermediary, and I was again allowed to give lessons.

She did in fact come by two or three times. Although I was far from sure it was proper, she even stayed the night once, and went back toward noon the next day. That was the end. A month passed, two months, the last of the O-tori festivals* was over, in Asakusa the New Year markets were opening. I heard nothing.

I shall not forget that night. It was the twentieth of December, there was a heavy snow, and I was on my way home in the evening from a lesson in the stock-market district. I had a drink against the cold, and meant to take a boat across the river. But as I looked out at the snow I felt less like going, and instead stopped by the Fusahana on the strand. All three girls, including Kosono, had been called out, it seemed. The master too was away, as well as the elderly geisha who served as his wife. The man smoking by the brazier, still in his cloak, was Yamazaki the broker. He was in his forties, and he it was who had brought Kosono to this house. I knew him by sight. I asked how he had been.

He dislodged a cat from a cushion that seemed to be the master's and offered it to me. "You must be very busy. What a shame that there had to be snow just at the busiest time of the year." His thin lip curled in an obsequious smile to show an array of gold teeth. "As a matter of fact, sir, there's something I've been thinking I must talk to you about. I would have gone to see you this evening if the snow hadn't frozen me up."

---

* Twice or three times in November.

"I've come at the right time, then. What's the problem?"

"It's about Kosono, sir. There seems to be no one at home, so perhaps we can have our talk now."

It was hard to know which of them had taken the initiative, but shortly after Kimi had come to the Fusahana she had become the master's woman, and, after some squabbling, the old geisha who had functioned as lady of the establishment had been evicted. Yamazaki had therefore been asked to see me about giving Kimi up. The master would pay whatever I wanted.

I sat staring at the man.

"I quite understand, sir," he went on, "but unless I make a rather embarrassing confession you won't see why. The truth is that I once had a bit of trouble with her myself."

"Oh? You're one of us, are you?"

"It was before she came to Tokyo. I've had little to do with her since, but I've known her for a long time—she couldn't have been more than fifteen—and I don't think I'm completely without information about the sort of person she is. It won't last in any case, sir, so why don't you just take whatever money he has to offer and let her go? He'll be lucky if it lasts till the cherries bloom."

"Whatever happened to that Shinnai man, Shimezō?"

"The master here is only worried about you, sir, and has said nothing about Shimezō. I haven't gone to look for him. I suppose he's the same as ever."

"Has she been called out to a party?"

"She's been away on a trip for several days, I'm told. The other two girls say that before they'll let her be their mistress they'll move away. I found a place for one of them yesterday in this same district, and I think I'll have a spot for the other at Ōmori before the end of the year."

"I see," I said. "I had thought I'd have a talk with her before I decided what to do, but what you say makes it clear that I'll only lose face the more time I let go by. Suppose I just withdraw and leave you to do what you can. Come and see me in Honjō when you find time."

I spoke quietly, and went out into the snow. In the course of the conversation I had made up my mind. I had of course known what to expect when I let her become a geisha again. If a patron had ransomed her I would have had nothing to say, though I might very well have

been annoyed. But to give herself to her master and, without a thought for her debts, to take her place by the brazier and play the grand lady—that I could not allow. I bought a knife as I came out on the main Ningyō-chō street. Meaning to take advantage of the snow and hunt her down in the course of the night, I walked the district until my hands and feet were frozen. I found no trace of her. I went back to Honjō to rest, started out again in the morning, and spent the next days and nights on her trail. All in vain. Maybe she had sensed what was happening. To throw her off guard, I withdrew for several days.

It was the twenty-eighth, three nights from the end of the year. Tonight I would surely find her. I started out as if to have a look at the street stalls, and when the lights were on I did every alley and every lane in all Yoshi-chō. Not a trace of her. The wench was a sly one, I said to myself. She had managed to live beyond her time. I went into a bar, drank from sheer exasperation, and staggered toward home.

It was on the Honjō strand, exactly where I had run into her after being evicted from Shimbashi. About the place where they put the approach to Kuramae Bridge after the earthquake. A crowd had gathered, and I wandered over to see what had happened. There were various rumors: a woman had jumped into the river; she had been stabbed and thrown in; no, it had been a try at double suicide, and the woman had been held back by the police after the man had jumped in. For no reason at all, my heart was racing. When I reached home I found a penciled note on my samisen scores: "I wanted to talk to you, but you were out. I have to run. I will stop by on the evening of the thirtieth on my way from the hairdresser's. Take care of yourself. Kimi."

My chest tight, I ran to the police station. I had not been wrong. The murdered woman was Kimi. Stabbed in the back, she had fallen into the river, and she was dead when the police pulled her out. I had a knife in my kimono and no alibi. I was about to be arrested when a man was brought in. He had given himself up at a police box: the Shinnai singer Shimezō. From his confession it was apparent that he had seen Kimi several times while she was living with me. He had been driven to murder by exactly what had infuriated me: he could not tolerate the idea of her having given herself to her keeper, of her planning to set herself up as mistress of a geisha house.

Many of Shiga's early short stories were written under the spell of high-minded Shirakaba idealism. After a number of years, however, his essentially down-to-earth approach inclined him toward a more realistic form of expression and, like many other members of the Shirakaba school who were to become important writers (e.g., Satomi Ton), he outgrew its rather woolly idealism and launched into his own style of literature with his own ideas. The realism of Shiga's fiction, especially after 1920, has exerted a particular influence on modern Japanese literature.

Shiga Naoya is an intensely personal writer. Most of his principal works are virtually autobiographical. Although he did not originate the "I-novel" or the "I-story," he achieved an unusual degree of literary success in the genre. This inspired many younger writers to follow his example by pouring out on paper the details of their personal experience. All too often their results have been banal or irksome, and in this respect at least it may be said that Shiga's influence has not always been fortunate.

Even when Shiga does invent plots, they are usually of a simple, uncontrived nature and almost invariably we are aware of the author's own powerful personality. His approach is concrete, calm, self-confident. Shiga's writing reveals an explosive hatred for the various manifestations of falsehood and injustice, and a constant search for the means whereby the individual can attain harmony. There is very little in the way of abstract speculation and theory and, despite the preoccupation with human emotions, a minimum of sentimentality.

Shiga is one of the few important modern Japanese authors who is mainly a writer of short stories. He has now been producing short stories for over four decades. They cover a wide field. Many of them are introspective and autobiographical. Others, like "Seibei's Gourds," are brief, delicate, simply-written stories with an undertone of mellow, ironic humor.

Shiga's best-known work, however, is a novel "A Dark Night's Journey" (Anya Kōro); it is considered by many critics to be the great masterpiece of modern Japanese literature, but few foreign readers would share this view. It is a long book written in two parts between the years 1921 and 1937. Strongly autobiographical, it explores the themes of conflict, search, and final serenity. Despite the constant quest for harmony, the dominant mood is one of profound gloom; in this sense it reflects a spirit which was prevalent among Japanese intellectuals during the Taishō and early Shōwa periods, and which also sets the tone of Natsume Sōseki's famous novel Kokoro.

It may seem surprising that despite the relative paucity of his work Shiga

*Naoya should have achieved such an important position in Japanese letters.
The main reason lies in his development of literary style. Shiga spends immense effort on each story and novel that he produces and he always aims at
obtaining the best results with the fewest possible words. The result is writing
of exceptional beauty and deceptive simplicity which has become known as
the "Shiga style." His language is clear, terse, delicate—and often unusually
difficult to translate. Thanks to his sensitive perceptivity, he is able to achieve
the most subtle effects by means of simple, objective descriptions. "Shiga
Naoya," as the literary critic Yoshida Kenichi has written, "is one of the
pioneers in the creation of a literary style in which to express forcibly and
precisely the working of the modern Japanese mind . . . . Only an original
writer like Shiga could weld the disjointed elements of current speech into a
literary vehicle adequate for a true and detailed description of the life going on
about him."*

*The present story (Seibei to Hyōtan in Japanese) was first published in
1913, when the author was thirty. The collection and preparation of gourds is
a well-established practice in Japan, where curio shops often offer gourd bottles
of considerable antiquity and price.*

THIS is the story of a young boy called Seibei, and of his
gourds. Later on Seibei gave up gourds, but he soon found something
to take their place: he started painting pictures. It was not long before
Seibei was as absorbed in his paintings as he once had been in his gourds.

*   *   *

Seibei's parents knew that he often went out to buy himself gourds.
He got them for a few sen and soon had a sizable collection. When he
came home, he would first bore a neat hole in the top of the gourd
and extract the seeds. Next he applied tea leaves to get rid of the unpleasant gourd smell. He then fetched the saké which he had saved up
from the dregs in his father's cup and carefully polished the surface.

Seibei was passionately interested in gourds. One day as he was
strolling along the beach, absorbed in his favorite subject, he was
startled by an unusual sight: he caught a glimpse of the bald, elongated
head of an old man hurrying out of one of the huts by the beach.
"What a splendid gourd!" thought Seibei. The old man disappeared
from sight, wagging his bald pink pate. Only then did Seibei realize

his mistake and he stood there laughing loudly to himself. He laughed all the way home.

Whenever he passed a grocery, a curio shop, a confectioner's, or in fact any place that sold gourds, he stood for minutes on end, his eyes glued to the window, appraising the precious fruit.

Seibei was twelve years old and still at primary school. After class, instead of playing with the other children, he usually wandered about the town looking for gourds. Then in the evening he would sit cross-legged in the corner of the living room working on his newly acquired fruit. When he had finished treating it, he poured in a little saké, inserted a cork stopper which he had fashioned himself, wrapped it in a towel, put this in a tin especially kept for the purpose and finally placed the whole thing on the charcoal footwarmer. Then he went to bed.

As soon as he woke the next morning, he would open the tin and examine the gourd. The skin would be thoroughly damp from the overnight treatment. Seibei would gaze adoringly at his treasure before tying a string round the middle and hanging it in the sun to dry. Then he set out for school.

Seibei lived in a harbor town. Although it was officially a city, one could walk from one end to the other in a matter of twenty minutes. Seibei was always wandering about the streets and had soon come to know every place that sold gourds and to recognize almost every gourd on the market.

He did not care much about the old, gnarled, peculiarly formed gourds usually favored by collectors. The type that appealed to Seibei was even and symmetrical.

"That youngster of yours only seems to like the ordinary looking ones," said a friend of his father's who had come to call. He pointed at the boy, who was sitting in the corner busily polishing a plain, round gourd.

"Fancy a lad spending his time playing around like that with gourds!" said his father, giving Seibei a disgusted look.

"See here, Seibei my lad," said the friend, "there's no use just collecting lots of those things. It's not the quantity that counts, you know. What you want to do is to find one or two really unusual ones."

"I prefer this kind," said Seibei and let the matter drop.

Seibei's father and his friend started talking about gourds.

"Remember that Bakin gourd they had at the agricultural show last spring?" said his father. "It was a real beauty, wasn't it?"

"Yes, I remember. That big, long one. . . ."

As Seibei listened to their conversation, he was laughing inwardly. The Bakin gourd had made quite a stir at the time, but when he had gone to see it (having no idea, of course, who the great poet Bakin might be) he had found it rather a stupid-looking object and had walked out of the show.

"I didn't think so much of it," interrupted Seibei. "It's just a clumsy great thing."

His father opened his eyes wide in surprise and anger.

"What's that?" he shouted. "When you don't know what you're talking about, you'd better shut up!"

Seibei did not say another word.

One day when he was walking along an unfamiliar back street he came upon an old woman with a fruit stall. She was selling dried persimmons and oranges; on the shutters of the house behind the stall she had hung a large cluster of gourds.

"Can I have a look?" said Seibei and immediately ran behind the stall and began examining the gourds. Suddenly he caught sight of one which was about five inches long and at first sight looked quite commonplace. Something about it made Seibei's heart beat faster.

"How much is this one?" he asked, panting out the words.

"Well," said the old woman, "since you're just a lad, I'll let you have it for ten sen."

"In that case," said Seibei urgently, "please hold it for me, won't you? I'll be right back with the money."

He dashed home and in no time at all was back at the stall. He bought the gourd and took it home.

From that time on, he was never separated from his new gourd. He even took it along to school and used to polish it under his desk during class time. It was not long before he was caught at this by one of the teachers, who was particularly incensed because it happened to take place in an ethics class.

This teacher came from another part of Japan and found it most offensive that children should indulge in such effeminate pastimes as collecting gourds. He was forever expounding the classical code of the samurai, and when Kumoemon, the famous Naniwabushi performer, came on tour and recited brave deeds of ancient times, he would attend every single performance, though normally he would not deign to set foot in the disreputable amusement area. He never minded having his students sing Naniwabushi ballads, however raucously. Now, when he found Seibei silently polishing his gourd, his voice trembled with fury.

"You're an idiot!" he shouted. "There's absolutely no future for a boy like you." Then and there he confiscated the gourd on which Seibei had spent so many long hours of work. Seibei stared straight ahead and did not cry.

When he got home, Seibei's face was pale. Without a word, he put his feet on the warmer and sat looking blankly at the wall.

After a while the teacher arrived. As Seibei's father was not yet home from the carpenter's shop where he worked, the teacher directed his attack at Seibei's mother.

"This sort of thing is the responsibility of the family," he said in a stern voice. "It is the duty of you parents to see that such things don't happen." In an agony of embarrassment, Seibei's mother muttered some apology.

Meanwhile, Seibei was trying to make himself as inconspicuous as possible in the corner. Terrified, he glanced up at his vindictive teacher and at the wall directly behind where a whole row of fully prepared gourds was hanging. What would happen if the teacher caught sight of them?

Trembling inside, he awaited the worst, but at length the man exhausted his rhetoric and stamped angrily out of the house. Seibei heaved a sigh of relief.

Seibei's mother was sobbing softly. In a querulous whine she began to scold him, and in the midst of this, Seibei's father returned from his shop. As soon as he heard what had happened, he grabbed his son by the collar and gave him a sound beating. "You're no good!" he bawled at him. "You'll never get anywhere in the world the way you're carrying on. I've a good mind to throw you out into the street where you belong!" The gourds on the wall caught his attention. Without a word, he fetched his hammer and systematically smashed them to pieces one after another. Seibei turned pale but said nothing.

The next day the teacher gave Seibei's confiscated gourd to an old porter who worked in the school. "Here, take this," he said, as if handing over some unclean object. The porter took the gourd home with him and hung it on the wall of his small, sooty room.

About two months later the porter, finding himself even more hard pressed for money than usual, decided to take the gourd to a local curio shop to see if he could get a few coppers for it. The curio dealer examined the gourd carefully; then, assuming an uninterested tone, he handed it back to the porter saying: "I might give you five yen for it."

The porter was astounded, but being quite an astute old man, he replied coolly: "I certainly wouldn't part with it for that." The dealer immediately raised his offer to ten yen, but the porter was still adamant.

In the end the curio dealer had to pay fifty yen for the gourd. The porter left the shop, delighted at his luck. It wasn't often that the teachers gave one a free gift equivalent to a year's wages! He was so clever as not to mention the matter to anyone, and neither Seibei nor the teacher ever heard what had happened to the gourd. Yes, the porter was clever, but he was not clever enough: little did he imagine that this same gourd would be passed on by the curio dealer to a wealthy collector in the district for six hundred yen.

*　　　*　　　*

Seibei is now engrossed in his pictures. He no longer feels any bitterness either toward the teacher, or toward his father who smashed all his precious gourds to pieces.

Yet gradually his father has begun to scold him for painting pictures.

TATTOO

BY Tanizaki Junichirō

TRANSLATED BY Ivan Morris

  Tanizaki Junichirō was born in Tokyo in 1886. He belonged to the old Japanese merchant class, which had developed during the Edo period; his father was a rice broker. Despite his deep roots in traditional ways, he was from an early age fascinated with the West and its innovations; this dualism was to play an important part both in his life and in his writing.

  Tanizaki studied classical Japanese literature at Tokyo Imperial University and during his student days he and a group of literary friends published a magazine called New Thought. *Many of Tanizaki's earliest stories, including "Tattoo," appeared in this magazine. These stories were mostly written in a strongly romantic vein and showed the full force of the contemporary reaction against naturalism. Their publication brought the author's name to the attention of the critics and, together with Nagai Kafū, Tanizaki soon became known as a leader of the so-called neo-romantic school.*

  "Tattoo" exhibits many of the European influences, notably those of Poe, Baudelaire, and Oscar Wilde, that helped to shape Tanizaki's early writing and to direct his romanticism into sensual, aesthetic channels. At this period Tanizaki was obsessed with cruelty, sexual aberration, and the mysterious "demonic" forces that had fascinated Poe. Japanese critics, with their fondness for classification, lost no time in labeling Tanizaki as a "satanic" writer.

  The stories of the early period are marked by a rather un-Japanese form of aestheticism, liberally flavored with hedonism and sado-masochism. One of the

*principal motives appears to have been a sensuous adoration for women—
adoration of a type, it may be added, that is rarely found in Japanese literature.
The girl in "Tattoo" is typical of Tanizaki's early heroines: she possesses a
peculiar sensuous beauty which, combined with her latent sadism, is capable of
arousing a perverted form of excitement in the artist-observer.*

*Tanizaki lived in the Tokyo area until the great earthquake of 1923,
when he moved to the gentler, more cultured region of Kyoto. It was here
that he steadily became absorbed in the Japanese past. In the following years he
seems to have lost some of his fascination with the West and also to have
abandoned his pursuit of "satanism." The brilliant, sensuous writing of his
early years gave way to a more subdued and natural style. It should not, however, be suggested that there was any profound break in Tanizaki's literary
development. His increasingly Japanese, conservative outlook did not mark
the end of his interest in the West. Indeed, the conflict between the lure of
Western innovations and the nostalgia for traditional Japanese ways received
its finest, most sensitive treatment in* Tade Kuu Mushi *("Some Prefer
Nettles"), published in 1928.*

*After 1931 Tanizaki wrote a series of short novels, many of which were
inspired by nostalgic, traditionalistic themes. Traces of the earlier aestheticism
and sado-masochism still remain in works like Shunkinshō ("The Tale of
Shunkin, 1933), which tells the story of a blind woman musician whose
pride and arrogance are coupled with strong sadistic leanings and of her life-
long admirer who finally blinds himself out of love for her. Among Tanizaki's
major literary works is his masterly translation into modern Japanese of the
great eleventh-century classic, "The Tale of Genji"; this was started before
the war, but only recently completed. The literary success of this immense
undertaking was largely a result of the purity of style that characterizes all
Tanizaki's best work. The theme of nostalgia dominated Sasameyuki ("The
Makioka Sisters," 1934-38), another of Tanizaki's lengthy novels. This
is a roman fleuve which gives a meticulous recreation of middle-class life in
pre-war Osaka. Like much of his fiction, it has a pronounced autobiographical
element. Tanizaki's most recent novel Kagi ("The Key," 1958) describes
the marital relations of a middle-aged couple; its preoccupation with certain
perverted and grotesque aspects of sex is in some ways reminiscent of the
writings of his youthful period.*

*The present story (Irezumi in Japanese) was first published in 1910,
when the author was twenty-four.*

THESE things happened at a time when the noble virtue of frivolity still flourished, when today's relentless struggle for existence was yet unknown. The faces of the young aristocrats and squires were darkened by no cloud; at court the maids of honor and the great courtesans always wore smiles on their lips; the occupations of clown and professional teahouse wit were held in high esteem; life was peaceful and full of joy. In the theater and in the writings of the time, beauty and power were portrayed as inseparable.

Physical beauty, indeed, was the chief aim of life, and in its pursuit people went so far as to have themselves tattooed. On their bodies, brilliant lines and colors were raveled in a sort of dance. When visiting the gay quarters, they would choose as bearers for their palanquins men whose bodies were skillfully tattooed, and the courtesans of Yoshiwara and Tatsumi gave their love to men whose bodies boasted beautiful tattoos. Frequenters of the gambling dens, firemen, merchants, and even samurai all had recourse to the tattooer's art. Tattoo exhibitions were frequently arranged where the participants, fingering the tattoo marks on each other's bodies, would praise the original design of one and criticize the shortcomings of another.

There was a young tattooer of outstanding talent. He was much in fashion and his reputation rivaled even those of the great masters of old, Charibun of Asakusa, Yakkohei of Matsushimachō, and Konkonjirō. His works were greatly prized at the tattoo exhibitions and most admirers of the art aspired to become his clients. While the artist Darumakin was known for his fine drawings and Karakusa Gonta was the master of the vermilion tattoo, this man Seikichi was famous for the originality of his compositions and for their voluptuous quality.

Previously he had achieved a certain reputation as a painter, belonging to the school of Toyokuni and Kunisada and specializing in genre paintings. In descending to the rank of tattooer, he still preserved the true spirit of an artist and a great sensitivity. He declined to execute his work on people whose skin or general physique did not appeal to him, and such customers as he did accept had to agree implicitly to the design of his choosing and also to his price. Moreover, they had to endure for as long as one or two months the excruciating pain of his needles.

Within this young tattooer's heart lurked unsuspected passions and pleasures. When the pricking of his needles caused the flesh to swell and the crimson blood to flow, his patients, unable to endure the agony, would emit groans of pain. The more they groaned, the greater was the artist's strange pleasure. He took particular delight in vermilion designs, which are known to be the most painful of tattoos. When his clients had received five or six hundred pricks of the needle and then taken a scalding hot bath the more vividly to bring out the colors, they would often collapse half dead at Seikichi's feet. As they lay there unable to move, he would ask with a satisfied smile: "So it really hurts?"

When he had to deal with a fainthearted customer whose teeth would grind or who gave out shrieks of pain, Seikichi would say: "Really, I thought you were a native of Kyoto where people are supposed to be courageous. Please try to be patient. My needles are unusually painful." And glancing from the corner of his eyes at the victim's face, now moist with tears, he would continue his work with utter unconcern. If, on the contrary, his patient bore the agony without flinching, he would say: "Ah, you are much braver than you look. But wait a while. Soon you will be unable to endure it in silence, try as you may." And he would laugh, showing his white teeth.

*　　　*　　　*

For many years now, Seikichi's great ambition had been to have under his needle the lustrous skin of some beautiful girl, on which he dreamed of tattooing, as it were, his very soul. This imaginary woman had to meet many conditions as to both physique and character; a lovely face and a fine skin would not in themselves satisfy Seikichi. In vain had he searched among the well-known courtesans for a woman who would measure up to his ideal. Her image was constantly in his mind, and although three years had now elapsed since he started this quest, his desire had only grown with time.

It was on a summer's evening while walking in the Fukagawa district that his attention was caught by a feminine foot of dazzling whiteness disappearing behind the curtains of a palanquin. A foot can convey as many variations of expression as a face, and this white foot seemed to Seikichi like the rarest of jewels. The perfectly shaped toes, the iridescent nails, the rounded heel, the skin, as lustrous as if it had been washed for ages by the limpid waters of some mountain brook—all combined to make a foot of absolute perfection designed to stir the heart of a man and to trample upon his soul. Seikichi knew at once that this was the foot of the woman for whom he had searched these many years. Joyously he hurried after the palanquin, hoping to catch a glimpse of its occupant, but after following it for several streets, he lost sight of it around a corner. From then on what had been a vague yearning was transformed into the most violent of passions.

One morning a year later Seikichi received a visit at his house in the Fukagawa district. It was a young girl sent on an errand by a friend of his, a certain geisha from the Tatsumi quarter.

"Excuse me, sir," the girl said timidly. "My mistress has asked me to deliver this coat to you personally and to request you to be so good as to make a design on the lining."

She handed him a letter and a woman's coat, the latter wrapped in a paper bearing the portrait of the actor Iwai Tojaku. In her letter the geisha informed Seikichi that the young messenger was her newly adopted ward and was soon to make her debut as a geisha in the restaurants of the capital. She asked him to do what he could to launch the girl on her new career.

Seikichi looked closely at the visitor who, though no more than sixteen or seventeen, had in her face something strangely mature. In her eyes were reflected the dreams of all the handsome men and beautiful women who had lived in this city, where the virtues and vices of the whole country converged. Then Seikichi's glance went to her delicate feet, shod in street clogs covered with plaits of straw.

"Could it have been you who left the Hirasei restaurant last June in a palanquin?"

"Yes, sir, it was I," she said, laughing at his strange question. "My father was still alive then and he used to take me occasionally to the Hirasei restaurant."

"I have been waiting for you now for five years," said Seikichi. "This is the first time that I have seen your face but I know you by your feet. . . . There is something that I should like you to see. Please come inside, and do not be afraid."

So saying, he took the hand of the reluctant girl and led her upstairs into a room which looked out on the great river. He fetched two large picture scrolls and spread one of them before her.

It was a painting of Mo Hsi, the favorite princess of the ancient Chinese emperor, Chou the Cruel. Languidly she leaned against a balustrade, and the bottom of her richly brocaded gown rested on the steps of the staircase leading to a garden. Her tiny head seemed almost too delicate to support the weight of her crown, which was encrusted with lapis lazuli and coral. In her right hand she held a cup, slightly tilted, and with an indolent expression she watched a prisoner who was about to be beheaded in the garden below. Secured hand and foot to a stake, he stood there awaiting his last moment; his eyes were closed, his head bent down. Pictures of such scenes tend to vulgarity, but so skillfully had the painter portrayed the expressions of the princess and of the condemned man that this picture scroll was a work of consummate art.

For a while the young girl fixed her gaze on the strange painting. Unconsciously her eyes began to shine and her lips trembled; gradually her face took on a resemblance to that of the young Chinese princess.

"Your spirit is reflected in that painting," said Seikichi, smiling with pleasure as he gazed at her.

"Why have you shown me such a terrible picture?" asked the girl, passing her hand over her pale forehead.

"The woman depicted here is yourself. Her blood flows through your veins."

Seikichi then unrolled the other scroll, which was entitled "The Victims." In the center of the picture a young woman leaned against a cherry tree, gazing at a group of men's corpses which lay about her feet; pride and satisfaction were to be discerned in her pale face. Hopping about among the corpses, a swarm of little birds chirped happily. Impossible to tell whether the picture represented a battlefield or a spring garden!

"This painting symbolizes your future," said Seikichi, indicating the face of the young woman, which again strangely resembled that of his visitor. "The men fallen on the ground are those who will lose their lives because of you."

"Oh, I beg you," she cried, "put that picture away." And as if to

its dreamy light over the rooftops on the other side of the river. The tattoo was not yet half done. Seikichi interrupted his work to turn up the lamp, then sat down again and reached for his needle.

Now each stroke demanded an effort, and the artist would let out a sigh, as if his own heart had felt the prick. Little by little there began to appear the outline of an enormous spider. As the pale glow of dawn entered the room, this animal of diabolic mien spread its eight legs over the girl's back.

The spring night was almost over. Already one could hear the dip of the oars as the rowboats passed up and down the river; above the sails of the fishing smacks, swollen with the morning breeze, one could see the mists lifting. And at last Seikichi brought himself to put down his needle. Standing aside, he studied the enormous female spider tattooed on the girl's back, and as he gazed at it, he realized that in this work he had expressed the essence of his whole life. Now that it was completed, the artist was aware of a great emptiness.

"To give you beauty I have poured my whole soul into this tattoo," Seikichi murmured. "From now on there is not a woman in Japan to rival you! Never again will you know fear. All men, all men will be your victims. . . ."

Did she hear his words? A moan rose to her lips, her limbs moved. Gradually she began to regain consciousness, and as she lay breathing heavily in and out, the spider's legs moved on her back like those of a living animal.

"You must be suffering," said Seikichi. "That is because the spider is embracing your body so closely."

She half opened her eyes. At first they had a vacant look, then the pupils began to shine with a brightness that matched the moonlight reflected on Seikichi's face.

"Master, let me see the tattoo on my back! If you have given me your soul, I must indeed have become beautiful."

She spoke as in a dream, and yet in her voice there was a new note of confidence, of power.

"First you must take a bath to brighten the colors," Seikichi answered her. And he added with unwonted solicitude: "It will be painful, most painful. Have courage!"

"I will bear anything to become beautiful," said the girl.

She followed Seikichi down some stairs into the bathroom, and as she stepped into the steaming water her eyes glistened with pain.

"Ah, ah, how it burns!" she groaned. "Master, leave me and wait upstairs. I shall join you when I am ready. I do not want any man to see me suffer."

But when she stepped out of the bath, she did not even have strength to dry herself. She pushed aside Seikichi's helping hand and collapsed on the floor. Groaning, she lay with her long hair flowing across the floor. The mirror behind her reflected the soles of two feet, iridescent as mother-of-pearl.

Seikichi went upstairs to wait for her, and when at last she joined him she was dressed with care. Her damp hair had been combed out and hung about her shoulders. Her delicate mouth and curving eyebrows no longer betrayed her ordeal, and as she gazed out at the river there was a cold glint in her eyes. Despite her youth she had the mien of a woman who had spent years in teahouses and acquired the art of mastering men's hearts. Amazed, Seikichi reflected on the change in the timid girl since the day before. Going to the other room, he fetched the two picture scrolls which he had shown her.

"I offer you these paintings," he said. "And also, of course, the tattoo. They are yours to take away."

"Master," she answered, "my heart is now free from all fear. And you . . . you shall be my first victim!"

She threw him a look, piercing as a newly sharpened sword blade. It was the look of the young Chinese princess, and of that other woman who leaned against a cherry tree surrounded by singing birds and dead bodies. A feeling of triumph raced through Seikichi.

"Let me see your tattoo," he said to her. "Show me your tattoo."

Without a word, she inclined her head and unfastened her dress. The rays of the morning sun fell on the young girl's back and its golden gleam seemed to set fire to the spider.

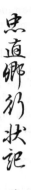

菊
池
寛

ON THE CONDUCT
OF LORD TADANAO

BY Kikuchi Kan

TRANSLATED BY Geoffrey Sargent

*Kikuchi Kan (1888–1948), though a prolific writer to
the year of his death, produced his most distinguished work—mostly short
stories and one-act plays—in the brief period from 1917 to 1920. A realist and
skeptic in literature and a shrewd businessman in life, he subsequently scan-
dalized the purists by turning to the production of literature for the masses,
writing magazine serials (with one eye on the cinema), extremely popular
dramas, and even (during the China Incident) government propaganda; and
the financial success he thus achieved has had an adverse effect upon his posthumous reputation.*

*The present story (Tadanao-kyō Gyōjō Ki in Japanese) was first pub-
lished in 1918, when the author was thirty. It immediately attracted wide
attention and set the fashion for a spate of imaginative reinterpretations of
episodes in Japanese history or legend, expounding a clear thesis, which were
known as "theme novels" (tēma shōsetsu). The story deals with a cause
célèbre of the seventeenth century—the dispossession and banishment in 1623
of the young Daimyo of Echizen, lord of one of the greatest fiefs in the land—
and its rather paradoxical theme is the inhumanity of the feudal system, not
toward the oppressed vassals but toward the exalted daimyo.*

I

Lord Tadanao's councilors were summoned before Ieyasu at his headquarters and treated by His Excellency to an eloquent burst of abuse.

"When Ii Tōdō's forces were in trouble today, were the Echizen retainers taking a midday nap? Did no one tell them what was happening? If they had moved forward, covering the rear of the main attack, Osaka Castle would have fallen this very day. But, no. Thanks to your general's youth, and thanks to his councilors' being the biggest cowards in Japan, we have thrown away a battle! A precious battle!"

Ieyasu did not wait for an answer. Livid with rage, he rose at once and left the room.

The senior councilor, Honda Tomimasa, had come prepared with several excellent excuses for the Echizen forces' failure to take part in the day's fighting, but this perfunctory dismissal took him by surprise. He had not had a chance to utter a word.

There was obviously nothing more they could do, but the mood of the councilors, as they withdrew from headquarters and returned to the Echizen camp, was very far from one of philosophic resignation. They were in a panic. One thought tormented them all. How on earth could they phrase this matter when they made their report to Lord Tadanao?

General Lord Tadanao, Daimyo of Echizen, was twenty-one. He had inherited his huge fief, with its annual revenue of almost three and a half million bushels of rice, at the tender age of thirteen upon the death of his father, Hidéyasu. His father had died in the intercalary fourth month of the year 1607, and never, from that moment until now, had the general suspected the existence, this side of heaven, of a will stronger than his own.

The natural strength of will—or perhaps one should say the natural willfulness—which the general had brought with him into the world had since been cultivated by him to a growth of towering proportions, like a lone cedar shooting skyward from the peak of a lofty mountain. The councilors remembered the trepidation with which they had entered his presence, the gingerly fashion in which they had broken the news, when the order to join the present campaign had first reached the Echizen household.

"Letters have been received from His Excellency the Shogun's father," they had reported. "He cordially requests your appearance before Osaka, with your forces." The custom of representing to their young master that his will was absolute had by that time become second nature.

And today it was their inescapable duty to convey Ieyasu's words of rebuke to Lord Tadanao. What reactions might be set in motion by such outspoken criticism—for the sensation of being rebuked had had no part in their master's experience, waking or dreaming, since the day he was born—was a question which naturally afforded them the liveliest misgivings.

Lord Tadanao called them to his quarters as soon as he heard of their return.

"And what did His Excellency my grandfather have to say? The usual set phrases of thanks for our labors, I suppose?" Lord Tadanao was in high spirits, and he smiled pleasantly as he put his questions. But this affability only increased the embarrassment of his councilors. It was some time before one of them gathered up sufficient courage to make a reply, and when he spoke his voice trembled.

"I fear your lordship is mistaken. The fact that the Echizen forces took no part in today's fighting seems to have aroused his excellency's anger, and . . ." He ventured no more. The color drained from his face, and he prostrated himself on the ground.

Never having known how it felt to be crossed or scolded, Lord Tadanao had developed no mechanism of resistance to the sensation, and no means of controlling himself when under its influence.

"Eh! What did he say?" he bellowed. "When I begged to lead the attack he forbade it. And does he still affront me? Tadanao, die!—that is the meaning of my grandfather's riddles. To all of us, to you as well as to myself, he says—die! Tomorrow, then, lord and vassal alike, we shall drench the enemy's swords with our blood! Our corpses will whiten and rot beneath the castle walls! Tell this to my soldiers, and let them prepare themselves for death!"

Tadanao's hands, folded on his lap, were visibly trembling. With a sudden movement, as if he could bear the restraint no longer, he snatched his Nagamitsu sword from the hands of a page boy, unsheathed the blade, and thrust it forward before the councilors' faces.

"See! On this Nagamitsu I shall spike the head of Hidéyori, and thus shall I thrust it into my grandfather's face!" Seated on the floor though he was, he brandished the sword above his head and cut a series of wide circles in the air.

Lord Tadanao, not much over twenty, was still subject to occasional half-lunatic tantrums of this sort. His councilors, whose experience of such outbursts dated back to the days of Tadanao's father, merely shut their ears to the noise and lay prostrate on the ground, as if waiting for a gale to blow over.

* * *

The leaden skies of the last few days had vanished, and the seventh day of the fifth month of the year 1615 dawned exceptionally clear and still.

The fall of Osaka castle was now simply a question of time. Most of the more distinguished captains among its garrison—men like Gotō Matabei, Kimura Nagato, and Susukida Hayatonoshō—had been killed in the desperate fighting of the previous summer, and now only Sanada Saemon, Chōsokabé Morichika, Mōri of Buzen, and a handful of others were left to face the final onslaught.

The Shogun, Lord Hidétada, rose early this day and set out from his quarters an hour before dawn. At once he ordered the detachments of Matsudaira Toshitsuné of Chikuzen, Katō Samanosuké Yoshiaki, and Kuroda Nagamasa of Kai to move forward to the Okayama pass and take up positions as the first line of attack.

Shortly after dawn Ieyasu appeared, borne from his quarters in a palanquin. He wore a short jacket of brown silk, a thin white kimono, and formal overskirts bound tightly at each ankle. Tōdō Takatora, meeting him by chance, expressed concern at this unwarlike mode of dress.

"Today, surely, Your Excellency should be wearing armor?"

Ieyasu grinned, and in his eyes was the usual glint of sly mockery.

"Armor?" he said. "I need no armor to finish off the little fellow in Osaka."

In one hand he held a priest's horsehair flapper, and with this he beat off the flies which kept swarming about him. Some thirty of his most trusted retainers, including Naitō Kamon-no-Kami Masanari, Uemura Iemasa of Dewa, and Itakura Naizen-no-sho Shigémasa, walked in attendance upon the palanquin. And at the end of the procession, dressed exactly like Ieyasu and carried in a similar but lighter palanquin, came Honda Masanobu of Sado.

Drawn up across the plain, between the Okayama and Tennōji highways, lay an army of more than a hundred and fifty thousand men. Banners fluttered in the early summer breeze, and polished helmet-graces flashed in the sun. Each detachment, drawn up in orderly ranks in its allotted position, stood waiting for the now overdue word of attack. But the handing down of this word was apparently no simple matter. Three messengers from Ieyasu, on white chargers, now wove their way through the assembled units.

"Room is being made in the ranks for Lords Yoshinao and Yori-nobu," they announced. "The forces in the van are not yet to open the engagement. They will withdraw their horses a distance of one to two hundred yards, dismount, hold their lances at the ready, and await further orders."

This was not to the liking of Lord Tadanao of Echizen. His mind had been in a fever of excitement ever since the shock of the previous evening, and he had passed an almost sleepless night waiting for today's battle. Now, as soon as he heard this last order, he sent Councilor Yoshida Shuri ahead to prepare the way and then moved forward himself with his whole force of near thirty thousand men—sixteen battalions headed by those under his two senior councilors, the brothers Honda. Pushing through the center of the lines occupied by the Kaga detachment, deaf to the angry protests of the Kaga men, he pressed on recklessly to the very foot of Chausu Hill, and there, a little to the left of the front line forces under Honda Tadayori of Izumo, he deployed his troops in extended formation for attack.

Just at that moment an order from the Shogun was transmitted to all units: "The defenders are evacuating their advanced posts and appear to be waiting for night. The order to attack will shortly be given."

But Lord Tadanao was waiting no longer for orders. As two or three exploratory shots were directed at the enemy from Honda Tadayori's forward positions, the Echizen forces suddenly let loose a salvo from seven or eight hundred muskets, and, screened beneath billowing clouds of smoke, all sixteen battalions advanced simultaneously, like a moving forest, upon Chausu Hill.

The defense of the sector from the Aoya pass to Chausu Hill was entrusted to Sanada Saemon and his son, supported a little to the south by Iki Shichirōémon Tōotaka, Watanabé Kuranosuké Tadasu, and Ōtani Daigaku Yoshitané; but the combined strength of these units amounted to little more than six thousand men.

Among the forces which confronted them, the great Echizen army stood out at once for its splendor and immensity. Its general, too, Lord Tadanao, was a conspicuous figure. He gave the impression of a man resolved to achieve glory this day at any cost. His general's baton had been cast aside, and, brandishing in its stead a huge cavalry lance, he was urging his horse at the gallop closer and closer to the enemy, paying no heed to the caution of his lieutenants.

With their general setting such an example, the rank and file fought with furious enthusiasm, each determined to outshine his neighbor, and the enemy forces facing the Echizen army swayed and broke like trees in a gale. The first great triumph came when Honda Tadamasa of Iyo slew Nenryū Sadayū, the champion swordsman of the castle garrison, and similar feats of arms, by men like Aoki Shinbei, Otobé Kurobei, Ogita Shumé, and Toshima Shuzen, followed in quick succession. Sanada Saemon's troops, defending the line from Chausu Hill to the Kōshin Temple, were routed in a single assault, Saemon himself falling to Nishio Nizaemon, and his chief lieutenant to Nomoto Ukon. The Echizen forces, pressing close upon the fleeing castle troops, then forced their way through the Senba pass to the Black Gate, raised their standard on the gate itself, and set fires ablaze at a number of places inside the castle.

Three thousand six hundred and fifty-two enemy heads were taken. In the battle-honors of this day there was no one whose share was comparable to that of Lord Tadanao.

Lord Tadanao had drawn up his horse on the crest of Chausu Hill. From there he saw the Echizen banners and war pennants sweep like a tidal wave across the castle moat, overflow into the perimeter beyond, re-form into a narrow triangular salient which jutted conspicuously from the main attacking lines, and drive on like a wedge into the interior of the castle. And as he watched he leaped up and down in his saddle in a transport of simple, boyish glee.

A soldier from the front line came running back.

"Aoki Shinbei was the first inside the castle, sir!"

Lord Tadanao's face beamed as he heard the report.

"Shinbei's the bravest of them all!" His voice was shrill with excitement, and he was obliged to quiet his horse, which had taken alarm at the sound and was urging itself forward. "Return at once and tell Shinbei that his revenue is increased by twenty-five thousand bushels!"

What manner of glory was his, as a general, now? That he should be able to offer up the head of Sanada Saemon, the man who had wrought such havoc among the besieging forces—this was enough in itself. But now the supreme distinction of setting first foot within the castle walls had been won, among all these detachments from so many fiefs, by a soldier of his own army! What manner of glory, thought Lord Tadanao, might this be?

Pondering the miraculous achievements of his retainers, Lord Tadanao felt all to be but a reflection of his personal strength and power of will. The wound to his self-respect dealt him yesterday by his grandfather Ieyasu was now completely healed. But it was more than just that: Lord Tadanao's faith in himself was now many times stronger and more fervent even than before.

Almost one hundred daimyo had taken part in the attack on Osaka Castle, and when Lord Tadanao reflected that not one of them could have won laurels to match his own, he experienced a glow of immense satisfaction. He could almost have believed a halo of glory hovered about his person. But he felt far from surprised. Indeed, as the son of the peerlessly courageous Hidéyasu, and as a blood relation of the Tokugawa family, it seemed to him that such deeds of martial valor as he had performed today were perfectly natural, almost disappointingly so. Lord Tadanao's exultation became mingled with a feeling of complacency which he found it difficult to keep in check.

"My grandfather was a little too hasty in his estimate of this Tadanao. I must see him and hear what he has to say." He hurried off at once to seek an audience with Ieyasu, whose headquarters had now been moved up to the Okayama pass.

Ieyasu, seated on a campstool, was receiving the formal congratulations of a succession of daimyo, but when Lord Tadanao appeared he rose from his seat—a signal honor—and grasped him by the hand.

"Splendid! The hero of the day, and a true grandson of Ieyasu!" He drew Lord Tadanao close, praising him unreservedly to his face. "In military valor you have shown yourself worthy of a place beside Fan Kuai of China. Yes, truly, you are the Fan Kuai of Japan!"

Lord Tadanao was of an ingenuous, uncomplicated nature, and as he heard himself extolled in this manner tears of happiness welled in his eyes. The fact that he had been insulted by this same person only the day before was instantly forgotten. Not the slightest tinge of resentment remained.

On returning that evening to his camp he mustered his retainers for a great celebration. He knew himself now to be the strongest and bravest of all men. Even that flattering reference of Ieyasu's to "the Fan Kuai of Japan" seemed to him, as he recalled it, only partially adequate.

Darkness had fallen, and in the night sky he could see the ruddy reflection of scattered fires still raging within Osaka Castle. Those fires, he idly imagined, were bonfires lit in honor of his own exploits. He drank to them, refilling his great wine cup again and again. Except for a certain hazy exhilaration, Lord Tadanao's mind was empty of all thought and feeling.

*   *   *

On the fifth day of the following month, when all the feudal lords who had assisted in the final assault were reassembled at Nijō Castle in Kyoto, Ieyasu took Lord Tadanao by the hand and addressed him as follows:

"When your father Hidéyasu was still alive you always behaved toward me with the utmost respect, as became a filial grandson. Now you have shown your loyalty on the field of battle, excelling all others, and my satisfaction is complete. I had considered offering you a written address of thanks, but this is a family matter and such ceremony might not be fitting. Rest assured, then, that as long as my own family line continues, the household of Echizen shall remain in undisturbed peace, as firm as the ageless rocks." With these words he presented to Lord Tadanao a flower-patterned tea canister from his private collection.

Overwhelmed by the honor, Lord Tadanao fancied for a moment that there radiated from his person—from his person alone in this vast assemblage of his peers—shafts of dazzling light. Inside him there was a throbbing, flooding warmth of limitless satisfaction, as if there were nothing more he could ever wish for in this world.

Satisfaction, of course, was by no means an entirely novel sensation for one whose will had not normally encountered obstacles, and who was able, more often than not, to gratify his emotional impulses to the full. Since early childhood his will and his emotions, being subject to no form of discipline from without, had developed at their own pace and run riot as they pleased. Lord Tadanao carried no memories of inferiority or defeat in anything he had ever undertaken. In his childhood, shooting toy arrows at toy targets in competition with his playmates, he had always been the winner. Whenever a tournament of court football was held within the castle—for courtiers from Kyoto had introduced the art even to the garrison of Fukui—the player who kicked with the greatest skill had invariably been Lord Tadanao. Even in trifling board games like Gobang, Chinese Chess, and Double Six, he was victorious in nine cases out of ten. He had naturally, too, shown precocious ability in all the arts which were essential to a military man—in archery, horsemanship, jousting, and swordplay—and after outclassing his companion pages, who had started on equal terms with himself, he gave regular proof of his amazing prowess by defeating, with ease, even those young samurai who were acknowledged within his household as the champions in their respective fields.

In this way, with the passage of the years, a sense of superiority over his immediate circle had taken firm root in his mind. And, deep down, he had come to cherish the conviction that he was, in fact, of a superior species, possessing characteristics quite distinct from those of his retainers.

But, although Lord Tadanao was sufficiently convinced of his preeminence over his own retainers, he had, despite himself, fallen prey to certain melancholy misgivings since setting out for the Osaka campaign. His competitors in the struggle for glory would now be daimyo, men of his own class. Was it possible that he might find himself outshone by some among their number? Worse, now that he was to be tested in that very business of war to which men of his class were dedicated, might he, unawares, commit some error of judgment as a general? In actual fact, in the engagement of the sixth of the fifth month, by deferring his entry into the battle until too late, he had committed just such an error, and had dangerously shaken even his own deep-set faith in himself. But the glory he had won on the very next day, in the storming of the castle, had completely healed this wound to his self-esteem. It had done more. The Echizen forces had been first inside the castle, and their battle-honors had been overwhelmingly greater than those of any other detachment; Lord Tadanao's comparatively modest conviction that he was a better man than any of his retainers had consequently grown more comprehensive in scope, and changed to a conviction that he was a better man than any of the sixty noble lords who had joined in the storming of the castle. The forces which had taken three thousand seven hundred and fifty enemy heads in the Osaka campaign, and the forces, moreover, which had taken the head of General Sanada Saemon, belonged to Lord Tadanao. There was no doubt of that.

The flower-patterned tea canister and the title of "the Fan Kuai of Japan" had made a deep impression on Lord Tadanao's mind. He regarded them together as a twin testimonial to his preeminent merit. It was exhilarating. He felt as if all one hundred and twenty daimyo and lesser lords in that room were gazing upon Lord Tadanao in wide-eyed wonder and admiration.

Until now he had been proud to think himself a finer man than any of his retainers. But it was not really satisfactory, this measuring himself only by those who were his subordinates. Now, taken by the hand and cordially welcomed by no less a person than His Excellency, he was being singled out for praise before all the lords in the land.

Lords Yoshinao and Yorinobu, who were his own uncles, had won no particular distinction. Another uncle, Lord Tadateru, Chamberlain of Echigo, had failed to take any part in the fighting on the seventh and had positively fallen into disgrace. Even the honors won by the great and celebrated clans of Daté, Maeda, and Kuroda paled to insignificance, to less than the gleam of fireflies before a full moon, when set beside those of the Echizen household.

When he thought in this way, Lord Tadanao's sense of superiority, which had been momentarily unsettled on that one occasion by Ieyasu's cutting rebuke, not only miraculously recovered all its former strength, but went on, by a process of violent reaction, to become something far more splendid and unshakable than it had ever been before.

Thus Lord Tadanao, Daimyo of Echizen, taking with him the proud consciousness of being the foremost hero in the land, withdrew from Kyoto in the eighth month of that year and returned in a most exalted frame of mind to his castle seat at Fukui.

II

Hundreds of candles, set in silver candlesticks, blazed in the great hall of the castle at Echizen Kitanoshō. The evening's festivities, as clearly shown by the solid masses of white wax which had already climbed high about the base of each candlestick, were well advanced. It had been Lord Tadanao's custom, since returning to his province, to gather together his young retainers during the day for tournaments, and at night, as soon as the games were over, to invite the whole company to a huge informal banquet.

The title of "the Fan Kuai of Japan," so flatteringly conferred upon him by his grandfather Ieyasu, was a source of immense happiness to Lord Tadanao. His heart beat quicker at the mere thought of it. And by thus competing with the young warriors of his household, measuring his own skill with the spear and the sword against theirs, and soundly defeating all comers, he was providing this proud new boast of his with the daily sustenance it demanded.

The young warriors, ranged at this moment in a deep curve around the great hall below the step of the slightly elevated section on which he himself was seated, had been specially selected from among his numerous young retainers for their prowess in the military arts. Among them he could see some who were still mere youths, their hair not yet trimmed to the styles of manhood, but one and all were powerfully built, and their eyes shone vigorously.

But an even nobler and more gallant spectacle was presented by the master of the castle himself, Lord Tadanao. Though lean and trim in figure, his eyes glowed darkly with an almost uncanny quality of penetration, and in the set of his brow there was an overwhelming suggestion of dauntless courage.

Lord Tadanao was a little intoxicated. Everything had a tendency to revolve before his eyes. Nevertheless, he steadied himself and gazed slowly around the whole assembly. The one hundred or more young men seated in the hall below him were every one of them slaves to his will. As the thought passed through his mind he could not check a sudden surge of that special pride known only to those who wield great authority.

But the pride he felt this evening was not that alone. It was twofold. For in his prowess as a fighting man, too, he had proved himself superior to all these young men seated before him.

Earlier today he had assembled his retainers for yet another great tournament. He had chosen from their number those judged most proficient in the art of wielding the spear, and had divided them into two teams, the Reds and the Whites.

He himself had taken command of the Reds. But from the very start his teammates had fared badly. One after another they had retired from the arena in defeat, and when it came to the deputy commander's turn, and he too was laid low, there still remained five members of the White team who had not yet been obliged to fight.

It was at this juncture that Lord Tadanao, as commander of the Reds, strode valiantly and imposingly into the arena, brandishing his huge six-yard spear with masterful ease. The White warriors were cowed at the mere sight. His first opponent, the head page boy, who had been so overawed by Lord Tadanao's warlike appearance that he seemed of two minds whether to join battle or flee, had his spear struck from his grasp before he had really started, and upon receiving a blow in the stomach, he collapsed in the semblance of swoon. The following two contestants, a stable overseer and an officer of the treasury, were stricken to the ground in rapid succession. The deputy commander of the Whites next took the field. This was Ōshima Sadayū, eldest son of the castle's fencing instructor, Ōshima Sazen, and rated second to none in the whole Echizen household in his skill with the spear.

There was a murmur of excited whispering among the spectators. "Even his lordship, for all his strength, may find Sadayū a stiff proposition." But after some seven or eight vigorous exchanges Sadayū too was humbled. Recoiling from a glancing blow to his thigh, and momentarily set off balance, he lowered his guard and exposed himself to a crippling thrust from directly in front, which landed squarely on the vital region of his chest. His downfall was greeted with wild cheering from the spectators' seats, where the whole of Lord Tadanao's household was gathered. Lord Tadanao, gasping a little for breath, stood quietly awaiting the appearance of the rival commander. He was experiencing, not for the first time in his life, a glow of sublime and exhilarating self-satisfaction.

The White commander was a young man called Onoda Ukon. At the age of twelve he had become a pupil of Gondō Saemon, the celebrated Kyoto master of spearmanship, and at the age of twenty, demonstrating the good use which he had made of his training, he had defeated his own teacher. But Lord Tadanao held no one in awe. At Ukon's sharp cry of challenge—"Ei!"—he leveled his spear and went furiously in to the attack. There was more than the confidence of skill behind his onslaught. There was, it seemed to the onlookers, the whole power and majesty of the lord of a province, of the daimyo of a fief of almost three and a half million bushels. The battle was hotly contested for some twenty exchanges, and then, suddenly, Ukon staggered beneath a powerful blow to his right shoulder, retreated a few steps, and, prostrating himself before Lord Tadanao, signified his surrender.

The spectators cheered until the very walls of Kitanoshō Castle trembled. Lord Tadanao felt once more that glow of sublime self-satisfaction. Returning to his seat of honor, he announced, in a great voice:

"Gentlemen, my sincere thanks to you all. It is now my wish that, as some compensation for your labors, you should join me in a feast."

He was in even greater spirits than usual. As the banquet proceeded, his most trusted retainers came before him, one after another, and offered their compliments.

"My lord! Since your experiences amid the arrows in the Osaka campaign you have advanced yet further in your skill. People like ourselves are no longer worthy opponents for you."

The merest mention of the Osaka campaign was enough to make Lord Tadanao childishly happy. But even Lord Tadanao was by this time feeling very much unsteadied by the wine. Looking about the assembly he could see that a large number of his guests had already lapsed into some kind of drunken stupor. Some had reached the stage of incoherence. Others were softly murmuring sentimental songs. It was obvious that there was little life left in the evening's entertainment.

Lord Tadanao recalled suddenly the aura of feminine refinement which pervaded his own apartments, and he sickened at the boorishness of this all-male carousal. Abruptly he rose.

"Gentlemen, I beg your leave!" Without further ceremony he left the hall. Even the most heavily intoxicated of his guests managed somehow to straighten their disarray and make a low obeisance. The small page boys, who had been fast asleep until this moment, opened their eyes with a start and hurried out after their master.

Lord Tadanao, emerging onto the long open veranda which led to his apartments, sensed with pleasure the cold caress on his cheeks of the early autumn air. Beyond, from where thick clusters of lespedeza flowers showed faintly white in the dim glow of a tenth-day moon, he could hear the singing of autumn insects.

Lord Tadanao decided to take a stroll in the garden. He dismissed the serving-maid sent from his apartments to meet him, and, accompanied only by a single page boy, stepped down from the veranda. The surface of the garden was moist with dew. The dim moonlight made the town beneath the castle seem like some chiaroscuro painting afloat in a vast luminous space of night air.

It was long since he had found himself in surroundings of such utter quietness. All heaven and earth was sad and still. There was only a faint, confused sound of revelry, drifting across from the great hall he had just left. Since his departure the party seemed to have grown more boisterous, for he could hear, mingled with the other sounds, someone singing to the accompaniment of an Azuma zither. But the hall was distant, and the sounds reached him too faintly to be an annoyance.

Lord Tadanao followed a narrow path through the lespedeza thicket, skirted the rocky spring, ascended a miniature hill, and arrived before a small thatched pavilion. He went inside. From here the mountains of the Shin-Etsu range could be dimly seen, floating high in the moon-drenched air. Lord Tadanao fell into a sentimental reverie, seized by an emotion he had never before experienced in all his life as a daimyo; and he stood where he was, unconscious of the passage of time, for almost an hour.

Suddenly he heard men's voices. In the stillness which, until now, had held only the sad voices of insects, the voices of men sounded. There were two people, it seemed, and as they talked they drew closer and closer to the pavilion.

Lord Tadanao was loath to have the pleasant serenity of his feelings at this moment shattered by casual intruders. But he could not, on this particular night, summon up sufficient indignation to have his page order the men away. Gradually, still talking, they drew nearer. The interior of the pavilion was in darkness, untouched by the light of the moon, and the two men could have had no idea that their lord was standing there. He felt no curiosity to know who these intruders were. But as they came slowly nearer he could hardly help recognizing their voices. The man who sounded a little the worse for drink was Onoda Ukon, the White commander in today's tournament. The other, the one with the sharp, nervous voice, was the deputy commander, Ōshima Sadayū, who had been so quickly beaten to submission this day by Lord Tadanao. The two of them seemed to have been talking for some time about the battle of the Reds and Whites.

This was Lord Tadanao's first experience, since being born into this world as a daimyo, of the strange fascination of eavesdropping, and, despite himself, he listened intently.

The two men had apparently halted by the spring, not more than six yards from the pavilion. Sadayū was speaking, in a confidential tone.

"Tell me, what do you think of the master's skill?"

Ukon's reply was spoken with a certain jocular bitterness.

"Gossip about his lordship! It's suicide for us both if we're heard!"

"We gossip about the Shogun, too, on the sly. Come, what do you think? His lordship's prowess in arms. . . . What is your real opinion?" Sadayū sounded in earnest. He was completely silent for a moment, as if waiting tensely for Ukon's assessment.

"Well, it's as they say. He's pretty good." Ukon paused abruptly.

Lord Tadanao felt as if, for the very first time, he was hearing himself praised without deceit by a retainer. But Ukon continued.

"I allowed him the victory, as usual, but I didn't exactly exert myself."

There was a significant silence, during which the two men were doubtless smiling wryly at each other.

Ukon's words, naturally enough, had a devastating effect upon eavesdropping Lord Tadanao. A great whirl and tumult of emotions suddenly raced within his breast. Lord Tadanao had never known this feeling before. It was as if he had been trampled on and kicked from head to toe by muddy feet. His lips quivered, and the blood in every vein of his body seemed to be boiling over and rushing to his head.

Ukon's brief words, with their indescribable shock, had hurled Lord Tadanao down from the loftiest heights of human dignity, from the pedestal on which he had stood exalted until this moment, and cast him ignominiously into the dust. His mood was certainly near to violent rage. But it was very different from the violent rage which stems from a heart bursting with superabundant strength. His anger raged furiously on the surface, but it arose from the sudden creation, at the very core of his soul, of a terrible, desolate emptiness. He was overwhelmed by the bitter discovery that the world was a fraud, that his whole life until now, and all his proud boasts, had been built upon a false foundation.

For a moment he felt an urge to take the sword from his page boy's hands and kill the two men on the spot; but the strength for such desperate resolutions was no longer within him. Besides, it would only double his humiliation. For a lord to pride himself on false victories granted in flattery by his own retainers was shame and folly enough. But was he to cut down these two men now and reveal to his whole household that he knew of his own stupidity? Lord Tadanao fought against the tumult of emotions in his breast and tried to consider calmly what course of action might be most fitting. But, because the experience had come upon him so unexpectedly, and because, to make matters worse, Lord Tadanao was of such an excitable disposition, his emotions continued for some considerable time longer in wild disorder, refusing to be arranged.

The page, who had been squatting at Lord Tadanao's side all this while, as motionless as a piece of furniture, was a boy of some intelligence, and he was not unaware of the critical nature of the present situation. If, he felt, he failed to warn the two men of their master's presence, there was no knowing what might happen. Noting in alarm the thunderous expression on his master's face, he coughed lightly, three times.

The page boy's coughing was, on this occasion, most efficacious. Ukon and Sadayū, realizing that someone was nearby, abruptly concluded their seditious conversation. As if at a prearranged signal, the two men hurriedly departed in the direction of the great hall.

Lord Tadanao's eyes were flashing with anger. But his cheeks were ominously pale. The whole world of emotions in which he had lived since boyhood had gone wonderfully bankrupt at a word from Ukon.

As a child, in childish pastimes, he had always been cleverer than any of his companions. When he shot his toy arrows he had always scored more bull's-eyes than the others. During calligraphy classes the old teacher had frequently patted him on the knee and praised his brush-work. These, and other such incidents, came momentarily back to his mind now as unhappy memories.

It had been the same in military arts. As a swordsman, or with the spear, he had reached in an amazingly short time the stage of defeating any of his retainers who offered to oppose him. And he had believed in himself right up to this moment. He had had the firmest faith in his genuine ability. Just now, for instance, even while listening to the derogatory remarks which Ukon and his friend were making behind his back, he had almost been able to convince himself that this was merely their chagrin at defeat.

But, when he had considered the circumstances under which they were spoken, he had known that Ukon's words were neither jest nor lie. Even Lord Tadanao, with all his buoyant self-confidence, had felt obliged to accept what he heard as a statement of the honest truth.

Ukon's words were with him still, echoing loudly in his mind. Lord Tadanao tried to calculate just how much of each splendid feat today had been due to himself, and how much to deceit. But it was no use. And it was not only about today that he would never know. Among all the countless victories and distinctions he had gained since childhood, in every variety of contest or skill, he would never know what had been the proportion of reality and of pretense. The thought was an agony, tearing at his heart. Not everything had been sham, he knew. Not all his retainers had given him victories which were not his by right. No, by far the great majority of his opponents had been fairly beaten. But the taint was there. Simply because there were people, insolent people, like Ukon and Sadayū, every one of those past triumphs was now tainted with an aura of impurity. He felt himself beginning to hate Ukon and Sadayū.

But the wound went deeper. Even the glory he had won three months ago on the Osaka battlefield seemed now no longer wholly credible. And as he recalled that fine title which had been his pride—

"the Fan Kuai of Japan"—he began to wonder whether even this did not carry with it the sort of exaggeration which makes a man ridiculous. He had been humored like a child by his retainers. Had he also been manipulated like a puppet by his grandfather? At this thought Lord Tadanao's eyes began at last to dim with tears.

III

The banquet continued informally long after Lord Tadanao departed, but when the castle bell tolled the hour of midnight all the young warriors accepted it as the signal to rise and prepare to retire. At this moment, however, a chamberlain came hurrying into the hall from the lord's apartments.

"Gentlemen!" he cried, raising both arms for silence. "Your attention please! His lordship has this moment ordered a change in the plans for tomorrow. In place of the hunt which he had previously announced, there will be tomorrow, just as today, a great tournament of spearmanship. The time and the combat arrangements are to be as before."

There were some who felt a little disgruntled at the prospect. There were some, too, who smiled to themselves. His lordship, it seemed, was eager to enjoy today's triumph in duplicate. But the majority, pleasantly exhilarated by the wine, accepted the change with great good humor.

"Let it go on for days and days," they cried. "All the more wine to celebrate on! Tomorrow, again, we can get gloriously drunk."

*   *   *

On the following day the castle drill-hall was once more swept spotlessly clean, and white and red awnings were draped along its walls. Lord Tadanao, as before, occupied the seat of honor, but throughout the proceedings he gnawed ceaselessly at his lower lip, and his eyes blazed.

There was little difference in the results of the contests. But, with yesterday's victory or defeat still fresh in the memory of each contestant, most of the bouts were, for one of the parties, battles to redeem lost honor, and a far fiercer note was detectable in the shouting and challenges.

The Reds fared, if anything, even worse than they had on the previous day. When their commander, Lord Tadanao, took the field, there remained six members of the White team, including the com-

mander and deputy commander, who had not yet been called upon to fight.

Lord Tadanao displayed a curious tension which at once puzzled the spectators. He seemed almost delirious with excitement as he stood there whirling his great leather-tipped spear wildly about his head. His first two opponents approached him as gingerly as if they were feeling the region of an ulcer, but were quickly dealt savage blows which sent them reeling to the floor. The next two were no less overawed by their lord's terrible ardor, and offered only a formal show of resistance.

The fifth to appear was Ōshima Sadayū. Sadayū entertained certain private misgivings, slight though they were, as to the causes which underlay Lord Tadanao's seemingly eccentric behavior this day. Of course, he did not imagine for one moment that it might have been his lord himself who had been standing nearby the previous night, listening to that conversation. But he did wonder, a little anxiously, whether the owner of that cough, which had sounded last night in the darkness of the garden, might not have reported what he had heard. It was with a bow of even more than usual solemnity that he now saluted his lord.

"So it's you, Sadayū!" Lord Tadanao gave the impression of a man striving to sound unconcerned. But his voice was strangely shrill.

"Sadayū! Be it sword or spear, unless it is a real sword or a real spear we can never know our true skills. Combats with leather-capped practice spears are fake combats. If we can lose without suffering injury, then we may, perhaps, permit ourselves to lose too easily! Tadanao is tired of false battles. I propose to use the spear which served me so well at the siege of Osaka. And it is my wish that you, too, shall this time face me with a naked weapon in your hands. You are not to think of me as your lord. If you see an opening, strike without hesitation!"

Lord Tadanao's eyes smoldered with rage and his voice trembled as he spoke these last few words. Sadayū paled. Onoda Ukon, too, standing a little behind Sadayū, grew pale.

The family retainers in the spectators' seats were completely at a loss to understand what possessed Lord Tadanao. Many were seized with a sudden fear that their master had lost his reason.

Lord Tadanao had had his fits of temper before this. He was, by nature, highly strung, and there were times when he was excessively rude. But he had never, in the slightest degree, shown himself tyrannical or cruel. Observing Lord Tadanao's behavior today, his retainers were, not unnaturally, aghast.

But, although it was true that in calling for the use of real weapons Lord Tadanao was activated by a consuming hatred of Sadayū and Ukon, he was moved also by the hope that at last he might discover what were his true capabilities. If obliged to face up to a real spear, even these two might not so readily suffer defeat. They would use every art they knew to defend themselves. And then he would know the truth about his own skill. He might, of course, have himself to admit defeat. But even that, he felt, was infinitely better and cleaner than foolishly exulting over a prearranged victory.

"Ho there! Get ready a spear!" At Lord Tadanao's order—so promptly that it seemed they must have been well prepared in advance—two small page boys brought forward a great spear, seemingly no easy weight for them to carry, and laid it between Lord Tadanao and his retainer.

"Sadayū, use that!" said Lord Tadanao, and at the same moment he removed the sheath from the blade of his own trusted, six-yard weapon. The murderous glint leaping from the seven inches of steel tip, the work of the master spearsmith Bingo Sadakané, cast an oppressive chill upon the spirits of the whole assembly. At the uncovering of the blade Senior Councilor Honda Tosa, who had chosen to overlook his lord's behavior until now, rose suddenly from his place and hastened before Lord Tadanao.

"My lord, have you taken leave of your senses? To expose your valued person in such reckless sport with naked weapons, and to court injury from your own retainers! If the Shogun hears of this it will be no light matter! I beseech you to desist." The councilor wrinkled his old, tired eyes and pleaded desperately.

"Old man, it is useless to interfere," said Lord Tadanao, with an air of stern finality. "I am resolved upon fighting today with real weapons, even if it cost me Tadanao's three-and-a-half-million-bushel province. It is utterly impossible to stop me." There was a crushing authority in his manner, and one might as well have sought to argue away the autumn frosts. Thus absolute, in his own household, was the will of Lord Tadanao. The councilor offered no further advice and retired dispiritedly.

Sadayū had already made up his mind to raise no objection. This, he was now convinced, was a punishment for his talk last night, which must have reached the ears of his master, and there was nothing further to be said. As a retainer he had no alternative but to accept his punishment. And when he considered that it was to be administered secretly, under the pretext of a contest with naked weapons, he even felt that in this Lord Tadanao was showing him considerable favor. To die on his lord's spear would be an atonement, a noble death, and it was now his only wish.

"My lord," he said firmly, "no matter what the weapons, Sadayū is ready to oppose you."

There was a murmur of disapproval from the spectators at Sadayū's disloyal presumption. Lord Tadanao smiled bitterly.

"Well then, you are a true retainer of Lord Tadanao. But do not think of me as your lord. If my guard is down, do not hesitate. Strike!" Lord Tadanao withdrew five or six yards, brandishing his spear as he spoke, and took up his position.

Sadayū now picked up the spear brought by the pages and removed the sheath from its blade.

"Your pardon!" he cried. And he stood at the ready, facing his lord.

All eyes were fixed upon the scene in dreadful fascination and horror. The watchers sat tensed and breathless, as if entranced, following every move in the battle being fought to a finish between master and man.

Lord Tadanao was obsessed by one thought. If he could only find out—find out with certainty—the real extent of his strength and skill, he could want nothing more. He was not conscious of himself as daimyo of a province, nor did he think of his opponent as a retainer. He merely fought, with courage and determination.

But Sadayū had, from the outset, determined the issue. After three brief exchanges he took the point of Lord Tadanao's spear high on his left thigh, toppled backward, and crashed to the floor.

The spectators, one and all, heaved a deep sigh of relief. The body of the wounded Sadayū was quickly borne from the arena by a group of his colleagues.

Lord Tadanao, however, felt no joy of victory. Sadayū's defeat, he saw only too clearly, was of the same self-inflicted variety as his defeat of yesterday, and in Lord Tadanao's heart there was now an aching loneliness far worse, even, than last night's words had brought. The realization that the wretched Sadayū was ready to feed his lord with false victories, even if it cost him his very life, had reimplanted at the core of Lord Tadanao's being, even more deeply than before, his terrible uneasiness, loneliness, and sense of lost faith. He felt bitterly toward his true inner self which, even if he imperiled his own person and sacrificed the lives of his retainers, he could never know.

At Sadayū's fall Ukon had taken up the discarded spear; with this in his hand, he now stood at the ready. He showed no trace of fear. His face, it is true, was pale, but the eyes glowed with fierce resolution.

Lord Tadanao felt that Ukon at least, the man who had dared to speak so frankly last night, would surely offer a determined resistance, and, summoning back his will to fight, which had been fast evaporating, he turned to face him.

But Ukon, no less than Sadayū, was deeply moved by a sense of his own guilt. And he too was resolved to expiate his crime upon his lord's spear.

In the course of five or six exchanges Lord Tadanao noticed that his opponent repeatedly contrived to leave the vital region of his breast unguarded. This fellow too, he realized with a sudden mortifying return of his sense of loneliness, was prepared to throw away his very life to cheat his lord to the end. The idea of vanquishing an opponent who thus artfully assisted him was a sickening absurdity.

But Ukon, as if sensing that he must accomplish his wish without further delay, suddenly maneuvered his body into the path of a feint from Lord Tadanao's spear, and was pierced through the right shoulder.

Lord Tadanao had most wonderfully vented his rancor of last night. But it had merely created a new sadness in his heart. Both Ukon and Sadayū, at the risk of their lives, had maintained their pretense.

When Lord Tadanao heard late that night that the wounded Ukon and Sadayū, upon being carried to their respective homes, had both, at a chosen time ripped open their stomachs, he lapsed into a mood of even deeper despondency.

Lord Tadanao pondered the matter carefully. Between these men and himself there stretched a solid, dividing tissue of deceit. This tissue, this barrier of pretense, they were striving desperately to keep in existence. The pretense was no idle one: it was something to which they were irrevocably committed. Today, with his naked spear, Lord Tadanao had made a supreme effort to pierce this tissue, but these men had repaired the gaps at once with their blood. And now, between himself and his retainers, the tissue stretched as intact as ever. Beyond it men were living as men, in genuine human relationships with each other. But if any of those men turned for a moment to face their lord, they at once dropped down before themselves this protective tissue of pretense. As Lord Tadanao suddenly realized that on this side of the barrier there was absolutely no one but himself, the terrible sense of loneliness redoubled its strength and invaded every corner of his being.

IV

The alarming intelligence that, since the day of the contests, the master had become increasingly subject to fits of evil temper soon made Lord Tadanao an object of terror to everyone in the castle. When on duty in their master's presence the page boys hardly dared breathe, their eyes started from their heads, and they would avoid the slightest unnecessary movement. Even the companions of honor took care to stand most particularly upon protocol, never moving a step in advance of, nor taking a step of greater length than, their lord. The feeling of ease which had existed to a considerable degree between master and retainers was completely lost, and the prospect of an audience with the lord filled one and all with gloomy apprehension. On withdrawing from his presence the retainers would feel physically and mentally exhausted, as never before.

The deterioration in this relationship was not remarked solely by the retainers. One day, when a companion of honor brought him a letter from the family councilors, Lord Tadanao noticed that the man was preparing to crawl to him on his knees from a point some four or five steps away.

"Don't be afraid to come close," he said. "There's no need for all that ceremony."

But this was really spoken less in friendliness than in irritation. The retainer was sufficiently encouraged by the remark to make an effort to recover some of his old sense of ease. But it was a self-conscious easiness, and underneath there was still a hard core of restraint.

Ever since the contests with naked spears Lord Tadanao had refrained, as completely as if he had forgotten their existence, from any form of practice in the military arts. It was not simply that he discontinued the tournaments, tournaments which had been held so regularly that they had seemed almost like a part of the daily routine; he was never even seen to take a dummy sword or spear in his hand.

He had been bursting with martial pride, but always gentle; rough-mannered, but basically a most innocent and harmless young lord. Now that he had abruptly withdrawn his interest from swordplay and archery he devoted more and more of his days to drinking. Though he had been addicted to wine since early youth, it had never adversely affected his behavior. Now, as he drained cup after cup, day after day, signs of dissipation and disorderliness began slowly to appear.

*   *   *

It was at a banquet one night. Lord Tadanao was in an unusually cheerful mood. His favorite page boy, Masuda Kannosuké, ventured to make a remark while replenishing his lord's great wine cup.

"Why have we not seen your lordship lately in the military drill-hall?" he asked. "We wonder whether your lordship's satisfaction over your recent exploits has not made you negligent." By speaking in this way Kannosuké fancied that he was demonstrating, clearly enough, a friendly concern for his master.

Lord Tadanao went white with rage. Seizing a tray for wine cups which lay at his side he hurled it with the speed of an arrow toward Kannosuké's face. The violence was unexpected, and Kannosuké blanched; but, rigidly trained as he was in the code of loyalty, he made no attempt to dodge. He took the impact of the tray full on the front of his face and fell prostrate where he was, the blood slowly trickling down his pallid cheeks.

Lord Tadanao rose without so much as a word and went straight to his quarters.

A group of fellow pages ran to Kannosuké's assistance and gently raised him. Kannosuké, excusing himself from further duty that night on a plea of sickness, retired to his lodgings, and before the dawn of the new day he committed suicide.

When Lord Tadanao heard the news he only smiled, sadly and bitterly.

Some ten days after this event Lord Tadanao was playing Gobang with his old family councilor Koyama Tango. The old man and Lord Tadanao ranked equal in Gobang, but over the last two or three years the councilor had tended to lose his touch. Today he was defeated three times running.

"My lord," he said, with a good-natured smile, "lately you have become exceedingly proficient. An old man like myself is no longer a match for you."

Lord Tadanao had been in good spirits until now, apparently highly pleased at his run of victories, but at Tango's words an expression of melancholy stole across his face; and then, suddenly, he rose and viciously kicked over the small Gobang table set between himself and his opponent. The white and black ivory pieces arrayed on the table flew off in all directions, and one or two struck Tango in the face.

Why his lord should burst into such a fury, especially when he was winning, was something which Tango was utterly unable to understand. As Lord Tadanao was stalking from the room the old man caught at the hem of his overskirts and addressed him in a voice which quavered uncontrollably.

"What are you doing? Is your lordship out of his mind? For what reason does he offer such insults to Tango?" Indignation at the impropriety of this treatment blazed uncontrollably in the old man's stubborn breast.

But Lord Tadanao was not in the least moved by the old man's anger. With a curt exclamation he pushed away the hand that clutched at his overskirts and abruptly walked through to his private apartments.

The old man's eyes filled with tears. He was mortified that the lord to whose upbringing since his earliest days he had devoted such loving care should have thus outrageously insulted him. As he recalled the respect and kindness shown him by Lord Tadanao's father during his lifetime, he bitterly repented that he had ever lived on to know such shame. The idea of faking defeats on the Gobang board to flatter his lord was a servile notion which would never for one moment have entered Tango's honest head.

But by this time Lord Tadanao had come to interpret every act and gesture of his retainers in only one light.

That day, on returning to his house, the old man put on formal robes and, with due observation of ceremony, plunged a dagger into his wrinkled stomach, thus ending an existence which had become too shameful to bear.

*   *   *

Rumors of Lord Tadanao's disorderly conduct gradually spread throughout and beyond his domains.

Lord Tadanao, avid for victories of any sort, had always been an enthusiastic player of board games, finding real satisfaction in demonstrating to himself his superior skill, but after this incident he suddenly desisted from such pastimes.

It was natural under the circumstances that Lord Tadanao's mode of life should grow gradually more wild and uncouth. Within the castle he did nothing but eat, drink, and make love. When abroad his sole pastime was hunting. He hunted birds on the moors and beasts in the mountains. Birds and beasts did not, simply because it was the master of the province come to hunt them, rush voluntarily within range of Lord Tadanao's arrows. Away from the world of men, in the world of nature, Lord Tadanao felt refreshed, as if he had escaped from behind that barrier of deceit.

V

Lord Tadanao until now had always listened attentively to the advice of his senior councilors. At the age of thirteen, when he was still known only by his boyhood name of Nagayoshimaru, he had been called to the bedside of his dying father, and his father had said: "When I am gone listen carefully to whatever the councilors say. Think of their words as if they were your father's." He had always respected this last injunction.

But lately he had begun to place a perverse interpretation upon every word they uttered, even if it concerned matters of the fief's administration. If his councilors recommended a person for a certain post and lauded his abilities, Lord Tadanao felt convinced the man must be an impostor, and he would stubbornly refuse to make use of the man's services. If his councilors complained of a person's conduct and strongly urged punishment by house arrest, Lord Tadanao felt convinced of the man's honesty and usefulness, and he would forbid them to issue, at any time, an order for his detention.

The harvest throughout the Echizen fief was leaner this year than it had ever been in recent memory, and this imposed severe hardships upon the peasantry. The councilors appeared before Lord Tadanao in strength and pleaded for some alleviation of the burden of rice taxation. But the more eloquently they expounded their case, the more distasteful to Lord Tadanao grew the idea of acting upon it. In his heart he sympathized with the peasants. It was simply the thought of doing what his councilors wished him to do which troubled him. They droned on with their lengthy explanations until Lord Tadanao could bear it no more.

"No!" he thundered. "I say it cannot be done, and you will do as I say!" Why he refused was something he did not clearly understand himself.

The emotional impasse between master and retainers continued unresolved, and meanwhile rumors of the Lord of Echizen's eccentric behavior reached even the innermost council rooms of the Shogunate at Edo.

But Lord Tadanao's distemper now proceeded little by little to gnaw its way into more fundamental compartments of his life.

One night Lord Tadanao had been drinking steadily from an early hour in the privacy of his own rooms, accompanied only by a small group of his favorite ladies of the bedchamber. Included in the group was the girl called Kinuno, a beauty procured for him from faraway Kyoto, who had recently come to monopolize the whole of Lord Tadanao's amorous passion and affection.

The evening light had faded, the dark hours had slipped by, midnight was almost come, and still Lord Tadanao drank on. For the ladies, who did not drink, the time had been occupied solely in the monotonous and endlessly repeated business of keeping their lord's cup replenished.

Lord Tadanao suddenly roused himself from his dim-eyed, half-drunken torpor and glanced across at the dearly cherished Kinuno, seated there in attendance upon him. But these nightly drinking sessions had seemingly exhausted her. In the very presence of her lord she appeared to have lost all consciousness of what she was doing. Those superb double-folded eyelids were slowly falling, and Kinuno was about to slip drowsily away to a moment of sleep.

As he gazed intently into her face Lord Tadanao was seized by yet a new anxiety. He thought he saw there, clearly revealed in that unguarded weariness of expression, all the sadness of a woman at the beck and call of a great lord whose power is absolute, a woman unable for one moment of the day to exercise her own will, moving only to her master's wishes, like a puppet.

Lord Tadanao considered things further. It was unlikely that this woman, any more than other people, felt any genuine affection for him. Her smiles, her alluring glances—these were all tricks of art, things which had no deep significance. Having been sold, body and soul, for a sum which made any refusal on her part impossible, and set down, whether she liked it or not, to serve a great and powerful daimyo she had no choice but to act as she did. Her last chance of escape from the misery of her present situation lay in doing everything she conceivably could to win the affection of that powerful person who controlled her fate.

But it was not only this woman whose love Lord Tadanao now questioned. He began to wonder whether any single woman, among all those others he had loved in his life, had ever loved him in return.

He had lately become increasingly aware that throughout his life he had been denied the normal, everyday sympathy which men feel for their fellow beings. He had never known even the sympathy extended to a friend. From his childhood days numbers of page boys of his own age had been selected to keep him company. But they had not associated with Lord Tadanao as friends. They had merely offered submission. Lord Tadanao had loved them. But they had never returned that love. They had been merely submissive, from a high sense of duty.

And what, if this was the nature of his friendships, was he to think of his relationships with the opposite sex? Since early youth he had had about him, at his disposal, many beautiful women. Lord Tadanao had loved them. But how many had loved him back? Though Lord Tadanao had given them love they had not offered love in return. They had merely offered him their submission. Just that. He had still about him, in his service, a large number of these human creatures. But, in place of human feeling for a fellow human, they offered only that one token —submission.

It had become clear to Lord Tadanao that he received submission as a substitute for love, submission for friendship, and submission for kindness. Of course, there might have been cases, somewhere in the midst of all this, of true love based on human feeling, of true friendship, and of sincere kindness. But these, as Lord Tadanao tried to recall them in his present frame of mind, became hopelessly confused in the general pattern. The ramifications of that one word, submission, seemed to have robbed him of all else. A man raised by his fellows one degree above the normal world of human feeling, a man in daily association with a multitude of retainers, yet conscious of complete isolation—that was Lord Tadanao.

He saw that even his home life, the life he lived in the intimacy of these rooms, had been a dreariness of solitude. The impurity of every love he had ever known from women seemed now clearly revealed. If ever he had set his heart on a woman she had gratified his wishes to the full, without hesitation. But, for her, this had had nothing to do with love. It had been simply the fulfillment of a duty, the retainer's duty to the master. He was sick and tired of receiving dutiful submission in the place of love.

*   *   *

From this time there was a change in the settled pattern of Lord Tadanao's private life, corresponding with the change in other spheres. He began to think that, instead of the usual passive puppets, he should like to love some more spirited, resilient type of woman. If such a woman loved him in return, well and good. But, even if she did not, at least she would show some resistance. She would treat him like a human being.

By way of experiment he caused a succession of the daughters of his more highly placed retainers to be sent to him in his apartments. But to these women, too, Lord Tadanao's words were simply the words of the lord of the castle, and they did as they were told in complete resignation, as if obeying an order which it was beyond anyone's power to question. Feeling only the nobility of their own sacrifice, like maidens offering themselves upon the altar of some awesome divinity, they lay down beside Lord Tadanao. And Lord Tadanao, even as he held them in his arms, felt not the slightest sense of illicit pleasure.

After things had continued for some time in this unsatisfactory state it occurred to Lord Tadanao that he might achieve better results from women already promised to some particular person in marriage. Surely they, at least, might resist, if only a little. Accordingly he obliged a selection of the girls in his household who were shortly to be married to attend him. But these too proved a disappointment. They held the will of their lord to be absolute, and they offered their services to Lord Tadanao in untroubled serenity, as to someone quite distinct from the human male.

From about this time criticism of Lord Tadanao's unseemly conduct began to be voiced even among the lord's own retainers. But Lord Tadanao's disorder had not yet run its course.

The experiment with girls promised in marriage having brought no relief, he proceeded to an even more shocking defiance of morality. He ascertained, by private enquiries, which of the wives of his retainers in the Echizen fief possessed the greatest beauty and most lovable dispositions; he summoned three of these ladies, as if on urgent business, to the castle; and he refused to return them to their husbands.

To many this action seemed the final, incontrovertible proof that his lordship was truly mad. The husbands made repeated entreaties to Lord Tadanao, but their wives were not returned to them. The senior councilors strongly urged their lord to reconsider an action so manifestly inhuman; but the more loudly they remonstrated, the more pleasure Lord Tadanao derived from persevering in his project.

The three retainers whose wives had been stolen soon discovered the true nature of the cruel deceit practiced upon them by Lord Tadanao. Two of them, apparently believing that even this sort of thing did not absolve them from their samurai duty of obedience, thereupon committed suicide.

When notification of their deaths arrived, forwarded from the district inspectors, Lord Tadanao drained at a gulp the cup of wine he was holding, smiled wearily, and said nothing. The members of his household, however, were loud in their expressions of sympathy and admiration for the two deceased retainers. "True faithful warriors!" "Magnificent deaths!"—their eulogies even included phrases of this kind. But, as for the cause of these two noble deaths, there was no one who thought of this as anything but a heaven-sent mischance, a visitation of ineluctable fate.

Now that these two were dead the attention of the whole household was concentrated upon the solitary injured husband who lived on, a man called Asamizu Yojirō. There were many who bewailed the cowardice of a fellow whose wife had been stolen and who yet hesitated to plunge a dagger into his stomach.

Four or five days later the man himself appeared abruptly at the castle and informed the reception official that he desired an audience with Lord Tadanao. The official did his best to dissuade him.

"Whatever has happened, the other party is your lord. If you were to see him now it could only result in your attempting revenge. His lordship has behaved most improperly, and we all realize that. But, whatever he has done, he remains your lord."

But Yojirō was insistent.

"That is as it may be," he flashed back, "but I request an audience. I must see Lord Tadanao, whatever the consequences. Please forward my application."

The official, left with no choice, passed on the request to a councilor who was then conducting some business in the anteroom.

"This Yojirō fellow seems to have lost his wits," muttered the old councilor when he had heard the official's explanation. "His lordship has used him badly, but in a case like this the proper thing for a retainer to do is to register his protest by a formal suicide. The other two understood that perfectly, but his losing his wife seems to have completely deranged Yojirō's mind. I had thought better of him."

Still grumbling away to himself the councilor summoned a page boy and, with evident distaste, communicated the request to Lord Tadanao.

Lord Tadanao's reaction was surprisingly good-natured.

"What!" he cried. "Has Yojirō come to see me? This is indeed a welcome visit. Show him in at once! The audience is granted." He was shouting loudly but his features were animated, for the first time in many days, by a flickering, playful smile.

Moments later, Yojirō, lean and wasted like a sick dog, appeared before Lord Tadanao. The man seemed to have worn himself out in the last few days by the intensity of his anguish: he was deathly pale, and the expression on his face was sullen and murderous. His eyes were streaked with lines of red.

For the first time in his life Lord Tadanao saw before him an Echizen retainer revealing in his looks, without any attempt at concealment, his true feelings toward him.

"So, it's you, Yojirō. Come closer!" Lord Tadanao spoke amiably.

He felt somehow that he was now dealing as one human being with another, and he was even conscious of a kind of affectionate yearning for Yojirō. It was as if the barrier separating lord from retainer had been removed, and he and Yojirō now faced each other directly, simply as fellow men.

Yojirō slid himself forward on his knees over the smooth straw matting until he was only a few steps from his master, and then cried out, in a voice which might have risen from a tormented soul in the depths of hell:

"My lord! Even the code of loyalty is a trifle beside the great law of humanity! You have stolen my wife, and this is how I show my hatred!"

With the speed of a swallow in flight he sprang to his feet and rushed upon Lord Tadanao. A blade gleamed in his right hand. Even so, Lord Tadanao was too agile for his attacker. He caught the upraised arm with consummate ease, twisted it, and forced Yojirō to the floor. An attendant, acting with what he imagined to be considerable tact, took Lord Tadanao's great sword from the boy sword-bearer and proffered it to his master. But Lord Tadanao brusquely pushed the man back.

"Yojirō! It is you alone who have shown yourself a true warrior!" He released his hold on Yojirō's arm as he spoke.

Yojirō, still grasping the dagger, did not even raise his head, but prostrated himself in submission.

"Your wife, too, refused on every occasion to comply with my wishes. In this household of mine you are indeed rare creatures!" Lord Tadanao broke into loud and joyous laughter.

Yojirō's rebellion had afforded Lord Tadanao double cause for rejoicing. First, he had been sincerely hated as a man, even to the point of an attempt on his life, and this gave him the feeling that he had been permitted for the first time to step down into the world of human beings. Secondly, he had been attacked in full earnestness by a man reputed to be the foremost swordsman in the whole fief, and he had most convincingly beaten down that attack. He could not believe that there was in this victory, at least, any element of deceit. He was able once more, untroubled by the doubts which had plagued him so long, to savor his old sense of exultation in victory. Lord Tadanao felt as if a gap had opened in the oppressive cloud of melancholy which had settled of late about his life, and he had caught a glimpse of the radiance beyond.

Not only did he permit Yojirō, who begged piteously that his lord's vengeance might fall on him alone, to depart without a word of reproof, but he at once gave Yojirō's wife her liberty.

Lord Tadanao's joy, however, was short-lived.

On their first night at home after returning from the castle Yojirō and his wife, resting their heads close together on their pillows, killed themselves. For what reason they died was not made clear, but it was perhaps from a sense of shame, in that Yojirō had raised his hand against their hereditary lord, or perhaps because they were overwhelmed with gratitude at Lord Tadanao's merciful kindness in granting them their lives.

However that may have been, Lord Tadanao heard the news with not the slightest gratification. Even Yojirō's armed attack upon him, viewed in the light of his subsequent suicide, seemed to Lord Tadanao to have been a strangely incredible act. He wondered whether it had been no more than a calculated attempt to achieve a noble death at the hands of the master. If this were so, then Lord Tadanao's amazing feat in seizing Yojirō's arm before he could strike and forcing him to yield was not so very different from those amazing victories over the enemy commanders in the battles of the Reds and the Whites. After a little more of such reflection Lord Tadanao lapsed once more into a state of black despair.

The steady worsening of Lord Tadanao's disorder from this point is just as recorded in the histories. In time he was not only casually murdering his own retainers but he reached the point of imprisoning and putting to the sword numbers of completely innocent countryfolk. The tale of "The Stone Chopping-Block" in particular, a story which has come down to us over the centuries in oral tradition, still produces in the listener a shudder of aversion. But, if Lord Tadanao perpetrated such cruelties, it may well have been because his retainers failed to treat Lord Tadanao as a human being, and Lord Tadanao, on his side, ended by treating his retainers in the same way.

VI

But this outrageous behavior was not to continue without end. While Lord Tadanao, in Echizen, proceeded freely from excess to excess, in Edo the Shogun's ministers Lords Doi Toshikatsu and Honda

Masazumi were privately revolving plans for his overthrow. Frontal measures against so hotheaded a daimyo, and one, moreover, who was closely related to the Tokugawa family, might have given rise to a serious disturbance. Accordingly, the ministers decided to send Lord Tadanao's mother, who had taken Buddhist vows and was now known as the nun Seiryo, on a mission to Echizen to convey indirectly the resolve of the Shogun's household.

Lord Tadanao received his mother, whom he had not seen for many years, with great affection. And, strangely enough, when told of the Shogun's desire to dispossess him, he cheerfully signified his compliance, and very soon after, abandoning his great fief as calmly as if it had been a pair of outworn straw sandals, he set off for his place of exile, the town of Funai in northern Kyūshū.

On his way, at Tsuruga, he formally took Buddhist orders and assumed the priestly name of Ippaku. This was in the fifth month of the year 1623, when Lord Tadanao was a little past thirty years of age.

From Funai he later moved to Tsumori, another town in the same province of Bungo, and at this place, on a small fifty-thousand-bushel fief granted him for his maintenance by the Shogunate, he passed the remainder of his days uneventfully, dying in 1650 at the age of fifty-six.

No systematic account of Lord Tadanao's life in this latter period has been transmitted to us. But the lord of Funai Castle, Takenaka Shigétsugu, whose duty it was to watch over Lord Tadanao, caused his retainers to keep a record of the exile's behavior to be forwarded to the Shogun's minister Lord Doi Toshikatsu, and this small volume, entitled "Report on the Conduct of Lord Tadanao," survives. The following is an excerpt:

". . . Since his removal to Tsumori in this province, Lord Tadanao has passed his days quietly, showing no signs of violent disposition. His lordship has frequently remarked that when he lost his great family heritage he felt only an immense relief, as if he had awakened from a bad dream. He prays that he may never, in any future reincarnation, be born again as lord of a province. Though surrounded by vast numbers of people, he avows that he very often experienced the torments of a soul fallen into a hell of solitude. Concerning the matter of his dispossession, he appears to harbor no resentment toward anyone. . . . At times of relaxation he occasionally invites a village elder or a priest to a game of Gobang in his private rooms. It had been previously rumored that, when absorbed in this pastime, his lordship was prone to fits of temper more terrible than the tantrums of King Chou of the Yin dynasty, but of such behavior there has been no sign. When, on one occasion, the priest Rōnō of the Jokon Temple, a person with whom his lordship has established a particularly cordial relationship, ventured to remark that 'Any man who had a fief of 3,350,000 bushels would have been tempted to model his behavior on the tyrant Chou—it was no fault of your lordship's,' Lord Tadanao merely laughed and was not in the least angry. Of late His Lordship has called into his presence even lowborn peasants and townspeople, and he appears to take great pleasure in listening to their rough and unaffected talk. When people observe his respectful bearing on all occasions, the consideration with which he treats his attendants, and his constant solicitude for the welfare of the ordinary people on his estate, they never cease to wonder that this was the lawless monster who lost his family a province of 3,350,000 bushels. . . ."

THE CAMELLIA

BY Satomi Ton

TRANSLATED BY Edward Seidensticker

*Satomi Ton, born in 1888, was early associated with a
group of well-to-do young literati who proclaimed themselves rebels against the
materialism and pessimism of the naturalists. The leaders of the group espoused
a sort of Tolstoian idealism, but their emphasis on the importance of the individual—again as a protest against the naturalists and their leveling impulses—
meant that the group had almost as many philosophies as members. Satomi
himself was something of a heretic from the start. In particular, a richness in the
texture of his prose and a preoccupation with the senses set him apart from his
more ascetically minded fellows. He later developed what he described as a
"philosophy of sincerity," and his mature works, essentially Confucian in
their affirmation of the natural rectitude of man, seem to hold that no act is to
be condemned if the whole heart of the actor is in it.*

*The present story (Tsubaki in Japanese) was first published in 1923, when
the author was thirty-five. It illustrates another part of Satomi's philosophy—
his belief in the validity of literary values. It was written shortly after the great
Tokyo-Yokohama earthquake and its announced purpose was to demonstrate
that formal beauty was possible even then. The source of the young women's
hysteria will be clearer if it is remembered that the Japanese have a superstitious
fear of the camellia, whose blossoms fall, not petal by petal, but whole, like
severed human heads.*

SHE was past thirty and still unmarried. She lay facing
left, and she was reading a magazine romance by the light of a lamp
with a low, scarlet shade. The night was still and cold: there was not a

138

suggestion of wind. One would guess that it was not yet midnight, though the sounds of the last passers-by in the street had faded as the night wore on. The very lack of noise struck the ear with a special sharpness.

As she turned a page, she glanced over at her twenty-year-old niece. Their beds were perhaps six inches apart, and the girl lay facing her. The sleeping face was remarkably beautiful. Only the nose and forehead were visible, clean, above the velvet border of the quilt. The aunt gazed as though she were seeing the face for the first time.

"Aren't you calm, though." She wanted to tease the girl, to laugh with her. But the girl was like a thing modeled, so quiet that not even her breathing was audible. The aunt laughed silently. The floor matting, freshly changed just before they had moved in, rustled a little as she shifted her weight, and a wave of warm air rose over her neck and face.

For a time she thought of nothing but the progress of the story. Unfortunately she was not sleepy.

Far away a steam whistle blew a short blast. The night was really too quiet. She could not remember such quiet. She thought of waking the maid and having her move them upstairs so that the three could sleep together. But it would be a nuisance to get up. She went on reading.

The relations of the hero and heroine approached a crisis, and nothing happened. The men were unexciting—she was not likely to remember any of them. Her mind taking in almost nothing, she read on.

Slap.

It was by her pillow. Nothing before and nothing after, only the one sound. Something had fallen on the matting, that much was clear. What would it be? She could not bring herself to look. Laying the magazine down softly on the bed, she pulled her left hand in and clasped her two hands to her breast. The icy cold of the left hand sank into the other.

Her niece was staring over with narrowed eyes.

"What is it?" The aunt started up. "What is it, Setchan?"

"No!" The girl jumped up quilt and all, and buried her head on her aunt's knee.

"I asked you to tell me what was the matter. What is it, Setchan?"

Setchan raised her head a little. "Don't!"

The older woman threw the weight from her knee and resolutely looked beyond the head of the bed. In the alcove, several feet farther away than she would have guessed, a large crimson camellia had fallen. It lay on the matting like a turned-down bowl. They had hated to leave the camellias in their old garden and had had the agent break off an armful, which they had brought with them. The celadon vase in the alcove was full of week-old camellias.

"Behave yourself, Setchan." There was relief in her voice. The girl too raised herself from the bed.

"What's the matter?" she asked.

"I'm the one who should be asking that."

"But you—"

"I didn't do anything."

"Didn't do anything! You screamed at me."

"The way you stared. And your eyes were half closed."

"You were already terrified," said the girl. "You stopped reading and pulled your hand under the quilt. Don't deny it."

"You saw me, did you?"

"I thought we had robbers."

"Don't be silly. But what woke you up?"

"You called me."

"I did not. Why should I call you?"

"You didn't?"

"I didn't."

"Then I must have been dreaming."

"It was a camellia. A camellia fell."

"Don't!" Again the girl threw herself on her aunt. "Don't. Don't. Don't say such things."

"Setchan, please. I'm surprised at you."

"But why do you say such things?"

"What did I say to upset you? Look for yourself."

"No, no, no."

"Don't be foolish, child. One of the camellias fell, and that's what woke you up."

"Oh?" At length the girl pulled her face away and looked timidly over her aunt's shoulder toward the alcove. "Isn't it awful. Bright red."

"Red or white, it falls when its time comes. What if it is bright red?"

"It's repulsive."

"Suppose you throw it away, then."

"I can't. You throw it away."

"It's doing no harm. We can leave it till morning."

"Swollen with blood."

"Stop it, Setchan." A frown wrinkled the beautiful eyebrows. The rebuke was in earnest. "You're talking nonsense. I'm going to sleep."

She pushed her niece away, turned over, and pulled the quilt up over her face.

"You're cheating." The girl lay where the force of the push had left her. Bundled from head to foot in the quilt, she held her breath and listened.

Silence.

She lay still for a time. Finding it hard to breathe, she timidly pulled her head up. Her aunt lay facing left, the quilt as always tight around her shoulders. "Isn't she nasty!" The girl rolled away. The lampshade sent a violet light into the far corners of the room and planted a seal of death upon the face of the familiar seventeenth-century beauty on the screen.

"How awful." The girl rolled over again. Her aunt in front of her was laughing convulsively. It was so unlike her—she laughed so little. But now she laughed, the bright quilt pulled hastily over her nose. Her body shook from shoulders to hips, her eyes were closed, she laughed on. At first the girl did not see. Then she saw as in a mirror, and she too was laughing helplessly. She laughed, she laughed. She could not say a word, she only rolled over laughing. The night was dead quiet. They had to control their voices, and the effort made it so much funnier. It was so funny, it was so funny. The more she thought of it the funnier it was. What could she do, it was so funny.

mouth open in disbelief, its head a deep green, wriggling on the three strong points. A flip of a trout's tail sends needles up the arm. One slap from Akaza, however, and the trout lay still in his hand like a woman's foot.

Even at the bottom of the river the workers were unable to cheat. Under Akaza's watchful eye they would dive, come up for air, dive again. In early spring the river too would seem to have come into leaf. Small fish and even the rocks would be a pleasant green for the season. Annoyed at something, Akaza would plunge into the water, give one of the men a shove or a rap on the head, send down the big rocks for the paving that is so important in breaking a current. That hoarse voice seldom stopped. However strong the undercurrent, Akaza would plunge down through it, slender as a flatfish. None of the workers was longer-winded than he. In the water they had a healthy respect for that angry face, but once out again, Akaza would be in good spirits. He thought it less a river of which he was master than a lake he had built for himself.

On payday twice a month his wife Riki appeared at the shelter—so quiet and understanding a woman that she was known as "the saint." Riki would show no mercy in an argument, however: "That's the sort of person he is, and you'll just have to take him for what he is. No amount of talking will make him listen to what he doesn't want to hear."

But Akaza would only snort and turn away.

The payment was remarkably precise for river work. Riki avoided the usual trimming of fractions. She added to her popularity by paying for job-work in advance, and when on payday she came over the dike with packages of biscuits the rough laborers would all wave at her. Gathered around for their afternoon tea, they would chatter happily, and as they put their money inside their shirts or wrapped it in kerchiefs the river rang with their voices. Akaza only received a report from his wife. He had long made it a practice to leave money matters to her. Even during tea he would stare at the river cutting between its two banks. He had come to work. As is the way with men who work in the sun, he was sunburned even to his eyes—eyes that seemed to have been made for the river. When the river was high from days of rain he would go out to gaze at the boiling, muddy waters. Turned sadly on

the river, his eyes would cloud over. The boats would be high against the dike, and the whole expanse under muddy waters that had washed away the shelter. However much he might command the respect of his fellows, Akaza could do nothing now. He had lived with the river since he was six, he was a full-fledged stoneman at fourteen, he came to manhood with his feet lacerated by bamboo splints. Even so, the terror of the flood was new each year. How did it manage to take away a hundred massive rock-baskets? Since he had become his own master at nineteen, he had seen his baskets go in less than a year. Yet those at the bottom of the river always remained. "Akaza's baskets," his colleagues would say admiringly.

"Has Mon come home yet?" he would ask as Riki was about to leave. His voice showed no emotion.

"Not yet."

"Has Inosuké gone to work?"

"He's asleep, just as you left him."

"No good in him."

With that Akaza would turn and walk off toward the men, back at their posts. He carried himself in powerful strides, the stout walk of a stout man.

Akaza had three children. Inosuké was undeniably Akaza's son, but though he was now twenty-seven and had finished his apprenticeship and become a stonecutter in his own right, he was not a hard worker, and it was hard to imagine where he found the dubious women he was always having trouble with. Even among accomplished stonecutters no one could do an epitaph quite as Inosuké could. He would have made good money if he had worked steadily, but he would work for a week or so, go off with the money, and not be seen for some days. The horns and the streetcars of Asakusa were in his ears, said his sister Mon, though perhaps not in exactly those words.

Presently he would return, go to work, and leave again when he had a little money. He listened to nothing Riki said, and he managed to be out of the house when his father came home in the evening.

Inosuké had two sisters, both younger than he. The older was Mon. She had gone to work as a maid in a Tokyo temple and had struck up a liaison with a student. When she became pregnant he fled to the provinces and she heard no more from him. She took lover after lover, and soon was doing the rounds of Tokyo as a barmaid. She came home not once in six months, and when she did appear she would lie sprawled on the floor, breathing in noisy, sluggish gasps, and order Riki about. Riki would grumble a little: the child had her troubles, but couldn't she let well enough alone? Riki's manner suggested revulsion, and at the same time it suggested the deepest pity as she cooked the things Mon liked and left her to sleep as she would. Mon slept until her face was blanched from sleep. She never got a decent night's sleep, it would seem. Riki thought she understood. Inosuké too, back from his nights out, would sleep the whole day through, as though he meant to sleep himself to extinction. When one or the other finally awoke, he would prop himself drowsily up and, eyes still narrow from sleep, look dully at the bustling Riki. Occasionally it occurred to Inosuké that he would have to leave home if she were to collapse from overwork. He would then look at her with real compassion, but he soon managed to forget the matter.

And Mon would say: "At least I'll never bother you for money." To her that seemed to be the most important question.

A year had passed when Kobata, her student friend, came calling at Akaza's house. Mon was working in Tokyo, but as usual she had left no address. She had only said that she would come home some day. Riki went down to call Akaza. Silently, Akaza left the shelter, climbed the dike, and hurried toward the house. The boy was only a student, said Riki, and Akaza was not to be rough with him.

"Probably he's come to ask about the child," she added. "He must think it's still alive."

"Does he seem like a slippery sort?"

"He's only a boy."

Akaza tried to talk, but Kobata was overawed by his appearance and manner.

"Let's hear what you have to say," said Akaza.

There was no answer. At length the boy said that he should at least have written, he knew, and that it was hardly proper of him to come calling now. His father in the country had kept such a close watch over him, however, that he had had no chance to sneak out. Now that he had made his way back to the capital he hoped to take care of all the expenses. There was no mention of the main problem: of whether he wanted to marry Mon, whether he wanted to see her again. Indeed

Akaza sensed that the fellow was relieved at finding her away. There was an appearance of honesty about him that made one want to dismiss him as another spineless but well-meaning student, and yet he could calmly retire to the country and not say a word for a whole year, in spite of a flood of letters. Not one to be led into a bad bargain, thought Akaza as he watched the pale youth make his show of forthrightness.

"The baby was born dead. Mon's lost control of herself since."

Akaza caught a suggestion of relief in the startled look that greeted his remark. The fellow had played it clever. It had been worth the trouble of making his way up the river—the thought came from deep inside Akaza's stout frame.

Where might Mon be, Kobata asked. Might he have her address? He had so many things to apologize for, he wanted to apologize and start over with clean conscience. His voice became strangely excited as he gathered momentum. Akaza was annoyed at the transparent complacency in the child, now so pleased with himself. He remembered the day he had heard from Riki that Mon was pregnant. How many of his men had he hit that day, he wondered. Akaza must be tired, he had heard them mutter.

Mon had taken to her bed in the back room. The girl had been defeated, she had been made a plaything and then sent home. Akaza, who had never in his life been defeated, did not want to see her.

The woman-chasing Inosuké for his part lashed out at Riki whenever he found the chance. Hadn't he said exactly what would happen? Hadn't he said it would be dangerous to let her leave home? Riki listened in silence. Sometimes, as Mon lay with an ice-bag on her forehead, he would stand by the bed and bawl at her as if he had stumbled on something filthy.

"So you fasten yourself on some pretty little schoolboy, do you, and he starts slobbering for his mother's milk, and now look at what you've got pushing at your belt. Well, get rid of it before it jumps out on you, whatever it is. I'm not going to have any damned schoolboy's squalling brat waking me up in the middle of the night."

"You're going too far." Riki would try to intervene. "And it's none of your business. Come on outside."

But Inosuké was again having trouble with a woman, and this bellowing was his revenge.

Riki was finally stunned into silence. Trouble between brother and sister could descend to such abuse, then, could it?

Inosuké was beginning to hit his stride, and the abuse flowed without interruption. "Makes me want to throw up, thinking of that face snuggling up to some schoolboy. Well, he's ten times as smart as you, that's a fact. He knew from the start that when he'd had his fill of you he could make his getaway. And as a matter of fact who could stand looking at that face year after year? Off he goes without telling you his name or his address, and not a peep from him afterwards. And you think he's so sweet and you want to protect him. God. Are you in love with him or are you feeble-minded or both? You're a fine piece anyway, that much is sure. And that thing inside you, getting fatter and fatter. Nobody's going to have much use for you the day it gets in shape and pops out on you. Take it and get on a boat and go straight to Tokyo and have it squashed like a frog."

When Riki again tried to intervene he turned on her. "You're her mother, aren't you? She's the sort of daughter you had, and now you try to shut me up. I'm feeling sorry for San, that's all." Inosuké's other sister, San, was working soberly as a maid somewhere, and occasionally she came home with appropriate gifts. At the mention of San everyone fell silent.

"There are good, quiet children like her," said Riki at length, "and look at you, not doing an honest day's work and eating off your father and then saying things like that. There are times when it's right to get worked up and times when it isn't, and this isn't your time. If someone has to be after her, let it be your father. He hasn't said a word. None of us should say a word. We should just leave her alone." Riki could make remarks the sharpness of which was out of keeping with her soft voice.

Mon's face was twisted from a headache, but she too had her say. "You should talk! How many times have you waddled off like a duck and left them to hatch for themselves, and Mother to clean up after you? How about the time you dragged that woman to the back door and Father found out and I had to go out and hide her? You almost knelt down to thank me out there in the dark. Remember? And now when I'm in trouble you don't lose a chance to shout at me like some mongrel puppy. Well, I've had enough of it. You're not the one who's feeding me, and I don't see that you have much right to talk. Once I've had the baby I'll pay for eveything, whatever I have to do while I'm about it, and I don't mean to worry Mother or Father again. I may not be a girl any more, but now that I've gone this far at least I'm my own boss, and I'm not taking any advice. Didn't Father tell me to look after myself? He didn't even want to see me, he said. Well, I don't need anyone like you standing there looking like my big brother. You make the headache worse, that's all. Whining at me because you're having trouble with some woman—no wonder women don't like you."

Now Akaza remembered how it had been to live with all that. He could hardly believe that the child here before him, almost on the point of weeping, could have been Mon's partner. Riki had said not to be rough. She need not have worried: Akaza felt his irritation recede. This was only a boy in trouble. Akaza had thought of taking him out to the dike and giving him full payment for what he had done to Mon. But the boy was only a boy and Akaza was no longer up to such roughness. The baby was dead, Mon herself had not been blameless. It might be best to let Kobata go.

"I doubt if Mon will want to see you. Suppose we just say goodbye." Akaza got up, indicating that he had work to do. As he glanced at the boy again, he too seemed on the verge of tears. "You'd better not commit any more crimes," he said, as if more important things must remain unsaid. "You came out on top this time."

In confusion, he hurried up the dike. The weather had been good for some days, and the strand—here shining a pure white, there broken into patches of weed-fringed stone, and yet farther on colored a rich tan by seeping water—the whole wide expanse came into his eyes, the shining white spots first. The seven boats out in the current were like so many white moths. They had reared Mon and Inosuké and San too. Riki was still young when she bore Mon and San, and she had softly pointed breasts. While she was waiting for him to empty his lunch box she would nurse a child or gather herbs along the dike. It did not seem such a very long time ago, and yet Mon had had her baby and gone on, and Akaza could not find it in him to roar at the man who was responsible—a sign, surely, that the affair had hurt him.

Riki knew from the surprisingly genial conversation that Akaza wanted only to tear his thoughts away. She was a little grateful. He had improved, he had become more understanding. She had expected to see him use his fists before the interview was half over. It had been one of his rules that a good punch was ten times as effective as any number of words. When a discussion with his wife became even a little circumspect and wordy he knew nothing better than to hit her. Riki had gone on being hit through the years, but the frequency of blows had decreased, and some time had passed now since the fear of being hit had last troubled her. She was glad he had not hit Kobata. Kobata had been too lightly punished, it was true, but to Riki it seemed that the heedless act had been his and Mon's too. In her heart she still hoped that the two might somehow be brought together. Now that Mon had fallen so low, however, no man was likely to take her, and Kobata seemed too quiet and docile for a good argument. Riki thought she understood why Mon had loved him and she was sorry to see him leave.

"I'll tell Mon when she comes again that you were good enough to call."

"And find out where she's living, please." Kobata took out a packet of money and pressed it upon her.

She would never see him again, thought Riki as she went with him to the gate. Kobata seemed to feel something motherly in her, and he was slow to leave the garden for the street. He looked at the summer chrysanthemums and the irises, asked what color the chrysanthemums were, and seemed to be taken by a strange, wistful sadness.

"How old are you?" she asked abruptly.

"How old am I? Just twenty-three."

Pale and nervous, he looked younger. It was in the spring of his twenty-second year, then, that he had had the affair with Mon. Only a year separated their ages. Riki had married Akaza when she was twenty-one. She had been no better informed than a baby on what it meant to be a woman.

A year had passed since the affair, and clearly the boy had come in good faith. How foolish of her not to have seen the purity of his motives earlier! A really bad one would surely be clever enough not to come calling at this late date.

Kobata took out a pen and wrote his address on a calling card. Give this to Mon, please." After repeated bows, the tall young figure went off through the paddies toward the dike.

Inosuké had been away for two or three days. At the worst moment he could have chosen, he came wandering back. He looked at Kobata with narrowed eyes. Riki told him that it was Mon's student friend, and a spasm of anger passed over the pale, drawn face. As Kobata climbed from the paddies to the dike Inosuké went after him, taking care that his mother did not see. Kobata knew who it was. Recognition quickly changed to fear. Inosuké followed for a hundred yards or so and remained silent even after they were abreast. Their shoulders almost brushed. The face, so like Akaza's, was twisted in open, animal anger. Kobata wondered when the man would leap. Spasms of fear went through his legs. If only he would speak; but Inosuké was in fact so strangled with malice and resentment that he could not speak. His ears were ringing.

"Just a minute." That was all he said, but the words meant release for Kobata.

"Yes?" Kobata tried to make his tone as unprovocative as possible.

"I'm Mon's brother."

Kobata was a ghostly white.

"I want to talk to you. Sit down. Over there. I want to talk to you." It was an order, and Kobata obediently sat down on the dike.

Inosuké asked if he had seen Mon. Kobata said he had not.

"You played with Mon and you as good as wrecked our family. You have your nerve coming here now. Let me tell you something. I used to sleep with Mon when we were little. Every night I woke her up to go to the toilet and I used to go with her because the hall was dark. I carried her on my back when she was a baby. I couldn't go out-doors unless I took her along. Until she was sixteen or so there wasn't a day I didn't see her or a meal we didn't have together. I knew where she had a mole she didn't know about herself until I told her about it, and that was after she was grown up. We were closer than brother and sister, Mon and I. When she came home with that brat of yours inside her, I did everything I could to hurt her. I got to treating her like some dirty mongrel puppy. Mother thought it was the real me saying those things and she used to look at me like a snake. She always took Mon's part. I could see why. If she hadn't, we'd all have been treating Mon like someone we had to get rid of. I knew all along you'd be coming around some day, damn you, and I wanted to let you know how close

Mon and I were. I brought her up myself, from when she was a baby. You're nothing but a spoiled schoolboy, and because you were lucky enough to be born a man you thought you could do what you wanted with her and not give a damn afterward. You could see by looking at her that she was a farmer's daughter. It happens all the time, you didn't see why you shouldn't do it too. Well, it won't work. I'm not letting you off as easy as my old man."

As he talked Inosuké took Kobata by the wrist and pulled and twisted at his arm. Tears came into his eyes. They had seemed to strike out at his adversary like whips, but now they had lost their strength. He was torn at by feelings of wounded affection so violent that he wondered himself how a confirmed profligate could be so moved. Kobata for his part felt his hand go numb. He sat there like a dunce, overcome by more than fear, wondering what sort of violence was coming next, yet unable to deny whatever it might be and unable even to think of escaping.

"And you just came to apologize?"

"I can't do anything but apologize."

"You mean to let Mon go on as she is?"

"I'd like to see her and talk things over."

"Will you marry her?"

"I might."

"Damned liar!"

Inosuké slapped him full in the face and in almost the same motion kicked him to the ground.

"Just say what you have to say. What will you gain by hitting me?"

But Inosuké, putting his whole strength into it this time, struck him a blow on the jaw. "I know damned well that whatever happens to you here it won't make a better man of you. Not as long as you live. But remember Mon. You have this much coming. You ruined her, you left her good for nothing at all, before she was even a woman. But don't go around thinking she'd marry the likes of you. If you went and asked her, she'd snap her fingers at you. You may think she's ruined, but her mind's sounder than ever. You won't find any trace of the girl that was so easy for you. Not a trace. All that's gone. And you did it. If you'd kept your hands off of her she wouldn't have turned into the woman she is. Don't come again. And don't go cheating her again."

"I was wrong. I admit it. I'm not making any excuses."

Inosuké stood up. The fellow was too docile. The incentive disappeared, and Inosuké began to feel a little ashamed of himself. "Go on home. I'm Mon's brother. If you have a sister yourself, you'll understand what I've done."

"Well, goodbye, then." Kobata felt that he did indeed understand, and as the other's face softened he began to feel something like friendliness in spite of what had happened.

Inosuké seemed to want to say something. Kobata was sure that he wanted to apologize.

"You can get a bus in town," said Inosuké finally. "Wait at the main intersection."

*   *   *

A week later Mon came home. San too was at home on a visit. The two of them took Akaza's lunch to the shelter. He only glanced at them. He had nothing to say about the remarkable chance that the two of them were home together. As they climbed the dike, however, he gazed after them for a time.

Mon listened with no show of surprise as Riki told of Kobata's visit. She seemed worried only about her father and how he had behaved during the interview. He had said nothing, said Riki. Indeed he had seemed sorry for the boy.

"Oh? But it was wrong of him to come. He needn't have come. And did he see Inosuké?"

Riki thought not.

"That's good." Mon lay down, relieved. "There might have been trouble if he had. But didn't you think he was handsome, Mother? Didn't you think he had nice eyes?"

"Don't be a fool. How can you go on praising the man who left you with a child?"

"There've been others since, but none I've been able to like the way I liked him. I let him do things I would never let another man do. Some have been a good deal handsomer, but when they're so handsome they're always pleased with themselves. He had just the right amount of handsomeness. But if he were to come back I wouldn't marry him." She laughed. "I just like to think about him. If I saw him again, he'd be just another lukewarm man."

"Can't you talk about anything but men?" San objected. "I could never say things like that. Why, I can't say half the things I'm thinking. And I don't know anything about men."

"You wouldn't. But when you've turned into a hussy like me you soon learn everything. Men are dirty. They're dirty when you think about them, but then as time passes you forget what you've been thinking. You're on your guard, but somehow it doesn't last."

At noon Inosuké came home. "So the slut's here again, as bold as ever. You'll eat off of us for a week or so and then leave, I suppose. Better leave before we're all sick of you. You're better off away having fun with your coolies. We may not look it, but we're a respectable family and we don't want you dirtying the place up."

"You shouldn't talk to her like that," said San. "She hasn't been home in such a long time."

"Shut up, brat. With a woman like Mon you can go on saying what you want and it won't bother her a bit, and you don't need to think it'll reform her either. She's not that kind of animal. Let's not have any more foolishness from you." He saw that Mon was still glaring at him. "When the hell do you mean to settle down and make yourself an honest living? We don't want you around here as long as you're in that business. And we don't need to see that schoolboy of yours either. He had his nerve coming here. You can tell what he thinks of us."

"You saw him, did you?" Mon turned pale and looked questioningly from her mother to her brother. San and Riki too were startled.

"That I did. I saw how he was going home and I followed him."

"What did you do?"

"Just what I wanted to." Inosuké looked insolently down at her and a sneer came to his lips.

"I don't suppose you hit him?" Mon held her breath.

"That I did. He knew he couldn't win and didn't fight back. I felt fine afterward."

Mon was stunned into silence. As they watched, her features began to collapse. Her nose and mouth twisted, her face seemed to lengthen. Then she spoke, as if dragging the words from the top of a reeling mind. "Say it again, please. Say again what you did." Her white fingers like coiled snakes, she clutched at the neck of her kimono. She had half risen from her seat, and there was a cold, murderous quality about her that made it hard to believe she was a woman. Neither Riki nor San had seen this Mon before.

Inosuké laughed softly. "I half killed him."

"Half killed a man who didn't fight back. Damn you." She leaped up. "Damn you. Who the hell ever asked you to show off your rough business? And what do you have to do with him? I gave myself to him of my own free will, and I don't need to listen to the likes of you. Who told you to kick him and step on him? Why did you have to hit a man who wouldn't fight back? Coward! Pig! Whore-chaser!"

She lunged at him and shot a plump hand at his face. There were three nail marks from his eye down over his cheek. Then, as if from a swollen berry, the red blood trickled down.

"And just what do you think you're doing?" said Inosuké. Though somewhat taken aback, he pushed her to the floor. She jumped up again and clutched at his shoulder. As he shook her off, his big hand struck her full in the face. "Bitch! Whore!"

"Kill me," screamed Mon. "Go ahead and kill me!" It was like the croak of a frog.

"All right. You asked for it. I'll break every bone in your damned body."

He had thought Mon would try to run. She did not move. "Hit me," she screamed. "Go ahead. Kill me!"

Riki and San tried to stop him, but he only grew more violent—if he didn't show the bitch now, she'd get into the habit. When at length the timid San burst out weeping, however, he decided that he had done enough.

But Mon would not have it. "Excuse me, but I'm different from you, running around with your snotty whores. You're good enough to say that I'm a whore myself. A drunken whore, a slut no decent man would marry, the leavings of a woman who can't tell her own mother and father where she's living. All right. But let me tell you something. When someone pushes my man so far that he can't fight back and then half kills him—I don't care who it is, my own brother or who, he's not going to get away with it. Go on back to your rock pile. You call yourself a man, do you? You had your nerve hitting him.

Now I know the sort of brother I have, and I'm ashamed. Ashamed before the whole world. Pig! Skirt-chasing pig!" Her voice rose into a piercing wail.

That was no way for a woman to talk, said Riki. What would the neighbors think? But Mon told her to be quiet. Mon had not thought they had a bully in the family. Was she to let him go on playing big brother to her?

"You want more, do you, bitch?"

"Go ahead, damn you. You're wrong if you think those fists of yours can change me. That's all over long ago. A farmer rotting away in the rice paddies doesn't have much idea what a person like me is up to."

Inosuké was about to lunge at her again, but Riki stopped him, and he saw that it was time to go back to work. "Just get the hell away from here, that's all," he growled as he turned to leave.

Mon began sobbing the moment he was out of the house.

What sort of life was the girl leading, thought the horrified Riki. Where had she learned such language? "You're quite a woman, aren't you?"

The tremble in her voice struck at Mon's heart. "No, Mother. I'm all right. You needn't worry about me."

"But I've never heard a woman talk like that before. Please, for my sake, find yourself a good job and be an ordinary woman. You're even worse than your brother."

"I'm not as bad as you think. But there's nothing I can do."

Riki showed her Kobata's card. She gazed at it for a time. "I don't have any use for this sort of thing," she said, tearing it to small bits. She sat sobbing quietly, her head bowed. When she had had her cry, she was the old Mon again, sprawled sluggishly on the floor as if she found herself a nuisance.

"Something must be wrong with me. I have no energy."

"Surely it's not that again!"

"Oh, Mother." Mon laughed. It was rather a forced laugh, and somehow it touched Riki. "I wouldn't be coming home if that was the trouble. I came because I wanted to see you." There was sincerity in her voice. "Whether I'm good or whether I'm bad, somehow I want to come home. I even want to see that Inosuké."

While all this was happening, Akaza was with his boats, the seven of them tied together, their decks almost under water from the weight of the rocks they were hauling downstream. He was irritably hurrying the work in preparation for the early-summer rains, only a few days off. Once that work was over there would be a vacation. Akaza disliked vacations. Anyone who wanted to work on into the summer should come ahead, he shouted.

"Raise your hands if you want to."

As they approached the jetty, he called out a hearty invitation to the half-naked men in the boats. Akaza was in good spirits. They all raised their hands, in favor of going on to the next job. Good, good—they'd all keep busy, and the dog days wouldn't dry them out. Then Akaza gave the order to lower the rocks. The river rocks, like steel, poured from the worker's hands into the baskets, and even as they watched it the current pulled up and stopped, almost sadly. When a little of the water found an outlet, it roared angrily through. "Rocks over there, rocks over there," shouted Akaza. The hair on his chest seemed to stand on end. He bent forward like a bronze statue, tense to the point of breaking.

西班牙犬の家

佐藤春夫

THE HOUSE OF
A SPANISH DOG

A STORY FOR THOSE FOND OF DREAMING

BY Satō Haruo

TRANSLATED BY George Saitō

Satō Haruo, the eldest son in a physician's family, was born in Wakayama Prefecture in 1892. From his early youth Satō aspired to become a writer. Upon graduation from school he entered Keiō University in order to study literature under Nagai Kafū.

He started his literary career as a poet. His early poems show a strong socialistic tendency, which can be accounted for partly by the social disorder of the time. This stage, however, lasted only for a short period; Satō's later poems were written in the characteristically elaborate style which was the outcome of his profound knowledge and passionate love of Japanese classical literature. Some critics have even gone so far as to declare that Satō's poems will survive and be treasured so long as the Japanese language exists.

As a novelist Satō was mainly influenced by Nagai Kafū and Tanizaki Junichirō. His poetic talents led his early prose writings into the realm of fantasy. "The House of a Spanish Dog" (Supein-inu no Ie, 1916) was the first of several stories that were composed in a strongly lyrical vein. In his effort to escape from the melancholy of youth, Satō attempted to produce modern versions of the "hermit literature" so important in ancient Chinese and Japanese writing.

"Pastoral Melancholy" (1919) represents the culmination of Satō's literary art; in it he develops the style of fantasy already revealed in "The House of a Spanish Dog." Satō's critical mind, however, did not permit him to remain a

writer of simple prose poetry, but led him to adopt a more realistic approach to his material. At the same time he tried to depict the land of Japan in the style of Western painting. To this end he used the works of such writers as Edgar Allan Poe and Oscar Wilde, interpreting them after his own fashion.

FRATÉ starts running all of a sudden and waits for me at the parting of the road that leads to the blacksmith's. He is a very clever dog and has been my friend for years. I am convinced that he is far cleverer than most men, not to mention my wife. So I take Fraté with me whenever I go for a walk. Once in a while he leads me to some quite unexpected spot. That is the reason that when I go for a walk these days I do not have any set destination in mind but follow obediently wherever my dog leads me. So far I have never been down the side street that goes to the blacksmith's. Very well, today I shall follow the dog down there. So I turn in that direction.

The narrow road is on a gentle slope which occasionally makes sharp twists. I walk along behind my dog, not looking at the scenery, nor thinking, but simply letting myself indulge in idle fancies. Now and then I look up and observe the clouds in the sky. Suddenly some flowers by the roadside catch my attention. I pick a few and hold them to my nose. I do not know what they are called but they smell good. I walk along twisting them between my fingers. Fraté happens to notice them. He stops for a moment, tilts his head to the side and gazes into my eyes. He seems to want them. I throw them down for him. He sniffs at the flowers and then glances up at me as if to say that he wishes they were dog biscuits. Then he starts running down the road once more.

I walk along like this for nearly two hours. We seem to be climbing considerably and before long I can command quite a good view. Below the open fields that stretch out before me I can vaguely make out some town in the distance between the mist and the clouds. I stand there for some time gazing at it. Yes, it is certainly a town. But what town can possibly be lying over there with all those houses? There is something rather peculiar about the whole scene. I am totally ignorant about the geography of these parts, however, and there is really nothing so surprising about seeing an unfamiliar town. I look down the other side of the hill. It slopes down gently into the distance. The entire surface is covered with dense thickets. It is shortly before noon and the gentle spring sun shines like smoke, like scent, through the fresh green foliage and onto the slender trunks of oaks, chestnut trees, and silver birches. The balance of shade and sun on the tree trunks and on the ground is beautiful beyond words. I feel like going into the depths of that forest. The undergrowth must be very dense, but it is surely not impenetrable.

My friend Fraté seems to be thinking along the same lines. He advances merrily into the forest and I follow him. When we have gone a little over a hundred yards, the dog begins to walk in a different way. He abandons his easy gait and busily moves his legs forward as if he were weaving. He thrusts his nose forward. He must have found something. Is it a rabbit's footprints, or can he have found a bird's nest in that thick grass? For a few moments he hurries to and fro restlessly. Then he seems to find the right path and walks straight ahead. My curiosity is slightly aroused and I follow him. From time to time we startle wild birds who are mating amidst the branches.

After we have walked along at a rapid pace for about half an hour, Fraté suddenly comes to a halt. At the same moment I seem to hear the gurgling sound of running water. (This part of the country abounds in springs.) Jerking his ears irritably, Fraté walks back a few yards, sniffs the ground once again, and then sets off to the left. I am surprised to find how deep the forest is. I had never imagined that there were such vast thickets in this part of the country. From the look of it there must be almost seven hundred acres of woods. My dog's peculiar behavior and the endless forest combine to fill me with curiosity. After another half an hour or so of walking, Fraté stops once again. He gives out a couple of staccato barks. Until this moment I had not noticed it, but now I see that a house is standing directly in front of me. There is something very strange about it. Why should anyone have a house in a place like this? For this is no ordinary charcoal shed such as one finds in the forests.

A quick glance tells me that there is nothing in the way of a garden; the house blends abruptly into the woods. "Blends" is indeed the only word, for as I have said I came upon the house all of a sudden and could not catch a glimpse of it from the distance. The house has clearly been built in such a position that it can be seen only when one is standing directly before it.

As I walk closer I see that it is quite a commonplace sort of house. At the same time, it is rather hard to put my finger on exactly what type of house it is. It has a thatched roof, but it is not like an ordinary farmhouse. The windows are all glazed in the Western style. Since I cannot see any entrance, I gather that we must be facing the back. From where I stand I notice that the two side walls are half covered with ivy. This is the only embellishment to give the house any interest or character.

At first I thought it was a lodge, but it is too big for that and, besides, this wood doesn't seem large enough to require a keeper. Well, if it isn't a lodge, what can it be? Whatever happens I must go in and have a look. I can say that I have lost my way. No doubt they will offer me a cup of tea, and Fraté and I will eat the box lunch that I have brought.

With this in mind I walk round to the front of the house. Until now my sense of sight seems to have submerged my sense of hearing, but suddenly I realize that there is a stream nearby. The gurgling sound that I heard earlier must have come from near here. When I reach the front, I find that, like the rest of the house, it directly faces the forest. There is one peculiar thing about it, however: it is far more luxuriously built than the other parts of the building. Four fine stone steps lead up to the front door. This stone is far older than the remainder of the house and it is thickly overgrown with moss.

The house faces south and beneath the front window a row of small red roses grows along the wall. The roses stand there with a proprietary air. They are in full bloom and I have the impression that they blossom regardless of the season. And that is not all. From under a clump of roses flows a stream of water, the width of a sash, glittering brightly in the sun. At first glance it looks as if the water were flowing out of the house itself. My retainer Fraté starts lapping the water avidly; he evidently finds it delicious.

Now I walk quietly up the steps. I can clearly hear the sound of my shoes against the stone, but they do not really disturb the quiet of the surrounding scene. Playfully I mutter to myself: "I am now visiting the house of a hermit, or perhaps of a magician." I look round and see Fraté standing there nonchalantly with his pink tongue hanging out and his tail wagging.

In the Western manner I knock on the Western-style door. There is no answer. I have to knock again. Still no answer. This time I call out: "May I come in?" There is not the slightest reaction. Is the owner out, I wonder, or is the house completely unoccupied? I am overcome by a rather weird feeling. I go to the front window where the roses are growing—for some reason I walk as quietly as possible—and standing on tiptoe look inside the house.

The window has a heavy, dark-maroon curtain decorated with blue lines. Obviously of very good quality, it does not go with the rest of the house. The curtain has been partly pulled aside and I can see clearly into the room. To my surprise I see a large stone basin, about two feet high, standing in the middle of the room. Water is gushing up from the center of the basin and pouring constantly over the sides. The basin is overgrown with moss. The floor, too, is of stone and it looks rather damp. (When I think about it later, I realize that the water spilling over the edge of the basin is the same glittering water that I saw slithering out like a snake from among the roses.)

That basin really amazes me. Although I have felt from the beginning that there was something rather peculiar about the house, I never expected to find such a weird arrangement inside. A new surge of curiosity comes over me and I start carefully examining the inside of the house through the window. The floor is made of some pale stone whose name I do not know. Round the basin where it is wet it has taken on a beautiful blue color. In laying out the floor they evidently used the stone just as it came from the quarry; there is something peculiarly natural about the surface. On the wall furthest from the entrance there is a fireplace also made of stone, and to the right I notice three bookshelves with what look like dishes piled on top. At the other end of the room, near the window where I am standing, is a large plain desk, and on the desk—yes, what *is* on the desk? I bring my face as close to the glass as possible, but the window is so shaped that I cannot see. Oh, wait a moment! This house is far from being deserted. Indeed, someone must have been here only a moment ago. For on the corner of that desk lies a cigarette butt and from it, very gently, rises a thread of smoke; it goes up vertically for about two feet, then starts wavering and, as it goes higher, becomes more and more disturbed.

Amidst all the unexpected happenings of today's walk I have completely forgotten about smoking. Now I am reminded of it and I take a cigarette out of my pocket and light it. At the same moment my desire to enter the house and have a look becomes quite irresistible. I think carefully for a few moments and make up my mind. Yes, I shall go in. Even if the owner happens to be out. In case he comes back and finds me, I'll explain my reason to him honestly. Since he is leading such a peculiar existence in any case, I am sure he won't object to my uninvited visit. He may even welcome me. The paintbox, which have taken along on my walk and which has begun to be rather a uisance, will now turn out to be useful since it will prove that I am not a thief. No, nothing will stop me: I'm going into this house. Once again I climb the steps to the entrance. As a final precaution I call out: "Is anyone there?" No answer. Quietly I open the door. It is un- ocked.

As soon as I have walked in, I draw back a few steps. For there, lying in the sun under the window, is a coal-black Spanish dog; the dog, who has been dozing with his chin touching the floor and his body curled in a ball, opens his eyes in a sly, furtive manner when he hears me and sluggishly stands up.

At this, Fraté starts growling and walks up to the black dog. For a time they both growl at each other. But the Spanish dog seems to have a peculiarly gentle disposition: after the two dogs have sniffed carefully at each other, it is he who starts wagging his tail. My dog joins in and soon they are both wagging busily. Then the Spanish dog lies down in the same place as before. Fraté lies down directly beside him. Strange indeed to see such a friendly attitude between two dogs of the same sex who have only just met each other! Of course Fraté has a very amiable nature, but the Spanish dog deserves the main praise for his amazing magnanimity in welcoming a stranger. I feel reassured and walk into the room.

This Spanish dog is unusually large for the breed. He has the characteristically thick, tufted tail and when he winds it up on his back he looks very impressive indeed. From the little I know about dogs I can tell from the luster of his fur and the look of his face that he is quite old. I walk up to him and pat him on the head by way of paying my respects to my temporary host. From past experience I know that dogs (so long as they are not strays who are in the habit of being badly treated by human beings) tend by nature to be friendly to people. This is especially true of dogs who live in lonely places. Such dogs will never hurt people who are nice to them, even if they are complete strangers. Besides, their instinct tells them instantly whether a man is a dog lover or the type that is likely to treat dogs unkindly. My theory proves to be correct, for the Spanish dog now starts happily licking my hand.

This is all very well, but who on earth is the owner of the house? And where is he? Will he be back soon? Despite my resolutions, now that I am actually in the house I am beginning to have compunctions. I am free to examine the place from top to bottom, but instead I remain standing by the large stone basin. Just as I had expected when I looked through the window, it comes up only to my knees. The brim is about two inches across and is provided with three grooves. The water runs along the grooves, round the outer edge of the basin, and then spills onto the floor. Yes, to be sure, in places situated like this house, this is one possible way to draw water. No doubt the people who live here use the water for drinking. The basin is certainly no mere ornament.

From the look of things this room seems to be serving several purposes at once. There are one, two, three chairs. Yes, just three— one by the basin, one by the fireplace, and one next to the table. They are all practical, down-to-earth chairs; neither they nor anything else in the room bespeaks the slightest effort at elaboration. As I continue looking round the room, I feel myself gradually becoming emboldened. I notice that a clock is ticking away the time. Tick-tock, ticktock—like the pulsation of the quiet house itself. Where can the clock be? It is nowhere on the dark reddish-yellow wall. Ah yes, there it is, standing on the table that I saw from the window. With a slight feeling of diffidence toward the Spanish dog, the temporary master of the house, I walk up to the table. There on the corner lies the cigarette that I saw from outside. By now it has completely burned out and is nothing but a cylinder of white ash.

Above the dial of the clock is painted a picture. This gives it a toy-like appearance which contrasts curiously with the generally uncouth aspect of the room. I examine the picture. It shows a lady of noble deportment standing next to a gentleman. There is a third member in the party—a bootblack who polishes the left shoe of the gentleman once each second. A childish picture, but nevertheless interesting. I

am no expert where foreign matters are concerned, but from the lady's wide skirt that trails its lace frills on the floor and from the gentleman's top hat and side whiskers I gather that the scene depicted on the clock must be some fifty years old. Well, well—what a pathetic fellow that bootblack really is! There he has to crouch in this quiet house, and in the smaller world contained inside this house, and day and night he has to keep on polishing a single shoe. As I observe the monotony of his ceaseless movements, I feel my own shoulder becoming stiff. The clock says quarter past one; it is one hour slow.

Some four or five dozen dusty books are piled on the table and a couple of others are lying by themselves. All the books are rather bulky—they might be albums of pictures, or books of architecture, or again, atlases. The titles seem to be in German and I cannot understand them. On the wall hangs a heliochrome seapiece. I've seen this picture before somewhere—isn't that Whistler's coloring? I strongly approve of having such a picture here. Anyone secluded among the hills like this would probably forget that the world contained such things as the sea unless he had a picture to remind him.

I decide to leave the house and go home. Perhaps I'll call again one of these days and meet the real owner. Still, I feel a little uneasy about having entered the house while it was empty and to be leaving now while it is still empty. On second thought, perhaps I'd better wait until he comes back. I watch the water gushing out of the basin and light another cigarette. For some time I stand there gazing at the water. Now that I really absorb myself in it, I seem to hear some sort of music coming from the distance. I listen with admiration and rapture. Can it be that music is actually coming from the depths of this constantly gushing water? The owner of such an unusual house must be an extremely eccentric individual. . . . Wait! Is it possible that I have become a sort of Rip Van Winkle? Shall I return home to find that my wife has turned into an old woman? I imagine myself leaving the forest and asking a passing peasant where the village of Kurosaka is. "Kurosaka?" he answers. "There's no such place in these parts." A queer feeling comes over me and I decide to hurry home at once.

I go to the door and whistle for Fraté. The Spanish dog, who seems to have been following my every movement, now gazes at me as I prepare to leave. I become frightened. Perhaps that dog has only been pretending to be gentle, and now that he sees me going he may jump on me from behind and bite me. I wait impatiently for Fraté to follow me, then I hurry out of the door, carefully watching the Spanish dog, and shut it with a bang.

Before setting out for home, I decide to have a final glance inside the house. I stand on tiptoe by the window and look in. The Spanish dog gets slowly to his feet and walks toward the table.

"Well, that was quite a startling visit I had today," he seems to say to himself in a human voice, evidently unaware of my presence. He yawns in the way that dogs so often do—and then in a twinkling he becomes a middle-aged man in glasses and a black suit who stands leaning against the chair by the desk with a still-unlit cigarette in his mouth, and who slowly turns the pages of one of those large books.

It is a very warm spring afternoon. I am in a thicket of trees that nestles among the hushed hills.

AUTUMN MOUNTAIN
BY Akutagawa Ryūnosuké

TRANSLATED BY Ivan Morris

Akutagawa Ryūnosuké was born in Tokyo in 1892 and lived all his life in the capital. He committed suicide in 1927 by carefully administering an overdose of veronal.

While still a student in the English Literature Department of Tokyo Imperial University, Akutagawa collaborated with his friends (among them Kikuchi Kan and Kumé Masao, both of whom later also became well-known writers) to produce a literary magazine. His short story, Hana ("The Nose") appeared in the first issue and its importance was immediately recognized by Akutagawa's mentor, the great novelist Natsumé Sōseki. Rashōmon was published in 1915 in another student magazine and the young man was rapidly acclaimed in literary circles for the power and brilliance of his conception and for the vivid, individual quality of his style. During the remaining twelve years of his life he devoted himself entirely to writing and became famous as the leading figure among the so-called neo-realists.

Although he produced a number of poems and essays, and also one brief novel, his creative energies were largely devoted to the short story. He wrote a total of some 150 stories, which were published in seven collections; a considerable number have been translated into English, French, German, and Spanish.

Akutagawa's writing, like that of so many authors in the present anthology, represented in part a revolt against the naturalist school, whose influence predominated in Japan until a very late date. In Akutagawa's case this revolt took two main forms. In the first place, he abandoned the confessional type of writing. Whereas the naturalists deliberately narrowed their range of material to what was covered by personal experience, Akutagawa, except toward the

173

end of his career, very rarely introduced himself in his work. Instead he used his literary erudition (he was thoroughly familiar with the classical literature of China and Japan, as well as with nineteenth-century Western writing), to provide inspiration and material for an immensely wide range of scenes and subjects. A large number of his stories derive from classical tales, which Aku-tagawa reinterprets in the light of modern psychological insight, thereby im-buing them with new and complex meanings. He had a particular penchant for strange, vaguely disturbing stories. Yet, however weird his material may have been, his vivid, realistic method of presentation prevents the stories from lapsing into the obscure or the "quaint."

Apart from the novelty of his subject matter, Akutagawa differed from the naturalists in his absorption in literary style. He was a painstaking perfec-tionist in matters of wording and construction. His language is original and often highly colored; at the same time it has the economy that is so essential for successful short stories. Occasionally Akutagawa's overwhelming concern with style led to a type of preciosity, but on the whole his struggle with literary form was remarkably successful.

Though in most of his stories Akutagawa avoided anything in the way of autobiographical outpourings, his personality and his outlook on life emerge throughout his work. Akutagawa had a powerful, critical intelligence and a nature that since his youth had been sensitive to the point of neurosis. He looked hard and clearly at the people about him, as well as at the people whom he knew from his study of history and literature, and on the whole he did not like what he saw. In his writing an increasing pessimism about human nature is combined with a harsh irony as he describes the devious, and usually un-pleasant, motives that drive his characters. Apart from this pessimism, Akuta-gawa was plagued by doubts about his own artistic abilities and by a tem-peramental inability to face the practical aspects of life. All this culminated in the "vague uneasiness" which he enigmatically gave as the cause of his suicide.

The only positive ray to relieve the growing darkness of Akutagawa's thought was his belief in aesthetic values. This is exemplified by the present story (Shūzanzu in Japanese), first published in 1921, when the author was twenty-nine, and one of the stories most valued by his admirers. Even here there is a powerful touch of irony, inasmuch as the painting about which the story centers appears to have been merely a figment of the imagination. The important point for Akutagawa, however, is the fact that supreme beauty has actually existed, even if only in the mind of the observer. The story ends on a sanguine note as the two old Chinese sages, having realized the significance of the elusive painting, laugh and clap their hands with delight.

"AND speaking of Ta Ch'ih, have you ever seen his Autumn Mountain painting?"

One evening, Wang Shih-ku, who was visiting his friend Yün Nan-t'ien, asked this question.

"No, I have never seen it. And you?"

Ta Ch'ih, together with Mei-tao-jen and Huang-hao-shan-ch'iao, had been one of the great painters of the Mongol dynasty. As Yün Nan-t'ien replied, there passed before his eyes images of the artist's famous works, the Sandy Shore painting and the Joyful Spring picture scroll.

"Well, strange to say," said Wang Shih-ku, "I'm really not sure whether or not I have seen it. In fact. . . ."

"You don't know whether you have seen it or you haven't?" said Yün Nan-t'ien, looking curiously at his guest. "Do you mean that you've seen an imitation?"

"No, not an imitation. I saw the original. And it is not I alone who have seen it. The great critics Yen-k'o and Lien-chou both became involved with the Autumn Mountain." Wang Shih-ku sipped his tea and smiled thoughtfully. "Would it bore you to hear about it?"

"Quite the contrary," said Yün Nan-t'ien, bowing his head politely. He stirred the flame in the copper lamp.

* * *

At that time [began Wang Shih-ku] the old master Yüan Tsai was still alive. One evening while he was discussing paintings with Yen-k'o, he asked him whether he had ever seen Ta Ch'ih's Autumn Mountain. As you know, Yen-k'o made a veritable religion of Ta Ch'ih's painting and was certainly not likely to have missed any of his works. But he had never set eyes on this Autumn Mountain.

"No, I haven't seen it," he answered shamefacedly, "and I've never even heard of its existence."

"In that case," said Yüan Tsai, "please don't miss the first opportunity you have of seeing it. As a work of art it's on an even higher

hung in his own house—not even Li Ying-ch'iu's Floating Snowflakes, for which he had paid five hundred taels of silver—could stand comparison with that transcendent Autumn Mountain.

While still sojourning in the County of Jun, he sent an agent to the Chang house to negotiate for the sale of the painting. Despite repeated overtures, he was unable to persuade Mr. Chang to enter into any arrangement. On each occasion that pallid gentleman would reply that while he deeply appreciated the master's admiration of the Autumn Mountain and while he would be quite willing to lend the painting, he must ask to be excused from actually parting with it.

These refusals only served to strengthen the impetuous Yen-k'o's resolve. "One day," he promised himself, "that great picture will hang in my own hall." Confident of the eventual outcome, he finally resigned himself to returning home and temporarily abandoning the Autumn Mountain.

"About a year later, in the course of a further visit to the County of Jun, he tried calling once more at the house of Mr. Chang. Nothing had changed: the ivy was still coiled in disorder about the walls and fences, and the garden was covered with weeds. But when the servant answered his knock, Yen-k'o was told that Chang was not in residence. The old man asked if he might have another look at the Autumn Mountain despite the owner's absence, but his importunacy was of no avail: the servant repeated that he had no authority to admit anyone until his master returned. As Yen-k'o persisted, the man finally shut the door in his face. Overcome with chagrin, Yen-k'o had to leave the house and the great painting that lay somewhere in one of the dilapidated rooms.

*　　　*　　　*

Wang Shih-ku paused for a moment.

"All that I have related so far," he said, "I heard from the master Yen-k'o himself."

"But tell me," said Yün Nan-t'ien, stroking his white beard, "did Yen-k'o ever really see the Autumn Mountain?"

"He said that he saw it. Whether or not he did, I cannot know for certain. Let me tell you the sequel, and then you can judge for yourself."

Wang Shih-ku continued his story with a concentrated air, and now he was no longer sipping his tea.

*　　　*　　　*

When Yen-k'o told me all this [said Wang Shih-ku] almost fifty years had passed since his visits to the County of Jun. The master Yüan Tsai was long since dead and Mr. Chang's large house had already passed into the hands of two successive generations of his family. There was no telling where the Autumn Mountain might be—nor if the best parts of the scroll might not have suffered hopeless deterioration. In the course of our talk old Yen-k'o described that mysterious painting so vividly that I was almost convinced I could see it before my eyes. It was not the details that had impressed the master but the indefinable beauty of the picture as a whole. Through the words of Yen-k'o, that beauty had entered into my heart as well as his.

It happened that, about a month after my meeting with Yen-k'o, I had myself to make a journey to the southern provinces, including the County of Jun. When I mentioned this to the old man, he suggested that I go and see if I could not find the Autumn Mountain. "If that painting ever comes to light again," he said, "it will indeed be a great day for the world of art."

Needless to say, by this time I also was anxious to see the painting, but my journey was crowded and it soon became clear that I would not find time to visit Mr. Chang's house. Meanwhile, however, I happened to hear a report that the Autumn Mountain had come into the hands of a certain nobleman by the name of Wang. Having learned of the painting, Mr. Wang had despatched a messenger with greetings to Chang's grandson. The latter was said to have sent back with the messenger not only the ancient family documents and the great ceremonial cauldron which had been in the family for countless generations, but also a painting which fitted the description of Ta Ch'ih's Autumn Mountain. Delighted with these gifts, Mr. Wang had arranged a great banquet for Chang's grandson, at which he had placed the young man in the seat of honor and regaled him with the choicest delicacies, gay music, and lovely girls; in addition he had given him one thousand pieces of gold.

On hearing this report I almost leaped with joy. Despite the vicissitudes of half a century, it seemed that the Autumn Mountain was still safe! Not only that, but it actually had come within my range. Taking along only the barest necessities, I set out at once to see the painting.

I still vividly remember the day. It was a clear, calm afternoon in early summer and the peonies were proudly in bloom in Mr. Wang's garden. On meeting Mr. Wang, my face broke into a smile of delight even before I had completed my ceremonial bow. "To think that the Autumn Mountain is in this very house!" I cried. "Yen-kʻo spent all those years in vain attempts to see it again—and now I am to satisfy my own ambition without the slightest effort. . . ."

"You come at an auspicious time," replied Mr. Wang. "It happens that today I am expecting Yen-kʻo himself, as well as the great critic Lien-chou. Please come inside, and since you are the first to arrive you shall be the first to see the painting."

Mr. Wang at once gave instructions for the Autumn Mountain to be hung on the wall. And then it all leaped forth before my eyes: the little villages on the river, the flocks of white cloud floating over the valley, the green of the towering mountain range which extended into the distance like a succession of folding-screens—the whole world, in fact, that Ta Chʻih had created, a world far more wonderful than our own. My heart seemed to beat faster as I gazed intently at the scroll on the wall.

These clouds and mists and hills and valleys were unmistakably the work of Ta Chʻih. Who but Ta Chʻih could carry the art of drawing to such perfection that every brush-stroke became a thing alive? Who but he could produce colors of such depth and richness, and at the same time hide all mechanical trace of brush and paint? And yet . . . and yet I felt at once that this was not the same painting that Yen-kʻo had seen once long ago. No, no, a magnificent painting it surely was, yet just as surely not the unique painting which he had described with such religious awe!

Mr. Wang and his entourage had gathered around me and were watching my expression, so I hastened to express my enthusiasm. Naturally I did not want him to doubt the authenticity of his picture, yet it was clear that my words of praise failed to satisfy him. Just then Yen-kʻo himself was announced—he who had first spoken to me of this Autumn Mountain. As the old man bowed to Mr. Wang, I could sense the excitement inside him, but no sooner had his eyes settled on the scroll than a cloud seemed to pass before his face.

"What do you think of it, Master?" asked Mr. Wang, who had been

carefully observing him. "We have just heard the teacher Wang Shih-ku's enthusiastic praise, but . . ."

"Oh, you are, sir, a very fortunate man to have acquired this painting," answered Yen-k'o promptly. "Its presence in your house will add luster to all your other treasures."

Yen-k'o's courteous words only seemed to deepen Mr. Wang's anxiety; he, like me, must have heard in them a note of insincerity. I think we were all a bit relieved when Lien-chou, the famous critic, made his appearance at this juncture. After bowing to us, he turned to the scroll and stood looking at it silently, chewing his long mustaches.

"This, apparently, is the same painting that the master Yen-k'o last saw half a century ago," Mr. Wang explained to him. "Now I would much like to hear your opinion of the work. Your candid opinion," Mr. Wang added, forcing a smile.

Lien-chou sighed and continued to look at the picture. Then he took a deep breath and, turning to Mr. Wang, said: "This, sir, is probably Ta Ch'ih's greatest work. Just see how the artist has shaded those clouds. What power there was in his brush! Note also the color of his trees. And then that distant peak which brings the whole composition to life." As he spoke, Lien-chou pointed to various outstanding features of the painting, and needless to say, a look of relief, then of delight, spread over Mr. Wang's face.

Meanwhile I secretly exchanged glances with Yen-k'o. "Master," I whispered, "is that the real Autumn Mountain?" Almost imperceptibly the old man shook his head, and there was a twinkle in his eyes.

"It's all like a dream," he murmured. "I really can't help wondering if that Mr. Chang wasn't some sort of hobgoblin."

*   *   *

"So that is the story of the Autumn Mountain," said Wang Shih-ku after a pause, and took a sip of his tea. "Later on it appears that Mr. Wang made all sorts of exhaustive enquiries. He visited Mr. Chang, but when he mentioned to him the Autumn Mountain, the young man denied all knowledge of any other version. So one cannot tell if that Autumn Mountain which Yen-k'o saw all those years ago is not even now hidden away somewhere. Or perhaps the whole thing was just a case of faulty memory on an old man's part. It would seem unlikely, though, that Yen-k'o's story about visiting Mr. Chang's house to see the Autumn Mountain was not based on solid fact."

"Well, in any case the image of that strange painting is no doubt engraved forever on Yen-k'o's mind. And on yours too."

"Yes," said Wang Shih-ku, "I still see the dark green of the mountain rock, as Yen-k'o described it all those years ago. I can see the red leaves of the bushes as if the painting were before my eyes this very moment."

"So even if it never existed, there is not really much cause for regret!"

The two men laughed and clapped their hands with delight.

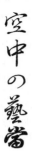

THE HANDSTAND

BY Ogawa Mimei

TRANSLATED BY Ivan Morris

*Ogawa Mimei was born in 1882 and graduated from the
English Literature Department of Waseda University in 1905. His first published work appeared in the following year. Waseda was at that time the
academic center of Japanese naturalism. Ogawa's temperament, however, inclined him toward an idealistic form of romanticism. In a period when naturalism predominated in literature, Ogawa's romantic approach had little chance
of success and his early years as a writer were marked by great difficulties.
The humanitarian socialism that inspired many of his subsequent works no
doubt derived to some extent from the practical hardships that he experienced
at this time.*

*In 1920 (the year of "The Handstand"), Ogawa Mimei joined the inci-
pient Socialist Union and for a time the socialistic content of his work became
pronounced. As may be judged from "The Handstand," however, there was
always a sentimental streak in Ogawa's socialism. His approach (fairly typical
of the period) was that of an intellectual who looked sympathetically from the
outside at the sufferings of the working class; his writing has little of the brash
tough-mindedness that characterizes later proletarian literature. Ogawa's attitude was not that of a scientist or an ideologist, but of a poet with a violent
loathing for the injustice he saw about him. It is, perhaps, not altogether surprising that he should gradually have become dissatisfied with the materialistic
stand of the Socialist Union. After a brief period of anarchism, he parted with*

185

the organization. Thereafter his writing returned to the pure simplicity of his earlier work and was largely devoted to poems and to children's tales.

Already since 1910 Ogawa Mimei has written humorous children's tales and it is for this genre that he is best known today. These tales, which are frequently marked by a moving lyricism and considerable artistry, helped to set a new standard for juvenile literature in Japan; several of them have been translated into English. Although the romantic mood is predominant, Ogawa creates his children's tales largely out of everyday material and many of them reflect the deep concern for human welfare that characterized his earlier "socialistic" writing.

"The Handstand" (Kūchū no Geitō) was first published in 1920, when the author was twenty-eight.

IT WAS at a time when I had been reduced to painting street signs for a living. My days were spent entirely in drawing huge advertisements on billboards for tooth paste, circuses, bottled beer, and ladies' underwear. At first the novelty of my new life made it tolerable, but soon I came to loathe it and to long for some form of escape even if only temporary.

Formerly when I had worked as a serious painter I had, of course, never taken the slightest interest in the pictures on billboards, let alone given any thought to the people who painted them. If anything, these pictures had struck me as an insult to my artistic sensibility. Yet now when I saw the little drawings printed on the covers of notebooks in the stationer's, or the designs glazed on the lids of paintboxes, or even the billboards outside theaters, I would stop and look, and sometimes I found myself actually being moved by them. I suppose it was because I had come to realize that among the people who produced these drawings there must be many who, like myself, had once aspired to be real artists but had been forced by circumstances into this drudgery.

What made me begin to hate my new occupation, however, was not just the feeling that I was prostituting such talents as I might have; it was the relentless monotony. I soon learned that almost all the workers with whom I had now come to spend my time suffered to a greater or lesser extent from this same sense of monotony. They were forever discussing possible ways of breaking the tedium of their lives.

We would gather in the evening by the benches near the suburban tenements where we lived. One by one we arrived from different directions, exhausted at the end of a long day's work in the heat. We sat down heavily on the benches or, if there was no longer any room, squatted beside them on the gravel, and indolently fanned ourselves as we chatted away, oblivious to the passing of time.

Along came a couple of young street-acrobats. One of them danced round with a lion's mask while the other accompanied him on a tambourine. A girl wearing a red sash came out of the ice-cream parlor opposite where we sat and gave the boy a copper. Later a young woman strolled past with a samisen, her hair fastened in a bun with a green comb, and carrying a baby on her back.

"Not bad looking, eh?"

"I bet she's an ex-geisha or something. What do you think?"

She walked up and down the street in front of us. Occasionally she stopped and strummed on her samisen. Later a huge, dirty-looking woman in an advanced state of pregnancy waddled past us. We looked at her in fascination. She was the most repulsive woman we had ever seen. So that day drew slowly to an end.

"A good job? Hell, there's no such thing as a good job! It's all a lot of sweat! If anyone thinks it's fun making a living, he's crazy."

"No, we'll never get anywhere this way. Just sweat away till we croak, that's all! The only way to make money is gambling."

"Gambling, eh?" said a large, dark-skinned bricklayer who was squatting next to the bench in his undershirt. "I'll tell you about gambling. When I lived in Shitaya, there was a girl in the neighborhood about twenty-four years old. She was a pretty little piece, I can tell you! I used to watch her passing outside my window. She strutted past in her straw sandals with her head high in the air. She wore a big gold chain over her breast and always carried a shining patent-leather handbag. She had a gold chain on the bag also. She lived in a poor-looking sort of house and I got to wondering how she could afford to doll herself up like that. Then I heard she'd been gambling and made quite a pile. 'That's how to get rich,' I thought to myself. 'Even women can do it.' Then early one morning on my way to work I saw a girl hurrying out of a low-class brothel. I just saw her back but there was something familiar about the way she walked. I followed her for a while and then saw her face as she got on a tram. It was the girl with the gold chain, all right! So much for gambling!"

"That's right," said a serious-looking man on the bench. "You can't always hit it lucky. And even if you do, it doesn't always work out. Why, only last week I saw in the paper that a certain man won a gambling pool or something. He'd been hard up all his life and then all of a sudden about half a million yen fell in his lap. What did he do? He went stark raving mad and murdered his wife with a hatchet! No, it's no good when things change too much. . . . I'm not so sure it isn't best to jog along the way we do." The man sat looking straight ahead after he had spoken. He seemed quite moved by what he had said. After a while he got up and left. Then one by one the others began to leave, some to start their night shifts, some for the public baths, some for home. Soon they had all gone except myself, a tinsmith called Chō, and two others.

"Is it hard to learn the flute?" said Kichikō, an engineer's mate. "I'd like to play the flute."

"What an idea!" said Chō with a smile. "How's a clumsy ox like you going to play the flute? Anyhow it takes years before you can play an instrument."

"I suppose you're a great hand at the flute," said Kichikō.

"No, I can't play. I like listening, though," said Chō.

"Well, you're a fine one to tell me I can't play the flute. You're a clumsy brute yourself."

"I may not be able to play, but at least I know what it's all about. You haven't got the vaguest idea what art is. It's not something you can learn like playing tiddlywinks!"

"Oh yes, I'd forgotten. You're a great artist, aren't you?" said Kichikō laughing. "A great artist when it comes to singing songs in the beer parlor, I mean!"

"I'm good at standing on my hands," announced Chō, beaming all over but with a touch of genuine pride. Chō was a rather silent man. He had a large round face—almost bloated, in fact. There was something about his expression that made one feel he was smiling inwardly all the time in a warm, pleasant way.

"Standing on your hands? What a very original art!" I said without thinking. We all laughed, including Chō.

I did not know why, but for some reason Chō's handstanding excited my curiosity. In time I came to learn from Chō himself and from some of his friends how he had acquired this avocation. It appeared that he had once seen a girl doing a handstanding stunt in the circus. Standing upright on her hands, she had crossed a long narrow plank suspended between two platforms high over the arena. Chō had been greatly impressed. There seemed to be no catch in this as in so many other circus tricks; it was purely the result of long practice. Suddenly it occurred to him, as he sat there in the circus, that he could learn the trick himself.

From then on, he began practicing handstands whenever he had time—after meals, in the evenings, and in the brief rest periods between work. At least it broke the monotony.

Often he was discouraged and felt that he would never be any good. Yet he persevered. "It's that girl," he told me once, "that girl at the circus. I just can't get her out of my mind. She was a real beauty, you know. Fine white teeth, red lips, lovely breasts, big, dark, mysterious eyes—she's the prettiest girl I've seen."

He had never seen her again but by his handstanding he kept her memory alive. Apart from this there was, I guessed, a hidden motive that made him continue his exhausting pastime. By becoming an expert handstander himself, as great as this girl if not greater, was he not in some way derogating from the perfection which he had originally seen in her, thereby making her, in this respect at least, less wonderful? By surpassing her in the art of handstanding, by taking for himself the praise that had originally all been hers, was he not somehow punishing her for being so completely unattainable?

"The trouble was," said Chō, "I didn't have a high narrow plank to practice on. But I got round this in the end. I found a straw mat with a thin black border to do my handstands on. This black border becomes the plank and both edges become sheer drops hundreds of feet high. So when I practice walking along the edge of the mat on my hands, I'm as frightened of falling as I would be in the circus. Well, I've got now so I can do it every time without even swaying. And if I can do it on the mat, I don't see why I couldn't do it in the circus like she did. . . . But of course I'll never really know."

"That girl certainly did something to you," I said to Chō one day.

Chō looked at me seriously. "It's the same as painting," he said. "When you see something beautiful, it gets you in some way, doesn't it, and that makes you want to paint it. You'll work away like mad trying to paint it, won't you? Well, it's the same with me. Only I can't paint so I've got to imitate what I've seen. Is that so strange?"

His explanation struck me as quite reasonable.

"Look, Chō," said Kichikō that evening when I first heard about the handstanding, "why don't you let us see you do it now?" He laughed and looked round. The last rays of the summer sun were fading; the sky had lost its brightness and become a light transparent blue. A slight wind had blown up and dull, vaguely colored clouds scudded past high above us.

"Would you really like to see?" said Chō cheerfully. He stood up, and leaned forward on one of the benches. As he put his weight on it, the bench shifted slightly on the gravel.

"I'd better do it here," he said. He planted his hands firmly on the ground next to the bench and raised himself a couple of times, falling back lightly in the same place. Then, keeping both legs closely together, he moved slowly up until he was standing vertically in the air. The soles of his straw sandals faced the surface of the limpid evening sky. His plump arms were slightly bent as they supported his heavy, squat body. As the blood ran to his head, his face became so dark that one could hardly distinguish it from the earth.

Kichikō whistled with admiration. "That's good," he said. "That's pretty damned good!" Quite a few people had gathered from the neighborhood to watch Chō's performance and they were all exclaiming their admiration as he held his feet immobile in the air. When he stood up again, a couple of the local errand boys and a few other enterprising young fellows began to try the trick. After I left, I turned back and saw them all in their light shirts standing upside down by the benches in the gathering dusk.

*   *   *

There was a large steelworks in the neighborhood. Most of the workers were regular employees, but there was also quite a number of casual laborers who drifted in from the other factories or from the mines and usually left again after a time. One evening as we were gathered

by our benches, a small, intelligent-looking man joined us. "You're new around here, aren't you?" I said.

"That's right. I've just got myself a job as a lathe man in those iron-works over there. I've got lodgings near here, too."

He soon established himself as one of our group. We all found him interesting because he had spent his life moving from place to place and could describe all sorts of things that were unfamiliar to us. Although uneducated, he was a good talker and, as he told us of the hardships he had undergone, the strange places where he had worked, the odd customs he had observed in other parts of Japan, and the efforts of workers to improve their conditions, we felt that we were being lifted out of the prisons of our narrow lives.

His lively eyes shone as he described life underground in the Aso mines where he had formerly worked. "To get to the first pit, you go down a hundred and fifty feet in the cage. Then down you go another hundred and fifty feet to the next pit. There are twelve pits altogether. In the bottom pit the temperature was nearly a hundred degrees just from the heat of the earth. There was a whole lot of us working down there. The air was pumped down from the pit-head. But after you'd been down there a while, it got so damned hard to breathe your lungs were fit to burst. I was in the war and I can tell you that to spend eight hours down there in that mine was worse than twenty-four hours under enemy fire.

"And don't let them tell you mining isn't dangerous! Down there you're at the mercy of machines and they're always going wrong. One of the fellows I knew was pulling a loaded trolley onto the elevator. At least he thought the elevator was there but something had gone wrong and instead he stepped backward into the empty shaft and went shooting down hundreds of feet with the loaded trolley on top of him. You could hear him screaming right down to the bottom.

"You see, the strain down there makes you careless in the end. Lots of the fellows get blown to smithereens by the dynamite they've planted themselves. Sometimes they even knock down the props when they're working and get buried alive.

"But I'll tell you something funny. While you're down there in the mine, you're so busy with your work, you're so damned glad you haven't had an accident yourself and trying so hard to watch out in the future, that you don't have time to worry about anything else. It's when you come out on the surface after a day's work that you start thinking. You see other people walking about up there who've never been down a mine in all their lives. And you get to asking yourself: 'What the hell! I'm no different from them. What do I spend all day down in that damned hole for?'

"That's the way lots of us began figuring. It wasn't hard to get the other fellows to see our point of view. What the hell, we were risking our lives down there every day to make profits for the company. We all got together and were going to make a set of minimum demands for our safety—not wages, mind you, just for our safety. But we had an informer among us. Our plan leaked out and the company put a stop to it all.

"Later on, a couple of smooth, well-dressed men came along and told us how we ought to organize ourselves. They'd never been further down a mine than the pit-head but they pretended to know all about it. Well, we miners were a pretty uneducated bunch but we could tell fakes when we saw them. If these men really had our interests at heart, we'd have felt it and gone along with them all the way. But it didn't take us long to see they were the type who make their living out of our troubles—and a damned good living too. 'Better honor than life,' they used to teach us in the army. Well, these men wanted honor *and* life— and plenty of both—all at our expense. The dirty rats—what could they teach us? It's lucky for them they cleared out before I got my hands on them!

"No one who hasn't really been a worker knows what it's all about. You can't learn it out of a book. You've got to be a worker, you've got to live like a worker, day after day, year after year. That's the only way to get to understand the 'labor problem.'"

"We weren't born to live like slaves or animals! We workers deserve the same share of the country's wealth as everyone else. That's what I'd like to tell society."

"A socialist," I thought to myself and wondered whether all the others realized it. They used to sit listening to him in silence and occasionally I noticed Chō sighing as if moved by something the man had said.

One day as I was strolling down the sunlit street, I stopped dead in my tracks. Some of the things the little man had said suddenly came back to me with extraordinary force. It was as if I had been walking along a narrow single-track railway bridge and had abruptly been struck by the thought "What shall I do if a train comes rushing toward me?" Perhaps the time would come when I'd have to make such a decision. The idea made my heart pound like a hammer.

The little man told us one day about a derelict mine. The ore had given out and the miners had all moved to other pits. The power was still connected, however, and one morning the lights were turned on for a party of visiting journalists. One of the men got separated from the rest of the group and, before he knew it, he was hopelessly lost in the maze of tunnels and passages which twisted about underground like the coils of some immense serpent. He must have rushed round, gradually becoming panic-stricken, in those weird, deserted corridors hundreds of feet below the ground. His shouts for help would have been deadened by the thick walls. And then he ran headlong into the open elevator-pit and fell hundreds of feet into pitch darkness.

This story made a great impression on me and it was long before I could rid my mind of the terrifying vision.

Gradually I came to think that, however monotonous and unrewarding my present work might be, I should at least be grateful that it was safe. "After all," I said one evening, "why do we work anyway? When all's said and done, surely it's so we can earn enough to keep alive. In that case, it's a complete contradiction to take a job where you're risking your life."

It seemed unbelievable to me that anyone should be so mad as to do work in which he might at any moment be killed. Later I was to learn that such logic does not always apply and that to break the unendurable monotony of their lives, some people will in fact do things which can only be classed as insane.

Chō and the little man became friends and I often saw them together. One evening as I was calling for Chō on my way back from work, I found him standing outside his shop talking to the little man. They both nodded to me. The man had a map in his hands. "Here it is," he said, pointing to a small corner of land sticking out into the blue northern sea, "here's Nikolaevsk. That's where I'll be heading now. A friend of mine's working up there and he's asked me to join him." He looked up at the deep blue sky. "When I decided to leave the mines," he continued, "I first thought I'd try my luck somewhere really far away—Sakhalin, Kamchatka, or somewhere. But then I thought if I came to Tokyo, I'd meet a lot of interesting people, people I could talk to, people who felt like I did about things. I've always been a great talker, you know, ever since I was a youngster. Well, I've got to like a lot of you fellows, but I'm not really your type. So now I'm pushing on. I won't be going straight to Nikolaevsk. I'll spend the winter working in Hokkaidō and try crossing over to the mainland next spring." He paused for a while. "I suppose the fact is I'm just a born wanderer," he added laughing. We said goodbye, and Chō and I stood watching him walk away in the distance.

"He asked me if I wanted to go with him," said Chō. "And I would have, too, except for my old mother. She'd be lost without me."

We started walking along slowly. A few sprigs of wilted morning-glory stood in a black, unglazed vase in a window opposite the shop. It was really amazing how blue the sky was. Under this deep, weird, silent blue, the black-tiled roofs of the houses seemed to roll sadly into the distance like dunes along a seashore.

None of us ever saw the little man again. We heard that he had found a job in a factory at Ōi. No doubt he made his way to Hokkaidō and perhaps he even reached Nikolaevsk. Wherever he may be, I am sure he is heatedly expounding his theories.

I thought about him often. I remembered the clear look in his eyes when he was not talking. In them were reflected the images of far-away mountains, of clouds floating across distant skies, of infinitely remote stars, and sometimes of the dark, raging ocean. Yes, he was a wanderer and I felt that like the wanderers of old he had within him a song that comforted him in his weariness and that constantly spurred him on to discover new places and new ideas. Compared to him the members of our group, rooted here in our dreary suburb, seemed to me men exhausted by the monotony of work, men in whom all spirit of adventure had atrophied. At least, that is what I thought until the following incident.

*   *   *

I had spent all day painting a huge advertisement for women's dresses on a tin billboard. In the evening when I had finished, I decided to pass by Chō's shop. It was a close, sultry evening and although the summer was almost over, the sun was extremely hot. There was not the slightest breeze. When I arrived, Chō was standing in a shirt and a pair of khaki trousers working on a shiny tin bucket.

"Have you ever been to the girls' circus at Asakusa?" he said when he saw me.

"No, never. I've been to the opera once—that's all."

"I'd like to go to the amusement park at Asakusa," said Chō wiping the perspiration off his face.

"Asakusa," I said. "That shouldn't be too difficult. It doesn't take all that long to get there."

"It's all right if you've got money. Then you can go to the mountains for the summer. But when am I going to have time to go to Asakusa? I suppose that's what they mean by no leisure for the poor." His face was wreathed in smiles; he looked as if he was imagining the gay, bustling pleasure grounds of Asakusa.

Presently Kichikō, the engineer's mate, joined us. He had on a short workman's coat.

"Well, hot enough for you?" he said in his gruff voice. "What's happening? Anything interesting?"

"No," said Chō. "By the way, Kichi, where were you last night?"

"Last night? Oh yes, after work I went down to the river at Ryōgoku to cool off." He sat down on Chō's workbench and began fanning himself.

"Look, Chō," said Kichikō after a while. "What about you and me climbing that chimney over there by the spinning mill? We'd get quite a view."

"In this heat?" said Chō. "How high do you suppose it is?"

"Come on, don't be a coward," said Kichikō laughing. "It's two hundred and fifty feet."

"Heights don't bother me," said Chō. "I was always climbing trees when I was a kid."

"Well then, let's go."

"What about you?" said Chō looking in my direction.

I remembered how I had once peered out of the window from the fourth floor of an office building. The pavement below had looked white and dry in the glaring sun, and the heat seemed to be flashing from the hard surface. Suddenly I had imagined how my blood would redden those burned, white stones if I fell out of the window.

I glanced at Chō but did not answer.

Just then Kichikō looked at me. "Come on," he said. "You can have a go at painting the top of the chimney. It'll be more fun than those billboards of yours!"

I was too much of a coward to admit that I was frightened of heights. "All right, I'll come along," I said, even simulating a certain enthusiasm.

The three of us left Chō's shop. On our way we stopped at an ice-cream parlor and each had a glass of iced water. Then we set out for the spinning mill. It was on a huge dusty plain at the edge of the city. As we trudged along, the shriek of the crickets reverberated in my ears like the sound of a boiling kettle. The perspiration was streaming down my forehead. We were all looking ahead at the chimney which reared itself before us under the blue, cloud-speckled sky. It had only recently been completed and the scaffolding was still coiled round it all the way to the top like a monstrous snake. There was no smoke.

We reached the chimney in about fifteen minutes.

"Are you sure it's two hundred and fifty feet?" said Chō looking up. "It doesn't seem that high from here."

"Come on and see," said Kichikō. "You'll get dizzy just standing down here staring at it." He bent his head back and looked up to the top. "Imagine working up there, though," he added. "They wouldn't get me to work on a chimney like that for anything."

We took off our coats and threw them on the ground next to the solid-looking brick foundation; then we removed our shoes and socks and wet the palms of our hands with spittle. I put one foot on the rickety scaffolding and glanced back at the city: under the deep blue sky the rooftops stretched out in solid black rows; they looked very safe.

Kichikō started climbing first; after him went the rotund Chō and finally myself. The steps were not built straight, but circled round the chimney in an endless-looking spiral. The narrow iron rungs dug sharply into the soft soles of my feet.

I had not realized what this climb would be like. As the other two moved steadily upward round the chimney, I gradually began to fall behind. When I had reached about the halfway mark, I suddenly felt I could not continue. But glancing down, I realized that it would be at least as hard to start going down. From now on, I forced every muscle in my body to continue climbing. My feet no longer hurt, but my legs were trembling uncontrollably and although I planted myself firmly on each rung, I had the uncomfortable feeling that at any moment my body would float off into space of its own accord.

The wind was blowing quite hard up here and I could hear some of the looser boards of the scaffolding clatter noisily. If just one of these flimsy rungs should slip or break, I'd lose my footing and go plunging headlong into space. At the thought, a cold sweat ran over my whole body. My hands were particularly clammy and I was certain that they would slip as I grasped the rungs above. If only I could wipe them or rub them with sand.

Looking up, I saw that Kichikō had reached the top of the chimney. He was standing on the narrow bricklayers' platform that surrounded it and leaning with both his hands on a low, perilous railing. He looked round at the scenery. Now Chō reached the top and joined Kichikō in admiring the view. From time to time they glanced down the side of the chimney to see how I was getting on.

Finally I reached the top. It was broader than I had imagined while climbing—about six feet in diameter. My legs were twitching with a sort of cramp and I realized that I could not possibly stand on the platform with the other two. Instead I squatted down carefully on the wooden boards and held on to the bottom of the railing with both hands. My teeth chattered and my whole body was trembling.

I no longer cared in the slightest what impression I was making on my companions. My only object now was to elicit their sympathy so that they might somehow help me to reach the ground safely. Normally they would have laughed to see me in this condition and probably they would have teased me. But now they just glanced at me occasionally without smiling or saying anything, as if it was quite normal that I should be in such a state. In some way, this attitude of theirs added still further to my anxiety. I should almost have welcomed some normal bantering. Instead I heard Chō saying: "Take a look over there, Kichi. The sea's come right up close, hasn't it? And look at those trams. They're just like little crawling bugs. . . . What's that tower over there?"

"That's the twelve-story pagoda of Asakusa," answered Kichikō nonchalantly.

I just stared straight down at the wooden boards. My head was blank and there was a haze in front of my eyes. Yet I could not help noticing between the wide cracks of the boards people down below like tiny black beans. At this sight my throat became clogged and I could hardly breathe. I must stay still, I told myself. If I try looking at the sea or the twelve-story pagoda of Asakusa, I'm done for.

Gradually I noticed that the sun was sinking and that the whole sky had turned crimson. Why in God's name had I come up here? How would I ever get down? I was bound to lose my footing on those endless steps. As my mind darted back over my past life, which now seemed infinitely remote, I remembered with shame how I had cursed the monotony and never felt really grateful for its safety.

Only a few feet away gaped the huge, black, empty mouth of the chimney. I was aware of a distant rumbling sound coming from its depths, like the roar of some great monster. At the same time I suddenly realized that the entire chimney was swaying to and fro, even if only very slightly. I had forgotten that tall buildings and chimneys move in the wind.

A sense of despair came over me. Just then I heard an astounding remark from Kichikō.

"I don't suppose you could do that trick of yours up here?" he said.

I looked up at Chō, who was standing directly over me. His face at this moment seemed more enormous than ever. He smiled strangely and looked round.

"Of course I could," he said after a while. "I can stand on my hands anywhere. The trouble is, there's no proper place to rest my hands on up here. These damned boards bend every time you step on them. Besides, this platform's so narrow that the railing would get in the way when I raised my legs."

"Supposing we bet you? If you can do it up here, we'll each give you a yen," said Kichikō after a pause. "What about it?" he added looking down at me. "You'd give him a yen, wouldn't you?"

The whole thing was a joke, I realized. Chō was a determined fellow, but he wasn't crazy. He obviously knew that this would be

suicide. I nodded silently at Kichikō. I'd share in the joke, if that's what they wanted.

"You'd each give me a yen, eh?" said Chō. "That makes a whole day's wages."

"Only look here," said Kichikō laughing nervously, "if you make a mistake, it'll be the end of you. I'll have to go down and pick up the mess."

"You needn't tell me. I can figure that out for myself," said Chō. "The trouble is," he continued, as if speaking to himself, "where would I put my hands?" He looked all round the platform. Then his eyes came to rest on the thick iron mouth of the chimney. He bent over and looked into the great black opening.

"If I do it," he said, "I'll stand on this edge."

He felt the surface of the chimney top.

"The trouble is, it's damned slippery." Suddenly his expression changed, and with a sense of horror I knew that he was going to try the trick. I wanted to stop him and began to stutter out something, but the words wouldn't come. All I could do was to squat there gazing up at him intently with my sunken eyes. Surely, I thought, he could not be doing this for the two yen, however much he may have wanted to spend the day at Asakusa. Could it be that he was still trying in some strange way to get the better of that girl at the circus? Or was he emulating the little man and defying monotony in his own way? I never knew. The next moment I heard Chō say: "All right, I'll take the wager. I'll have a go." There was no longer the slightest trace of laughter in his voice.

"Wait a minute," said Kichikō, suddenly becoming dead serious. "You know what'll happen if you slip."

"If I slip, that's the end of me." There was a touch of defiance in Chō's voice as he threw out the words. He turned round in the direction of the city and stared at it for a few moments. The sun was rapidly disappearing now and strangely shaped tufts of cloud drifted past in the darkening sky. Yet the top of our chimney was brilliant red from the last rays of the sun, as if illuminated by giant flames.

Chō spat on his hands and rubbed his palms carefully with a handkerchief to remove any trace of greasiness. Then he hung the handkerchief on the railing and, bracing himself, planted both hands on the iron mouth of the chimney. For several moments he stood there peering down into the huge, black opening from whose depths emerged the continual roaring sound. I glanced at him. His eyes protruded from their sockets, his short fat back bulged, repeated tremors passed down his arms, and his close-cropped head was wet with perspiration. All this time the chimney swayed rhythmically to and fro in the wind.

Chō brought his legs together and drew them in as far as possible to avoid catching them on the railing. Once they were raised, it would be too late to make any adjustment. Should he then miscalculate and lose his balance, he would either fall headlong into the two-hundred-and-fifty-foot gullet of the chimney or backward over the railing and down to the hard ground below.

His legs had now left the platform and were already a few feet in the air. My head began going round and I had to look down. When I next glanced up, Chō was gradually straightening his legs. A moment later they were fully extended and now he stood there on his hands, his body a rigid line against the evening sky. A presentiment of relief ran through me.

Kichikō had not taken his eyes off Chō for a moment. He continued to gaze fixedly at him as he now slowly drew in his legs and began to retrace the line he had drawn in the air. Skillfully avoiding the railing, he gradually brought them back to the platform. For the first time since the performance had begun, I allowed myself to look straight at him. The strength of his entire body seemed to be concentrated in the bulging muscles of his arms. I noticed that a sort of spasm was passing from the nape of his neck to his shoulders. His hair was drenched.

The handstand was safely completed. For a while none of us spoke. Chō stood staring straight into space with unblinking, protruding eyes. His complexion was not even pale, but completely colorless like a dead man's. Round the corners of his mouth I detected a cool, dark, self-mocking smile.

In a flash I remembered seeing such a smile once before. A car had come hurtling along the street where I was walking and had almost run over a man working on the tram lines. By some miracle he had escaped, though the side of the car must have grazed his overalls. Afterward he had stood there rigid in the middle of the street still holding a large granite paving-stone. His eyes were wide open and there was a weird smile on his face. The car disappeared in the distance and the people who had stopped to look hurried on; but the man still stood there staring straight ahead into space.

Then I noticed a black bird skimming past directly over the chimney and silhouetted strangely against the dark sky.

Kichikō was the first to go down and I followed him. Glancing back, I saw Chō still standing there on the platform. His face was that of a dead man. He seemed sunk in thought.

セメント樽の中の手紙

葉山嘉樹

LETTER FOUND IN
A CEMENT-BARREL
BY Hayama Yoshiki

TRANSLATED BY Ivan Morris

Hayama Yoshiki was representative, both in his life and in his writing, of the so-called proletarian school. He was born in 1894 in Kyūshū. His father was a petty government official and his childhood was spent in genteel poverty. Hayama managed to enter Waseda University, but he was dismissed for irregular attendance. Thereafter he worked as a seaman on a cargo boat and later on a coal-carrier. The appalling labor conditions aboard these boats are graphically described in "Men Who Live on the Sea" (1928), his best-known novel.

Having abandoned the seafaring life, Hayama shifted from one occupation to another. He worked, among other things, as a printer's canvasser, a clerk in a school office, a cement-factory laborer and an operator in a hydroelectric power station. Much of the material in his novels and stories (including "Letter Found in a Cement-Barrel") was suggested by these experiences.

In 1919, Hayama began to take an active part in the incipient and pre-

*carious labor movement; in the same year he was thrown into prison for an in-
fraction of the police regulation governing the maintenance of public peace.
From then on he was almost constantly in and out of prison. His novels and
stories were usually written while in custody. In between his terms of imprison-
ment he was busy fighting in the abortive labor movement of the 1920's and
early 1930's. He died in 1945 in great poverty.*

*Given the inherent limitations of the proletarian school of writing, Ha-
yama's work is often remarkably effective. On the whole he avoids senti-
mentalizing his workmen-martyrs, and by his sparse, compact prose he
manages to keep the reader's interest in the story even when the plot is obviously
contrived to convey a message. It is inevitable, however, that his work should
rapidly have dated; much of what he wrote, like the story translated here, is
likely to strike the reader as a downright parody on "proletarian" literature.*

*"Letter Found in a Cement-Barrel" (Semento-daru no Naka no Te-
gami) was first published in 1926, when Hayama was thirty-two.*

MATSUDO YOSHIZŌ was emptying cement-
barrels. He managed to keep the cement off most of his body, but his
hair and upper lip were covered by a thick gray coating. He desperately
wanted to pick his nose and remove the hardened cement which was
making the hairs in his nostrils stand stiff like reinforced concrete; but
the cement-mixer was spewing forth ten loads every minute and he
could not afford to fall behind in its feeding.

His working day lasted for eleven hours and not once did he have
time to pick his nose properly. During his brief lunch break he was
hungry and had to concentrate on gulping down food. He had hoped
to use the afternoon break for cleaning out his nostrils, but when the
time came he found that he had to unclog the cement-mixer instead.
By late afternoon his nose felt as if it were made of plaster of Paris.

The day drew to an end. His arms had become limp with exhaustion
and he had to exert all his strength to move the barrels. As he started
to lift one of them, he noticed a small wooden box lying in the cement.

"What's this?" he wondered vaguely, but he could not let curiosity
slow down the pace of his work. Hurriedly he shoveled cement onto
the measuring frame, emptied it into the mixing boat, and then began
shoveling out more cement again.

"Wait a minute!" he muttered to himself. "Why the hell should there be a box inside a cement-barrel?"

He picked up the box and dropped it into the front pocket of his overalls.

"Doesn't weigh much, damn it! Can't be much money in it, whatever else there is."

Even this slight pause had made him fall behind in his work and now he had to shovel furiously to catch up with the cement-mixer. Like a wild automaton, he emptied the next barrel and loaded the contents onto a new measuring frame.

Presently the mixer began to slow down and eventually it came to a stop. It was time for Matsudo Yoshizō to knock off for the day. He picked up the rubber hose that was attached to the mixer and made a preliminary attempt at washing his face and hands. Then he hung his lunch box round his neck and trudged back toward his tenement. His mind was absorbed with the idea of getting some food into his stomach and, even more important, a powerful cup of rice brandy.

He passed the power plant. The construction work was almost finished: soon they would be having electricity. In the distance Mt. Keira towered in the evening darkness with its coat of pure-white snow. The man's sweaty body was suddenly gripped by the cold and he began to shiver. Next to where he walked the rough waters of the Kiso River bit into the milky foam with a barking roar.

"Damn it all!" thought Matsudo Yoshizō. "It's too much. Yes, it's too damned much! The old woman's pregnant again."

He thought of the six children who already squirmed about their tenement room, and of the new child who was going to be born just as the cold season was coming on, and of his wife who seemed to give birth pell-mell to one baby after another; and he was sick at heart.

"Let's see now," he muttered. "They pay me one yen ninety sen a day, and out of that we have to buy two measures of rice at fifty sen each, and then we have to pay out another ninety sen for clothing and a place to live. Damn it all! How do they expect me to have enough left over for a drink?"

Abruptly he remembered the little box in his pocket. He took it out and rubbed it against the seat of his trousers to clean off the cement. Nothing was written on the box. It was securely sealed.

"Now, why the hell should anyone want to seal a box like this? He likes to act mysterious, whoever he is."

He hit the box against a stone, but the lid still would not open. Thoroughly exasperated, he threw it down and stepped on it furiously. The box broke and on the ground lay a scrap of paper wrapped in a rag. He picked it up and read:

"I am a factory girl working for the Nomura Cement Company. I sew cement-bags. My boyfriend used to work for the same company. His job was to put stones into the crusher. Then on the morning of October 7th, just as he was going to put in a big rock, he slipped on the mud and fell into the crusher underneath the rock.

"The other men tried to pull him out, but it was no use. He sank down under the rock, just as if he was being drowned. Then the rock and his body were broken to pieces and came out together from the ejector looking like a big flat pink stone. They fell onto the conveyor belt and were carried into the pulverizer. There they were pounded by the huge steel cylinder. I could hear them screaming out some sort of a spell as they were finally crushed to bits. Then they were put into the burner and baked into a fine slab of cement.

"His bones, his flesh, his mind had all turned into powder. Yes, my boyfriend ended up entirely as cement. All that was left was a scrap of material from his overalls. Today I've been busy sewing the bags into which they'll put him.

"I'm writing this letter the day after he became cement, and when I've finished I'm going to stick it into the bag in this barrel.

"Are you a workman, too? If you are, have a heart and send me an answer. What is the cement in this barrel used for? I very much want to know.

"How much cement did he become? And is it all used in the same place or in different places? Are you a plasterer or a builder?

"I couldn't bear to see him become the corridor of a theater or the wall of some large mansion. But what on earth can I do to stop it? If you are a workman, please don't use the cement in such a place. . . .

"On second thought, though, it doesn't matter. Use it wherever you want. Wherever he's buried, he'll make a good job of it. He's a good solid fellow and he'll do the right thing wherever he happens to end up.

"He had a very gentle nature, you know. But at the same time he was a brave, husky fellow. He was still young. He'd only just turned twenty-five. I never had time to find out how much he really loved me. And here I am sewing a shroud for him—or rather, a cement-bag. Instead of going into a crematorium, he ended up in a rotation kiln. But how shall I find his grave to say goodbye to him? I haven't the faintest idea where he's going to be buried, you see. East or west, far or near—there's no way of telling. That's why I want you to send me an answer. If you're a workman, you will answer me, won't you? And in return I'll give you a piece of cloth from his overalls—yes, the piece of cloth this letter's wrapped in. The dust from that rock, the sweat from his body—it's all gone into this cloth. The cloth is all that's left of those overalls he used to wear when he embraced me—oh, how hard he used to embrace me!

"Please do this for me, won't you? I know it's a lot of trouble, but please let me know the date when this cement was used, and the sort of place it was used in and the exact address—and also your own name. And you'll be careful too, won't you? Goodbye."

*   *   *

The din of the children once more surged about Matsudo Yoshizō. He glanced at the name and address at the end of the letter and gulped down the rice brandy that he had poured into a teacup.

"I'm going to drink myself silly!" he shouted. "And I'm going to break every damned thing I can lay my hands on."

"I see," said his wife. "So you can afford to get drunk, can you? And what about the children?"

He looked at his wife's bloated stomach and remembered his seventh child.

THE CHARCOAL BUS

BY Ibusé Masuji

TRANSLATED BY Ivan Morris

    Ibusé Masuji, who was born in 1898, started his literary career as a poet. Although he soon switched to fiction and essays, the strength, restraint, and economy of his prose style reveals the poetic influence. His first published prose work, "The Giant Salamander" (Sanshōuo), appeared in 1932; like "The Charcoal Bus," it is a sustained satire, and it is marked by a dry form of humor that characterizes much of Ibusé's writing. In the early 1930's Ibusé joined a group of authors who aimed both to free literature from the dominance of the proletarian writers, and at the same time to avoid retiring into an ivory tower by concentrating exclusively on stylistic perfection. This no doubt worthy movement was short lived, and it was in fact not until after the war that Ibusé's position in the world of letters was confirmed.

    Ibusé is known, on the one hand, for his historical works, which reveal the influence of the great Meiji writer Mori Ōgai, and on the other, for his realistic stories and novels of contemporary life. His writing is outstanding for its fine style and for its characteristic form of humor. He is not a humorous writer in the conventional sense: but an indirect and subtle humor pervades his novels and short stories and, among other things, serves to prevent his warm, often moving, accounts of the hardships of poor people's lives from lapsing into sentimentality. Ibusé's short stories are marked by a very special type of irony, sharp without being bitter, subtle without being pretentious, and also by a distinctive manner of conveying the savor of real life through the slightly distorted words and actions of the characters.

"The Charcoal Bus" (Noriai Jidōsha) *was first published in 1952, when the author was fifty-four. It may be read as a political satire, with the driver representing Japan's militarist leaders and the passengers the grumbling but obedient civilian population. The honeymoon couple may stand for the noncooperative minority and the four-mile stretch of road brings to mind the four-year stretch of war following Pearl Harbor. The remarks of the old man in a peasant smock provide a pungent comment on the "reverse course" trends in recent Japanese politics.*

ON A recent trip to the country, I rode once again on the Binan-line bus. I hadn't been on this bus for some time—not since the war, in fact. However, I remembered it well.

During the war, all the country buses were pretty decrepit, but the bus on the Binan route was in a class of its own. It rarely got through a run without a series of mishaps: first there would be a puncture, then the engine would break down, and when this had finally been repaired the gear box would give trouble. Almost all the windows were broken; some of the openings were covered with cellophane, others with wooden boards.

Now, five years after the war, the bus still ran on charcoal, though the body had been painted over and most of the windows repaired. The driver was a young fellow whom I recognized from the war days, when he had been the conductor. Apparently he had changed places with the mustachioed man who had previously occupied the driver's seat. I wondered whether this had any particular significance.

"Haven't the driver and the conductor switched round?" I said to a woman in the seat next to mine. "Surely this conductor used to be the driver. Has he had an accident or something so that he can't drive any longer?"

"No," put in the woman's companion, "he became unpopular during the war and had to be demoted. He was too strict with the passengers, you see. As soon as the war was over, people began to write the company complaining about his behavior and saying he should be purged. . . . Well, this is where we get off."

The couple nodded to me and left the bus. An old man in a peasant's smock, who had been listening to the conversation, took the woman's place beside me.

"That's all very well," he said as soon as he had sat down, "but the conductor will soon be back where he was before, mark my words. Of course, he was so unpopular after the war that they couldn't help purging him; they lowered his salary and made him a conductor. But nowadays the purgees are all coming back into favor. It's people like him who are going to get ahead now." The old man nodded his head and murmured, as if to himself: "Yes, that's how things are moving these days."

I glanced at the conductor. How well I remembered that little mustache! He was standing now at the back of the bus looking out the window. We crossed a bridge over a dried-up river; beyond the rice fields I could see the slopes of a barren-looking mountain. As we passed a Shinto shrine by the side of the road, the conductor removed his cap and wiped the perspiration from his forehead. As he did so, he bowed his head slightly, and I wondered whether this was intended as a mark of respect for the shrine. Such reverence had been unfashionable for some time after the war but was now gradually coming back into favor. The conductor's gesture seemed deliberately ambiguous.

My memories of the man were far from favorable. During his long term of duty as driver for the Binan-line bus, he had never missed an opportunity to hector the young man who was then conductor. The burden of his abuse was usually the alleged misdemeanors of the passengers, and among his favorite points of attack were rucksacks.

"No rucksacks inside the bus!" he used to roar at the conductor. "Kindly tell that passenger to remove his rucksack. You know perfectly well they aren't allowed. What are you waiting for anyhow? Make him get off!"

There was indeed a rule that each piece of luggage, including rucksacks, had to be checked, paid for, and piled on top of the bus. Occasionally the police would stop the bus at a crossroads and examine the luggage for black-market articles, such as rice or firewood, the discovery of which meant confiscation and a fine. Under the circumstances we preferred to take our baggage with us and push it under the seats, but such attempts were almost invariably frustrated by the mustachioed driver. He, on the other hand, did not scruple to transport large quantities of carrots, peas, and other contraband in the tool box next to his seat.

Not only did I and the other regular passengers regard the driver as a disagreeable bully, but we also despised him for his inefficiency in handling the bus. The constant delays and breakdowns used to leave him quite unperturbed. As soon as the engine failed, he would announce in a stentorian tone: "All passengers out! Start pushing!" When we had pushed for fifty or sixty yards, the engine usually started and he would order us aboard.

Toward the end of the war, however, these periodic breakdowns became more serious and the last time I had taken the bus (shortly before the destruction of Hiroshima) I had helped push it almost four miles. I had gone fishing in a mountain stream and after spending the night at an inn, had gone early next morning to the Otaki Bridge bus stop. About forty people were already waiting. The time for departure came but there was no sign of the bus. A few people gave up at once and left; others vented their annoyance by reviling the driver, a luxury that they certainly would not have permitted themselves had he been within earshot. Only about half of us remained when the bus finally arrived, over two hours late.

I gave the conductor my return ticket and luggage check, passed him my rucksack, and stepped aboard. There were seats for all of us. When the conductor had finished stoking the burner with charcoal, the driver pressed the starting button. Nothing happened. He pressed it again several times, but still the engine would not fire. This, of course, was a fairly normal occurrence and, without waiting to be told, we all got out of the bus—all, that is, except for a young couple who remained unconcernedly in their seats. They were obviously not familiar with the Binan-line bus.

With one accord we started to push. As the burner, which stuck out in the back, was extremely hot, we split into groups on each side. One enterprising passenger found a long board and used it to push the burner. The conductor also jumped down and began pushing. The road here was at a slight incline and the bus moved along without too much effort on our part. The driver sat calmly in his seat, hands on the steering wheel.

We had pushed the bus three or four hundred yards without the engine once firing, when suddenly we heard a hysterical voice from inside the bus. It was the driver, who evidently had just noticed the young couple.

"Hey, you two back there!" he roared. "What do you think you're doing? Can't you see that everyone else is pushing? Get out and lend a hand! Don't just sit there!"

A man's voice answered calmly: "Would you mind not shouting at me? I may not be much of a traveler, but I always thought that buses ran on their engines."

"I see," said the driver. "So that's your attitude! You're too good to push like everyone else, eh? Well, let me tell you something: I don't care if you're honeymooners or not, if you don't get out this minute and start pushing, you'll damned well wish you had!"

"If you want to continue this conversation," answered the man, "you'd better address me politely."

There was a pause. A little later, as the road passed through a quiet grove, the driver's voice again broke the silence.

"Hey, you two back there! Don't be so damned stubborn. How can you go on sitting there in comfort when all the others are sweating away on the road? We're beginning to go uphill now. Get out and help!"

"Why don't you pay attention to the engine?" said the young man loudly. "You're the one that's stubborn! You're so interested in making us get out and push that you aren't even trying to start the engine. Concentrate on your job like other drivers! You're a disgrace to the public-transport system!"

"Shut up!" said the driver. Then in a milder tone he added: "See here, young man, we're going up Sampun Hill now. You don't want to let the others do all the work, do you? Look at them back there sweating away!"

Sampun Hill was a steep cutting; both sides of the road were clay cliffs. It took all our strength to move the bus. From the top of the cutting the road went steeply downward, and if the engine didn't fire there, it was hard to see when it would. We all stopped at the summit and watched the bus gathering speed as it ran downhill. It passed a large irrigation tank on one side of the road and disappeared behind a clump of trees. We pricked up our ears for the sound of the engine, while the conductor ran down the hill after the bus.

A man in an open-neck shirt, a peaked cap, and a pair of khaki plus-fours stained with paint came up to me. "Can you hear if it's started?" he said.

"I believe it's started," replied a girl in slacks who was standing next to me. "I think I can hear the engine. . . . But maybe it's just my imagination."

"I can't hear a thing," said the man in plus-fours. "How many more miles is it to town?"

"About four and a half," said the girl. "But in just over two miles we come to Three Corners Crossing, where we can catch a decent bus."

"And I'm taking that bus for the rest of the way," declared the man in plus-fours. "I'm fed up with this charcoal contraption!"

Just then the conductor appeared at the bottom of the hill. He stood there waving his arms and shaking his head, before disappearing again in a clump of trees.

"We've never had to push this far before," said the girl in slacks as we started disconsolately down the hill. "That couple has annoyed the driver. He's taking it out on the rest of us."

"Yes, I bet he'll have us pushing the bus all the way to the end of the line," said the man in plus-fours angrily. "There's only one thing for us to do—look exhausted. We must make him think we're on our last legs; then maybe he'll change his mind." He pulled his shirt out of his trousers to give himself a disheveled appearance.

Finally we caught sight of the bus parked by a farmhouse near the trees. The driver was standing beside it with arms folded, while the conductor was busily turning the handle to stoke the burner. I could see a girl in a green dress drawing water from a well.

"Isn't that the girl who was in the bus?" I suggested.

"That's right," said a horse-faced man in an old army uniform with a mourning band. "I've got a feeling something's gone wrong. Look, the girl's carrying a bucket into the bus. Hey, what's got into you?" he called out to the driver. "What are you doing, just standing there looking up at the sky? Have you decided to give up driving or what?"

"That's right," said the driver, fingering his mustache. "I've resigned."

"What do you mean, you've resigned?" said the horse-faced man.

"That stubborn fool in there wouldn't get out and push when I told him. So I had to give him a good beating. But first I resigned, because employees aren't allowed to hit the passengers. Once I'd resigned, I was a private citizen and could give him the beating he deserved."

"Look here," said the horse-faced man, "you've gone too far this time. And who do you think is going to drive if you don't?"

The driver shrugged his shoulders. He glanced disdainfully at the passengers assembled beside the bus.

"I can't drive any more," he repeated stubbornly. "I tell you I've resigned."

At this point a tall old man stalked out of the farmhouse.

"I've had about enough of this!" he shouted to the driver. "I've seen everything that's gone on. I saw you attacking that peaceful couple. What do you mean by behaving like that in front of my house?"

"I'm a private citizen," said the driver. "I've got a perfect right to strike anyone I want to."

"Don't talk like a fool," said the old farmer. "And kindly get your bus away from my house. I'll help push the damned thing in place of the honeymoon couple if that's what's bothering you. My old woman can give a hand too. You get in and steer!"

We all followed the old couple to the back of the bus, and as I passed one of the windows, I glanced inside. The young man was lying back pale in his seat. He had some tissue paper stuffed in his nostrils and one of his eyes was red and swollen. The girl in the green dress had apparently just finished swabbing his face; she took the bucket to the back of the bus and handed it to one of the passengers, who returned it to the well.

The driver stood with his arms folded and refused to get into his seat. The old couple began pushing the bus with all their might. It would not budge.

"Hey, all you others," shouted the old man, "give us a hand!"

"Right you are," said the horse-faced man and ran to the back of the bus. "Come on, all of you," he shouted, "push away! Yo-heave-ho!"

We all pushed. The bus began to move. The driver opened his eyes wide in amazement. "Hey, wait a minute!" he shouted. "Don't be crazy! Wait till I get hold of the wheel."

He ran after the bus, jumped on to the driver's platform, and grasped the steering wheel before even sitting down. We all pushed now with redoubled vigor, spurred on by the feeling that we had taken matters into our own hands, at least temporarily. The road was fairly straight and the bus ran along at a steady speed.

"Hey, driver," shouted the horse-faced man, "can't you get the engine started? Are you sure you aren't doing it on purpose?"

"Don't be so suspicious," answered the driver. "It's not my fault it won't start. The engine's worn out. The battery isn't charging right either. But of course you people wouldn't know about such things."

"That's right," said a man who was wearing a light yellow shirt and a surplice inscribed with a Buddhist prayer. "We laymen are only good for pushing. 'Push and don't ask questions!' That seems to be the motto of this bus company."

"Yes, it's going a little too far," said the horse-faced man. "We've got to push whether we want to or not, and no one even bothers to tell us what's wrong with the damned bus. I'm exhausted!"

The driver turned round with a cigarette in his mouth.

"Hey there, you two," he shouted to the honeymoon couple, "did you hear what that passenger said just now? He's exhausted. They're all exhausted because of your damned selfishness! Aren't you ashamed of yourselves? Listen to the voice of the people back there! Get out this minute and push—both of you!"

"Are you still worrying about us, you poor fool?" said the young man. "I've told you already—leave us alone and concentrate on the engine or the battery or whatever it is. First you charge us high fares and then you try to make us do a lot of useless pushing. I'll have something to say about all this when we arrive, I warn you!"

"What's that, you bastard?" roared the conductor. "Do you want another beating?"

"You tell me to listen to the voice of the people," answered the young man calmly. "Well, by protesting like this, I'm trying to make it penetrate your ears too."

"So you still think you're pretty smart, do you?" cried the driver, shaking with fury. "You still think you're better than everyone else? All right, I'll show you! You've asked for it!" He got to his feet.

"Sit down, sit down!" shouted the horse-faced man, who had now become our spokesman. "Don't let go of the steering wheel!" Then turning to us, he said: "Come on, push harder! Don't let the driver leave the steering wheel. Push away!"

We pushed harder than ever and the bus moved rapidly along the straight, narrow road. On the left was a low stone wall beyond which was a steep drop to the paddyfields; on the right was a shallow river. The driver could ill afford to let the bus swerve in either direction. In the distance I noticed a car approaching.

"Stop a minute!" cried the driver. "I've got to give that fool another beating."

"Oh no, you don't!" said the horse-faced man. "Come on, everyone, push away! Let's really get this old crate moving!"

We pushed—in fact we almost hurled ourselves at the back of the bus. In our excitement we had forgotten that the driver could stop the bus whenever he wanted simply by applying the brakes. We were all out of breath by now, but this did not deter us.

"Hey, what's wrong with you all?" shouted the driver. "Why do you stand up for that insolent bastard anyway? It's his fault you're all worn out."

"Don't worry about us!" said the horse-faced man. "Just keep steering! If you let go of that wheel, you'll really have something to worry about."

"That's right," added the man with the surplice. "You'll be with your ancestors before you know it."

Just then a large van approached from the opposite direction. The bus jerked to a sudden stop which almost knocked us off balance; it was a moment before I realized that the driver had applied the brakes. We exchanged disappointed, frustrated looks.

"Well, at least we've arrived at the crossroads." remarked the horse-faced man. "We've pushed it four miles already. Quite an achievement, I must say! But I've had enough. I'm taking the proper bus from here on."

He gave his luggage check to the conductor, loaded his rucksack on his back, and started walking toward Three Corners Crossing. I also decided to take the other bus; so did the man in plus-fours, the girl in slacks, and a few others. The rest said they would continue pushing— some because they were convinced the bus was about to start, others to prevent the driver from attacking the honeymoon couple, still others because they did not want to lose their fares. The refractory couple decided to remain in the bus. The man in plus-fours went to fetch his luggage and joined us at the crossroads.

"They're sitting in there having lunch," he reported. "They've taken out a tin of dried beef."

"What about the driver?"

"It looks as if he's going to leave them in peace to enjoy their meal. They've got a bottle of whisky too."

I looked back at the charcoal bus. The driver had opened the hood and was tinkering at the engine with a wrench more for form's sake than anything, I imagined. The conductor put some charcoal in the burner and began turning the blower furiously. He seemed to have unbounded confidence in the engine. I noticed that the old farmer and his wife were trudging back toward their home.

機
械

横
光
利
一

MACHINE
BY Yokomitsu Riichi

TRANSLATED BY Edward Seidensticker

Like Kawabata Yasunari, Yokomitsu Riichi (1898–1947) gained prominence as a leader of the lyrical school which the Japanese call "neo-sensual" (shinkankaku-ha). The neo-sensualists revolted against two schools of "realism" popular in the mid-twenties: the autobiographical reporting of the naturalists and the special pleading of the proletarians. Relying for their effects on startling images, mingled sense impressions, and an abruptness of transition that sometimes calls to mind Gertrude Stein's automatic writing, the group derived on the one hand from Japanese haiku poetry and on the other from a jumble of European influences—Dadaism, futurism, expressionism, and the like.

Yokomitsu soon found it necessary to moderate the excesses of subjectivity to which this youthful revolt led. Beginning with "Machine" (Kikai) in 1930, he turned to psychological exploration under the influence of Joyce and Proust. From then until his death, his obsessive theme was the plight of the sensitive and receptive intellect assailed by a relentless, contradictory world and unable to know itself. "Machine" may be read as one statement of the theme; and Yokomitsu's last important work, an unfinished novel, treats of the modern Japanese intellect trapped between irreconcilable East and West.

AT FIRST I wondered sometimes if the master of the place was not insane. He would decide that his child, not yet three, did not like him. A child had no right to dislike its father, he would announce, frowning fiercely. Barely able to walk, the child would fall on its face. That gave the man cause to slap his wife—why had she

223

let the child fall when she was supposed to be watching it? For the rest of us this was all fine comedy. The man was in dead earnest, however, and one did begin to wonder if he might not be insane.

A man of forty, snatching his child up and marching about the room with it when for a moment it stopped crying! And it was not only with the child that he seemed strange. There was a suggestion of immaturity in everything he did. It was a home industry, and his wife naturally became its center, and it was natural too that her allies there gained strength from her position. Since my own ties were if anything with the husband, I was always left to do the work everyone most disliked. It was unpleasant work, really unpleasant work. Yet it was work that had to be done if the shop was not to come to a complete standstill. In this sense it was I and not the wife who was at the center of things; but I could only remain silent about the fact. I was among people who thought that the one given an unpleasant job was the one who was otherwise useless.

Still, the useless one can sometimes be strangely useful at a task that baffles others; and in all the many processes involving chemicals in this name-plate factory, the process entrusted to me was richest in violent poisons. My job was a slot made especially for dropping otherwise useless people into. Once in the slot, I found my skin and my clothes wearing out under the corrosive attacks of ferric chloride. Fumes tore at my throat; I was unable to sleep at night. Worse, my mind seemed to be affected, and my eyesight showed signs of failing. It was not likely that a useful person would have been put into such a slot. My employer had learned the same work in his youth, but no doubt because he too was a person who was considered otherwise useless.

Still, not even I meant to linger on there until in course of time I should become an invalid. I had come to Tokyo from a shipyard in Kyūshū, and on the train I happened to meet a lady, a widow in her fifties, who had neither children nor home. She meant, after presuming upon the kindness of Tokyo relatives for a time, to open a rooming house or some such business. I said jokingly that when I found work I'd come and take one of her rooms. She replied that she'd take me to see the relatives she had mentioned. They would have work for me. I had no other prospects at the time, and something refined in her manner told me to trust her. So I trailed after her and arrived here.

At first the job seemed easy. Then, gradually, I saw that the chemicals were eating away my ability to work. I'll leave today, I'll leave tomorrow, I would tell myself. But having lasted so long, I decided I should at least wait until I had learned the secrets of the trade. I set about becoming interested in dangerous chemical processes.

My fellow worker, a man named Karubé, promptly decided I was a spy who had crept in to steal trade secrets. Karubé had lived next door to the wife's family, and, since that fact gave him certain liberties, he responded by putting the interests of the shop above everything, becoming the proverbial faithful servant. He would fix a burning gaze upon me whenever I took a poison down from the shelf. As I loitered before the darkroom he would come up with a great clattering to let me know he was there watching. I thought all this a trifle ridiculous, and yet his earnestness made me uncomfortable. He considered the movies the finest of textbooks and detective movies a mirror of life, and there was no doubt that I, who had wandered in unannounced, was good material for his fantasies. He had ambitions beyond spending the rest of his life here. He meant one day to set up a branch establishment, and he most certainly did not mean to let me learn the secret of making red plates, an invention of our employer, before he had learned it himself.

I was interested only in learning and had not a suggestion of a plan for making my living by what I learned. Karubé was not one to understand such subtleties, however, and I could not in complete honesty deny that once I had learned the business I might consider making my living from it.

In any case, my conscience would be at rest if I could assure myself that it was good for him to be teased a little. Having reached this conclusion, I quite forgot about him.

His hostility grew, and even while I was calling him a fool I came to think that, precisely because he was a fool, perhaps he wasn't such a fool after all. It is rather fun to be made a gratuitous enemy, because you can make a fool of your adversary while the situation lasts; and it took me a long time to note that this pleasure left a crack in my own defenses. I would move a chair or turn an edging tool, and a hammer would fall on my head, or sheets of brass, ground down for plates, would come crashing at my feet. A harmless compound of varnish and ether would be changed for chromic acid. At first I thought I was being careless. When it came to me that Karubé was responsible for all this, I concluded that if I wasn't careful, I'd find myself dead. This was a chilling thought. Karubé, though a fool, was older than I, and adept at mixing poisons. He knew that if he put ammonium dichromate into a person's tea, the result could pass as suicide. I would see something yellow in my food, take it to be chromic acid, and have trouble making my hand move in its direction. Presently, however, this caution struck me as funny. Let him try killing me if it seemed so easy! And so I forgot him again.

One day I was at work in the shop when the wife came in to tell me that her husband was going out to buy sheet metal and that I was to go with him to carry the money. When he carried it himself, he invariably lost it. Her chief concern always was to keep him away from money. Indeed, most of our troubles could be traced to this particular failing of his. No one could understand how he always managed to drop whatever money he had. Lost money will not come back, however much one storms and scolds, but, on the other hand, one does want to protest when the money for which one has sweated disappears like foam upon water. If it had happened only once or twice, things would have been different; but it happened constantly. When the master had money, he lost it. Inevitably, then, the affairs of this house shaped up rather differently from the affairs of most other houses.

A man of forty taking money and promptly losing it—one wondered how it could happen! His wife would tie his wallet around his neck and drop it inside his shirt, but even when the wallet remained on him, the money would have quite disappeared. It seemed likely that he had dropped it when he took something from the wallet. Even so, one would think that as he took his wallet out or put it away again, he might occasionally have reminded himself to look and see if he had dropped anything. Perhaps he did in fact watch himself. If so, could one believe that he really lost all his money so often? Perhaps the story was a trick on the wife's part to delay paying our wages.

So I thought for a time, but finally his behavior was enough to convince me that the wife's reports were true. It is said of the rich that they do not know what money is; and in a somewhat different sense our employer was wholly indifferent both to the five-sen copper for the public bath and to the larger amount of money for sheet metal. There was a time in history when he would have been called a sage and a saint; but those who live with a saint must be alert. None of the shop work could be left to our master, and what he should perfectly well have been able to do by himself, two men had to go out to do. It is impossible to calculate the needless labor caused by that one man. All this was true; yet the place would have been far less popular had he not been there. The business may have had its detractors, but not because of him. Not everyone approved of his subservience to his wife, but he was so good-natured, so small and docile in his chains, that on the whole he pleased people. He was even more charming when, free for a moment from his wife's sharp eye, he scampered about like an uncaged rabbit and threw money in all directions.

I am therefore constrained to say that the heart of the house was not the mistress, nor Karubé, nor myself. Clearly I was an underling, with an underling's devotion to his master; but I liked the man and that was that. To imagine the sort of man he was, you must think of a child of, say, five who has become a man of forty. The very thought of such a person seems ridiculous. We wanted to feel superior to him, and yet we could not. The unsightliness of our own years was revealed to us paradoxically as something fresh and new. (These were not my thoughts alone. Much the same thoughts seemed to move Karubé. It occurred to me afterward that his hostility came from a good-heartedness that made him want to protect our master.) The difficulty I found in deciding to leave the shop stemmed from the unique goodness of the master's heart; and the dropping of hammers on my head seemed to come from the same source. Goodness sometimes has strange manifestations.

Well, the master and I went out that day to buy sheet metal, and on the way he said that he'd had an interesting proposal that morning: someone wanted to buy the red-plating process for fifty thousand yen. Should he sell or shouldn't he? I could not answer, and he continued: no question would arise if the process could be kept secret forever, but his competitors were feverishly at work. If he was to sell at all, he should sell now.

That might be true, but I felt no right to discuss the process on which he had worked so long. Yet if I were to leave him to his own devices, he would do as his wife told him, and she was a woman who could think of nothing not immediately before her eyes.

I wanted to do what I could for him—indeed that wish became an obsession. When I was in the shop, it seemed that all the processes and all the materials were waiting for me to put them in order. I came to look upon Karubé as a menial, and, worse than that, his somewhat histrionic manner annoyed me. But then my feelings began to move in another direction. I noted again how Karubé's eyes were fixed on my smallest action. When I was at work his gaze almost never left me. It seemed clear that the wife had told him of her husband's latest research and of the red-plating process. Whether she had also told him to watch me, I could not be sure. I had begun to wonder if Karubé and the wife would not one day steal the secret, and I was telling myself that it might be well to do a little watching myself. I was therefore under no illusion that the two of them did not have similar doubts about me. When I was the object of suspicious looks, I did, it is true, feel somewhat uncomfortable; but it amused me to think, perhaps impudently, that I was watching them in turn.

About this time the master told me of his new research: he had long been looking for a way to tarnish metal without using ferric chloride. So far he had found nothing satisfactory. He wondered if in my spare time I would help him. However good-natured he was, I thought he should not be giving out information on so important a matter. Still, I was touched that he should trust me. It did not occur to me that the trusted one is usually the loser, and that the master thus perpetually defeated us all. That infinite childishness was not something one could acquire; it gave him his worth. I thanked him from my heart and told him that I would do what I could to help him.

I thought that some time in my life I'd like to have someone thank *me* from his heart. But since the master had no petty thoughts about "doing and being done by," I could only bow lower before him. I was trapped as if hypnotized. Miracles, I found, are not worked from without; they are rather the result of one's own inadequacy. With me as with Karubé, the master came first. I began to feel hostile toward the wife who controlled him, hostile toward everything she did. Not only did I wonder by what right such a woman monopolized such a man, I even thought occasionally of how I might free him from her.

The motives that made Karubé lash out at me became clear as day. When I saw him I saw myself, and the revelation fascinated me.

One day the master called me into the darkroom. He was holding a piece of aniline-coated brass over an alcohol burner, and he began to explain. In coloring a plate, one must pay the most careful attention to changes under heat. The sheet of brass was now purple, but presently it would be brownish black, and when, at length, it turned black, it promised in the next test to react to ferric chloride. The coloring process, he said, was a matter of catching a middle stage in a given transformation. The master then ordered me to make burning tests with as many chemicals as possible. I became fascinated with the organic relationships between compounds and elements, and as my interest grew I learned to see delicate organic movements in inorganic substances. The discovery that in the tiniest things a law, a machine, is at work came to me as the beginning of a spiritual awakening.

When Karubé noticed that I had free entry to the darkroom (until then no one had been admitted), his attitude changed. He was thinking, no doubt, that the care with which he had watched me had been wasted, since what was not permitted to him—to him who thought only of the master—was now permitted to me, a newcomer. Still more, he was thinking that unless he was careful he might find himself completely in my power. I knew that I should be more circumspect, but who was Karubé that I need worry about him at every move I made? I felt no sympathy for him, only a cool, detached interest in what the fool might be up to next, and I continued to treat him with lofty indifference.

He was infuriated. Once when I needed a punch he had been using, it disappeared. Hadn't he been using it until a minute ago, I asked. What had disappeared had disappeared, whether he had been using it or not, he answered, and I could go on hunting until I found it. That was true; but hunt as I would I could not find it. Then I happened to glance at his pocket and there it was. Silently, I reached for it. Who the devil did I think I was, reaching into a person's pocket without permission, he wanted to know. Another person's pocket indeed! I retorted; while we were here in the shop everyone's pocket was everyone else's. Because that was the way I felt, he said, I was the sort that would go around stealing secrets.

"When did I steal anything? If helping the master with his work means stealing, then you're stealing too," said I.

For a moment he was silent. Then, lips quivering, he stammered: "Get out of here! Get out of this shop!"

"All right, I'll go. But I owe it to the master not to leave until the research has gone a little farther."

"Then I'm going."

I tried to quiet him. "You'll only be causing trouble. Wait until I leave myself."

But he insisted he would go.

"All right. Go ahead. I'll take on the work of us both."

With that he snatched up the powdered calcium at his elbow and threw it into my face.

I knew that I was in the wrong, but wrongdoing could be interesting. I understood his impatience clearly, the fretful irritation in the man's good heart. I felt like relaxing to enjoy the sport, but at the same time I knew that would not do; so I sought to quiet him a bit. I had been wrong to ignore him. But it would have taken more of a man than I was to cower before each new wave of indignation. The smaller one is, the more one does to make people angry. As Karubé grew progressively angrier, I recognized the measure of my own smallness. In the end, I no longer knew what to do, about myself or about Karubé. Never before had I found myself so unmanageable. It has been well said that the spirit follows the body's dimensions. In silence I reflected that mine seemed to match exactly.

After a time I went into the darkroom and, to precipitate a bismuth dye, began heating potassium chromate in a test tube. That too was an unwise move. The fact that I had free entry into the darkroom had already aroused Karubé's envy, and now here I was in there again. He exploded, of course. Flinging the door open, he pulled me out by the collar and threw me to the floor. I let him have his way; indeed, I almost threw myself down. Violence was the only thing that worked with a person like me. He looked into the darkroom to see whether the potassium chromate had spilled, and while he was about it he went in and made a hasty circuit of the room. Then he came back and stood over me, glaring—apparently the trip around the room had not calmed him. He seemed to be wondering what to do next; he might well decide to kick me if I moved. For a few tense moments I wondered what, exactly, I was doing; but soon I began to feel as if I was dreaming. I thought I must let him have a really good tantrum, and by the time I concluded that he was angry enough to be satisfied, I was quite at ease myself. I looked in to see how much damage he had done. The devastation, I decided, was worst on my own face. Calcium was gritty in my mouth and ears. Still not sure whether I should get up, I glanced at the shining pile of aluminum cuttings by my nose and felt astonished at the amount of work I had done in three days.

"Let's stop this foolishness and get to work," I said. "There's aluminum to be coated."

But Karubé had no intention to work. "Suppose we coat your face instead!"

Shoving my head deep into the cuttings, he rubbed it back and forth as though the metal were a washcloth. I visualized my face being polished by a mountain of little plates from house doors and thought how disturbing violence could be. The corners of the aluminum stabbed at the lines and hollows of my face. Worse, the half-dried lacquer stuck to my skin. Soon my face would start swelling. I concluded that I'd done my duty and started for the darkroom again. Thereupon he seized my arm, twisted it behind my back, and pushed my face against a window, thinking, apparently, to slash it with glass splinters.

The violence would not continue long, I was sure. But as a matter of fact, it did go on and on. Though much of the blame was no doubt mine, my feeling of contrition began to fade. My face, which I had hoped wore a diffident, conciliatory expression, was swelling more and more painfully, offering a pretext for new violence. I knew that Karubé was no longer enjoying his anger, but it was now beyond his control.

As he pulled me toward a vat of the most poisonous corrosive, I turned on him: "It's your business, of course, if you want to torture me, but the experiments I've been working on in the darkroom are experiments no one else has done. If they're successful, there's no telling what profits they'll bring in. You won't let me work, and now you've upset the solution I spent all that time on. Clean it up!"

"Why don't you let me work with you, then?"

I could not tell him that the decision was out of my hands, that a person who could not even read a chemical equation would be less of a help than a hindrance. It may have been a little cruel of me, but I took him into the darkroom, showed him the closely written equations, and explained them to him.

"If you think you'd find it interesting, go ahead—mix and remix, using these figures. Go ahead! You can do it every day in my place, all day long." For the first time, I had the better of him.

With the fighting over, I found life easier for a time. Then, suddenly, Karubé and I became extremely busy. An order arrived from a municipal office to make name plates for a whole city, fifty thousand plates in ten days. The wife was delighted, but we knew it meant that we would have to go virtually without sleep. The master borrowed a craftsman from another name-plate shop. At first I was overwhelmed by the sheer volume of work; but soon I began to see something strange in the manner of the new man, Yashiki. Although his awkwardness and his sharp glance did suggest a craftsman, I suspected that he might perhaps have been sent to steal our secrets. If I were to speak of my suspicions, however, there would be no way of knowing what Karubé might do to him, and I decided to keep quiet for a time and to observe. I noted that Yashiki's attention was always focused on the way Karubé shook his vat. Karubé's work was the second speciality of our shop, something no other shop could imitate. Yashiki put sheets of brass into a solution of caustic soda to wash away the varnish and glue that Karubé used with corrosive ferric chloride. It was therefore natural that Yashiki should be interested. Still, given my doubts, the very naturalness of it was cause for further doubt.

But Karubé, more and more pleased with himself now that he had an audience, was in great form as he shook his vat of ferric chloride. Since he had doubts about me, he should naturally have had even greater doubts about Yashiki. Quite the reverse was true: he explained the shaking of the vat in such esoteric terms that I wondered where he might have learned them. You always laid the inscription face down, it seemed, and let the weight of the metal do the work. The uninscribed surface corroded more rapidly—suppose Yashiki try for himself. At first I listened nervously to the chatter, but in the end I decided that it made no difference. One might as well teach the secrets to anyone who wanted them. I would no longer be on my guard against Yashiki.

My chief gain from this incident was the discovery that a secret leaks out because of the conceit of its possessor. But it was not only conceit that led Karubé to tell everything. Without a doubt, Yashiki was an able seducer. Though the light in his eyes was sharp, it had a strange charm, when it softened, that had the effect of making one's caution melt away. That same charm affected me each time he spoke, but I was so busy with all the jobs I had to rush through that I paid little attention: from early in the morning I had to lacquer heated brass and dry it, put metal coated with ammonium dichromate out to react in the sun, add aniline, and then rush from burner to polisher to cutter. There was little time for Yashiki to charm me.

About five nights after he came, I awoke and saw Yashiki, who should have been doing night work, come from the darkroom and go into the wife's room. While I was wondering what could be taking him there at such an hour, I unfortunately fell asleep again. But the first thought that came into my mind next morning was of Yashiki. The trouble was that I gradually became less sure whether I had actually seen him or whether it had been a dream. I had had similar experiences from overwork before, and I suspected that I had only been dreaming. I could imagine what reason he might have for going into the darkroom, but I had no idea how to explain his entry into the other room. I could not believe that the wife and Yashiki were carrying on in secret. The easiest solution, then, was to dismiss it all as a dream.

At about noon, the master began laughing and asking his wife if there had been anything out of the ordinary on the previous evening.

"I may be a heavy sleeper," she answered quietly, "but I know who took the money. If you have to steal it, you might at least do it more cleverly."

He laughed still more delightedly.

Had it been not Yashiki but the master I had seen going into her room? I thought it odd that the latter should be sneaking into his own wife's room, chronically short of money though he was.

"It was you I saw coming from the darkroom?" I asked.

"The darkroom? I don't know anything about the darkroom."

The confusion deepened. Had it been Yashiki, after all, in the darkroom? It seemed certain that the man who had stolen into the wife's room was not Yashiki but the husband; yet I could not think I had only dreamed Yashiki's emergence from the darkroom. The suspicions that had for a time left me began to gather again. I saw, however, that doubting in solitude was like doubting oneself, and did no good. I'd better ask Yashiki directly. But if I did and it had in fact been he, then he would be upset, and to upset him would be no gain.

Still, the matter was of such interest that I thought it a pity not to push it further. For one thing, the secret formula for combining bismuth and zirconium silicate—the process on which I had been so hard at work—and the formula for the red amorphous selenium stain that was the master's speciality were both kept in the darkroom. Not only would their loss be a severe blow to the business, but the loss of my own secret would take all the zest from life. If Yashiki was trying to steal the formula, there was no reason why I shouldn't try to keep it hidden. I suspected him more intensely. When I thought how, after having been suspected by Karubé; it had now become my turn to suspect Yashiki, I wondered if I'd be giving Yashiki the same prolonged pleasure I'd had in making a fool of Karubé. But then I thought it over and decided it would do me good to let myself be made a fool of for once. So I turned my full attention to Yashiki.

Perhaps because he noticed how my eyes burned at him, Yashiki began to look exclusively in directions where his eyes would not meet mine. I was afraid that if I made him too uncomfortable he might take flight. I must be more circumspect. Eyes are strange things, however. When glances that have been wandering at the same level of consciousness meet, each seems to probe the other to its depths.

I would be at the polisher, talking of this and that, and my glance would ask him: "Have you stolen the formulas yet?"

"Not yet, not yet," that burning eye would seem to answer.

"Well, be quick about it."

"It takes a devil of a long time, now that you know what I'm after."

"My formula is full of mistakes anyway. It wouldn't do you much good to steal it now."

"I can correct it."

So the imaginary conversations went, while Yashiki and I worked together; and gradually I began to feel friendlier toward him than toward anyone else in the place. The Yashiki charm that had excited Karubé and made him reveal all his secrets was now working on me.

I would read the newspaper with Yashiki, and on subjects that interested us both our opinions always agreed, especially on technical matters. I'd speed up reading when he speeded up and slow down when he slowed down. Our views on politics and our plans for society were alike. The only question on which we disagreed was the propriety of trying to steal another person's invention. He had his own views, and thought there was nothing wrong with stealing if it contributed to the advance of civilization. In such a case, the person who tries to steal may, in fact, be better than the one who does not. Comparing his spy activities with my own attempts to hide inventions, I concluded that he was doing more for the world than I. So I thought—and so Yashiki made me think. He seemed to approach nearer and nearer; yet I wanted to keep at least the secret of the amorphous selenium stain from him. So, even while I became his closest friend, I was also the one who most got in his way.

I told him that Karubé had suspected me of being a spy when I first came to work here, and had almost killed me. Karubé had not done the same to him, laughed Yashiki, because Karubé had learned a lesson with me.

"So that's why you found it so easy to be suspicious of me," he added mischievously.

"If you knew all along that I was suspicious, you must have come here prepared to be suspected."

"That's right," he said.

He was as good as admitting he had come to steal our secrets. I could not help being astonished at the openness with which he said so. Perhaps he had seen through me and was sure that in my surprise I would come to respect him. I glared at him for some seconds.

But Yashiki's expression had already changed. Somewhat loftily, he went on: "When you come to work in a shop like this, it's the usual thing to have people think you're up to something. But what could a person like me do? No—I won't begin apologizing now. Suppose we just work and let work. The worst thing," and he laughed, "is having someone like you look at me as if I ought to be doing something bad when I'm not."

He had touched a sensitive spot. I felt a certain sympathy for the man. I had borne the sort of treatment he was now getting.

"You can't be enjoying the work very much if it makes you say things like that," I said.

Yashiki pulled his shoulders back and shot a glance at me, then passed the moment off with a quick laugh.

I made it my policy to let him plot as he would. A person of his ability would no doubt have seen everything in a single trip into the darkroom, and, having let him see, one could do nothing, short of killing him, except take the consequences. Perhaps one should rather be grateful for having met such a remarkable person in such an unlikely place.

I went even further: I came to think that it would be a good thing if, in the course of time, he did succeed in taking advantage of the master and stealing our secrets.

One day I said to him: "I don't mean to stay here long myself. Do you know of any good openings?"

"I meant to ask you the same thing. If we're alike even in that, what right have you to be lecturing me?"

"I see what you mean. But don't misunderstand me. I don't mean to be lecturing and I don't mean to be prying. It's just that I respect you, and I thought you might let me be your pupil."

"Pupil?" He smiled wryly. Then, abruptly, he was sober again. "Go and have a look at a ferric-chloride factory, where the trees and grass have died for a hundred yards around, and talk to me again afterward."

I had no idea what the "afterward" might mean, but I thought I caught a glimpse of his reasons for thinking me rather simple. But what were the limits to which he would go in making me look foolish? They seemed far out of sight. Gradually I lost interest, and as I did so I thought I would have a try at making *him* look foolish. I had been attracted to him, however, and the effort was abortive—in fact it was comical. These superior people put one through a harsh discipline!

One day when we were about to finish the rush order, Karubé threw Yashiki on his face under the cutter. "Admit it, admit it!" he said.

Apparently he had caught Yashiki sneaking into the darkroom.

Astride Yashiki's back, Karubé was pounding at his head when I came into the shop. So it's finally happened, I thought. But I felt no impulse to go to Yashiki's rescue. Indeed, I was rather a Judas, curious to see how the man I respected would respond to violence. I looked coolly into Yashiki's twisted face. He was struggling to get up, one side of his head in some varnish that was flowing across the floor, but each time Karubé's knee hit him in the back he fell on his face again. His trousers were pushed up, and his stout legs were bare, threshing awkwardly at the floor. This rather spirited resistance struck me as utterly foolish, but revulsion was stronger than disdain, as if the face of the respected one, ugly from pain, showed an ugliness of spirit as well. I was troubled less by the violence itself than by the fact that Karubé could force a person to wear such an ugly expression.

Karubé had no eye for expressions, ugly or otherwise. He seized Yashiki's neck in both hands and pounded his head against the floor. I began to doubt whether my indifference to suffering was entirely proper, but I felt that if I were to make the slightest move to help one or the other, I would be guilty of still greater impropriety. I also began to wonder whether Yashiki, not prepared to confess in spite of the pain to which that ugly, twisted face testified, had actually stolen anything from the darkroom, and I turned to the task of reading his secret in the furrows of his distorted face. From time to time he glanced at me. To give him strength, I offered a contemptuous smile each time his eyes met mine. He made a really determined effort to overturn Karubé. He was helpless, however, and there was a new rain of blows.

Starting up whenever I laughed at him, Yashiki was showing his true colors. The more he moved himself to action, it would seem, the more he gave himself away. Though I tried to continue laughing at him, I began to feel something more like contempt, until, as the moments passed, I was no longer able to laugh at all. Yashiki had a way of choosing the least likely moments for his struggles. A most ordinary human being he was, no different from the rest of us.

"Suppose you stop hitting him," I said to Karubé. "Won't it do just to talk to him?"

"Stand up!" Karubé gave his victim a kick and poured metal fragments over his head, much as he had buried my head in similar fragments.

Yashiki edged away and stood with his back to the wall. He explained rapidly that he had gone into the darkroom in search of ammonia.

He had been unable to clean glue from sheet metal with caustic soda.

"If you needed ammonia, why didn't you ask for it?" said Karubé, and hit him again. "Anyone ought to know that there's no place in a name-plate factory as important as the darkroom."

I knew that Yashiki's explanation was absurd, but the thunder of Karubé's fists was too violent. "You ought at least to stop hitting him," I said.

With that Karubé turned on me. "It's a plot between the two of you, is it?"

"You can answer that yourself if you give it a little thought," I was about to say; but it occurred to me that our actions not only could be thought a conspiracy; they might, in fact, be something very like one. I had calmly let Yashiki go into the darkroom, and even thought myself less of a person for *not* stealing the master's secrets. The result was, in effect, a conspiracy.

As my conscience began to trouble me, I assumed a confident manner. "Plot or no plot, I think you've hit him enough," I said.

With that Karubé hit me on the jaw. "I suppose you let him into the darkroom."

I was less concerned about being struck than I was eager to show Yashiki, who had already been struck, how I was now being struck for taking his crime upon myself. I felt almost exhilarated. "Look at me now!" I wanted to cry. I had a strange feeling, however, that Karubé and I must now seem the conspirators. Yashiki must think that I could so unconcernedly allow myself to be hit only because we had arranged this in advance. I glanced up at him—he seemed to have come to life now that there were two of us.

"Hit him!" he cried, flailing away at the back of Karubé's head.

I was not particularly angry, but because of the pain I took a certain pleasure in the exercise of hitting back. I hit Karubé in the face several times. Thus assaulted from before and behind, he turned his main attention to Yashiki. I tugged from behind, and Yashiki, still flailing away, took advantage of the opening to knock him down and sit on him. I was astonished at how lively Yashiki had become. Doubtless it was because he thought that I, angry at having been hit without reason, was with him in the attack.

But I had no need of further revenge. I stood silently by and watched.

Effortlessly, Karubé overturned Yashiki, and began pounding him more fiercely than before. Again Yashiki was helpless. After Karubé had pounded Yashiki for a time, he suddenly stood up and came at me, perhaps thinking I might attack him from the rear. It was a foregone conclusion that I would lose in single combat with Karubé. I kept my peace once more and waited for Yashiki to help me. But Yashiki began hitting not Karubé but me. Unable to cope with even one adversary, I could do nothing against two. I lay there and let them hit.

Had I been so wrong? As I lay doubled up with my head in my arms, I wondered if I had so misbehaved that I must be hit by both of them. No doubt my conduct had been surprising, but had the other two not also chosen courses that could be called strange? At least, there was no reason for Yashiki to be hitting me. It was true that I had not joined him in the attack on Karubé; but he had been a fool to expect me to.

In any event, the only one who had not been attacked by the other two simultaneously was Yashiki. The one who most deserved to be hit had most cleverly escaped.

By the time I began to think I'd like to give him a cuffing for his pains, we were all exhausted. The cause of the whole senseless fight had clearly been less that Yashiki had gone into the darkroom than that we were exhausted from having made fifty thousand name plates in such a short time. Ferric-chloride fumes wore on one's nerves and disordered one's reason, and instinct seemed to reveal itself from every pore. If a man chose to be angry at each small incident in a name-plate factory, there would be no end to anger.

I had, nonetheless, been hit by Yashiki, and the fact was not to be forgotten. What was he thinking? If his behavior gave me the occasion, I'd find ways to make him ashamed of himself.

When the incident stopped—though one could hardly have said that it had an ending—Yashiki turned to me. "It was wrong of me to hit you, but I had to finish the business. There was no telling how long Karubé would go on hitting me. I'm sorry."

That was true, I had to agree. If I, the least guilty, had not been hit by both of them, the fighting would have gone on and on. I smiled wryly. I had, then, been protecting Yashiki in his thievery. And I must forego the pleasure of making him ashamed of himself. The man was an astonishingly able plotter.

In some chagrin, I said to him: "If you've been so clever at using me, I'm sure you've been just as clever at getting secrets from the darkroom."

"If even you think that, it's only natural that Karubé should have hit me." He laughed his practiced laugh. "Weren't you the one who turned him on me?"

I could offer no explanation if he chose to think that I had provoked the incident. Perhaps he had hit me because he suspected that I was in league with Karubé. It was becoming harder and harder to know what these two thought of me.

In the midst of all this uncertainty, however, there was one clear thing: Karubé and Yashiki, in their separate ways, were both suspicious of me. But however clear this fact might seem to me, was there any way for me to know how clear it *really* was? In any case, some invisible machine was constantly measuring us all, as if it understood everything that went on, and was pushing us according to the results of its measurements.

Even while we nursed our suspicions in this way, we were looking forward to the next day, when the job would finally be over and we could rest. Forgetting our exhaustion and enmity in pleasant thoughts of payment, we finished that day—and the next day a new blow hit.

On his way home, the master lost the whole of the money he had received for those fifty thousand name plates. The labors that had not allowed us a decent night's sleep in ten days had come to precisely nothing.

The sister who had first introduced me had gone with her brother, foreseeing that he might drop the money—and at least that much had run true to form. He had said that for the first time in a very long while he would like to have the pleasure of holding the money we had earned, all of it. Quite understanding, his sister let him have it for a few minutes. And in those few minutes the flaw worked like an infallible machine.

Though we did report the loss to the police, naturally none of us thought the money would ever be seen again, and we just sat looking at each other. We could no longer expect to be paid, and exhaustion suddenly overtook us. For a time we lay motionless in the shop. Then, smashing some boards that lay at hand and flinging away the pieces, Karubé turned on me.

"Why are you smiling?"

I did not mean to be smiling, but since he said I was, presumably I was. No doubt it was because the master was so comical—the comedy being probably a result of long years of exposure to ferric-chloride fumes. I felt anew that few things were to be so feared as mental disorder. What a wondrous system it was whose workings made a man's defects draw others to him, leaving them unable to fear!

I did not answer. It would do no good to explain.

Then Karubé stopped glaring at me. "We'll have a drink!" he said, clapping his hands.

He had spoken at a moment when one or another of us was to speak. Inevitably, our thoughts turned to liquor. At such times there is nothing for young men to do but drink. Not even Yashiki could have guessed that because of the liquor he would lose his life.

That night we sat drinking in the shop until after midnight. When I awoke I saw that Yashiki had mistaken leftover ammonium dichromate for water, had drunk from the jug, and had died. Even now I do not think, as the men from the shop that sent him here seem to, that Karubé killed Yashiki. Although it was I who had again that day done the gluing in which ammonium dichromate is used, Karubé and not I had suggested that we drink, and it was natural that suspicion should fall more heavily on him. Still, it did not seem likely that Karubé could have conceived the dark plot of getting him drunk and killing him unless we had thought of drinking much earlier in the evening. Karubé was nonetheless suspected, probably because of the threatening manner that revealed him as one who liked violence.

I do not say with finality that Karubé did not kill Yashiki. I can only say that my limited knowledge makes me able to conjecture that he did not. For I know he, like me, must have thought, upon seeing Yashiki go into the darkroom, that there was no way short of killing him to keep him from stealing the secrets. I had thought that the way to kill him would be to get him drunk and give him ammonium dichromate, and the same thought must have run through Karubé's mind. Yet not only Yashiki and I were drunk. Karubé was too. So it seems unlikely that Karubé gave Yashiki the poison. And if the possibilities that had troubled Karubé through recent days had worked in his drunken mind to make him offer Yashiki ammonium dichromate, then perhaps, by the same token, it was I who was the criminal.

Indeed how can I say absolutely that I did not kill him? Was it not I, rather than Karubé, who feared him? All the time he was there, was it not I who was most on guard to see if he went into the darkroom? Was it not I who harbored the deepest resentment at the idea of his stealing the bismuth and zirconium silicate formula I was working on?

Perhaps I murdered him. I knew better than anyone where the ammonium dichromate was. Before drunkenness overtook me, I kept thinking about Yashiki and what he would be doing somewhere else the next day, when he would be free to leave. And if he had lived, would I not have lost more than Karubé? And had not my head, like the master's, been attacked by ferric chloride?

I no longer understand myself. I only feel the sharp menace of an approaching machine, aimed at me. Someone must judge me. How can I know what I have done?

THE MOON ON THE WATER

BY Kawabata Yasunari

TRANSLATED BY George Saitō

Kawabata Yasunari was born in Osaka in 1899. His father, a physician with a special taste for literature and art, died when Kawabata was three years old; his mother died in the following year. Kawabata was then brought up by his grandfather and grandmother. The latter died when he was eight years old and his grandfather died in 1914. Kawabata was then put in the care of his mother's family.

In his primary-school days he wanted to become a painter, but when he was about fifteen he decided to become a novelist instead. In his fifth year in middle school he started contributing essays and stories to a private literary magazine and to local newspapers.

His diary, written just before the death of his grandfather, was later published as "Diary of a Sixteen-Year-Old." During the three years when he was a student at the First High School he devoted himself chiefly to reading Scandinavian literature and works of Japanese authors belonging to the Shirakaba school, which was strongly opposed to the simple approach of naturalism and sought a style suited to sensual expression.

Kawabata entered the English Literature Department of Tokyo Imperial University in 1920 and in the next year he started publication of a literary magazine in collaboration with other students. His story "A Memorial Day Scene," which was published in the second issue of the magazine, attracted the attention of Kikuchi Kan. At about the same time he also became a friend of Yokomitsu Riichi.

In 1923 Kawabata joined the staff of a leading literary magazine, Bungei Shunjū, and started writing book reviews. He was graduated from Tokyo Imperial University in March, 1924. In September of the same year he began the publication of the literary magazine Bungei Jidai, from which was started the new literary movement of neo-sensualism (shinkankaku-ha), discussed in the note on Yokomitsu Riichi.

"The Izu Dancer," which was published in the January and February, 1925, issues of Bungei Jidai, is representative of his early writing. It describes a young dancing girl belonging to a traveling entertainers' troupe which Kawabata as a high-school pupil happened to have met on a tour of the Izu Peninsula. The story recalls the writer's younger days and is wrapped in the sentimental atmosphere of youth.

In subsequent works, such as "The Kurenaidan of Asakusa" and "Flower Waltz," Kawabata deals chiefly with the lives of dancers and aims at evoking the ephemeral beauty of worldly things. In a short story entitled "Birds and Animals," published in 1933, he describes the psychology of a middle-aged man who in his loneliness raises dogs and birds. Solitude, loneliness, and a sense of the vanity of things cast their shadow over this work.

In his novel "Snow Country," which was started in 1935 and finished in 1937, Kawabata describes the relations of the hero, a specialist in Western ballet from Tokyo, with a geisha in a mountain village. The story is dominated by the sparkling love, mingled with the cold realization of actuality, between the hero, who has observed life only through art, and the woman, who has been leading a lonely life in this remote mountainous region.

Kawabata is also an important literary critic. He has discovered many promising young writers, including Mishima Yukio, and he has a keen interest in literature for young people.

In 1948, Kawabata was appointed chairman of the Japanese Center of the P.E.N. Club. After the war he declared that he would write nothing except elegies; in keeping with this resolve he has written several novels, such as "The Sound of the Mountain" and "Thousand Cranes," which are characterized by a deep sense of solitude and a consciousness of old age and approaching death.

The present story (Suigetsu in Japanese) was first published in 1953, when the author was fifty-four.

IT OCCURRED to Kyōko one day to let her husband, in bed upstairs, see her vegetable garden by reflecting it in her hand mirror. To one who had been so long confined, this opened a new life. The hand mirror was part of a set in Kyōko's trousseau. The mirror stand was not very big. It was made of mulberry wood, as was the frame of the mirror itself. It was the hand mirror that still reminded her of the bashfulness of her early married years when, as she was looking into it at the reflection of her back hair in the stand mirror, her sleeve would slip and expose her elbow.

When she came from the bath, her husband seemed to enjoy reflecting the nape of her neck from all angles in the hand mirror. Taking the mirror from her, he would say: "How clumsy you are! Here, let me hold it." Maybe he found something new in the mirror. It was not that Kyōko was clumsy, but that she became nervous at being looked at from behind.

Not enough time had passed for the color of the mulberry-wood frame to change. It lay in a drawer. War came, followed by flight from the city and her husband's becoming seriously ill; by the time it first occurred to Kyōko to have her husband see the garden through the mirror, its surface had become cloudy and the rim had been smeared with face powder and dirt. Since it still reflected well enough, Kyōko did not worry about this cloudiness—indeed she scarcely noticed it. Her husband, however, would not let the mirror go from his bedside and polished it and its frame in his idleness with the peculiar nervousness of an invalid. Kyōko sometimes imagined that tuberculosis germs had found their way into the imperceptible cracks in the frame. After she had combed her husband's hair with a little camellia oil, he sometimes ran the palm of his hand through his hair and then rubbed the mirror. The wood of the mirror stand remained dull, but that of the mirror grew lustrous.

When Kyōko married again, she took the same mirror stand with her. The hand mirror, however, had been burned in the coffin of her dead husband. A hand mirror with a carved design had now taken its place. She never told her second husband about this.

According to custom, the hands of her dead husband had been clasped and his fingers crossed, so that it was impossible to make them hold the hand mirror after he had been put into the coffin. She laid the mirror on his chest.

"Your chest hurt you so. Even this must be heavy."

Kyōko moved the mirror down to his stomach. Because she thought of the important role that the mirror had played in their marital life, Kyōko had first laid it on his chest. She wanted to keep this little act as much as possible from the eyes even of her husband's family. She had piled white chrysanthemums on the mirror. No one had noticed it. When the ashes were being gathered after the cremation, people noticed the glass which had been melted into a shapeless mass, partly sooty and partly yellowish. Someone said: "It's glass. What is it, I wonder?" She had in fact placed a still smaller mirror on the hand mirror. It was the sort of mirror usually carried in a toilet case, a long, narrow, double-faced mirror. Kyōko had dreamed of using it on her honeymoon trip. The war had made it impossible for them to go on a honeymoon. During her husband's lifetime she never was able to use it on a trip.

With her second husband, however, she went on a honeymoon. Since her leather toilet case was now very musty, she bought a new one—with a mirror in it too.

On the very first day of their trip, her husband touched Kyōko and said: "You are like a little girl. Poor thing!" His tone was not in the least sarcastic. Rather it suggested unexpected joy. Possibly it was good for him that Kyōko was like a little girl. At this remark, Kyōko was assailed by an intense sorrow. Her eyes filled with tears and she shrank away. He might have taken that to be girlish too.

Kyōko did not know whether she had wept for her own sake or for the sake of her dead husband. Nor was it possible to know. The moment this idea came to her, she felt very sorry for her second husband and thought she had to be coquettish.

"Am I so different?" No sooner had she spoken than she felt very awkward, and shyness came over her.

He looked satisfied and said: "You never had a child . . ."

His remark pierced her heart. Before a male force other than her former husband Kyōko felt humiliated. She was being made sport of.

"But it was like looking after a child all the time."

This was all she said by way of protest. It was as if her first husband, who had died after a long illness, had been a child inside her. But if he was to die in any case, what good had her continence done?

"I've only seen Mori from the train window." Her second husband drew her to him as he mentioned the name of her home town. "From

its name* it sounds like a pretty town in the woods. How long did you live there?"

"Until I graduated from high school. Then I was drafted to work in a munitions factory in Sanjō."

"Is Sanjō near, then? I've heard a great deal about Sanjō beauties. I see why you're so beautiful."

"No, I'm not." Kyōko brought her hand to her throat.

"Your hands are beautiful, and I thought your body should be beautiful too."

"Oh no."

Finding her hands in the way, Kyōko quietly drew them back.

"I'm sure I'd have married you even if you had had a child. I could have adopted the child and looked after it. A girl would have been better," he whispered in Kyōko's ear. Maybe it was because he had a boy, but his remark seemed odd even as an expression of love. Possibly he had planned the long, ten-day honeymoon so that she would not have to face the stepson quite so soon.

Her husband had a toilet case for traveling, made of what seemed to be good leather. Kyōko's did not compare with it. His was large and strong, but it was not new. Maybe because he often traveled or because he took good care of it, the case had a mellow luster. Kyōko thought of the old case, never used, which she had left to mildew. Only its small mirror had been used by her first husband, and she had sent it with him in death.

The small glass had melted into the hand mirror, so that no one except Kyōko could tell that they had been separate before. Since Kyōko had not said that the curious mass had been mirrors, her relatives had no way of knowing.

Kyōko felt as if the numerous worlds reflected in the two mirrors had vanished in the fire. She felt the same kind of loss when her husband's body was reduced to ashes. It had been with the hand mirror that came with the mirror stand that Kyōko first reflected the vegetable garden. Her husband always kept that mirror beside his pillow. Even the hand mirror seemed to be too heavy for the invalid, and Kyōko, worried about his arms and shoulders, gave him a lighter and smaller one.

* *Mori* means "grove."

It was not only Kyōko's vegetable garden that her husband had observed through the two mirrors. He had seen the sky, clouds, snow, distant mountains, and nearby woods. He had seen the moon. He had seen wild flowers, and birds of passage had made their way through the mirror. Men walked down the road in the mirror and children played in the garden.

Kyōko was amazed at the richness of the world in the mirror. A mirror which had until then been regarded only as a toilet article, a hand mirror which had served only to show the back of one's neck, had created for the invalid a new life. Kyōko used to sit beside his bed and talk about the world in the mirror. They looked into it together. In the course of time it became impossible for Kyōko to distinguish between the world that she saw directly and the world in the mirror. Two separate worlds came to exist. A new world was created in the mirror and it came to seem like the real world.

"The sky shines silver in the mirror," Kyōko said. Looking up through the window, she added: "When the sky itself is grayish." The sky in the mirror lacked the leaden and heavy quality of the actual sky. It was shining.

"Is it because you are always polishing the mirror?"

Though he was lying down, her husband could see the sky by turning his head.

"Yes, it's a dull gray. But the color of the sky is not necessarily the same to dogs' eyes and sparrows' eyes as it is to human eyes. You can't tell which eyes see the real color."

"What we see in the mirror—is that what the mirror eye sees?"

Kyōko wanted to call it the eye of their love. The trees in the mirror were a fresher green than real trees, and the lilies a purer white.

"This is the print of your thumb, Kyōko. Your right thumb."

He pointed to the edge of the mirror. Kyōko was somehow startled. She breathed on the mirror and erased the fingerprint.

"That's all right, Kyōko. Your fingerprint stayed on the mirror when you first showed me the vegetable garden."

"I didn't notice it."

"You may not have noticed it. Thanks to this mirror, I've memorized the prints of your thumbs and index fingers. Only an invalid could memorize his wife's fingerprints."

Her husband had done almost nothing but lie in bed since their marriage. He had not gone to war. Toward the end of the war he had been drafted, but he fell ill after several days of labor at an airfield and came home at the end of the war. Since he was unable to walk, Kyōko went with his elder brother to meet him. After her husband had been drafted, she stayed with her parents. They had left the city to avoid the bombings. Their household goods had long since been sent away. As the house where their married life began had been burned down, they had rented a room in the home of a friend of Kyōko's. From there her husband commuted to his office. A month in their honeymoon house and two months at the house of a friend—that was all the time Kyōko spent with her husband before he fell ill.

It was then decided that her husband should rent a small house in the mountains and convalesce there. Other families had been in the house, also fugitives from the city, but they had gone back to Tokyo after the war ended. Kyōko took over their vegetable garden. It was only some six yards square, a clearing in the weeds. They could easily have bought vegetables, but Kyōko worked in the garden. She became interested in vegetables grown by her own hand. It was not that she wanted to stay away from her sick husband, but such things as sewing and knitting made her gloomy. Even though she thought of him always, she had brighter hopes when she was out in the garden. There she could indulge her love for her husband. As for reading, it was all she could do to read aloud at his bedside. Then Kyōko thought that by working in the garden she might regain that part of herself which it seemed she was losing in the fatigue of the long nursing.

It was in the middle of September that they moved to the mountains. The summer visitors had almost all gone and a long spell of early autumn rains came, chilly and damp.

One afternoon the sun came out to the clear song of a bird. When she went into the garden, she found the green vegetables shining. She was enraptured by the rosy clouds on the mountain tops. Startled by her husband's voice calling her, she hurried upstairs, her hands covered with mud, and found him breathing painfully.

"I called and called. Couldn't you hear me?"

"I'm sorry. I couldn't."

"Stop working in the garden. I'd be dead in no time if I had to keep calling you like that. In the first place, I can't see where you are and what you're doing."

"I was in the garden. But I'll stop."

He was calmer.

"Did you hear the lark?"

That was all he had wanted to tell her. The lark sang in the nearby woods again. The woods were clear against the evening glow. Thus Kyōko learned to know the song of the lark.

"A bell will help you, won't it? How about having something you can throw until I get a bell for you?"

"Shall I throw a cup from here? That would be fun."

It was settled that Kyōko might continue her gardening; but it was after spring had come to end the long, harsh mountain winter that Kyōko thought of showing him the garden in the mirror.

The single mirror gave him inexhaustible joy, as if a lost world of fresh green had come back. It was impossible for him to see the worms she picked from the vegetables. She had to come upstairs to show him. "I can see the earthworms from here, though," he used to say as he watched her digging in the earth.

When the sun was shining into the house, Kyōko sometimes noticed a light and, looking up, discovered that her husband was reflecting the sun in the mirror. He insisted that Kyōko remake the dark-blue kimono he had used during his student days into pantaloons for herself. He seemed to enjoy the sight of Kyōko in the mirror as she worked in the garden, wearing the dark blue with its white splashes.

Kyōko worked in the garden half-conscious and half-unconscious of the fact that she was being seen. Her heart warmed to see how different her feelings were now from the very early days of her marriage. Then she had blushed even at showing her elbow when she held the smaller glass behind her head. It was, however, only when she remarried that she started making up as she pleased, released from the long years of nursing and the mourning that had followed. She saw that she was becoming remarkably beautiful. It now seemed that her husband had really meant it when he said that her body was beautiful.

Kyōko was no longer ashamed of her reflection in the mirror—after she had had a bath, for instance. She had discovered her own beauty. But she had not lost that unique feeling that her former husband had planted in her toward the beauty in the mirror. She did not doubt the beauty she saw in the mirror. Quite the reverse: she could not doubt the reality of that other world. But between her skin as she saw it and her skin as reflected in the mirror she could not find the difference that she had found between that leaden sky and the silver sky in the mirror. It may not have been only the difference in distance. Maybe the longing of her first husband confined to his bed had acted upon her. But then, there was now no way of knowing how beautiful she had looked to him in the mirror as she worked in the garden. Even before his death, Kyōko herself had not been able to tell.

Kyōko thought of, indeed longed for, the image of herself working in the garden, seen through the mirror in her husband's hand, and for the white of the lilies, the crowd of village children playing in the field, and the morning sun rising above the far-off snowy mountains—for that separate world she had shared with him. For the sake of her present husband, Kyōko suppressed this feeling, which seemed about to become an almost physical yearning, and tried to take it for something like a distant view of the celestial world.

One morning in May, Kyōko heard the singing of wild birds over the radio. It was a broadcast from a mountain near the heights where she had stayed with her first husband until his death. As had become her custom, after seeing her present husband off to work, Kyōko took the hand mirror from the drawer of the stand and reflected the clear sky. Then she gazed at her face in the mirror. She was astonished by a new discovery. She could not see her own face unless she reflected it in the mirror. One could not see one's own face. One felt one's own face, wondering if the face in the mirror was one's actual face. Kyōko was lost in thought for some time. Why had God created man's face so that he might not see it himself?

"Suppose you could see your own face, would you lose your mind? Would you become incapable of acting?"

Most probably man had evolved in such a way that he could not see his own face. Maybe dragonflies and praying mantises could see their own faces.

But then perhaps one's own face was for others to see. Did it not resemble love? As she was putting the hand mirror back in the drawer, Kyōko could not even now help noticing the odd combination of carved design and mulberry. Since the former mirror had burned with her first husband, the mirror stand might well be compared to a widow. But the hand mirror had had its advantages and disadvantages. Her husband was constantly seeing his face in it. Perhaps it was more like seeing death itself. If his death was a psychological suicide by means of a mirror, then Kyōko was the psychological murderer. Kyōko had once thought of the disadvantages of the mirror, and tried to take it from him. But he would not let her.

"Do you intend to have me see nothing? As long as I live, I want to keep loving something I can see," her husband said. He would have sacrificed his life to keep the world in the mirror. After heavy rains they would gaze at the moon through the mirror, the reflection of the moon from the pool in the garden. A moon which could hardly be called even the reflection of a reflection still lingered in Kyōko's heart.

"A sound love dwells only in a sound person." When her second husband said this, Kyōko nodded shyly, but she could not entirely agree with him. When her first husband died, Kyōko wondered what good her continence had done; but soon the continence became a poignant memory of love, a memory of days brimming with love, and her regrets quite disappeared. Probably her second husband regarded woman's love too lightly. "Why did you leave your wife, when you are such a tender-hearted man?" Kyōko would ask him. He never answered. Kyōko had married him because the elder brother of her dead husband had insisted. After four months as friends they were married. He was fifteen years older.

When she became pregnant, Kyōko was so terrified that her very face changed.

"I'm afraid. I'm afraid." She clung to her husband. She suffered intensely from morning sickness and she even became deranged. She crawled into the garden barefooted and gathered pine needles. She had her stepson carry two lunch boxes to school, both boxes filled with rice. She sat staring blankly into the mirror, thinking that she saw straight through it. She rose in the middle of night, sat on the bed, and looked into her husband's sleeping face. Assailed by terror at the knowledge that man's life is a trifle, she found herself loosening the sash of her night robe. She made as if to strangle him. The next moment she was sobbing hysterically. Her husband awoke and retied her sash gently. She shivered in the summer night.

"Trust the child in you, Kyōko." Her husband rocked her in his arms. The doctor suggested that she be hospitalized. Kyōko resisted, but was finally persuaded.

"I will go to the hospital. Please let me go first to visit my family for a few days."

Some time later her husband took her to her parents' home. The next day Kyōko slipped out of the house and went to the heights where she had lived with her first husband. It was early in September, ten days earlier than when she had moved there with him. Kyōko felt like vomiting. She was dizzy in the train and obsessed by an impulse to jump off. As the train passed the station on the heights, the crisp air brought her relief. She regained control of herself, as if the devil possessing her had gone. She stopped, bewildered, and looked at the mountains surrounding the high plateau. The outline of the blue mountains where the color was now growing darker was vivid against the sky, and she felt in them a living world. Wiping her eyes, moist with warm tears, she walked toward the house where he and she had lived. From the woods which had loomed against the rosy evening glow that day there came again the song of a lark. Someone was living in the house and a white lace curtain hung at the window upstairs. Not going too near, she gazed at the house.

"What if the child should look like you?" Startled at her own words, she turned back, warm and at peace.

NIGHTINGALE

BY Itō Einosuké

TRANSLATED BY Geoffrey Sargent

*The present work (Uguisu in Japanese) won a coveted
literary award soon after its publication in 1938 and is probably the best known
of Itō Einosuké's many stories of Japanese rural life. The author, born in the
northern city of Akita in 1903, was active for some years in Tokyo as a left-
wing literary critic before turning in 1931 to the writing of fiction. He writes
mainly of the impoverished farming people in northeastern Japan and Hokkaidō, and the series of stories with bird or animal titles (e.g., "The Owl,"
"The Crow," "The Swallow," "The Cow," "The Horse"), which he
has produced since 1937, has been widely popular. These stories are written
in a highly individual style, with speech and narrative closely intertwined,
and convey, in an amusing anecdotal form, the author's faith in the essential
goodness and simplicity of the Japanese peasant. The spoken parts, which
play a large part in Itō Einosuké's work, are in north-country dialect, and
the reader should bear in mind that the effect of this is largely lost in translation.*

*The uguisu, from which the story takes its title, is actually a bush war-
bler or mountain tit but is popularly called a Japanese nightingale because of
its melodious song.*

TOWARD evening, when the wind had dropped
and the dust had settled, a little old woman with a small cloth bundle
on her back came slowly up the street, dragging her feet wearily and
trailing loose ends of straw from the frayed heels of her sandals. After

every ten yards or so she would pause briefly, move on a few steps, and then stare intently at the front of a shop or at its signboard. She gave the impression of someone noting in amazement the changes which time had wrought in a once familiar town; or perhaps of someone searching out a strange house at which to call. On arriving before the Inspectorate of Agricultural Products—a building fronted by broad glass doors and a particularly prominent signboard—she stood motionless for an age, like a hawk hovering above a marsh, her neck strained toward the sign; and then, as if resolved at last, she stepped quickly forward and pushed back the glass doors.

"I'm from Akazawa." The black-uniformed clerk turned from his bored inspection of the street and waited for her to continue. "I want you to help me find where my daughter lives, sir."

The man leaned forward, not certain that he had heard correctly, but when the old woman went on—"They said she was at the Seifū Inn, so I came to see, but she's not there, so could you please help me find where she is, do you think?"—he broke in before she had finished: "Well, looking for people, you know—we don't do that sort of thing here. If that's what you want, you should go to the police station." He turned away to inspect the street once more.

"Oh, then this isn't the police?" The old woman cast her eyes slowly about the walls and furnishings of the room, and her face registered keen disappointment.

The police station was only two or three blocks farther up the street, but on entering it the old woman found the policemen all turned the other way, watching with evident amusement a pair who had arrived before her, and it was some time before anyone chose to look in her direction. The two people in question—one a sharp-featured woman of about fifty, the other a girl with plump cheeks and large eyes—were standing dejectedly, with bowed heads, before an officer whose hair had receded in a broad sweep from his temples. Both women wore bloomer-like work trousers, and through the side slits in the girl's a bright red undersash was visible.

"Now show us the money you stole." The girl, doing as the constable directed, reached into the folds of her sash and, after much rustling about, brought out a dirty striped-cotton purse. The constable examined the contents.

"Well, there it is. She hasn't spent a thing. Ten yen fifty sen—that's the lot, isn't it?"

He directed his question to the older woman, who nodded and gave a look as if of immense relief.

"This is a fine state of affairs, this is," continued the constable. "A mother robbed by her own daughter. A daughter robbing her own mother. You, young woman, you've gone too far. But you too"—addressing the mother—"isn't it time you stopped turning your daughter's husbands out of the house? Well? . . ."

He paused, but the mother offered no reply, managing to convey by her silence that, so far as that matter was concerned, she had her reasons. The policeman at the reception desk now intervened. His body was twisted around in his chair, and his ruddy-complexioned face was twisted yet further around on his shoulders, to enable him to view the scene.

"Hi!" he shouted, "How many sons-in-law have you thrown out now?"

When this produced only a long silence he put his question again, this time to the daughter.

"How many husbands have you had thrown out?"

The girl raised her eyes a moment to look at her mother, but quickly lowered them and stared once more at the floor.

"The last was the fifth," she whispered.

"What! The fifth! Five husbands at your age? That's no joke, I should say."

The policeman's gaze swept back around the room and came to rest upon the face of the old woman, who was standing directly before his desk. At once, as if at a sudden recollection of urgent business, he started writing something on a sheet of paper.

"Turned out five sons-in-law, eh?" resumed the first, the balding policeman. "What on earth makes you do it? If you intend to try any more of that sort of thing we certainly can't let your daughter go back home with you just like this. Stealing your purse is bad enough, but who knows what she might do next? Supposing she set the house on fire? What do you intend to do about it, then? Are you going to turn out any more? Well . . . are you?"

The mother was clearly shaken by the policeman's bullying tone.

She started to wipe her hands nervously with a piece of damp cloth. Her hands were black with grime, as if she had come straight from some sort of work in the fields.

"Yes, sir; I see, sir," she said. "I don't think I'll do it again." She spoke in a half-hearted mumble, keeping her sullen eyes glued to the floor.

"Don't think? That's not much good," said the policeman standing at her side, the patrolman who had brought the two women in. "If that's the best you can say, when it comes down to it you'll do it again, just the same as before."

Having administered this rebuke he turned to the daughter:

"You, now. How do you feel about that husband? Do you want him badly?"

The girl made no reply, but grew red in the face.

The policeman repeated his question: "Well, do you want him or don't you?" This time the girl nodded, very faintly, and the policeman turned at once to the mother.

"This money business is settled now," he said, "but that's not the important thing. You'll have to take your son-in-law back. Is that agreed? Well . . . is it?"

"Yes, I see," the woman said simply; but the policeman, observing in her face traces of some strong emotion which suggested she was far from convinced, now abruptly changed his tone and started shouting at her angrily.

"Look here! That's enough lip service! You can't go on and on—just because you're a widow—turning your daughter's husbands out of the house! You're old enough to know better. It's all very well wanting the youngster for yourself, but there's a limit. Tell me the truth. Are you really going to make it up with that last husband?"

At this point the young woman, her eyes filling with tears as memories of her dismissed husbands came crowding back upon her, burst suddenly into loud, convulsive sobs. Everyone turned in surprise and looked at her. She wept on unabashed, her mouth wide open, and in a matter of seconds her face was drenched in tears, which spurted from her eyes as if from a fountain.

"What on earth's the matter now?" The examining officer rose from his seat, turned his back to the girl, conversed briefly with the policeman at the reception desk, who was still immersed in his writing, and then walked aimlessly about the far end of the room with a disgusted look on his face.

"Mothers or daughters, there's not much to choose between them. Look here, you!" He approached the girl and pushed her on the shoulder. "That husband meant a lot to you, I dare say, but you can go too far with all this blubbering and stealing purses."

Still the young woman wept noisily. The mother, who had been distracted at the thought of her only daughter's love being taken from her by a son-in-law, now seemed for the first time to emerge from her trance. She patted her daughter on the shoulder.

"What is it, my dear?" she said soothingly. "Really, you know, in front of all these gentlemen. . . ."

The district patrolman, on being called to the woman's house to investigate the disappearance from a drawer of a purse containing ten yen, had found no signs of forced entry. He had known, moreover, that the woman, since losing her husband while still in the prime of her life, had been subject to violent fits of jealousy over her daughter, and had driven from the house a long succession of adopted sons-in-law, the latest being a particularly steady and respected young man called Naokura; and in view of this he had decided to question the daughter. He had found her working in the fields and, her answers to his questions proving evasive, had brought both women straight to the police station, where the examination had shown that his suspicions were correct. The thief was the daughter. She had stolen the money to suggest to her mother the insecurity of a house without a man, to get the dismissed Naokura recalled.

A door swung open noisily and the superintendent appeared, ready to go off duty. The policemen sprang to their feet, as if jerked upright by invisible strings, and saluted stiffly.

"What's all this crying? If you've given them a talking to, send them home," said the superintendent. He made as if to approach the crying girl, thought better of it, and walked out into the street. At once everyone appeared to relax. The policemen going off duty, chatting idly, started preparing to leave.

"Now, ma'am, you understand, don't you?" said the balding policeman, who took charge of all criminal matters. "And you, too, young woman. No matter how badly you miss your husband, this stealing and such-like has to stop. If you understand, you can go."

Hanging their heads, the two women moved toward the door. Constable Wakamatsu, the inspection officer, gazed idly after them as they went.

"I wish I had a way with the women," he said, tidying the things on his desk, "like that girl's husband seems to've had."

This gave rise to a discussion about which of the station staff had the greatest sex appeal.

"Whatever you say," said Constable Miyoshi, the military service officer, "Tange Sazen is the desperado the girls admire."

Miyoshi's left eyebrow and eyelid were marked by a scar. While angling for trout the previous summer he had slipped on a smooth, mossy rock, breaking his glasses, and because of the red scar that had formed when the wound healed, like some brand burned into his flesh to proclaim his overindulgence in fishing, his associates had secretly dubbed him Tange Sazen, after the celebrated murderer. One purpose of his remark was to let it be known that he was aware of this nickname.

"It's no good," said the balding criminal-affairs officer. "People like you and me don't stand a chance against the youngsters." He turned to gaze in ironic admiration at Constable Kobayashi, a young man fresh from the training depot. "Now, if only the 'ko' was knocked off his name, Kobayashi Chōjirō would certainly be our number-one glamor boy." He enjoyed his joke loudly.

"True, true," laughed the military-service officer. "If we had film-star Hayashi Chōjirō here, I should be only second best."

He raised his head as he laughed and, looking straight before him, noticed the old woman, who had seated herself on a bench before the reception desk. While waiting for the reception clerk to look her way, she had been overtaken by a sudden drowsiness and had dropped off to sleep.

The policeman called across to her. "Now, my old dear, what can I do for you?" At the sound of his voice she forced open bleared eyes and blinked vaguely about her for a few moments.

"Oh, I . . . I wanted some help to find my daughter," she said. Rising slowly to her feet she moved forward and pressed her face close to the handrail running along the rim of the reception desk. She was short, and only her eyes and the top of her head were visible. Constable Miyoshi, who, in addition to dealing with military-service matters, was the officer for general consultations, had a flair for listening sympathetically to the most trivial problems, and he now got down to business at once, speaking with genuine kindliness.

"Your daughter, eh? Has she run away from home?" he asked.

"Well, no; she was taken away by someone when she was ten years old, you see . . ." and the old woman started to tell her daughter's story. The old woman's name was Kin, and this daughter, Yoshié, was really an adopted child. Kin had decided upon adoption when she was past thirty and had lost hope of ever having a child of her own; but finding someone willing to offer a son or a daughter to a poor household like Kin's, where she and her husband earned the meagerest of livings as charcoal makers, had been no easy matter, and in the end Kin had been obliged to take in the bastard daughter of a woman called Sugi, a seller of dried seaweed, who came on business into that rather remote and mountainous locality once every five days. Sugi had been delivered of the child while her husband was away working in Matsumaé, and she had brought it to Kin's house very soon after the twenty-first day, carrying it all the way herself, strapped to her back. So to Kin, who had been fervently praying for a child for all these years, the girl Yoshié had seemed from the very beginning exactly like her own baby. And then, one day in autumn, when she was ten, Yoshié had suddenly disappeared. The village was searched in vain. Parties were sent out into the nearby mountains, directed by the divinations of a fortuneteller whom Kin consulted, but they discovered no trace of the missing girl. Then it was reported that someone had seen Yoshié going off with a woman who was possibly the seaweed seller, and Kin and her husband went at once to the woman's home, where there was a heated argument. Sugi, however, perhaps because her husband was present, stubbornly maintained she had no idea what girl they were talking about—that she had never even seen her—and the argument produced nothing. Some time later a rumor came to Kin's ears that Sugi had sold the girl to a traveling circus troupe which had passed through her town shortly after Yoshié's disappearance. In the years that followed, Kin had never been able to forget Yoshié. If ever there was a circus encamped in any of the towns at which she and her husband chanced to call when they brought charcoal down from the mountains, Kin would somehow find the money for a ticket, and she would sit in breathless attention throughout the performance, hoping against hope to catch a glimpse of her Yoshié. But no one in the least like Yoshié had ever appeared.

"Now, let me see," said Constable Miyoshi at this point, breaking into Kin's story, "would the husband of this seaweed-selling woman be a fellow called Kintarō? A horse dealer?"

Kin looked up in amazement. "Yes, that's right, sir. She was Kintarō's wife. But how do you know about Kintarō, sir?"

The constable made no reply to this question, but went on as if talking to himself, seemingly absorbed in recollections of the dim past. "If that's the case," he said, "I've seen that daughter of yours."

Fifteen or sixteen years back, when Miyoshi had been stationed in a neighboring division of the prefecture on his very first assignment in the police force, he had become involved in a squabble concerning a girl member of a circus troupe that had just arrived in town. The man who claimed at that time to be the girl's father had been, he could clearly remember, the horse dealer Kintarō, now deceased. Not only the girl's foster mother Kin, it seemed, but her real mother Sugi, had been watching out for the reappearance of this particular troupe; and Sugi—though it was difficult to know exactly what her feelings were in the matter—had, with better luck than Kin, managed to see the girl again. Her husband Kintarō had formerly been a day laborer, but when things were bad and his earnings had sunk below the level required for three square meals a day, he had switched to horse dealing, in which trade—with the help of the little capital provided by the sale of Yoshié—he had, in the optimistic tradition of horse dealers, assumed that he would soon make himself a fortune. But his various schemes had met with disaster, with the result, among other things, that he had been unable to buy Yoshié back.

His story was that the girl had been sold by Sugi for a mere thirty yen, which was not much more than the price of a cat; and when Constable Miyoshi heard this, being new to his job and anxious to win himself laurels by some startling feat, he had exclaimed in indignation at the idea of buying a human being at such a price, cruelly deceiving a poor, ignorant countrywoman, and he had gone so far as to say that the least the circus manager could do, if he wished to stay out of jail, would be to return the girl at once, together with a fair sum of money as compensation. Unfortunately the avaricious Kintarō had seized upon this suggestion only too readily, first of all proposing a hundred yen as a suitable recompense, then raising it gradually to two hundred, and finally insisting upon three hundred, at which point Constable Miyoshi had washed his hands of the affair and told the horse dealer, if he wanted to be that greedy, to settle things by himself. But Kintarō's impudence had been no match for that of the circus manager. That man had turned the tables on him, insisting that he would return the girl only if he, the circus manager, were given three hundred yen as compensation for his trouble in keeping and training her; and so Kintarō had come away with neither the money nor the girl.

"So you were the one who brought that girl up, eh? Is she still doing circus work?" asked Constable Miyoshi, recalling as he spoke, a girl in a flimsy green dress, her face thickly powdered, regarding him with dull, listless eyes. But the old woman Kin apparently had no idea what her daughter was doing now. After some years she had heard that Yoshié had run away from the circus troupe and was working at a textile factory in Shizuoka Prefecture; then, after a further lapse of years, news had somehow drifted her way that Yoshié was living with a man who worked at a cotton mill, and that she had a child. Just recently Kin had heard from a dry-goods salesman who visited her village about a woman with a child who was working in this town as a maid at the Seifū Inn. When she had questioned the man more closely she had learned that the woman seemed to have moved recently from somewhere in the midlands, and, when asked about her relatives, the woman had said she knew only a foster mother and was not sure whether she was dead or alive. From all this Kin had concluded that the woman must be Yoshié. She did not know what Yoshié intended, but even if she could not get her to return to her old foster mother, at all events she had to see her, just once. So Kin had come here today, no easy journey at her age, and had discovered that the woman was indeed Yoshié. But she had not seen her. Yoshié had stayed only two months at the inn, leaving again with her child at about the time the snows had started to melt, and no one knew where she had gone.

The off-duty policemen had all left by this time, and the room had grown quiet. A single electric light shone down dimly on the antiquated chairs and desks.

"Well, if we make inquiries, we should find her," said Miyoshi, "but it will take a day or two, you know. Where is it you live?"

He looked up in surprise when Kin said she was from Akazawa. "What? Do you mean to say you've walked from Akazawa?"

The place was some thirty miles distant, in the mountains. Added to this, Kin told him that she had no relatives or acquaintances of any kind in this neighborhood; but when he suggested that she stay overnight at a cheap lodginghouse, the old woman shrank back toward the bench as if he had threatened her.

"Whatever next!" she cried, with unexpected vehemence. "It would be wicked, paying good money to sleep at a lodginghouse. Please, just let me stay where I am until morning." She made no move to go.

Miyoshi disappeared into the night-duty room. Returning a little later, he found the old woman still standing by the bench. She was taking various articles from her cloth bundle, apparently preparing to sleep where she was, but the constable led her, much against her will, to the night-duty room. When she saw the room she drew back at once.

"Oh no, really," she said. "I've never slept on a nice matted floor like that in all my life. The wooden boards back there will do me just as well."

Eventually, however, when the policemen started opening up the supper boxes their wives had brought them, she advanced hesitantly into the room and began to untie her own bundle. Two eggplants tumbled out, rolling smoothly over the yellowing straw mats, and the old woman pursued them fussily as if she were chasing escaped chickens.

"Would any of you gentlemen care for one?" she asked, as she retrieved them.

"Well, thanks all the same, old lady, but we've got plenty. Keep them for yourself," said Miyoshi. Glancing up he saw that, with wrinkled, dirt-lined hands, she was picking at a hash of millet, cold boiled rice, and bean paste, folded in a wrapper of bamboo bark.

"Here, you try a bit of this instead," he said, holding out the round lid of his own chinaware supper box, on which were set several morsels of soy-flavored turbot.

"On dear, no," protested the old woman, keeping her hands where they were. "After getting you to put me up for the night I can't take your food too." At that moment a strange, choking noise sounded in her throat, and she stared straight ahead, her bleary eyes suddenly tense.

"What's the matter, old girl?" The policemen were alarmed. Kin hiccupped.

"It's nothing," she said. "My stomach's a bit queer, that's all." She sat holding a ball of rice in her hand, making no further move to raise it to her mouth.

The night drew on. The old woman had dropped off to sleep, snoring loudly, and the policemen, squatting on the floor at her side, were playing checkers. The station's detective officer, who had been on duty in the other room, called to them, passing by on his way to the toilet.

"We've got him!" he said. "The poultry thief!" At this the policemen hurriedly slipped on their jackets and, fastening the buttons as they went, trooped out to look. In the custody of the constable from a village three miles down the road stood a surprisingly tall, vacant-looking farm laborer. The case was no direct concern of Constable Miyoshi's, but he had often heard Yajima, the officer for penal offenses, grumbling about it: poultry had been disappearing at an alarming rate, from villages all over the district, for three or four months now; and in all this time the thief had managed somehow to escape arrest.

"Is this the man, then? The poultry thief?" he asked, gazing up at the lanky rustic overtopping him by a head. At the same moment he noticed another man, a short, dumpy fellow who looked like some sort of day laborer, standing to the rear of the village constable.

"Yes, this is the man who's been taking them all. But while he was out stealing chickens . . ." Constable Sasaki turned and glanced behind him. "Hey, you! It's no good trying to hide yourself!" He pulled a muffler away from the short man's face. "While he was out stealing chickens, this fellow was passing the time with his missus. What do we do about it?" He put the question to Miyoshi, who was his senior.

Until lately the lanky Kisuké had enjoyed a spotless reputation. He had never even been suspected of filching a sheaf of rice. But his earnings as a hired man on wretchedly small farm holdings had begun to seem hardly worth the trouble, and when faced recently with expenses for his mother's funeral and for the support of a newborn child, he had began stealing chickens to help out—just two or three fowl on isolated occasions at first, but in time it had become a habit, so that he was out stealing or selling chickens practically every night. Naturally the neighbors had grown suspicious, and, being sensitive to their remarks, Kisuké had at length stayed away completely from his own house. Deciding finally that, with things as bad as they were, he might as well take his wife and child with him and leave the district altogether, he had slipped back home tonight, after an absence of forty days, to carry out his plan. The hour was late and people everywhere were asleep, but from within his own house he had heard the sound of a man's voice. Turning aside into the garden and peering through a knothole in the drawn shutters, he had caught a glimpse of a face in profile and recognized it as that of Izumiya, formerly a railway laborer in the village over beyond the bridge, but now a gang leader in agricultural assistance work. Kisuké, even without this, was already overexcited, having hurried back in feverish anticipation of the joys of homecoming, and his immediate impulse had been to rush in and beat the life out of the man—but if he was to catch him, he had at once reflected, he might as well catch him in the act: so he had sat himself down in the dark to watch and wait.

"Do you admit this—about you and Kisuké's wife?" asked Miyoshi, turning to Izumiya.

"Whether he admits it or not," said Kisuké, assuming an expression of solemn righteousness, as if he had come to the police station expressly to complain of this very matter, "I saw it, with my own eyes. Saw it plain and jumped in on him. Saw it plain"—he asserted once more—"with my own eyes."

At this point Constable Wakamatsu returned from the toilet.

"Did you, then?" he shouted at Kisuké. "And I suppose you didn't see yourself stealing chickens?"

In contrast with the lanky Kisuké, whose pallor was probably the result of malnutrition and who seemed already resigned to his fate, the round-cheeked, plump little Izumiya was clearly anxious about what was to come, and the beadlike eyes in his swarthy face gleamed with apprehension. After suffering a merciless hiding from Kisuké, who had burst in from the rear of the house without a moment's warning, Izumiya had run off, dazed and mortified, toward the local policeman's house, shouting "The poultry thief! The poultry thief!" and yelping like a whipped dog; then, on returning boldly behind the policeman to glory in Kisuké's downfall, he had suffered the further discomfiture of hearing the arrested man calmly register a formal complaint against him.

"You must write an apology," said Constable Miyoshi.

"Oh, is that all you need, then?" said Izumiya, his expression brightening at once.

Kisuké, however, looked utterly amazed. "Here!" he protested. "Isn't this wretch going to be charged?"

"The one who ought to be charged," said the constable, "is you. If you hadn't left your wife alone to starve, this would never have happened!"

Kisuké looked suddenly dispirited and said no more. With everyone in the village talking about her husband's misdeeds, Kisuké's wife had soon found it impossible even to borrow a bowlful of rice from a neighbor, and it was in these straits that she had yielded to the smooth-tongued Izumiya, who had apparently promised her a job in agricultural assistance work.

"What sort of thing shall I write?" asked Izumiya, turning his diminutive round eyes on Constable Miyoshi, and taking up a pen.

"First of all," said the constable, "you write 'Guarantee.' "

"Is that the address?" asked Izumiya earnestly.

"Blockhead!" thundered the local policeman. "A guarantee's a promise! You have to promise you won't misbehave again. That's the regulation."

Izumiya was thoroughly abashed, and his next remark was spoken in a low whisper.

"But, you see," he said, "fellows like me, with no education, can't very well write complicated things like this . . . ."

Constable Miyoshi wrote out the guarantee for him, and Izumiya, having pressed his thumbprint on the document and bowed obsequi-ously to all the officers, withdrew toward the door.

"And if you do it again, you wretch,"—suddenly roused to a fury, Kisuké thrust his unwieldy form across the room after the disappear-ing Izumiya—"I'll damn well murder you!"

Izumiya, who was by this time just beyond the street entrance, whirled around defiantly and, like a beaten small boy calling names and making faces from a safe distance, shouted back: "Yah, dirty thief! I don't give a damn for a fellow like you! I never want to see your ugly face again! D'ya hear me?"

Kisuké, not to be outdone, was about to improve on this when Con-stable Wakamatsu intervened. "Get home, you fool," he bellowed at Izumiya. "You'll say too much!" And Izumiya promptly vanished.

When Miyoshi returned to the night-duty room, having first lodged Kisuké in the detention cell, the old woman Kin, who lay huddled in a corner beneath a padded quilt, was making noises that sounded like stifled moans.

"What is it, old girl?" he called across, as he poured hot water into an earthenware pot to make tea.

"It's nothing. Just pains in my stomach—I've always suffered from them," she replied; and at once she fell quiet. Presently, in the still darkness, coming from somewhere in the direction of the cell at the far end of the cement passageway which separated the night-duty room from the caretaker's lobby, there sounded the clucking of a hen. The old woman, apparently too exhausted by her stomach pains even to sleep, stirred beneath the quilt.

"My!" she said, without raising her head or turning it from the wall. "So you keep hens, too—even in the police station!"

Two or three days ago a young man of eighteen, a farm hand em-ployed by one of the leading families in a neighboring village, had spent a night in the detention cell. The young man had lately, for want of money, been obliged to discontinue his visits to a certain girl in one of the town's bawdyhouses, and on that night, unable to contain himself longer, he had grabbed three of his employer's chickens, stuffed them quickly into a basket, not even stopping to secure their legs, and carried them straight off to town. But, while hurrying toward a butcher's shop with the basket slung across one shoulder, he had suddenly noticed a policeman on patrol duty coming directly toward him down the street. Checking a rash impulse to turn and flee down a side alley—behavior which he realized would have been altogether too suspicious—he had walked boldly on past the policeman, luckily not a man of experience in these matters, and was just heaving a sigh of relief when the birds in the basket had started to cluck. He had been stopped at once and taken to the police station. There, while he was being questioned, the hens had broken loose and wandered idly about beneath desks and chairs, and when the policeman at last noticed this, after finishing his brief ten-line report, and tried to get them back into the basket, the hens had shown a desperate determination to avoid recapture, as if convinced that this time, with no shadow of doubt, they were to be sold to the butcher. After fluttering wildly from desk to desk in the office they had scampered through an open door into the superintendent's room, jumping up on the table used for entertaining visitors. The whole night staff had turned out to join in the hunt, leaving the thief to look after himself, but, even so, one of the birds, a white Leghorn, had slipped past them into the corridor and, reaching the open space between the caretaker's lobby and the wash house, had disappeared into the night. No one had seen it since. Constable Miyoshi, feeling certain in his own mind that the noise he had just heard was that same bird still loitering about somewhere outside, went out toward the cell to investigate, and as he did so a further series of clucks greeted him from the darkness at the end of the passage. The owner of the voice, however, was no hen. It was the newly arrested poultry thief, Kisuké.

"What's all this?" Miyoshi shouted indignantly. "You in there, this is no place for making stupid noises!"

"But the constable asked me." Kisuké's aggrieved voice floated out from the blackness of the boxlike cell. "The constable himself said to make a noise like a hen."

The policeman assigned to duty at the door of the cell turned to Miyoshi. "That's right, sir," he said. "I told him to do it. According to what he says, it's imitating the cluck that's the secret in stealing hens. I was just investigating, trying to find out what sort of noise it was."

Kisuké had been telling him that the only sure method in stealing hens was to creep up close to a bird, clucking expertly all the while, and then, in one movement, seize it and wring its neck. That way, it seemed, the bird never got away and never even scratched you.

At this moment there was a sound of voices at the front entrance, and Constable Miyoshi hurried back to the office to find a group of policemen gathered around a solitary dejected-looking woman. Her hair, bound backward and upward in the Shimada style, was badly mussed and disheveled, but there was nevertheless a certain professional elegance about her appearance. She wore a muslin kimono of a bold checked pattern, topped by a black neckpiece, and was carrying a samisen. Miyoshi summed her up at a glance as some sort of strolling entertainer.

"What is it? What's that woman here for?" he called out from across the room; and then, moving nearer, he noticed a face he recognized, the face of a man called Sakutarō, peeping out from behind the back of Constable Kobayashi, the officer who had brought the woman in.

"You here again?" he bawled at the man. "Have you seduced this one, too?"

Sakutarō had given the police, at various times, a great deal of trouble on matters pertaining to women, and Miyoshi remembered his face only too well. Sakutarō beat a big drum while his wife sang, and together they went the rounds of the local villages begging for money. Until the autumn of the previous year they had based themselves in this town, where they had rented a house. At about that time, however, on a visit to a town some thirty miles distant, the customary terminus of their man-and-wife singing tours, they had met up with another group in the same line of trade, and while traveling in company with these fellow artistes (both groups having decided that business would be better for all concerned if they joined forces and made one big, noisy party), Sakutarō had formed an intimate relationship with a girl named Sayo in the other troupe. His wife had caught them together one night, and had raised no end of a commotion, but Sakutarō was not the man to resign himself easily to defeat, and finally he and the girl had run away together to a distant part of the prefecture. Sakutarō's wife and the girl's uncle had then come to the police to request a search, and before long, thanks largely to the pains of Constable Miyoshi, the runaway couple had been returned. The girl was severely lectured and then handed over at once to her uncle, but Sakutarō, before being dismissed, was locked in the cell for a night. Within an hour from the time of his release the next morning, however, Sakutarō had come running back to the station in a state of great agitation.

"What is it now?" Miyoshi had chaffed him. "Do you want another spell in the lockup?"

Sakutarō had feigned alarm at this. "That's only a joke, officer, isn't it?" he had said, cringing. "You see, something awful has happened."

On returning to his house, it seemed, Sakutarō had found the place stripped bare. His wife, and everything from the furniture to the implements of their trade, was gone; and now he had come to ask for police assistance in tracing the woman.

"So this time it's your wife we're asked to look for, is it? Do you think the police force has nothing better to do all day than chase after you and your wife?" Constable Miyoshi, heartily sick of the business, had refused to help, and Sakutarō had soon afterward shut up his house and had apparently, ever since, been moving about from one cheap lodginghouse to the next.

"That's right," said Constable Kobayashi. "The fellow's back to his old games. Picked this woman up. Thought he'd seduce her. But . . ." Constable Kobayashi, who was fresh from the training depot and had lately, with admirable thoroughness, been reporting everything from a bicycle without lights to a public urination, now assumed an expression of intense seriousness, saluted his senior colleague Miyoshi, and continued: ". . . the thing is, this woman's a man. I found them together at a lodginghouse, in the course of my patrol, and brought them in."

Miyoshi looked at the woman. The skin on her face and neck was hidden beneath a thick layer of powder, but the bushiness of the eyebrows and a certain directness in her gaze did seem somehow more appropriate to a male. The hips, too, were surprisingly narrow.

"So this is a man, eh? Hi, you! Lift those skirts a bit and let's see your legs."

The woman fidgeted about, pleading with her eyes to be spared this indignity.

"Come on, pull them up!" Constable Wakamatsu now intervened, rising from his desk. Seeing the look of obstinacy on the woman's face, however, he took an abacus from a nearby desk, and with this quickly lifted up the skirt himself. A thick, hairy skin was revealed. The man in female guise clutched at the disordered skirts in a flutter of coquettish modesty and gave a little shriek.

"Now really"—the voice was shrill and feminine—"whatever are you gentlemen doing?"

Miyoshi was taken aback. "Well, listen to that! Are you sure this is a man?" he queried.

The same momentary doubt was clearly registered on the faces of his colleagues.

"Hi, let's hear some more like that," urged Constable Wakamatsu. "Speak in that womanish voice again."

But the ambiguous person stood silent with downcast eyes. Constable Kobayashi took the abacus from Wakamatsu's hand.

"Where," he cried, delivering a resounding and well-timed blow with the flat of the implement, "would you find a woman with breasts as hard as this?"

His surprised victim tottered backward and fell to the floor. Constable Wakamatsu tugged roughly at a sleeve of the man's kimono.

"And how did you get hold of these woman's clothes?" he demanded. "Pinched 'em?"

Still the bogus woman made no reply but fumbled fussily with the material at the base of one sleeve, where a seam had split. The hand was delicate, like a woman's, but the wrist, peeping out from the edge of the yellow sleeve, was decidedly large-boned.

"Well, that's as you say, I suppose," said Miyoshi, turning now to look at Sakutarō. "But what's this other fellow done?"

Constable Kobayashi resumed his posture of stiff formality.

"Ha. This fellow, of course, is a fellow having a relationship with the person masquerading as a woman, and I found him in heated argument with that person at a cheap lodginghouse near Sengen Temple and brought him in."

All this was delivered in one breath. Then: "Hi, you! Come here!" he shouted, and he pulled the man forward. Sakutarō, his hair thinning and his skin burned almost black—both conditions the result of his restless, year-round wanderings up and down country roads—was painfully embarrassed, and he gazed with apprehension at Constable Miyoshi, whom he had given so much trouble in times past.

"Where and when did you fall in with this person?" he was asked.

"It was this evening, sir," he replied. "We met at Iwasaki."

The two of them had walked back together to the town after that, singing and begging from door to door as they went, had done a further round of the gay quarters in town, and then, late at night, had put up at a cheap lodginghouse, where they had drawn their hard, wafer-thin mattresses together and lain down side by side like man and wife. So far all had gone smoothly; but Sakutarō, utterly woman-starved since the decampment of his outraged wife after that last unfortunate affair, had even at this late stage failed to observe the truth about his partner. And, out of the warmth of his feelings, he had not only treated her this evening to a bowl of rice and fried prawns, but had even, when she complained of having no money for face powder, allowed himself to be wheedled out of the whole of his day's takings.

"You damned swine!" he had shouted in his moment of disillusion-ment. "Give me back that money!"

But his companion had been stubborn—what had been given, she said, was given to keep—and before long the quarrel had roused the whole house, and a toffee vender, a clog repairer, and a hawker of drugs had joined in, protesting vigorously against this disturbance of their night's repose.

It was just at this moment that Constable Kobayashi had come by on his patrol. On reaching the otherwise deeply stilled neighborhood of Sengen Temple and hearing the angry shouts emerging from this lodginghouse, he had been prompted to investigate at once, and what had particularly roused his curiosity was the fact that earlier this year, at the time of the snows, he had run across a similar sort of disturbance at this house. It had been at this very hour, and the culprit on that occasion, grown wild and disorderly with drink, had been one of those begging priests who walk about playing a bamboo pipe. Kobayashi had been horrified at what he had seen on forcing his way into that room. The priest was grappling furiously with the toffee vender, who was attempting to restrain him from further drunken violence, and on seeing the constable he had stumbled across to embrace him, fixing him with glassy, befuddled eyes, and had wailed sorrowfully and incoherently: "Constable, ah Constable, haven't touched a drop for years. Not for years. Is this a divine punishment, Constable, for drink-again after all these years? Ah, Constable, Constable."

The money he had spent on the saké had been an allowance for his child's funeral. His wife, who was lying on a mattress, still suffering from the aftereffects of her recent confinement, had a moment before been hurling venomous abuse at her drink-sodden husband, but now, with a vacant expression on her pallid, sickly features, as if she had completely forgotten the cause of all this commotion, she was gazing fixedly at a sliding door, where the paper had been torn in the recent scuffle. Close by her pillow, however, in an orange crate before which there burned a single half-ounce offering candle, lay her child, born less than half a month ago, and dead since yesterday. According to the toffee vender's account, this now drunk and incapable priest, having no money to bury his child, had gone in tears to the district welfare man to plead for help, and as a result had received a grant of five yen from the Town Office. But he had come home swinging a half-pint bottle of saké in one hand, which, though little enough in itself, had been quickly augmented by a pint bottle and then by a quart bottle; and when he had finished them all off and was in a most exhilarated frame of mind, his wife had started to cry, saying how could they ever send the child to the cemetery now that all the money had been drunk, and he had shouted "If it hadn't been for you lazing about in bed all day, the child would never have got ill!" and had shaken and kicked her so violently that the toffee vender, unable to bear the sight any longer, had rushed to the woman's rescue. The next morning, after a night in the cell, the priest had been brought before the super-intendent. In the days before drink and women had ruined him, it turned out, he had been the resident curate of a small branch temple. "And what," the superintendent had exclaimed before dismissing him, "do you think of a temple priest who can't even bury his own child?" "Ah, I don't know what to say," the man had replied, as he backed toward the door, pale and heavy-eyed, almost doubling himself up in apology. "I don't often see a wad of money like that nowadays, you see, and I just lost my head. It's unforgivable."

Memories of that affair had been in Constable Kobayashi's mind as he had rushed in to investigate this second disturbance. At his entry

Sakutarō, seeing that it was the police, had at once stopped his shouting.

"It's nothing, officer," he had said, composing himself. "This woman here made some remark I couldn't understand, and then she started a row. That's all."

But the woman, seated on the flimsy mattress and now hastily rearranging her dress, was showing considerable agitation, and while Kobayashi was eyeing her suspiciously, the toffee vender, who had as usual been seeing all that he could, had sidled up to him.

"Constable, Constable," he had whispered confidentially, bobbing his glistening, prematurely bald head up and down in an obsequious manner and assuming the expression of one about to render a great service, "that's a Kabuki actor. A female impersonator."

"Hi, you! You're a man, are you?" Kobayashi had demanded.

But there had been no reply. The person on the mattress, readjusting a disarrayed neckline with meticulous care, had silently fixed the officer with the sulky stare of a woman wronged. Young Kobayashi had experienced a moment of panic, during which he stood rooted helplessly to the floor, but, with sudden resolve, he had thrust a hand inside the person's kimono, in the region of the breast. And, sure enough, it was a man.

"Do you still pretend you're a woman, then?" he had shouted, feeling considerably relieved. "You come along with me to the station."

"Hi, come over here!" Constable Kobayashi moved across to his own desk, took out his notebook, and began a leisurely interrogation, making notes as he proceeded. "When did you start dressing up like this? . . ."

It was much as the toffee vender had said. The man had formerly been an actor of female parts, going by the stage name of Kawakami Yoshio, in the "New Kabuki" troupe of Hanamura Masao, which had done a tour of the northeast on foot some two or three years past. It had been at a time of depression for farming people, and the company had broken up after a series of disastrous failures—whereupon Kawakami Yoshio, stranded in the wilderness, had exploited his dramatic gifts and training off-stage, walking from village to village in the guise of a female entertainer, complete with samisen and dancing kimono. He had done well by comparison with the ordinary kind of strolling beggar, but circumstances had obliged him to engage as a side line in the risky business of flaunting his charms and wheedling money out of male admirers. For the poisonous white powder with which he habitually plastered himself in order to conceal his sex from the public had unfortunately worked itself into his system, and life had lately come to seem intolerable without morphine.

"And you"—Constable Kobayashi turned banteringly to Sakutarō —"what technique did you use in attempting to seduce this woman? A demonstration, please!"

Sakutarō looked as if he had just stepped on a pile of cow dung. When they told him he could go, he merely pursed his lips, and continued to loiter about.

"Look here," he said at last, "I'm not going till you get that fellow to give me back my money."

But Kawakami Yoshio had already spent it on morphine, and they could find nothing in his purse except a solitary brass sen.

"That's a just punishment," Sakutarō was told, "for being too sexy." And, glumly scratching his sparsely covered head, he shuffled away.

In the small, old-fashioned station building, where the only room of any distinction was the superintendent's private office, there was considerable confusion and overcrowding during the remainder of that strangely eventful night. The old woman Kin, who had passed the whole time in the night-duty room, left at about seven, her ceaseless moaning having effectively deprived Constable Miyoshi of all rest. Again and again she had risen to go to the toilet, and each time, on returning, she had settled herself down for no more than a few moments before stirring and departing once more. It was clearly a case of severe diarrhea, with violent stomach pains, and Miyoshi, kept awake by her sounds of distress, had at one time half risen from his mattress and called across: "Here, old lady, if it hurts that much shall I fetch a doctor?"

But the old woman had scorned the idea. "It's nothing," she had answered. "I'm used to these stomach-aches. Sometimes they go on for four or five days. And as for calling a doctor, the bills finish you off quicker than the disease."

Miyoshi rose at dawn, and Kin rose too, with much fussing and rustling, and started preparing at once for the journey back.

"Hold hard, old lady, are you going to walk back on an empty stomach? Will you be all right?"

But Miyoshi's concern was wasted on Kin, whose will, for all the weakness of her flesh, was of manly strength.

"I'll be all right," she said. "So do what you can, please, to find Yoshié. I'll come again."

She folded her cloth wrapper about the remains of the millet and boiled rice, fastened the bundle across her shoulders with a cord, and left. The interrogation of the bogus woman had proved a fairly simple matter, and soon after the superintendent arrived a written report was ready for his inspection, but in the case of the poultry thief it was clear that little headway could be expected, no matter how many hours the penal officer devoted to his task. The number of chickens stolen ran into several hundreds, and Kisuké, who had never taken more than one from one place, found it impossible to recall each individual house he had robbed. The first twenty or thirty he managed to identify smoothly enough, but for every case after that the sieve-memoried Kisuké would mumble "Well, let me see, what house might that be? . . . what day was that, I wonder?" and lean his head sideways for interminable periods of vacant, open-mouthed silence.

Miyoshi was worrying, in a vague and drowsy way, about Kin—had she collapsed, perhaps, somewhere along the road?—and was stifling yawn after yawn as he listened at the same time to the vapid, painfully slow replies of Kisuké immediately behind him, when a gentleman in a dark-blue jacket entered the room and bowed with stiff formality before the reception desk. Miyoshi, glancing at the title of "Junior School Instructor" on the card handed him by the reception clerk, rose to attend to the visitor.

"Please, please," he said, "come this way."

The owner of the card, Onozaki, rose and slowly approached.

"The fact is," he began, after a brief bow, "one of my girl pupils is being sold as a factory hand, and is due to leave on the next south-bound express. I've just come from seeing her at the railway station. It didn't look" he continued, with signs of annoyance, "as if I had any chance of stopping things by myself, so I hoped someone might come along with me and talk to them."

"Much obliged, sir," said Miyoshi, accepting the information as if it had been offered with no other purpose than to assist the police in their efforts to suppress this sort of traffic. "Very good of you, taking the trouble to let us know. Fujioka!"—he turned to one of his subordinates—"get along quickly to the station with this gentleman."

The two men had scarcely gone before another visitor arrived, a woman of forty in a serge kimono, with her hair bound tightly back, and with the ample girth of a Sumo wrestler. Judging by the way she puffed and panted, and by the redness of her face, she had walked no little distance to get here. It was the unlicensed midwife Ueda Yaé, who had been served with a summons two days ago. Immediately she sat herself down before the legal-affairs officer. Her flesh bulged over the chair's rim and whenever she moved the chair swayed to one side or the other, creaking alarmingly as if in imminent danger of collapse.

"About how many births have you assisted at?" she was asked.

Yaé, who had just carried her considerable weight some six miles on foot, wiped the sweat from her brow with a neatly folded hand towel, probably a token of someone's gratitude for recent assistance, and replied quite frankly: "Well, I couldn't give you the exact figure. I've had any number of children myself, you see, so I know a lot about these things, and if ever there's a birth in the neighborhood, I'm asked in to help, and nowadays it seems people won't have anyone else."

Just lately a qualified midwife had come to work in the district, sponsored by the Prefectural Health Authority, but until her arrival it had been the universal custom at the time of a birth—unless a midwife was called in from the neighboring district, or the patient brought about her delivery unaided, heaving on a rope suspended from the ceiling—to go running off for help to Yaé's place. After the death of her husband, Yaé had come to rely for her subsistence almost entirely on the rice or bean curd given her in appreciation of those services, and gradually had come to feel that this was her profession. Even now, when a fully qualified midwife was available, the women in the village still went only to Yaé. They shrank from the newcomer, convinced that her fees must be exorbitant. Until recently there had never been any talk behind Yaé's back, nor any feeling that it was wrong to give payments to a person like that; but when the new midwife appeared— having returned to her native village after long years of nursing in a succession of large city hospitals, resolved to settle down quietly in the country for the rest of her days, even if it meant being a midwife—and discovered that there was surprisingly little demand for her services, she at once took a strong dislike to Yaé and started to create trouble. Realizing that she could not overthrow her rival merely by calling her an unqualified amateur, she had spread the rumor that Yaé was unlawfully practicing as a doctor—and it was this charge that the legal-affairs officer now wished to investigate.

"Now then," he continued, slowly coming to his point by a purposely devious route, "what sort of payments do you receive for this work?"

Yaé, who had no idea what was in the constable's mind, prattled on as if she were enjoying the conversation immensely.

"Payment? There's not many who bring me anything like that, I can tell you. Times are bad, of course, so you can't blame them, but like as not they'll just promise to bring a present over after the next good harvest, or say the child will give me something when he gets older, or could I please let them do a bit of work for me instead? Or, at best, they'll send me over a bag of bean curd or a pound of rice. In fact, far from getting paid, I often have to provide all the cloth and cotton wool from my own stocks, free of charge."

Hawkers occasionally came peddling their wares even inside the police station, and at this juncture a woman in work trousers, with a cotton towel draped over her head and fastened beneath her chin, entered hesitantly and called out: "Would any of you gentlemen like to buy a bird?"

"Buy a bird?" said a policeman, glancing up from a bowl of noodles. "To eat, do you mean? Or to keep in a cage?"

"It's a beautiful songbird," the woman replied. "A nightingale." And, looking thoroughly pleased with herself now, as if she had already found a buyer, she advanced further into the room and began to untie a cloth-wrapped bundle.

"Well, look at this!" The policemen, sitting or standing idly about and delving with chopsticks into their lunch boxes, peered into the smoke-blackened wooden cage resting on the floor. "It's a nightingale, right enough. But, does it sing?"

"Well, really, would I try to sell a bird that doesn't sing?" The woman looked genuinely shocked.

They asked her the price.

"Well, now, how much is it worth, I wonder?" she said, looking inquiringly around at their faces. "I don't know what they sell for, myself, but if any of you gentlemen will say what you think is a fair price, anything will do."

"Anything will do, eh?" laughed one of the policemen. "You're the first hawker I've met who doesn't know the price of his goods!"

"I'll give you fifty sen," said another.

"How much did you say?" The woman's face fell. "Can you buy a nightingale for fifty sen?"

"I thought you said you didn't know about these things," said the policeman who had just named the price. "In any case, you can't expect much from poor fellows like us."

But the woman was not to be put off so easily.

"If officials like you, with monthly salaries, haven't got any money," she retorted, "just where is the money in this town, I should like to know."

Constable Miyoshi had meanwhile joined the group, and now, catching sight of the woman's face, he looked suddenly annoyed and shouted: "You again! Have you come to talk more of that silly nonsense?"

"Oh, no, not this time, sir—I'm trying to sell a bird," she said, evidently flustered.

"You are, eh? Well, if that's all. . . ." Miyoshi peered into the cage.

Miyo was the woman's name, and when her husband had been arrested two months back for the unlicensed brewing of saké and had been given a spell in the workhouse in place of a fine, Miyo had come along to the police with the awkward request that she and her children, since they now had no idea where tomorrow's meals might come from, should be sent to the workhouse too. She had argued obstinately in this room for the best part of half a day, giving Miyoshi no end of trouble. The brewing of a rough, cloudy saké from crushed rice was a time-honored custom among the impoverished petty farmers roundabout, any form of refined saké being hopelessly beyond their means; since it was impossible to stop this practice, the police had abandoned imposing fines and, instead, merely consigned offenders to the workhouse. Miyoshi, recalling now the pinched, sad-eyed faces and soiled kimono of the three children Miyo had brought with her on that occasion, felt strongly inclined to make some sort of offer for the bird himself.

"My, now, it's a nightingale!" he exclaimed, bending over the cage. "How much are you selling it for?"

But at that moment Constable Fujioka, who had been to the railway station, reappeared with the teacher Onozaki and some other people, and Miyoshi returned to his desk. Yaé was still being questioned by the legal-affairs officer, but on seeing her neighbor Harukichi with his daughter Haru enter in the custody of a policeman, she beamed at him with her fat, moonlike face and cried: "Just fancy! You here too! What have you been up to, then?"

Harukichi had intended to accompany his daughter on the train as far as Owari, and now, dressed for the trip in a dark-blue kimono, with the white sleeves of his knitted underwear showing for several inches on each arm, he was following behind Onozaki in evident dejection at this sudden confusion of his plans. But when he saw Yaé's face he appeared to recover his spirits a little, as if he had found an ally.

"I've done nothing wrong as far as I can see," he said, "but just as I was thinking to send this girl off to a job in the central provinces, along came somebody and said I mustn't do it."

He studiously avoided looking at either Onozaki or the policeman as he spoke.

"Nothing wrong, do you say?" broke in Miyoshi. "Do you call it right to sell a girl that age into forced service?"

Onozaki, too, looked highly incensed. "This time I've had enough!" he said angrily. "You asked me to help, so I got in touch with the employment clerk, and now you've done this. You just don't know a promise is a promise!"

It was some time before that Harukichi, embarrassed by an excessively large family of small children, had first told Onozaki he wanted to put Haru out to service; but the girl was a promising student, and on that occasion Onozaki had managed to persuade Harukichi to let her stay on and proceed to high school, arranging meanwhile that she should receive a grant, and covering all minor expenses himself. Shortly after the start of this term, however, there had been expenses for the grandmother's funeral, and Harukichi, now desperate for money, had once more come along to say that he wanted to send his daughter out to work. Onozaki had reluctantly agreed, and, enlisting the help of the employment clerk at the Town Office, had undertaken to find a suitable opening. But Harukichi, whose visits on this matter had been fairly frequent for some time after this, had just lately ceased to appear, and yesterday morning (by which time Onozaki was already growing suspicious), Harukichi's sister-in-law had come to the school in his stead on some business connected with Haru. The school's spring excursion was only four days off, and it had been decided that the students of Haru's class should take the two-hour train journey to the prefectural capital. It had also been decided that certain money held in trust at the school, the proceeds of a sale of straw rope made at home by students, should be used for the children who could not afford the fares. Haru was one of those children. But Haru—her father's sister-in-law said—would unfortunately not be able to go on the excursion, so could they please have her share of the rope money now? When pressed for a further explanation, the woman had merely shaken her head as if she knew nothing more. Onozaki had felt almost sure then that Harukichi must have fallen for the smooth talk of some commission agent and sold his daughter into service, and on inquiry at the Town Office he had found —as he had expected—that the procedure there, at any rate, was not yet completed. Today, to add to his uneasiness, Haru had failed to appear at school and when he had heard her classmates, during recess, mention seeing Haru and her father set out that morning in the direction of the town, he had ridden off on his bicycle at once, asking a colleague to take over his class, and had discovered the two of them at the railway station, waiting idly for a train that was not due for almost another hour.

Onozaki had felt that now he really knew what people meant when they talked about the foxy cunning of these rustics. If the man was going to do this, why hadn't he come along decently and asked him to stop his inquiries? To treat their private agreement as if it had never existed, to go slyly behind his back and carry on secret negotiations, to pretend he wasn't doing a thing. . . . Inwardly seething, he had controlled his temper and tried to reason quietly with the man. But Harukichi had stubbornly refused to move from the waiting-room bench, claiming, with the despairing look of a man hounded by fate, that the twenty yen advanced to help with the preparations had already been spent on family needs and on payments to creditors. It was then that Onozaki had gone to the police for help. Haru, wearing an apron of red muslin over her cheap, gaudily patterned kimono, and white cotton socks with holes at the toes, was gazing up in awe at the faces of Onozaki and the policemen, making herself inconspicuous behind her father's back; but when Constable Miyoshi, who was a fearsome sight with the red scar running across one eyebrow, started severely lecturing her father— "What! When this gentleman takes all this trouble on himself to find a good job, you go to an agency? And don't you think it's hard on the poor girl, eh, sending her off to years of forced labor?"—she trembled suddenly, as if on the verge of tears and, turning abruptly away, pressed her hands to her face.

The job the employment clerk had been recommending was with a certain large spinning factory, but it had offered an advance payment of only ten yen, and, since Harukichi's situation had moved hopelessly beyond the stage where that sort of money could be of any use, he had decided, even if the working conditions should be a trifle rough, there was nothing for it but to sell the girl's services for a fixed period to some small factory which would give him a good lump sum of ready cash in advance. And he had not had the face to mention this to Onozaki, who had busied himself in so many ways to help his daughter.

"Ah, what can I say?" Harukichi began. "There were the debts, you see, and nothing to eat in the house, and when, on top of that, my third boy, Zenkichi, fell off a ladder and broke his leg and we had to have the doctor. . . ."

Children in Harukichi's household, whether there was anything for them to eat or not, sprouted into being like baby potatoes, and the eighth had been born at the end of the last year. Harukichi had been vaguely thinking, therefore, that with a family of eleven to support (for, although the grandmother could now at last be counted out, there were still, in addition to the eight children, two parents and a grandfather), and not the remotest chance of managing it on the scanty produce of his single acre of land, he might reasonably be excused if, in order to reduce the number of mouths by one at least, he considered some arrangement for Haru now that she had finished junior school;

and in any case—he had reasoned—no matter what sort of job the girl was sent to, she could hardly be worse off than she was now, living on starvation rations in a jerry-built shack crawling with children. And when the boy Zenkichi had injured his leg, and the bone had become infected so that expensive treatment became necessary, Harukichi had finally made up his mind to go to an employment agent and beg an advance on the security of his daughter's services.

"Here, how old are you?" asked Miyoshi suddenly.

"Thirty-four, sir," Harukichi replied, with a puzzled air.

"Thirty-four"—Miyoshi looked at the man in amazement—"eight children at thirty-four! That's good work, eh? Is it the truth, though?"

Yaé leaned across at this. "Eight it is, sure enough," she said. "Starting with this girl here, I've helped to bring out every one of them, so there's no mistake. He's not telling lies. If ever you go to his house there's always two rocking baskets there, side by side."

Miyoshi, who had been gazing in surprise at Yaé as she rattled briskly on, looked suddenly annoyed and shouted: "Hi, that's enough! Who asked you to talk?"

"Yes, that's how it is," said Harukichi, glancing apologetically to-ward Yaé, who had lapsed into a pained silence. "And we've never given you a thing, have we, for all that trouble? It isn't right?" He turned and indicated his daughter. "I was thinking, though, that when we'd sent this girl out to work we might have a chance to do something for you."

The hundred yen he had expected to receive on delivering Haru at the Owari weaving factory was to have been applied chiefly to the settlement of certain pressing debts, contracted on the security of the house, and to provision of the family's immediate needs; but Harukichi's plans for the money were laid in some detail, and even things like a gift for Yaé had not been forgotten.

Miyoshi, on being told that the twenty yen advanced as preparation money was all gone and knowing, moreover, that every penny in the Office's various relief funds was already out on loan, could think of no answer to the present problem, and he retired to confer with the superintendent; but there too, it seemed, no solution presented itself.

"Well, I really don't know," Miyoshi mumbled as he came back from the superintendent's office. "What's it best to do, I wonder."

Onozaki had at first listened to the excuses of the nervous, shifty-eyed Harukichi with unconcealed disgust, but as he came to learn more of the circumstances behind the case, his angry, tense features had gradually relaxed, and now he turned abruptly to Miyoshi and said: "That's it. I'll lend him a little money. If I do that"—he looked across at Harukichi—"you can manage all right, eh?"

"Well, seriously, you know, I just can't take it." Harukichi recoiled at the offer, his yellow, wizened face becoming momentarily resolute. "I'm not going to put you to any more trouble, sir, not on my account."

But Miyoshi was looking immensely relieved. "Now you," he said quickly. "That's no way to talk. You should accept a kindness in the proper spirit. Let's settle things the way the gentleman says, and let's hear no more about sending this girl into service."

Miyoshi was obliged to devote a large part of each day to people who came to the police to beg help of some sort, getting them cards for free medical treatment, arranging for assistance to be given from the Town Office, and so on, and Onozaki's simple solution seemed to attract him strongly, for he now added, as good measure: "And tomorrow I'll go to the Town Office myself and see if they'll let you have a bale of rice."

At that moment there was the sound of a motor car drawing up outside the entrance. Visitors in cars were rare, and as the policemen turned curiously toward the door there emerged from the vehicle a man whose face was a familiar sight to everyone in town. It was Dr. Yokota. He entered without removing his hat and, leaning unceremoniously across the handrail of the reception desk, cast affable, beady-eyed glances about the room from behind his thick-lensed spectacles. After a few bantering remarks—"Hello, Miyoshi, has the fishing started yet?"—his expression grew suddenly serious and he turned to Saitō, the hygiene officer. "I've just had a call from that prayer-mongering priest at Tora-no-kuchi," he said, "and I find there's a case of dysentery."

The hygiene officer rose from his chair. "Is it the priest, then?" he asked.

"No such luck," said the doctor. "It's an old woman stopping at his house. No one knows where she comes from. And, what's more, the so-called medicine he's giving her is stewed pine-leaf juice, or something of that sort, so you'll have to investigate this thoroughly."

With surprising suddenness Dr. Yokota now resumed his former cheerful manner and started gossiping with the other policemen. From across the room, where someone—to see whether the nightingale would sing or not—had lifted the cage onto a window ledge, there now sounded a single, brief, melodic call—"Ho-o-kekkyo!"

"Did you hear that?" cried the countrywoman excitedly. "Isn't that a lovely voice now?" She moved across to where Dr. Yokota was sitting. "How about it, sir? Wouldn't you like to buy that bird?"

The doctor, it so happened, wasted a great deal of time and money on pet birds, boasting quite a collection of them in his house.

"Eh, what sort is it?" he asked. He rose and walked over toward the window, moving around the rear of the small group centered about Harukichi. On the way he passed Constable Saitō. The constable, with great zest, was pulling out the sterilization equipment for use in case of infectious diseases, rejoicing that a time of action had at last arrived; for he had long been meaning to check up on this priest, a mendicant holy man who had established himself last spring in a shack near the Tora-no-kuchi cremation ground and, after acquiring a devoted flock of followers by the recitation of weird prayers for long life and happiness, had even, just lately, been credited with miraculous healing powers.

"I hear there's any number of sick people nowadays going to that priest," the doctor called out as he passed; and then, drawing up some two or three yards short of the window, lest the bird should take fright and refuse to sing, he peered from that considerable distance at the little creature fluffing its glossy yellow-green feathers inside the cage. Turning to the countrywoman, he said: "How much do you want?"

"Well, first of all, sir," said the woman, gazing hopefully at the doctor in his smartly cut lounge suit and clearly expecting a handsome offer, "how much would you be prepared to give?"

As she stood waiting for his reply, the nightingale apparently finding the warm spring sunshine to its liking, gave vent to yet another full-throated, high-pitched burst of song. Constable Miyoshi looked up sharply at the sound. His face was now stern, as if some irregularity had just occurred to him, and striding quickly across the room, he stood directly before Miyo and glared at her accusingly.

"Here you," he said, "this is a protected bird. Where did you get it, eh? It's against the law to catch birds like this."

"I didn't catch it, sir," Miyo replied. "It flew into my house all by itself."

But Miyoshi had already formed his own opinion on the matter and was obviously prepared to listen to no excuses. "Now then, no lies!" he scolded. "Who ever heard of a bird flying into a house of its own accord? You caught it with a net, there's no doubt about it."

In truth, however, Miyo had done nothing by design. That morning, shortly after dawn, a small bird had come flying into her house, beating its wings noisily against the walls, and when she and the children, after a wild and disorderly chase, had eventually trapped it inside a bean-paste sieve they had discovered that it was a nightingale. Miyo was in ill health, unable to do heavy work as a laborer, and after her husband's departure to the workhouse and the rejection of her tearful request to be put in there with him, she had racked her brains in desperation for some means—when there was not even food in the house for tomorrow —of keeping herself and the children alive for the next three months, until her husband came out again. Eventually she had decided, rashly, to borrow ten yen from a moneylender, at a daily interest rate of five sen, and with this as her capital had walked about the town selling apples; but although she had been able, for a few days, to buy some-times five and sometimes ten small measures of rice, in less than a month she had run through both capital and profits, and after that she could find nothing but occasional odd jobs here and there, at the more well-to-do houses, helping in the kitchen or weeding the garden; and the three children had eaten rice scarcely once in ten days. When the bird, in the midst of these misfortunes, had flown of its own free will into her house, Miyo had felt convinced that this was the work of providence. "Today," she had told her dejected and starved-looking children, "I'm going to town to get you some presents. So just be good and wait."

First she had gone the rounds of the shops, choosing those which looked likely to have old people somewhere on the premises, living in retirement, but no one had wanted a bird and her hopes had been sadly dashed. Then, thinking that the salaried workers in public offices might, after all, be more likely customers, she had abandoned her tour of the shops and come to the police station.

"Why not forget about it, officer?" said Dr. Yokota, interceding on Miyo's behalf. "Let her sell the bird to me."

Miyoshi, however, ignored the remark. "We'll have to set it loose," he said, and he moved toward the cage.

"But, officer!" Miyo pleaded, turning red in the face and clutching at Miyoshi's coat, "even if it is against the law to catch these birds, I didn't catch it with a net or a trap or anything like that! If it really flew into the house of its own accord, it's all right, isn't it?" But by this time a shadow had darted across the square of pale blue sky framed by the window, and the bird was gone.

"What an awful thing to do!" wailed Miyo. "Just when this gentleman"—with a bewildered, mortified air she turned to gaze at Dr. Yokota—"was going to buy it, too! I've spent my whole day trying to sell this bird, and what shall I say now when I get home? Can't you gentlemen do something?"

No one had anything to say to this, and Miyo, realizing that the bird was irretrievably lost and growing steadily more indignant as she visualized the faces of her children, waiting impatiently at home for their mother to return from town with the presents, walked red-faced from the room. Soon Harukichi too departed, drifting aimlessly off like a kite from a snapped string; but Haru clattered hastily after him in her flaking red-lacquer clogs and, looking straight up into his face, cried: "Father will you let me go on the outing?" Having been told that if she went with her father to Owari she could have rice to eat on the train and could wear her red kimono, Haru had lost all interest in the school excursion, but now, after today's events, the thought of missing that too was unbearable. Harukichi's mind, however, was fully occupied by other matters—as far as the advance from the agent was concerned, he thought he could get Onozaki to settle that, so there was nothing much to worry about there; the railway fare, too, would have to be returned, but he had that intact in his pocket; and, before all else, something (though he couldn't imagine what) would have to be done about the debts on the security of his house.

"The outing, eh? Let me see, that's the day after tomorrow, isn't it?" he mumbled vaguely. And he walked on again.

The examination of Yaé, on which the legal-affairs officer was still engaged, was concerned not merely with her midwife activities but with the question of whether or not she was setting herself up as a doctor. But on this latter point Yaé had quite openly confessed that the neighboring countrypeople, rather than go all the way to a doctor and be asked to pay a fee which they could not possibly afford, frequently came to her house for advice on things like burns, stomach trouble, or boils, and that on these occasions—since she had done some nursing in her younger days and was not entirely uninformed—she only said to the best of her knowledge what treatment was good for this or that, and sometimes gave people medicines or ointments out of her own household stock, so it did not seem likely that there was any more than this to the charges of the qualified midwife that Yaé gave medical treatment and dispensed medicines.

While the examination was proceeding, and not ten minutes after the departure of Harukichi, a woman of middle age, big with child, came half running, half stumbling into the entrance way. Close behind her, clutching at her mother's sleeve, gripping a mud-splattered rubber ball in her other hand, and gaping up stupidly at the policemen, came a podgy girl of six or seven; but the woman seemed almost in a trance, completely oblivious of the child's presence.

"I need help, please, I need help," she managed to gasp, and then her pallid face twisted in pain and she sank down, as if crushed by a weight from above, and crouched low on the floor.

Even at this the reception clerk remained stolidly motionless in his chair, but Miyoshi, who had been watching from the rear of the room, now came up shouting "Here, here! What's all this? What's all this?" and peered over the handrail of the reception desk.

The woman, letting her kimono flap loosely open at the front, began pacing up and down the stone-floored porchway like a caged animal, apparently in agony.

"Help me, please," she was crying. "It's dreadful! The birth has started!"

Miyoshi, who at first merely gaped at the woman in wide-eyed bewilderment, now seemed for the first time to grasp the situation.

" A baby, eh? Oh, this is serious, this is! What shall we do?" He ran out onto the porch, and then, in a panic of indecision, began to follow the woman wherever she moved. Suddenly a surprising thought appeared to strike him, and he dashed back into the room toward the desk of the legal-affairs officer.

"Hi, you're a midwife, aren't you?" he called out to Yaé. "Just give us a hand, then. It's you or nobody, so come on. Quick!"

"Oh, a birth? Here?" said Yaé, used to these things and rising unhurriedly. Realizing, however, after a brief glance at the woman, who was hovering about distractedly in her almost crawling posture, that the baby's head must already be more than half way out, she said: "We'll have to lay her down some where on a matted floor. And you!" —with a calming gesture to Miyoshi—"stop running round in circles and lay out a mattress as quick as you can."

Leading the woman by the hand, she followed Miyoshi into the night-duty room. Two other policemen hurried across to help Miyoshi, and the old caretaker also came out to lend a hand, and when the four of them, with a tremendous amount of fussing, had got the woman safely stretched out on the mattress, Yaé lowered her own massive form ponderously onto the matting and, sitting there in rock-like solidity, moving only her head, directed a stream of instructions at the policemen—to get boiled water, to go out and buy cotton wool, and so on—and, having taken her hand towel from her pocket and spread it out ready, in case the cotton swaddling cloth should not arrive in time, drew the sliding door across behind her. For a time there was only the sound of Yaé repeating again and again, in a school-teacherly tone: " Don't strain, now; don't strain." This was very soon followed by the thin, uneasy wail of a baby.

"It's arrived!" one of the policemen cried out involuntarily.

"I wonder who the woman is?" said another, in a low voice. "Let it go pretty late, didn't she?"

But the legal-affairs officer rose quickly from his chair and said: "The child's safely born, that's the important thing. Even an unlicensed midwife comes in useful at a time like this, eh?" And he walked excitedly up and down, beaming with pleasure, as if it was his own child that had just been born.

At this moment, however, he saw Constable Saitō and a patrolman, just back in the station's car from their job of disinfecting the room of the dysentery patient, enter in the company of the prayer-chanter, garbed in black robes like a genuine priest. He turned to greet them.

"What's this?" he asked. "So he's really been doing doctor's work, has he?" Constable Saitō saluted and, setting a bundle of roots, weeds, and tree bark on the table, together with a large bottle of cloudy-white liquid which he had hastily transferred to his left hand before saluting, said: "Doctor's work? I wouldn't call it that. This is the sort of stuff he doses his patients with, he says. Hi you! That's right, isn't it?"

He turned sharply to the priest standing behind him. The scanty remnants of the man's hair were cropped close and his eyes were cold and dull. He had formerly been an itinerant beggar, walking from village to village with an alms bag strung about his neck, but, instead of spending his takings on drink and tobacco, he had economized assiduously, and last spring he had built a ramshackle hut for himself on the outskirts of the town at Tora-no-kuchi, banged away on a big drum, and commenced chanting prayers. The sound of the drum had drawn large numbers of old women to his place for secret consultations, and in a very short time it was widely believed that you could be cured of chronic diseases if you asked this priest to pray for you, so the fame of the Tora-no-kuchi prayer-chanter had spread even to the remotest mountain villages.

When Constable Saitō had arrived in all haste at the hut, the priest had shown no trace of agitation, greeting him with foolishly elaborate ceremony. On an altar raised in the hut's dim interior were offerings of apples and other fruit, set on dishes of chipped red lacquer, and, as a further decoration, there was displayed a volume entitled "One Hundred Sutras" or something of that sort, from which the priest apparently gave recitals to his assembled flock twice each year, in the spring and autumn; but it was in the three-mat room next to this, beneath a thin cotton quilt, that the sick woman lay. She was breathing very faintly and showed no sign of seeing Saitō's face when he bent low and peered at her. He saw that it was Kin, the old woman who had passed the previous night at the police station. Like all those other old women—too poor and too settled in their ways to think of consulting a doctor—who had come from far and wide on hearing of the priest's mystic powers, Kin too had called in here for a cure on her way back. Even when Miyoshi had been vainly urging her to see a doctor, she had probably already secretly decided on this course. As for the priest, he had started his drum-beating and prayer-chanting immediately, thinking that this was just another fine bird flown into his net, but he soon saw that he had taken on a difficult proposition, and, realizing that things might be very awkward if the old woman should thoughtlessly pass away on him, he had called in Dr. Yokota to make an examination.

"Up to now, about how many patients have come to see you?" he was asked.

"Well, even if you put it as low as one every three days," the priest replied, without a moment's hesitation, "that would make it about a hundred."

"And have they all been cured?"

At this question the priest assumed a look of humility and said: "Ah, whether they have really recovered completely or not is something I can't say. But any number of them have come back and said that, thanks to me, they are feeling much better."

The legal-affairs officer picked up some of the plantain leaves and pieces of tree bark that had been thrown onto the table and thrust them under the priest's nose.

"Do they get better by swallowing stuff like this?" he shouted angrily. "Are you serious?" Taking the written report handed him at that moment by Saitō, he vanished immediately into the superintendent's office, returning in a few moments to say briefly: "For today, just lock him up."

Constable Saitō led the priest to a corner of the room, where he obliged him to remove his waistband.

"Come on, down here," he said, and, pushing his way toward the corridor through the crowd of policemen gathered outside the night-duty room to see the new baby, he dragged his charge without ceremony to the detention cell. There was a melancholy grating of bolts; then the constable returned and went over to speak to Miyoshi.

"It's a shame, you know," he began. "The patient up at that priest's place was the old lady who stayed here last night."

Miyoshi was leaning forward, gazing intently at the woman in the night-duty room. Now that the afterbirth, too, had been removed, she was lying perfectly still, and her eyes were shut.

"Eh, the old lady?"—he swung around, opening his eyes wide— "I told her to see a doctor, didn't I? And she wouldn't listen! Will she pull through?"

"At her age it's unlikely," said Saitō. "They've moved her to the isolation hospital, but she's in a bad way and there's not much hope."

From beyond the front section of the main office, deserted now except for the policeman on reception duty, there had sounded the steady beat of a rubber ball being bounced, but now, the noise ceasing abruptly, a girl came running in with a loud clatter of wooden clogs. Poking her head through the barrier of policemen, she yelled at the top of her voice: "Mum, I'm hungry! Give me something!" But when her ravenous gaze lighted on the wrinkled face of the new-born infant, wrapped in her mother's cloak and silently wriggling its hands and feet at her mother's side, she rounded her eyes and stared in blank, speechless astonishment.

"How is it?" one of the policemen called across to Yaé. "Everything all right?"

Yaé, squatting on the floor and looking as massively immovable as ever, wrinkled the narrow corners of her eyes in a brief smile.

"You don't often get a birth as easy as this one," she said. "It's a little on the small side, but it's a fine, strong baby." She adjusted the edges of the woman's bedding and then, turning to the old caretaker, called out: "Hi, dad, I suppose you haven't any oil, have you? Camellia hair-oil or anything like that will do."

"Well, a bald-headed fellow like me doesn't keep fancy things like camellia oil." The old man laughed, but he soon returned from the pantry with a bottle of sesame oil, and Yaé, after rubbing a little of it over the baby's body, started to bathe the infant in a pail of warm water. Constable Saitō, however, seeing that the mother continued to lie inert with eyes closed, now burst out angrily, in a voice so loud that everyone standing at the woman's side jumped in surprise: "Hi, all you people, where have you come from? What are you doing here?"

The woman, who had apparently been lying so still, with eyes tight shut, from some overwhelming sense of shame at her mismanagement, feeling that she would like to creep into a dark hole and hide herself, now opened her eyes with a start, and at once commenced to apologize.

"Forcing myself on you in this state, and giving you gentlemen so much trouble. I don't know what to say . . ." she began.

"Now, that's all right," said Miyoshi, restraining her as she attempted to rise. "You get some sleep. Don't try to move yet."

But the woman seemed not to hear him and, making no attempt to return to her former position, went on: "I've been at Higashiné until now, but I couldn't stay there any longer, you see . . ." Two broad tearstains appeared unexpectedly on her face, a face so emaciated and drained of color that one would imagine its owner no longer capable of feeling any misfortune or suffering; then suddenly, like streams swollen by a cloudburst, the tears came flooding down in glistening torrents. ". . . And I had nowhere to go, so I thought I'd come here for help."

Miyoshi had been studying her face intently. "Here," he now asked abruptly, "did you work in a circus troupe when you were a girl?"

The woman was clearly shaken. "Well, how did you know that?" she exclaimed, staring at him in blank astonishment.

"So it's true, eh? You had a child with you, too, so I thought you might be the one. And it's true, eh?" Miyoshi repeated.

When he had told her the complete story—how her foster mother, Kin, had come on foot the whole thirty miles from Akazawa just to find her, had fallen sick with dysentery, and was now lodged in the isolation hospital—Yoshié, who had raised herself on the mattress to a sitting position and was now staring straight ahead with a dazed look on her face, said "Then I must see her just once; it would be awful if she died" and rose unsteadily to her feet.

"Hi, stop!" cried Miyoshi. "You can't go anywhere in that state!"

"I'm all right," she replied obstinately. "And I must see her, just once, you see."

But, for all this display of determination, within a few moments her face turned deathly white and she crumpled exhausted to the floor. In January of the previous year, having been left without means of support by the death of the man who worked at the cotton mill, Yoshié had decided that if times were to be bad she would prefer to be in her native village, where she hoped she might also see her foster mother; so, selling her few household possessions to provide money for the journey, she had come all the way back to these parts after an absence of twenty years. But the snows had checked her progress, falling, as they had always fallen, until it seemed the houses would be buried up to their roofs; and since, in any case, she had no idea what to do next in the aimless quest for a person called Kin, who might or might not be alive, and whose village was no more to Yoshié than a vague childhood memory, she had taken a room in this town at a cheap lodginghouse near the railway station. Her landlady, seeing her sit for days perplexedly staring out at the snowy skies, had eventually taken pity on her and, employing Yoshié as a serving maid, had allowed both her and the child to remain as long as they pleased.

Then, taken in by the usual promises of marriage, Yoshié had foolishly allowed herself to be got with child by a traveling timber dealer who stopped briefly at the lodginghouse each month. As soon as her condition became obvious, the man ceased to call any more. The thought of showing herself in this state before her kind landlady was more than she could bear, and, carefully draping a sleeve of her kimono across the now prominent bulge in her figure, she had moved to the Seifū Inn; there, with the time of the birth steadily approaching and with no idea where she could stay when it came, she had met up with a ready-tongued sympathizer called Yashichi, who, unlike the timber dealer, had very soon taken her back home to live with him; but he too, it seemed, had wanted no more than a little temporary amusement, and, as if worried that things might get even worse if he waited until after the birth, he had seized as an excuse upon the bickerings between Yoshié's daughter and his child by his late wife and the resulting deterioration of his relationship with his mother-in-law, and, thrusting a single five-yen bill into Yoshié's hand, he had driven her forcibly from the house. In a deep calm following upon the tremendous labor of giving birth, Yoshié, with an abstracted and rather troubled look in her eyes, had turned to regard in silence the baby at her side, which was crying continuously and wrinkling up its face.

But now Miyoshi came hurrying back from the inner office, where he and the legal-affairs officer had been discussing matters with the superintendent, and called to Yaé: "Look, it's all right for you to go now, so do you think you could take this woman with you and put her up at your place? How do you feel? Will you do that? We'll talk about the details later, eh?"

Yaé, squatting on the floor, turned cumbrously to face Miyoshi.

"That'll be fine, officer. If you've no objection, there's plenty of room at my place," she replied, looking as if this was just what she had been hoping for; and at once she started making her preparations.

Soon the station car was noisily starting up its engine outside the crowded entrance way, and Yaé, holding the baby in her arms, squeezed herself through the car door with the greatest difficulty and settled down in the seat beside Yoshié and her daughter.

"Drive slowly," she exhorted Constable Kobayashi at the wheel; then, turning earnestly to the crowd of policemen gathered to see them all off, she called out: "If you need my help again, just send for me!"

MORNING MIST

BY Nagai Tatsuo

TRANSLATED BY Edward Seidensticker

Nagai Tatsuo, who was born in 1904, began writing short stories and plays while still in his twenties. Except for a period of silence during the war, he has followed a double career as journalist and writer. "Morning Mist" (Asagiri), which was published in 1950, is characteristic of the work for which he is perhaps best known today, half humorous, half pathetic sketches of unimportant people and their eccentricities.

Although it is somewhat nearer the objectivity of the conventional short story than most of Nagai's work, "Morning Mist" is nonetheless representative of a peculiarly Japanese genre, part essay and part fiction. Japanese writers of fiction have traditionally felt free to step forward and comment in their own voices, and the contemporary story-essay, if such it may be called, offers evidence that the break with the past in modern Japanese literature has not been so complete as many historians would have it.

"I SHALL see you later, then."

"Yes."

Having carefully tied his shoes, the solidly built old man stood up, deliberately turned around, and, as always, took a large watch from his pocket.

"This evening, I think I shall be home at about—five-seventeen."

"Yes."

In contrast to the elaborate formality of X's speech, this second quick "yes" from the old wife, who was seeing him to the door, was dry and terse as only long years of married life could have made it.

X's black briefcase was always puffed like a small pig. The question of what it contained will come up for discussion later; for the present, let us say that I imagined it to be stuffed with textbooks, reference works, examination papers, and the like.

He picked it up, put his hand to the glass door, and started out. There was a certain hesitation in his step, however. He laid the briefcase down again.

"I believe I said five-seventeen."

"Yes."

"That was a mistake. I shall be home at five-seven."

"Yes."

Briskly and quite without concern, the wife put away the shoe-horn and stepped into a pair of clogs. As if to follow him out or perhaps to chase him out, she went to the door, took a broom, and turned the corner of the walk toward the kitchen. She wasted neither time nor ceremony. The walk inside and outside the gate was to be swept.

The footsteps of X, who must by then have gone some distance, came nearer again.

"A little while ago—"

"Yes."

"I said five-seven. But today it will be five-seventeen after all."

"Yes. I see."

Shifting the heavy briefcase to a hand constantly exposed to the ravages of chalk, X set off at his usual pace. The sound of the broom had not stopped.

My description of this ritual from the distant past, repeated each morning when X set off for work, need not end here. Indeed the re-treating figure suggests that he may be back; but I shall eliminate the repetitions.

One knows that the wife's answers were not an expression of that drying up of love one so often sees. Quite the reverse: to shore up his feelings of security and to speed his decision, she had to make her answers as unvarying as possible.

It had taken her some time to hit upon the dry "yes." If the answer was even a little complicated—"I understand," or "Is that so?"—or if it was different from the answer of the day before, she would know the sorrow—she had known it more than once—of troubling his decision.

One day he had come all the way back from Shibuya to inform her of a change in his schedule.

He was under no obligation to specify the time of his return. No complications in his family life required it.

I myself have been working for nearly ten years now; and it rather amused me once to learn that carp in a fishing pond follow fixed and invariable paths. The working man is very much like the carp. He is most reluctant to move from the familiar rut. Except for pressing business or an emergency, he has no wish to change his route to work, even though he ought to be thoroughly sick of it.

If it were suggested that X's ritual was unhealthy, I think we could answer that he shared a disease from which all working men suffer to some extent.

X was living in a suburb of Tokyo.

He was ten minutes' walk from the station. At Shibuya he changed from the suburban electric to the government line, which took him to a certain middle school in the heart of the city.

As if pressed from a die, his teaching life had now gone on for seven or eight years since he bought his house on royalties from *Examinations Made Easy,* and we may therefore say that his everyday routine, of a sort that the reader will have no trouble in imagining from his own school days, had been rather a long one. If I had feared having X come into the mind as stereotype, I could have used an opening from a short story I happened to have on hand, by M. de Maupassant:

"Old M. Taille had three daughters: The oldest, Anna, of whom the family seldom spoke; Rose, the second, aged eighteen; and Claire, the youngest, a child of barely fifteen. M. Taille, a widower, was master mechanic in M. Lebrument's button factory. He was much respected, very honest, and very sober, a sort of model workman. The family lived on the Rue d'Angoulême in Le Havre."

Indeed it would have done my story no harm to be transported to a small city in France or America.

If, having come upon them, I had made use of these random sentences, I would have found that remark about honesty and sobriety quite appropriate. One is not to suppose, however, that X had three daughters, Anna, Rose, and Claire.

X was not my teacher, and it was by accident that I moved into a house very near his in the last years of his life. This little story really begins with a visit to his house at the invitation of his son, who had been my friend and classmate through high school and college, and whom I chanced to meet, for the first time in some years, on the platform of his suburban station. The war had just begun.

*　　　*　　　*

On the appointed Sunday afternoon, I was shown into the sitting room by the old wife. She said that her son would be home shortly. I was much impressed with her close-knit tidiness; then, when the husband sat facing me, I was still more impressed, somehow, by the simple fact that age had come upon him. It was not an impression of unhealthiness. It was a feeling of, literally, age. A general slackening had come over the well-fleshed and rather large figure.

Apart from that, the careful politeness of his speech was at least twice as pronounced as I had remembered.

"You know Mr. Iké," said the wife, introducing me. "He used to come often. A friend of Yoshihidé's."

"Is that so, is that so? It was extremely good of you to come. Yoshihidé is deeply in debt to you."

His place by a window seat had a well-used look about it. Clearly it was where the old man sat. Neatly piled by the wall in yellowed bindings were several of the familiar quick courses in mathematics of which he was the author, membership lists for academic societies, alumni registers for middle and high schools, and the like. But even more familiar was the black briefcase, showing some wear, it was true, but nonetheless staunch on the window seat where he could reach it, and puffed like a small pig, just as I had seen it the day before.

The wife said that her husband had resigned from a certain middle school three or four years earlier, and that he had now also given up his mathematics courses in Kanda.

During this brisk narrative, X sat with rigid formality, slightly bowed, hands on knees.

When his wife left the room, I had no choice but to talk as best I could of the old days, mostly of my friendship with Yoshihidé. He nodded and gravely answered "I see" each time I spoke.

The door opened. I thought Yoshihidé was back; but I soon knew, from the voice in the hall and the youthfulness of the footsteps, that it was someone else. At the door to the sitting room a loud voice announced that its owner was home. He roughly threw down a bundle, then saw that there was company. It was Yoshihidé's youngest brother, ten years younger than he. There could be no doubt about the identity of the still-growing boy, perhaps a middle-school student in his third or fourth year.

"Hello. It's been a long time."

I smiled at him. He stared for a moment, and seemed on the point of saying "Oh, it's you, is it?"

Instead he said "It *has* been a long time" and bowed.

X, who was sitting stiffly before me, returned the bow ceremoniously.

"It was extremely good of you to come."

The brother was already out of the room. X remained quietly in control of himself, but my own confusion was mounting. He spoke, again with great dignity.

"I'm very sorry, but might I know your name?"

"Iké Takeichirō, a classmate of Yoshihidé's. I called occasionally when you were living in Koishikawa."

"I see. A classmate of Yoshihidé's." It seemed to me that a touch of liveliness came over his face. He put on his spectacles and had no trouble finding our high-school register in the heap by the wall. Assiduously he ran his finger through the I's.

"Iké—Takeichirō. Here it is, here it is. Well, well. 15c, C-1, Nishi-kata-machi, Hongō."

"I lived with my father in Nishikata-machi until a couple of years ago."

His voice had suggested that reminiscences of Nishikata-machi were coming. Instead he flicked over the pages.

"Nishikata-machi—6E. Itō Shōtarō. Class of 1919, is it? You know him?"

"Nineteen nineteen. That was some years ahead of me."

"I see. Nishikata-machi. Here. Konuma Haruo. Was he near you?"

"I don't remember a Konuma in the neighborhood."

"I see. Nishikata-machi, 96A. Kawakita Chigusa."

So it went. I was offered name after name from Nishikata-machi and when one of them aroused a flicker of a memory, I took my stand.

I said I knew him. I thought I had seen the shingle of a doctor by that name. "I believe he was a doctor."

At last satisfied, X took his spectacles by the bow and smiled at me. "That's right. That's quite right. Tokyo Imperial University Medical School, class of 1928, it says."

"Was he one of your students, sir?"

I thought the question might interest him, but he answered: "Never met the gentleman."

He returned the register to its place, reached for the black briefcase in the window, and let it fall heavily at his knee.

"Something very, very good in here," he said, opening the briefcase as if it contained rare treasures and taking out several bundles of post-cards. "I suppose you know the famous novelist Ōmichi Saburō?"

"I've read his things in newspapers and magazines, I believe."

"Of course you have. This one is 1941. This one is 1938. And here —here is Ōmichi Saburō's New Year card for this very year. His real name is Noguchi Kunihiko—here, in parentheses. And here is Taka-hashi Goichirō. You must know him. He was elected to the Diet from Chiba last year. He was a hard one to manage, but he's done well for himself."

He shot them at me like the names in Nishikata-machi. I had to view card after card after card from his students. In the case of Ōmichi Saburō I saw cards for the last five years.

"I take them to school with me. To the lectures in Kanda too. I take them out when I have a minute to spare and look at them over a cup of tea. Endlessly fascinating. Why else would I have kept them these fifteen years?"

I felt a surge of I hardly know what—call it sympathy, call it pity. "A remarkably good way to entertain yourself," I was able to say with-out affectation.

Yoshihidé's brother came in with tea, apparently brewed in some haste. I pointed to a tennis racket on the veranda.

"You play tennis?"

"My brother does." Embarrassed, the boy stood up to leave. He turned back from the door. "It's time to heat the bath, Father," he blurted out, and almost fled from the room.

"Tennis is a good game. You let the ball go, and you drive it cross-court like this. That's when it's really good." X showed no sign of having heard his son. Gently raising his left hand with the elbow forward, he clenched his right hand and brought it diagonally down across his chest.

At this point a somewhat flustered Yoshihidé hurried in, apologizing for his tardiness. He had had business, and one interview had not been enough to finish it. X sat with the briefcase and several bundles of postcards before him, and remarked in the midst of the apology: "You let the ball go, and you drive it cross-court like this." He served again. I tried not to notice. I said that I was surprised to see how near we lived. I said that the brother was the image of the Yoshihidé of our high-school days. X raised his left arm, brought his clenched right hand diagonally forward, and half rose from his seat.

"You let the ball go," he said, "and you drive it cross-court like this."

Acutely uncomfortable, I fell silent. Yoshihidé stood up and put his arm around his father's shoulders.

"You let the ball go. . . ." The left hand rose again.

"It's time to heat the bath, Father. Suppose we go."

The old man got up without a protest.

"Suppose I go and heat the bath," he said.

After seeing him to the door, Yoshihidé pushed the postcards out of sight. "The old man's in his second childhood. We don't know what to do with him."

I left toward evening. As I passed the hedge, I saw X squatting by the boiler, busily shoving in wood. I spoke across the hedge to his wife, who was bustling about the kitchen. Though he was less than a yard away from me, X's attention did not leave the bath. I might as well not have been there.

*   *   *

Some two weeks later, Yoshihidé called me in for consultation. Thereafter I frequently visited the X house. Yoshihidé had chosen the girl he wanted to marry, but his parents would not give their consent.

To make quite sure of my ground, I met the girl and talked to her. She was bright and good natured, a girl in whom I could find no fault. Everything promised a happy marriage, and I concluded that I must help them. With the girl's permission, I went cautiously to work.

On my next visit, I introduced myself as before, and again was questioned about Nishikata-machi. This time Yoshihidé had told me what to do. I expansively admitted knowing everyone on the list. As Yoshihidé had predicted, X's happiness was extraordinary. His spirits brightened, his memory seemed to come back, and by fits he spoke of how it had been when I had come visiting as a school friend of Yoshihidé's.

I even went home with a present.

It was a commodity new on the market: the spring clothespin. Bringing a large cloth bundle from a back room, X dropped two bunches of clothespins into my hand. He had some days earlier passed a night stall by the station, Yoshihidé told me, and bought out the stock of clothespins.

I had heard that X was an expert calligrapher, and I next brought a doorplate to be inscribed. I have said that my name is Iké Takeichiró. Because it can be misread Ikétaké Ichiró, I asked him to leave a space between the first character and the other three. He happily agreed, and he did not again forget my name.

I had been reminded of his talent by the bath pails out drying in the garden. On the bottom of each round and oval wooden bucket, a beautifully written character—"Upper," "Lower," "Men," "Women," and so on—testified to X's love of hygiene and order. Somehow those round "Men" and "Women" made me think of masks for "good people" and "bad people" in a morality play—which subject reminds me of another performance.

X never missed his radio callisthenics. Hardly calisthenics—he moved his arms and legs at random, after a style quite his own. Sometimes he would sit on the parlor floor and flex his wrists, sometimes he would kneel and shake his head. The spectacle was effective comedy; but, for X, radio calisthenics were as serious as prayer.

Not only was he, like M. Taille "very sober," he was much attached to life, and he had long made a point of trying out everything said to be good for the body.

As the years passed, respect for details had become an obsession, and attachment to life a blind clinging; and the health prescriptions left to him had gradually dwindled to the bath and calisthenics.

The precision one noted in the bath buckets characterized the workings of the house. From the places at the table, to the setting of the tableware, to the arrangement of the bedding, there was nothing that had not had its order preserved for decades.

When, for unavoidable reasons, a rule had to be broken, X's uneasiness wrung one's heart.

One day I was discussing the marriage problem with Yoshihidé in the garden cottage that was later to be his and his wife's. There were persistent indications of quarreling out by the kitchen door. Summoned by the old woman as the tension mounted, Yoshihidé was slow in coming back. I slipped on a pair of clogs and went out through the garden for a look. In the narrow passage between the bath and the hedge, X was muttering something and walking back and forth in small, fretful steps, his hands clasped behind his back. His face registered the blackest dejection.

"But it's nothing an amateur can do, Father. The heater will have to be changed." Yoshihidé had his head in the oven.

"Can't something be done? Can't something . . . ?" There was a tremor in the old man's voice as he stopped behind Yoshihidé.

The old woman was standing in the kitchen door.

"It's exactly as I've been telling you," she said sharply.

"Will it kill you to go without a bath for a day or two?"

"Oh, Mr. Iké. Can't something be done?" The shattered face turned toward me.

To hide my confusion, I looked into the oven from beside Yoshihidé. The leak was large—that much anyone could see. X had been trying desperately to light a fire in the wet oven, and half-burned bits of paper and wood were scattered about as if to punctuate the long argument.

Yoshihidé and I quieted him and saw him into the sitting room. After turning on the radio and assuring him that the younger brother would be sent for a plumber, Yoshihidé signaled with his eyes that we should withdraw to the cottage.

Time after time we heard his father calling to his wife in the kitchen, asking if the boy had come back. When the sound of opening and closing doors stopped, there was a strange silence through the house.

I do not know how long it was before we heard a shriek from the old woman. "In bed already, and it's broad daylight. Whoever heard of going to bed without dinner, and you're no baby or invalid either! I won't have it! I won't!"

I remember the chill that passed over me: X might well be taking to his bed for good.

As long as order was preserved, life was preserved. Yoshihidé and I at length realized that this philosophy explained the complications in the way of his own marriage.

When the subject came up, the mother would say: "Whatever is all right with your father is all right with me."

And the old man would say, slowly and with great dignity: "We shall give the matter careful consideration, and let you know our decision." There the matter ended.

Though I was determined to act with restraint and deliberation, it was not always easy to hide my impatience.

Then one day: "Mr. Iké, there is something I greatly regret having to tell you."

Given the importance of my mission, I was naturally startled by these grave words.

"In the matter of the plate with which you entrusted me some days ago."

"I beg your pardon?"

"Since you told me you wanted a space left between family name and given name, I searched with considerable diligence for an example in Chinese texts and other materials at my disposal, and it now seems safe to conclude that precedents do not exist. I took responsibility upon myself, and have therefore been casting about for a solution. Now I have resolved to ask that you release me from the obligation. I must beg your forgiveness. I am truly sorry."

He bowed deeply. I could think of no way to apologize for having let such a trivial request cause him such pain.

"I see. My ignorance is appalling." I then asked if I might not have him write my name according to the rules, and happiness flooded his face. He would do it immediately—he was most engaging as he turned to his brush and ink.

A neighbor noticed the plate, which I hung out with slightly mixed feelings. It was the beginning of the war, and neighborhood associations were just being organized. As the praise was lavish, I mentioned the name of the calligrapher. My neighbor, who had a position in a Mitsubishi manufacturing company, said that he knew the gentleman—in fact had heard him speak of calligraphy when they chanced to be together two months before at the wake of a certain scholar. My neighbor was an authority on aeronautics, familiar to all of us as chief engineer for his company. I knew too that he lived between our station and the next.

"A fine old gentleman in an old-fashioned frock coat. He sat bolt upright half the night. A distant relative of the dead man?"

"Probably not a relative but a middle-school teacher," I answered.

"I think I understand, then. You remember the funeral in front of the station a couple of weeks ago? At the Hakusensha?"

"I don't believe I noticed. The laundry, is it?"

There was a shabby little business district by the station, no more than twenty shops in all. Toward the middle was the laundry, a blue shack probably painted by the owner himself.

"I came home on the last train and heard chanting. Five or six people from the neighborhood were in for the wake. And there was that same old man, I'm sure it was he, sitting bolt upright in his frock coat. It seemed odd, but I suppose it had something to do with his teaching."

I asked Yoshihidé, who frowned and broke in before I had finished.

"The old man has gone to the funeral of every last friend and acquaintance, near and far, rain and shine. You didn't know? And now that he's retired at home he goes to all the wakes in the neighborhood. Old residents call him the funeral man. He never has anything to eat or drink, though. The nickname means that he's a little odd, not that he's looking for free meals."

*   *   *

My friendship for Yoshihidé aside, I was more and more sure that both for Yoshihidé himself and for his family the girl he had chosen was the best he was likely to find.

The girl and I conspired in a harmless way to have her visit the house. The conspiracy went smoothly, but it did no good whatsoever. Time passed. I became aware of something besides the old man's irresolution. Though she may not have been conscious of the fact herself, the old woman revealed in her words and acts the maternal jealousy one sees when the moment arrives to decide upon a mate for a son. Yoshihidé had to be stirred to action.

Yoshihidé's absolute weapon was not of a violent nature, as I learned after he had used it. With the permission of a young uncle, his mother's brother, he hid himself for about a week in the uncle's house and made it appear that he had run away from home. The uncle and I were to solve his problem in his absence. As the uncle put it, there was no need for low comedy. He wanted to teach his sister a lesson, however, and he thought there might in the future be considerable advantage from "rebaptizing" the unworldly mother who would one day have to live with the young couple. And there was Yoshihidé's own view:

"It's because of my father's attachment to life that he's getting old in such a hurry. His obsession with fixed routines, his fear of letting anyone new into the house—it all comes from a blind fight to hold on to what he has left of life. Both my parents think a woman is out to steal their son; but as far as the old man is concerned, I'll really be playing the part of the affectionate son when I put an end to the nonsense for good."

Since the "low comedy" on the small stage of the X house made me a trifle uncomfortable, I shall describe only the essentials.

Yoshihidé disappeared, leaving a farewell letter behind. The next day I visited the silent house. The old woman came hesitantly to the door. She was most upset.

"Mr. Iké. Yoshihidé— But come in. Father, Mr. Iké is here." As she led me down the hall she gave me an emergency report. My own disingenuousness rather repelled me. The uncle had only that morning told me what I have recounted here, and I had come in disguise, so to speak.

"See? Look at him! He's completely useless when you need him most." The old man was sitting bolt upright at his usual place in the parlor. "Ask him what he's been thinking about since last night, Mr. Iké. He won't say a word to me. He won't understand how I feel."

X remained silent as I sat before him, though the upper half of his body swayed slightly. He would not usually have been guilty of such laxity.

"Mr. Iké. Rasselas—" grave words came from him, words for which my ears were not prepared—"Rasselas was too happy and went out to seek unhappiness."

It was not only *my* ears that were unprepared for this remark. Between us was the profile of the old woman, a trace of whiskers apparent on the upper lip. She was looking at her husband in complete bewilderment.

"Rasselas was too happy and went out to seek unhappiness."

His eyes were on the floor. Each word had its own special dignity, just as when he had first made the statement. After a short pause, he began again.

The wife suddenly turned to me. "Think of it! An oldest son, and not just an adolescent either, leaving two old parents and running away from home. Neither his father nor myself ever did a thing to deserve it." She spoke as if she could hold herself back no longer. For a moment she was choked with tears. "High school and college—you can't imagine the sacrifices we made for him."

"Rasselas was too happy and went out to seek unhappiness."

I do not know which of the two made me the more uncomfortable. Rasselas, Rasselas. Clearly it was the name of a person. Someone in Shakespeare? Horace? Homer? Rasselas, Rasselas. I looked at the ceiling and sought to distract myself with these queries.

"If he wants to get married, let him get married," said the old woman. "But why can't he come out and tell us, like a man? Weak, spineless, that's what he is."

Some one in Roman mythology? That was it. The name had the sound of Roman mythology. A calm satisfaction came over me. But X was speaking again:

"Rasselas. Rasselas was too happy—"

"Oh, shut up! What the devil does it matter if Rasselas was happy? Will that foreigner bring Yoshihidé back? You're useless enough anyway, and you're worse with Rasselas around. I say he can go to the devil."

Even X seemed a little surprised. He looked into his wife's face, over which tears were again streaming. I was pulled from my meditations.

"Right, Father? Have I even once objected to this woman he wants to marry? That I have not! I've been quietly encouraging him all the time. The trouble is with you—you and your indecision. Mr. Iké knows all about it."

The battle is won, I thought.

X had regained his self-possession. He was looking at the floor, and he seemed about to say something of Rasselas. I knew how to manage him. I put my arm around his shoulders, as Yoshihidé would have done, and spoke into his ear:

"Don't worry. I'll be responsible. I'll bring him back."

He nodded. The movement came to me warmly from his shoulders.

*   *   *

Having received a pretty young lady, the X house became more peaceful than ever. Yoshihidé told me that his father, so attached to fixed routines, took no notice of the cottage in which the young couple lived. All was quiet.

The old woman seemed to dry and shrivel, but she continued to bustle around the house.

We knew, as rations from the neighborhood association became smaller, that the war was approaching a crisis. The time came when Yoshihidé and I had as much spending money at the end of a month as at the beginning. There was nothing in the city to buy.

For six months X had been muttering something about dizzy spells. One day, before spring came, he fell dead of a heart attack. He was seventy-three or seventy-four, I believe. At the wake and the funeral there were probably people from the neighborhood who thought that only the February cold had kept the "funeral man" away.

The funeral was simple, as the times demanded. Tidying up afterward, Yoshihidé came upon his father's diary. A diary I call it, but it was in fact a series of brief, cryptic notes, many quite undecipherable, in an old memorandum book. Evidently he had disliked rain. On rainy days the entry was limited to a single word: "Rain."

But what most startled Yoshihidé was that there were entries for a full week after his father's death, written in his father's hand. Suddenly cold, Yoshihidé glanced over the last pages. He was unable to hold back tears at what he saw:

February 11.   Clear. Two rolls. Sweet.

February 12.   Very clear. By the calendar the cold season is over. Colder than ever. Fish chowder. Rice curry.

February 13.   Very clear. Three pieces of candy. Sweet. A pint of milk. No rations.

And so forth. I doubt if one can say that X picked too late a day to die. More terrible days were to come before the whole district was finally reduced to ashes.

When I heard of the diary from Yoshihidé, I thought of one morning late in the previous autumn when I had seen the old man and woman as probably no one else ever saw them. I never told this to Yoshihidé.

*   *   *

In October, my wife had had her first child.

Several hundred yards from the railway there was a fairly large hatchery; and the times were still such that a regular customer, if he did not mind risking a fruitless walk early in the morning, might every other week or so buy a few eggs. If he was very lucky, he might even go home with several ounces of chicken.

The appointed morning each week was the morning when life seemed most worth living.

I left home at about six. It was early November, and already chilly. Though I did think it rather a heavy mist, I did not realize, in the semi-darkness, how heavy it was. As the headlight of the earliest train moved slowly past the crossing, I saw that it was a fog such as we had not recently had. I crossed the tracks. I knew the road well, but I felt a childish thrill at each step. Only my head and shoulders floated above the fog. My heart raced at the thought of the hatchery, however, and I did not let the fog delay me.

I was to be disappointed. A military supply unit had advanced upon the place the day before and taken all the eggs. I had to be satisfied with three that had just been laid, indeed were still warm. Even so, I could hardly call myself unlucky.

The barracks-like hatchery was dark on the brightest day. Restraining the impulse to rush home and pass the spoils on to my wife, I started for an old chair far back in the dim earth-floored room and filled my pipe with the powdery war-time tobacco. The small eastern window suggested that day had at length come. I bent to look out.

The fog was hardly a fog any more, though the distant woods were still wrapped in white, and here and there a wisp sped to the west over the open fields. Lights faded and reappeared in the distance, marking the speed of the fog.

A human form passed from left to right, startlingly close to the window. A hunting cap and stick—it was X. A step or two behind, in the baggy trousers that were standard wear for women in those times, was his dry, shriveled wife.

Padding about in rubber boots, the owner of the hatchery wiped his hands, opened the wooden door, and came back into the empty building. As the two figures disappeared from the window, he spoke to them at the door.

"Good morning. Sorry, nothing today. But now that you're here, suppose you have a raw egg, each of you. . . . I beg your pardon?"

I first heard the old woman's thanks. Wondering whether to speak to them or wait for them to leave, I decided upon the latter course. I felt the eggs still warm in my pocket. As the rubber boots came near again, I walked to the door. I asked about the old couple as I paid for the eggs.

"That old fellow? He says his eyes are going bad on him, and he comes in to drink blood when I've been killing chickens."

I noticed that the cage usually full of chickens for the slaughter was missing. The place was quiet—there was not a single lamenting voice. If I had to see the old couple at the hatchery, I had picked a good day.

If I left now, I would overtake them, each with an egg; and overtaking them, I would have to speak. I finally turned to the left, choosing a slightly longer route through the cedar grove.

Among the trees, green with the last of the fog, the cold air washed my shoulders. I thought again of that soliloquy—I had almost forgotten it—and I said twice to myself:

"Rasselas. Rasselas was too happy and went out to seek unhappiness."

*   *   *

I am among those who were fortunate enough to return from the war. In the jungles and on the hills I called to Rasselas as to a guardian deity. I have never had the energy to find out who he was.

厭がらせの年齢

丹羽文雄

THE HATEFUL AGE

BY Niwa Fumio

TRANSLATED BY Ivan Morris

Niwa Fumio was born in 1904 into a family of Buddhist priests. When, on his graduation from Waseda University, he found that he was unable to support himself by literary work, he too joined the priesthood. He continued writing, however, and after 1932 his stories began to gain recognition.

Niwa's early works were stories and novels of manners, written mainly in the personal vein that had become usual for Japanese fiction. There was a strong sensualism in his writing, especially in his descriptions of feminine psychology and passion. "Superfluous Flesh" (1934), for example, portrays a young man's growing interest in his mother's sensual nature as he observes her relations with a lover. The subject of a mother eloping with her lover recurs in several of Niwa's novels and is taken from his own childhood experience.

In his more recent books Niwa has tended toward a form of objective realism and has frequently found his material in current social problems. Many of his postwar works consist of realistic descriptions of customs and circumstances in present-day rural and urban Japan. In particular, he has written a number of stories and novels dealing with the social confusion that followed the surrender of 1945. "The Serpent and the Dove" (1953), for instance, deals with one of the new religious sects that mushroomed in postwar Japan. *"The Hateful Age"* is a very explicit treatment of one growing social problem in modern Japan.

Niwa, an extremely energetic and prolific author, is constantly experimenting with new methods of expression and approach. His interest in Shinshū Buddhism and in the thought of the founder, Shinran Shōnin, adds depth to many of his writings. Niwa Fumio has one of the largest followings of the writers who started their work in the early Shōwa period.

"The Hateful Age" (Iyagarase no Nenrei) was first published in 1947, when the author was forty-three. It is an attack (almost unprecedented in Japan) on one facet of the family system. In this story, Niwa Fumio has criticized the traditional Japanese veneration for old people, and for longevity in general, which he considers to be both anachronistic and harmful. With the percentage of octogenarians in Japan increasing at a rapid rate (from 4.5 percent in 1950 to an estimated 10.8 percent in 1980), the story is, to say the least, topical. It has attracted considerable attention since its publication and the expression *"the hateful age"* has even passed into current usage.

Although this story is concerned specifically with conditions in postwar Japan, the general problem which it describes is, of course, far from unknown in the West. Apart from its sociologic interest, *"The Hateful Age"* gives an unusually penetrating picture of senility in its physical and psychological aspects.

With the permission of the author, certain cuts have been made in the present translation.

I

AT NIGHT, if anyone walked along the creaking passage to the toilet, he would invariably be startled by a voice from the darkness: "Who's there?" It was not the eager voice of someone longing to establish a human contact in the lonely night; nor was it the surprised voice of a person suddenly shaken from sleep. No, it was a cool, wide-awake voice and one could tell that its owner had not slept a wink all night. They all knew that the voice was old Umé's, and yet they could not help feeling a wave of revulsion.

The passer-by would identify himself—"It's I, Granny"—and that normally was the end of the exchange. Umé's granddaughters Senko and Ruriko had adapted themselves to this nightly ritual; their replies had become mere reflex actions. But in the case of Senko's husband, Itami, things did not always go so smoothly.

One night as footsteps sounded along the passage and Umé called out her usual challenge, an irritated voice shot back: "It's I—Itami. What do you want?"

Old Umé had expected no more than a word of identification, her question having been as automatic a reaction to footsteps as the creaking of the floor boards in the passage. Now in the darkness of her tiny room she sat up in bed, somewhat taken aback.

"All right, Granny," repeated Itami, "tell me what you want." Still no reply. There was, in fact, nothing for Umé to say. "It's intolerable!" cried Itami, growing angry. "Whose house do you think this is? It's my house, let me tell you, and I don't have to give an accounting if I want to go to the toilet at night. What's the matter with you, anyhow? You sleep all day long like a dead person, and then at night you stay awake spying on us. It gives me the creeps to think of you sitting there with your goggle-eyes listening to us breathing while we're peacefully asleep. Why can't you behave yourself like other old women?"

By this time the whole household was awake. The neighbors, whose house was separated only by a board partition, had also been disturbed by the angry shouts.

Itami strode back to his room, breathing heavily. His wife had turned on the light and was sitting up in bed.

"What's Granny done now?"' she said.

"I'm fed up," shouted Itami. "Fed up! I don't even feel I'm in my own house any longer. Why on earth should I have to get that old hag's permission every time I go to the toilet?"

"Of course you don't have to get permission," said Senko in a conciliatory voice. "Granny just calls out like that automatically whenever she hears footsteps. I suppose she gets bored lying awake all night. So she says 'Who's there?' to break the monotony."

"Well, you're her granddaughter," said Itami, pacing up and down the room, "so I suppose you can make allowances for her. To me she's just a hateful old woman. And an old hypocrite too. When people are watching, she pretends she's half crippled, and totters about groaning as if every step were pure torture. But when she thinks no one's looking, she walks along briskly enough. Then she's got this delightful habit of stealing. The moment we're out of our room, she rushes in, opens the drawers and helps herself to whatever she happens to find. I'm a pretty broad-minded fellow but I really don't see why I should have to support a thief in the house."

"But, Itami, you've got to remember she's eighty-six years old. She really doesn't know what she's doing half the time."

"I'm not so sure about that. I caught her taking money out of my wallet yesterday. All I know is that in that little body of hers the spite and hypocrisy and dishonesty of eighty-six years have coagulated into a solid core of wickedness. If she needs money, why on earth can't she tell me? What I can't stand is to have her stealing behind my back."

Itami sat down on the bed. His face was livid.

"That old woman is a real cancer. She's destroying our whole family. Your sister Sachiko and her husband shoved her on to us after their house was bombed and they moved to the country. They said they didn't have enough room, but of course the long and short of it is that they couldn't stand her any longer. So now you and your sister quarrel whenever you meet. She's a regular disease, that old woman."

"Oh come now, Itami," said Senko, "don't exaggerate."

"I only wish I were exaggerating. No, there's only one thing for us to do: get rid of her before she destroys us. If she starves on the streets —well, that's too bad. People who don't work and spend their time eating and being a nuisance don't deserve to live these days. In any case, she can't stay here any longer!"

"But if you throw her out, she'll simply go to the police and give our name and they'll bring her right back. There's no point trying to put her into an institution either; nowadays they only take people who have no families to look after them. It's not as easy as all that to get rid of her, you know."

"And don't think she doesn't realize it. She's a shrewd old thing and she knows that someone in the family is going to take care of her, no matter what she does. Well, it isn't going to be me any more! The greedy, ungrateful, dirty old pig! 'I want more rice, I want more rice!' —I can just hear her whining away at table. The other day I heard her say that we were trying to starve her and that she was going to get even with us by putting a curse on us all. 'My curses never fail,' she said. 'When I curse people, they die!'"

"She said that?" said Senko, sitting up abruptly. "Well, this time she's gone too far—even for me. I spend half my time looking after her and then I get cursed for my pains. We've done our duty for three months. Now Sachiko and her husband can take over again."

"Excellent," said Itami. "I'm glad you see things my way. There's no reason they should get out of their responsibilities, just because they've moved into the country. Your trouble, Senko, is that you're too kind to people."

With this comforting thought in mind, Senko began to make preparations the very next morning to transfer old Umé to her sister's place in the mountains. The practical problem of getting her senile grandmother to an unknown village hundreds of miles away was far from simple. Certainly the old woman never could have managed the trip by herself, even assuming that she had been willing to try. If only one could hang a label around her neck and hand l er to the postman for delivery!

Yes, thought Senko, Granny was just like some sort of a disease, visited permanently on the family, and now afflicting the third generation. Umé had outlived not only her husband, but her daughter as well. Now Senko and Sachiko, the two older granddaughters, were saddled with the care of someone who should have died years ago. As Senko thought of her comfortable existence with Itami menaced by that malicious old woman, she began to grow very sorry for herself. They had had luck, Itami and she: luck in that their house was not bombed to smithereens like that of Sachiko and her husband; luck in that absence of children allowed them living space enjoyed by few of their compatriots; luck in that they could still afford the luxury of a maid. But now their good luck was about to run out because she could think of no way of transferring her grandmother to Sachiko.

Finally she hit on a solution which satisfied the demands both of practicality and of social convention. Ruriko, her younger sister, was the answer. Yes, Ruriko, it seemed to Senko, had been put into the world for the express purpose of fulfilling this delicate mission. As the old woman was incapable of walking more than a few yards, Ruriko, a strapping girl of twenty, would carry her up the mountain road on her back. After all, old Umé weighed little more than a sack of charcoal. True, it would be a bit embarrassing for the girl to be seen walking along with a dirty old crone perched on her shoulders, but a desperate situation called for desperate measures.

"You've always taken a lot of trouble over Granny," said Senko to Ruriko that same morning. "Surely you won't mind doing this last thing for her. After all, we do give you a nice home here, don't we? You don't want it all to be ruined."

After much cajoling, abetted by sisterly authority, Senko prevailed on Ruriko to undertake the task.

II

And now came the morning of departure. Old Umé sat in the kitchen, seemingly unaware that a major change was impending. Senko and Ruriko busied themselves packing a bundle of their grandmother's clothes and her other scanty possessions.

"All right," said Senko, when they had finished, "we can start strapping her on now. Don't worry, Ruriko," she added, noticing her sister's accusing expression. "It'll all be ancient history by this evening. Remember, whatever Sachiko and Minobé say, you must leave her there. If they get angry with us—well, it can't be helped. They passed her on to us on the pretext of having lost their house. Well, that excuse is beginning to wear thin. Itami and I stayed here in Tokyo right through the war at the risk of our lives and managed to save our house from incendiary bombs. We didn't do it just to be saddled with Granny for the rest of our days."

Meanwhile old Umé sat with a blank look on her wrinkled face. Impossible to tell how much of this conversation she had heard or absorbed.

"Just look at her!" said Senko with disgust. "She hasn't even bothered to thank us for all the trouble we've taken over her. Itami's right. She really is a cancer. All she can do is destroy things."

"It's time to go," said Ruriko, standing up. Senko lifted Umé and strapped her to her sister's back.

"Well, here are the tickets," she said. "They're our parting gift to Granny."

As Ruriko trudged toward the station, she soon realized that though Granny weighed no more than a child, her body with its long legs and relatively short trunk was very much harder to carry. The thin lanky legs were clamped like a painful brace around Ruriko's waist, and by the time they approached the station, walking had become an agony. The ordeal was not only physical. In carrying someone eighty-six years old, one is supporting not just a body, but all the weight of a personal history that has accumulated ponderously over the decades.

The compartment was crowded, but one of the passengers, seeing Ruriko enter with her peculiar burden, offered his seat. Directly opposite her was a woman in her thirties, also accompanied by an old lady. Soon after the train started she addressed Ruriko:

"Excuse me, but where are you taking yours?"

"I'm leaving her at my sister's place in the country."

"Well, we seem to be in the same boat." said the woman, with a sigh. She and Ruriko exchanged the bitter smiles of people who share some painful illness. "How old is she?" the other woman asked.

"Eighty-six."

"Mine's eighty." She glanced about the carriage and went on in a lower voice. "Why on earth do they live on to be eighty? I just can't make it out. They live on and on and on, until they're of no use to anyone—until even they themselves are fed up with living. All that mine cares about nowadays is food, and she can't get it into her head that rice is rationed. She's always accusing us of being mean to her, even though she gets her full ration."

"Mine's the same," said Ruriko. "She's got the appetite of two normal people. I really don't know how she can eat so much, just sitting still all day."

"They're rice-eating spooks!" said the woman, with venom. "Just rice-eating spooks!"

Meanwhile the two "spooks" sat gazing vacantly out of the window at the changing scenery, evidently unaware that they were being discussed. The other passengers had overheard the conversation and were staring with undissembled curiosity at the two old women. From their expressions it was clear that they did not feel they were looking at human beings at all but rather at some strange species of superannuated plant or animal.

Apparently it did not occur to them that they all shared a common destiny with these old women, that unless their lives should be cut short by illness or accident, they too were condemned to become nothing but troublesome baggage carted along by their resentful families. With a little more imagination they might have regarded these two octogenarians not as members of some grotesque genus but as living warnings that they themselves would become old and useless, bereft of all joy of living and with only death to look forward to—yet still requiring three good meals a day. For some reason, the onlookers seemed to assume that they alone were immune to the scourge of senility.

After several uneventful hours, the train arrived at its destination. Gathering her courage, Ruriko set off on the four-mile trip to the farm where her sister and brother-in-law had made their home since leaving Tokyo. Soon she found herself on a rough country road which wound its way steeply over the hills; after less than a mile, her whole body was perspiring and her breath came in painful gasps. She set her teeth and trudged doggedly on. Abruptly she was startled by her grandmother's croaky voice.

"Oh, my legs hurt! Put me down by the road, child. I've got to rest a while."

"What's that?" said Ruriko. "I'm the one that needs a rest, not you. But I'm not stopping now till we get there."

"It hurts all over," said Umé. "My legs feel as if they're being torn right off. The straps are eating into my armpits."

"I'm sorry," said Ruriko, panting as she trudged up the hill, "but it's your own fault. If you hadn't threatened to put a curse on the family, you'd still be living comfortably in Tokyo with Senko. And I wouldn't be going through this agony."

"It hurts . . . it hurts!"

"Oh, stop it!" said Ruriko, giving her back such a shake that they both almost fell over in the dust.

It was a cold winter's afternoon, but Ruriko was unaware of the temperature; her face was flushed and beaded with perspiration. A man passed in the opposite direction and gaped at the girl.

"Let me down, for mercy's sake!" cried Umé. "My legs hurt so terribly. I beg you—dear little Ruriko, please let me down just for a minute."

"You needn't think you can get round me with that honeyed voice," said Ruriko. "You always speak like that when you want something."

They had reached the top of the hill now. Ruriko could see the rice fields, hills, and forests spread out under a lambent sky; she breathed in the clear country air. How she could have enjoyed it all had she not been saddled with an eighty-six-year-old crone!

"Put me down! Put me down! I'm dying, I tell you!"

Ruriko walked steadily on, paying no attention to her grandmother's desperate cries, which reached a crescendo as a man approached from the opposite direction. "Help, help! I'm dying!" she screamed at him. The man stopped, nonplussed by the hysterical voice and by the extraordinary apparition of an old woman riding on a girl's back far out in the country.

Ruriko looked at him with a wry smile. "Really, Granny, you must try and be patient," she said. "We aren't nearly there yet."

The man grinned sympathetically and continued on his way. Old Umé's first maneuver had failed, but she had evidently sensed a certain open kindliness among these countryfolk and the next time someone passed, she uttered her appeal with redoubled vigor. "Help! I'm dying! I'm being murdered! Help me, sir!"

Again the man stopped and again Ruriko had to smile reassuring[ly]. After this had happened three or four times, she felt that her face fixed into a sort of grimace.

"All right, Granny," said Ruriko, stopping suddenly. "I'll let you down, if that's what you really want. But don't think I'm going to pick you up again. I'm through!"

She unfastened the straps and roughly put Umé down by the side of the road. When the old woman tried to get to her feet, she promptly lost her balance and fell headlong into the ditch; though she struggled to raise herself, her arms were too weak to be of any use. The road was at an incline and Umé's head was pointing downward. She lay there at last without moving, as helpless as a trussed chicken. Her body was covered with mud and a dirty stream of water trickled over her; the blood oozed from her cheek and forehead, where she had grazed herself.

Ruriko stood by the road wiping the perspiration from her face; then she put a handkerchief under her dress and wiped her arms and breasts. The hair above her forehead was drenched, as if she had been caught in a rainstorm.

After a few minutes, Umé began to wriggle about in the ditch. She lacked the energy to call for help and her movements were so uncoordinated that she could not possibly sit up, let alone crawl onto the road. One of her legs stuck out at an odd angle, looking like an emaciated arm—and, indeed, for old Umé, the distinction between arms and legs seemed little more than academic. Her body had attained that peculiar thinness which denotes not starvation but a state in which food can no longer nourish the flesh and muscles. If one were to pinch her leg, the mark would remain for several minutes, and if one pulled the flesh on her arm, it would remain folded over, flaccid and inert.

"What's happened, miss?"

A man's voice startled Ruriko, and when she looked up she saw a middle-aged peasant standing by the ditch staring at Umé.

"Granny fell in," said Ruriko. "I'm carrying her to my sister's at the Shimomura farm."

"The Shimomura farm, eh?" said the farmer in his rustic dialect. "That'll be about another mile and a half, I reckon. Look miss, I'll be going most of the way myself. I'll carry her for you, if you like."

The man bent over and without any effort picked old Umé out of the ditch. She shook her long arms, as if to make sure that they were still properly attached, and her movements were as jerky and disconnected as those of a badly manipulated puppet. Lifting her onto his shoulders without a word, the man started walking briskly down the hill; he strode along freely, as if he were simply carrying a sack of rice.

"That'll be your sister's place," he said after about half an hour, pointing to a farm on the top of a nearby hill. "I'll leave you here."

Ruriko thanked him profusely and bent down while he shifted Granny to her own back. She climbed the hill with new vigor and soon reached the gate of the farm, where her three small nephews caught sight of her.

"Ruriko's here, Mummy! She's brought Granny. Is Granny coming to stay?" they shouted.

Ruriko quickly unfastened the straps and lowered the old woman to the floor. She was propping her against the wall as the door opened and Sachiko burst out:

"What do you mean by this? How could you bring Granny without even giving us warning?"

"Senko told me to."

"She did, did she? How old are you anyway, Ruriko? I should think you'd have enough sense not to bring a helpless old woman into the mountains like this without at least letting us know beforehand. Do you realize how we live here? There are five of us in two rooms. There isn't space for an extra chair, let alone for an old woman who needs constant attention."

"I had to bring her," repeated Ruriko dully.

"Had to! What do you mean, had to? Senko and Itami have a lovely big house; they don't have any children and they've even managed to keep a maid. We all know that Itami has made plenty on the black market. As for us, we have one eight-mat room full of cupboards, trunks, and packing cases where we all sleep. Then we've got a six-mat living room where we keep Minobé's painting equipment, the food stores, the tea chest, and the bookcases. Where on earth do you expect us to put Granny?"

Ruriko's face was red with indignation. After the four hours in the train and the grueling walk over the hills, this was more than she could bear. Her face twisted and she burst into tears.

"It's not my fault! It's not my fault!" she repeated between sobs.

The door opened and Minobé stepped onto the porch. After nodding to Ruriko, he glanced at Umé with a horrified expression.

"I really don't know how they could do such a thing," he murmured. "What goes on inside such people's minds, I wonder?"

"Itami threatened to move into his office if Granny stayed any longer," Ruriko said, still sobbing. "He swore that Granny was driving him mad."

"Well, so she probably was," said Sachiko. "But this was Senko's responsibility and she's got no right to wriggle out of it. A few years ago, when Granny could still be of some use for errands, Senko didn't mind having her around; now that she's become just a burden, Senko throws her out like a worn-out glove. . . ."

"Well, there's no use going into all that," Minobé interrupted. "She's here and I suppose we'll have to make the best of it. One's always at a disadvantage when dealing with people like your sister and Itami; patience, kindness, self-sacrifice—those are all so many words for them. As I said, though, we'll manage somehow. But good heavens, Ruriko, where did all that blood and dirt on Granny's face come from?"

"She fell into the ditch."

"H'm. She'll certainly need a good washing," said Minobé, studying old Umé's battered face. "Hello, Granny," he addressed her. "I'm afraid you're going to find life a bit primitive here after Tokyo. We don't have any electricity, you know."

Umé had been gazing with a bored expression at the unaccustomed fields and mountains. Now realizing that she was being addressed, she blinked vaguely at Minobé, put both hands on the porch, and began to lower and raise her head, rhythmically striking her forehead on the floor in the old-fashioned ceremonial manner.

"I'm just a nuisance," she said. "Forgive me, forgive me."

Everyone was amazed at this remarkable access of lucidity.

"Don't worry, Granny," said Minobé and went indoors.

Ruriko spent the night at the farm and left for Tokyo the following morning. She was delighted to be returning to Senko's household, where a large circle of acquaintances enlivened the days; also, she was glad to escape from the unpleasant atmosphere that had prevailed at the farm since Granny's arrival. She remembered that she was going back to a house with no old woman inside, and her step was springy as she hurried down the hill.

III

For some days after her arrival in the country, Umé complained of pains in her legs, in her chest, in her arms—in fact almost everywhere. Actually, her fall into the ditch had caused no more than a few bruises and after about a week she was as fit as ever. It would take more than a little fall to kill Granny!

They installed a bedroll for her next to the charcoal brazier in the living room and put a folding screen round it. The door of this room opened on the back porch, which the family had improvised as a kitchen. Now and then, Granny would peep from behind the screen and, if no one was about, shuffle out stealthily to the porch and appropriate whatever she happened to find—a box of matches, a dishcloth, a kitchen knife. At such times she would acquire a speed of locomotion and a nimbleness of gesture quite remarkable for a woman in her eighties; as her hand darted out toward the coveted object, she looked like someone whose whole life had been devoted to the art of pilfering. Stealing had become such a habit with her by now that she was hardly conscious of it.

On warm days, Sachiko used to carry her grandmother onto the front porch and leave her to bask in the sun. One morning as she sat there dozing, she suddenly rolled off the porch, hit her head on the ground, described a complete somersault in her sleep, and woke up—quite unscathed. Then she toddled back to her room and began poking the charcoal brazier. She was evidently unaware that anything had happened; nor had it occurred to her to wonder why she had awakened lying flat in the grass.

Often Minobé used to sit looking intently at old Umé for minutes on end, as though studying a model for his painting. The hair on top of her head was no more than a fuzz, but at the sides it grew in thick white tufts; her eyebrows, too, were white and bushy. She had an oval face with deep-set eyes, an aquiline nose, and a small, elegant chin. It was not hard to imagine that it had once been a beautiful face. Recently freckles had begun to spread from her forehead to the crown of her head.

After a while, becoming aware that she was being observed, Umé would laugh awkwardly. Then she would turn aside and gaze into the distance, as if she were quite alone. To Minobé there was something almost frightening about this instinctive movement of Umé's. It made him think of animals who can from one moment to another disregard the human onlooker. He felt that only someone who had lived an immense number of years could effect a gesture of such strange, almost inhuman aloofness; never could it be acquired by deliberate study or imitation.

One day a young friend come to visit Minobé from Tokyo. They

were talking in the living room when Umé tottered out from behind her screen. The guest gave a start—indeed, anyone would have been shocked at this strange, ghost-like figure.

"Is he from Echigo?" Umé demanded, and stared straight at the visitor.

"I'm afraid not, Granny," answered Minobé. "This is a friend of mine from Tokyo."

"Are you sure I didn't know him in Echigo?"

"Yes, quite sure, Granny," said Minobé. "You've never met him before."

After that, Umé was forever asking if people came from Echigo. It was her home province, which she had left over sixty years before, at the time of her marriage. Anyone whom Umé had known there would by this time be at least in his eighties. But such a detail did not bother her. Minobé wondered whether the approach of death brought vague memories of her distant youth to Granny.

Studying her with almost scientific objectivity, Minobé became more and more interested in his aged grandmother-in-law. Often he used to question Sachiko about her. It seemed that Umé's family was of ancient lineage; there was even a tradition that in the twelfth century the great military leader Minamoto no Yoshitsuné had lodged at their house. After her marriage Umé had moved to Tokyo, where her husband had died when she was thirty-two, leaving her with an only daughter. The next fifty-four years had been spent as a widow.

Now widowhood was certainly a worthy state, thought Minobé. But would not a woman be ashamed to face her husband in the grave after outliving him even for twenty years? By then she would have changed beyond recognition and, besides, her own memory of the man would be growing very dim; they would meet like two embarrassed strangers. Yet Umé had had the audacity to linger on more than fifty years, and even now there was no telling when she would take her place beside her husband. Their names had been engraved next to each other on the tombstone, with Umé's name colored in red, as tradition demanded, to show that she was still alive. The red had long since worn away—and still Umé survived. She was a stubborn old woman!

Among her more valued possessions had been a photograph of her husband taken shortly before his death. As she belonged to the Lotus sect of Buddhism, Umé had for years been in the habit of making offerings before this photograph; when she shared Minobé's house in Tokyo, he had often seen her prostrating herself before the dead man's image. Yet she had outlived her husband so long that any stranger would have taken this to be a picture of her son, or even her grandson. When the house was bombed, the photograph had disappeared, and from that moment Umé seemed to forget completely about it.

Apparently she had also forgotten the Lotus Sutra and religion in general. Perhaps she had passed the age when religion could any longer have real meaning. There were quite a few old women in the village where Minobé now lived in whom religion, and indeed all moral emotions, had long since atrophied. Bereft of higher feelings, some of them had sunk to levels of almost unbelievable squalor.

Only the other day an old hag had died at the age of eighty-eight. For the last two years she had spent nearly all her time by the manure piles, which seemed to have acquired a strange fascination; half blind and covered with dirt, she sat for hours rooting about in the filth. When finally she died, the neighbors did not bother to make the usual inventory of her possessions but took everything from her room, including the straw mats, and burned them by the side of the paddy fields. For the rest of the day the air was redolent with the smell of death and excrement.

Another old woman of seventy-nine, who lived with her family on a nearby farm, was equally sunk in filth. She used to take lumps of night soil and mold them into different forms as if they were clay. Then she would call to her grandchildren: "Come along, kiddies, here are some nice toys for you to play with." It was as though all that gives beauty to human existence had passed out of these old women into the hearts of younger, more sensitive people. Was it, Minobé wondered, that they had ended by rejecting the finer feelings of life, or did the feelings themselves abandon people when they became too old and too ugly?

IV

It soon became clear that Umé was going to be at least as much of a nuisance in the farmhouse as they had feared.

"You'll be the death of us all, Granny" moaned Sachiko. "We haven't had a proper night's sleep since you've been here. When will you get it into your head that the toilet is directly to the left when you go into the passage?"

Despite frequent injunctions of this kind, Umé almost invariably ended by going astray in the unlit house. Old age had evidently deprived her of all sense of direction, and as soon as she got out of bed, she began groping helplessly for the door to the passage. The room was small, but as she crawled around in all directions, it was like some vast deserted plain. She stretched her hands out into the darkness, hoping to touch the brazier, the table, in fact any object that would rescue her from this dreadful sense of isolation and link her once more to the safe world of human beings. Yet, though the room was crowded with furniture, she somehow managed to crawl about for minutes on end without finding anything.

"Where on earth can I have got to?" she muttered, as she changed her course once again. Then her forlorn voice echoed through the darkness: "Sachiko, Sachiko! For mercy's sake, child, come and help me! I'm completely lost! Help!"

In the next room, Sachiko and Minobé had already been awakened by the noise and were sitting up in bed. Suddenly there came a thump on the door and a moment later the sound of a handle being turned.

"Oh, Granny, that's the wrong door!" cried Sachiko, jumping out of bed. "You really are hopeless!"

Striking a match, she hurried into the next room, where she found Umé in a state of utter disarray, desperately grasping the handle of the door that led to the porch. With a sigh of resignation, Sachiko took the old woman by the hand, led her to the toilet, and then brought her back to bed.

On the following night they were awakened on three separate occasions; the routine was almost identical each time. When Umé had finally found the sliding door that opened to the passage, she would clutch the handle and lift herself to her feet, almost pulling the door out of its groove. Once in the passage, she started shuffling toward the toilet, dragging her left hand along the wall to orient herself. As soon as she felt the door of the toilet, she knew that she was nearing her goal. However, this did not end her trouble; the next hurdle was to find the door handle and that meant moving her hand all over the door, a process lasting several minutes. By this time Sachiko and her husband were wide awake. They would hear a voice croaking in the darkness: "Ah, here it is. Now all I've got to do is to turn it. Then I open the door—so—and walk right in."

Finally they heard the toilet door shut and all was blessedly silent. But not for long. A moment later Umé was again in the passage, lost and bewildered. She stretched out her left hand, remembering that she had used it on the journey from her room. Since she had turned round, however, what she now touched was the wall beyond the toilet, and this led her not to her door but to another wall, into which she bumped regularly every night. Thereupon she would let out a dismal wail: "Help, help, Sachiko! I'm lost! Which way do I go?" Once again Sachiko had to get up and rescue her.

These nightly excursions were only one of Umé's unpleasant habits. Despite strict orders to the contrary, she insisted on tampering with the charcoal brazier, with the result that she invariably managed to put it out. Then her querulous voice could be heard through the apartment: "The fire's gone out, Sachiko. Do come and light it, child. I'm cold. I'm dying of cold!"

Almost every morning when Sachiko made Umé's bed, she would come upon some object—a button, an envelope, a ball of string—that Granny had stolen and carefully sequestered under the bedding. The fact that these things would eventually be retrieved did not deter the old woman; the habit of stealing had become far too deeply ingrained for the most strenuous reprimands to have effect. Moreover, there seemed to be little use in lecturing her, as Umé apparently failed to hear or to understand; she simply stared ahead with a blank, bewildered look, and Sachiko assumed that in her old age Umé was becoming deaf. However, the children were not so easily deluded, and they took great delight in exposing their great-grandmother's pretense.

"Would you like a raw onion, Granny?" said one of the little boys, standing at the other end of the room, and speaking in a low voice which would normally fail to make the slightest impression on Umé. Onions were the old lady's favorite food and she immediately rose to the bait.

"An onion?" she said. "Oh yes, I'd love one."

"I caught you that time, Granny!" cried the boy, and ran out of the room laughing.

Umé was a tough old woman, but before long the strain of life in a primitive mountain village began to tell even on her. She missed the good food and comfort of Senko's house, and made no bones about telling everyone so.

"Oh, I wish I was back in Tokyo!" she muttered one day, as she sat with Sachiko and Minobé by the charcoal brazier.

"If you'd behaved yourself properly you'd still be there," said Sachiko. "You've got no one to blame but yourself."

"I want to go back to Senko's," continued Umé in a plaintive whine.

"If that isn't adding insult to injury," said Sachiko to her husband.

"Well, it doesn't worry me," said Minobé, and laughed. "If I let your grandmother annoy me, I'd have lost my sanity long ago."

V

A few days later occurred an incident which reduced still further Umé's popularity in her new home. The children were playing with toy dragonflies and one of the missiles by chance flew off in the wrong direction and struck the old woman on the forehead. Crying out, she glared into the garden and there caught sight of the young culprit. In a tone that would have sent shivers down the spine of a tough samurai, let alone a small child, she screamed: "Curse you, you little fiend! Curse you, I say!" Taking from the folds of her dress a recently stolen dishcloth, she began to wipe the blood from her forehead.

At lunch time a few days later, the boy said to his father: "Granny's keeping that cloth with the blood on it."

"Really?" said Minobé. "Why?"

At that, Umé again extracted the dish cloth from her dress and held it up for all to see. In the center was a dark stain that could be recognized as blood.

"I'm keeping this as a memento," she said. "I'll show it to people so that they'll realize how I've been treated here."

"You know perfectly well that it was a mistake, Granny," said Minobé.

"I'm not so sure about that," Umé said. She had abandoned her usual deferential tone and spoke defiantly, almost harshly.

"All right," said Minobé, "if that's going to be your attitude, I can be just as disagreeable as anyone else."

At once Umé lowered her head and gave out an old woman's cackle. "Of course it was a mistake," she said. "I was only joking."

Staring at Umé, Minobé suddenly remembered the Confucian teachings on filial piety and respect for one's elders. Was it possible that the Master had had sly, wicked old women like this in mind when he expounded his noble precepts? To respect an insensitive old woman like Umé, conscious as she was of only the physical aspects of life, was like worshiping a stone idol. Umé had become just a body, in which it was impossible to detect the slightest trace of soul, spirit, conscience, or anything that makes human beings worthy of respect. Her greatest worry in life was that her grandchildren or great-grandchildren might be getting better food than she herself.

To be sure, thought Minobé, there were people like Kōda Rohan, the great scholar, whose intellectual powers remained unimpaired until his death at the age of eighty. Such people, indeed, seemed as they grew older to become constantly more sensitive and intelligent. They were one in a thousand. The remaining nine hundred and ninety-nine were destined to become distasteful, useless lumps of flesh, the scourge of relatives and a burden to society. There was hardly a family in Japan that did not suffer from the system in which old people had to be either cared for by their children or committed to primitive and sinister institutions. People had been complaining for years, but the traditional family system still lingered on, with all its inefficiency, hypocrisy, sentimentality, and injustice. It was high time for something to be done— not by sociologists, but by people all over Japan who were themselves suffering from these anachronistic traditions. "Study the demeanor of your parents," Confucius had told Tzu-hsia, "and never fail to treat them with true deference and affection." That, thought Minobé, might be all right in the case of people like Kōda Rohan, but for old Umé and her kind the maxim seemed totally inappropriate.

That very evening Minobé was dismayed to hear a farmer's wife say to Sachiko: "My, my, your old lady's looking fit as a fiddle, isn't she? She seems to be putting on a bit of weight too."

"Are you sure she isn't swelling up with water?" said Sachiko hopefully.

"Oh no," said the woman, "it's the clean country air and plain food that's done it. She's good for another five or six years, mark my words."

"The question is," said Sachiko with a sigh, "are we?"

VI

Not long afterward, Minobé was able to take over a house in Tokyo from a friend. He hired a van for the day and piled it high with furniture, luggage, and the six members of his family. The people whom they passed on the road stared in amazement at the huge load, and occasionally Minobé detected a look of sympathy on their faces. Umé sat on a packing case, her body shaking rhythmically in response to the vibration. After a few hours, she began muttering querulously, and Sachiko had to lift her up like a baby and hold her over the side of the truck while she relieved herself. At that moment Sachiko could not help feeling bitter hatred for this old woman with her withered body and long, chicken-like legs.

In the new house Umé was assigned a small room of her own next to the toilet. Here she would sit quietly and give herself over to a new and particularly annoying habit that she had acquired since her return to Tokyo: taking any piece of material she could lay hands on—clothes, towels, or sheets—she would systematically tear it to shreds. In the case of clothes, she would first rip the material from the hem upward into strips about one centimeter in width, and then start on the sleeves; by the time she had finished, the pieces were so small that they could not even be used for dusters. Her usual expression while she did this was one of guileless vacancy, though as she tore up a particularly long piece or sat contemplating a huge pile of tatters, one could observe an enigmatic smile playing on her lips.

No one could make out the origin of this new quirk. Was it that Umé, whose entire youth had been devoted to the art of needlework (one of the few accomplishments then considered suitable for women of breeding), felt in some paradoxical way that by tearing material she was at least persevering in her speciality, even though she was now too old to do so constructively? Or was it that in an access of spite she had resolved that none of her clothes or other possessions should ever accrue to this family which had treated her so heartlessly in her declining years? Or was it just the sheer joy of vandalism? The result, in any case, was that, despite Sachiko's best efforts, Umé's wardrobe had soon dwindled to nothing. Because of the strict rationing, it was impossible to replace the shredded garments, so Sachiko had to give her grandmother some of her own castoff clothes. With their modern pattern and bright colors, they produced a somewhat ludicrous effect on the old lady. In the end they too were, of course, torn to bits.

"It's funny how Granny only likes things with salt," said Sachiko one day, "Most old people like sweet things, but she'll only eat things when they're salted or spicy."

"Let's hope she doesn't get pickled and live forever," said Minobé.

"Yes," said Sachiko, "the kindest thing she could do for herself and everyone else would be to die. Why do you suppose she goes on living like this?"

Minobé shrugged his shoulders. "In the Far East, longevity's supposed to be a wonderful thing," he answered. "For some reason it's considered a feat to grow very old, even though one doesn't have the slightest pleasure in being alive and is just a nuisance to everyone around. Take that old dog next door. Its owners go around boasting to everyone that they've got a dog who's lived to be fifteen. And yet the poor old thing is blind and lame, and should have died years ago. Evidently in Japan we can't even let animals die at the proper time.

"The fact is that once people are wrecks, like Granny, life becomes a spiteful force which turns on its owner, as if to punish him for hanging on to it so long. The blessings of old age, indeed! All Granny really cares about is eating, but because she's over sixty, the government will let her have only a reduced ration. That's what I mean by life turning on people if they live too long. And when they finally do die, what sort of memory do they leave behind? Just the memory of their last ugly, unhappy years. Granny once was a lovely woman, to judge from her photos, but what we'll remember is a hideous, wicked old hag. Surely people should fade out like music, leaving a beautiful melody in the air."

Almost all day, apart from mealtimes, Umé lay half-asleep by the charcoal brazier in the living room. At night, however, she was wide awake. As soon as the family had gone to sleep, she would wander out into the passage and start complaining raucously of hunger. Finally someone would have to get up and give her a piece of bread, a potato, or a rice ball.

She now visited the toilet four or five times a night; they left the light on permanently. Sometimes she would go and stand in the lavatory for ten or fifteen minutes, peering out the window. They could hear her muttering loudly to herself: "Ah, that's the moon over there. It's getting pale. It'll soon be time for breakfast. . . ." As she was gradually becoming incontinent, the first person to visit the toilet in the morning would usually find it in an appalling mess. Minobé wondered if this, too, was not an unconscious attempt to punish the family for imagined ill-treatment.

She occasionally suffered from hallucinations. One night Minobé awoke to the sound of fearful cries from Umé's room: "Help, help, I'm dying! Oh, they're killing me! Help, help!"

Jumping out of bed, he rushed to the rescue, but found Umé sitting up in bed as if nothing had happened. "What's wrong, Granny?" he asked, but she only shook her head, staring at him blankly. Minobé gave her a glass of water and went back to his room. He wondered if the old woman had been confronted with some horrible vision of death.

A few days later, she grabbed one of her great-grandsons by the arm as he was walking by, and held out a ten-yen note.

"Run down and buy me one yen's worth of rice and a yen's worth of tobacco," she said.

"I can't, Granny," answered the boy. "Everything's rationed. Besides, one yen wouldn't buy even a button."

"Nonsense, child!" said Umé. "Well, if you won't go, you can open the window and call for the errand boy down there by the corner. He did my shopping for me yesterday."

Evidently her mind had gone back to a time fifty years before when she had lived in Tokyo with her husband, and errand boys used to wait on the street corners. Now, understanding that she could expect no help from her great-grandson, Umé took down a small basket from the shelf; she wrapped her tattered dressing gown tightly about her and tottered out into the passage, clasping her ten-yen note.

"Where are you off to, Granny?" said Minobé, as he saw her passing the living room.

"I'm going out shopping."

"You'll have quite a job!" said Minobé. "But don't let me stop you."

This seemed to discourage her, for instead of going out, she visited the toilet, and no more was heard of the shopping expedition.

Later that day, Minobé heard the old woman's voice droning away monotonously in her room. He stopped and listened.

"Isn't that the Lotus Sutra Granny's reciting?" he said to Sachiko.

"No," she said, "it's *The Greater Learning for Women*. They had to learn it by heart at school. I suppose she's trying to see how much she can remember."

The Greater Learning for Women! That eighteenth-century classic which claims to set forth in one volume the essentials of a woman's moral training seemed to have profited Umé little in her long life. Minobé remembered the opening sentences: "Parents, rather than to bestow upon your daughters fine garments and divers vessels, better were it to teach them these precepts, which will guard them as precious jewels throughout their days. . . ."

She had begun reciting again, in a toneless, hurried chant which seemed almost entirely bereft of meaning. Only once in a while would an intelligible phrase emerge: "Not because of its height is yon mountain august. . . ." This, it seemed, was all that remained of Umé's arduous years of rote learning.

Then suddenly, with scarcely any change of expression, Umé said: "What about lunch? Haven't I missed my lunch?"

"Of course not, Granny," said Minobé. "You finished lunch an hour ago."

"Really?" said Umé. "I feel as if I hadn't eaten for ages."

The suspicion that she might have missed a meal, and was now being tricked into believing that she had eaten it, showed clearly on her face. And yet it was hardly surprising that Granny had forgotten about lunch, reflected Minobé. During her life she must have eaten almost one hundred thousand meals, and over thirty thousand of them had been lunches.

As soon as Umé awoke from one of her naps, she would start wailing: "Oh, I'm hungry! I'm dying of hunger! Bring me something to eat, for pity's sake—a rice ball, an onion pickle, anything. Only hurry!" Sometimes there were variations: "Help, the fire's gone out! I'm dying of cold. Come and light the fire, someone." Or: "Water, water! For mercy's sake, master, bring me a glass of water!"

An especially irritating habit was her referring to people in terms of exaggerated obsequiousness, as if to imply that only so could she prevail on them to help her. Thus Minobé became "master," Sachiko was "madam" or "mistress," and her great-grandchildren "young sirs." As he stood painting in his studio-room, Minobé would hear her shrill voice: "Oh, my dear mistress, may I crave a few grains of rice to calm my hunger?" or "Young sir, have mercy on an old woman and bring a glass of water." Despite his resolutions, Minobé would sometimes fling his paintbrush to the floor.

Her pilfering continued, and indeed had grown worse. If, on waking, she saw no one about, she would hurry over to one of the cupboards and take whatever she could find. Formerly, stolen objects had always been retrieved in her room, but Umé's pilfering had become far more serious since she had taken to tearing things to pieces.

"It's really going too far, Granny," said Sachiko one day. "You've gone and helped yourself to one of the best towels from the bathroom. Didn't I give you your own towel to play with?"

"A bath towel?" said Umé with an air of injured innocence. "I don't know anything about it."

"It's no use pretending, Granny. It's right there behind your foot warmer. At least you haven't started tearing it yet."

"My goodness!" said Umé. "So it is. I must have caught it on my shoulder by mistake when I went to the bathroom."

"That's quite an achievement," said Sachiko, "considering that it was firmly fixed to a towel rail."

Her appetite seemed to become more voracious as the weeks went by.

"Oh, good madam, take pity on me! I'm so hungry it hurts!" she started wailing one morning.

"Really, Granny!" said Sachiko, hurrying into her room. "I gave you five big rice cakes just a couple of hours ago. What have you done with them?"

"Rice cakes?" said Umé. "I don't remember any rice cakes."

Sachiko looked behind the foot warmer, under the bed, and in all the usual hiding places, but there was no trace of the rice cakes.

"Have you forgotten where you hid them?" said Sachiko. "Surely you can't have eaten them all already."

"Well, since you can't find them," said Umé dubiously, "I suppose I must have."

Sachiko left the room, shaking her head. And behind her Umé was sticking out her tongue contemptuously.

One day the children discovered a large piece of fresh bread in the dustbin and brought it to their mother.

"If that isn't the limit!" said Sachiko. "This is the piece I gave Granny a few hours ago. I know she doesn't like this cheap rationed bread, but it's all any of us can get these days. And I salted it specially for her."

She went into Umé's room and scolded her severely, but the old lady denied all knowledge of the bread. The following day a whole bowl of rice was found in the dustbin.

"How can anyone throw away rice these days when millions are starving!" cried Sachiko, glaring at Umé. "Such waste deserves to be punished."

"Good gracious!" said Umé. "Who could have done such a thing?"

"You know perfectly well it was you, Granny. You're the only one who throws things like this in the dustbin."

"Mercy me, no!" said Umé indignantly. "I'd rather die than throw rice away. It's a sacrilege. Let me tell you, I'd like to get my hands on whoever did it. . . . "

At this point Sachiko gave up.

In the evening she mentioned the matter to Minobé. "She's lost all judgment, hasn't she? If she wanted to get rid of the rice, all she had to do was to throw it down the toilet and none of us would have been the wiser. This way we were bound to find out."

"She was probably furious because the rice was cold," said Minobé.

"We all had cold rice today," said Sachiko. "She had the same as the rest of us."

"Yes, but nothing will ever convince her that we aren't getting better food than she is. I expect she purposely put the rice where we'd find it, as a sort of protest."

"I wonder if her mental powers are up to that," said Sachiko.

"When it comes to food, they certainly are," said Minobé. "Look at that awful habit she's got of bowing and scraping to us all, in the hope that we'll give her extra things to eat."

"Yes, I suppose she'll sink to anything to fill her belly. It's all that she lives for these days. It's as if she were under a curse. It really makes me sad, you know, when I think that she's my own grandmother."

When visitors came to the house, they would invariably be startled by the sudden apparition of old Umé, with her weird, white, wrinkled face and fuzzy hair.

"Are they from Echigo?" she would ask, and having been assured to the contrary, she would raise a piteous cry: "Oh, I'm so hungry! For mercy's sake, good people, let me have something to eat! I haven't had a morsel since last night. Help! I'm starving!"

Sachiko and Minobé would then be obliged to explain matters to the bewildered guests.

One day, when Umé had made a particularly ugly scene of this kind, Sachiko lost her temper and shouted harshly at the old woman. Umé listened in blank silence, vaguely shaking her head. That afternoon when Sachiko was doing the laundry at the garden well, she noticed a strange, spectral figure standing by the front gate; it was Umé, who had managed for the first time in years to make her way out of doors unaided. When the old woman realized that she was being observed, she raised one hand in a gesture of supplication and held the other to her throat as if about to slash it. She was barefoot and had thrown an old overcoat over her dressing gown. Obviously the aim of her maneuver was to have one of the neighbors discover her in this pathetic garb.

"Good heavens, Minobé," shouted Sachiko, "Granny's gone out!"

Minobé threw down his paint brush and ran to help her, but his wife had already managed to get the old woman back into the house. Umé stood by the door with a tragic look of frustration on her face, obviously exhausted by her feat. With one hand she was affecting jerky movements of obeisance; in the other, she held a gimlet menacingly. The end of the gimlet was broken off and Minobé recognized it as the one that he used to open his tins of paint and that had been missing for some days. No doubt it was part of Granny's recent loot.

"I'm afraid you won't be able to cut your throat with that, Granny," he said to her. "It's too blunt."

"What a hateful old woman you really are!" cried Sachiko bitterly. "All you wanted to do was to get even with me for scolding you this morning. The one emotion you haven't forgotten in all these years is —is spite!"

VII

In his spare time Minobé unpacked the numerous trunks and cases which they had brought from the country. One day he came upon a small photograph that had lain hidden for years among some old papers. He examined it for a moment, then took it to Umé's room.

"I expect you'll remember this, Granny," he said.

Old Umé was busy tearing to pieces a pair of her great-grandson's pants. She was having some trouble with the elastic band around the waist. She looked up and took the photograph which Minobé handed her, and suddenly a strange, choked cry escaped her throat.

"Oh, oh, I've missed her so terribly! It's my darling little girl. My only daughter! I've missed her for so long!"

She put her hand to her forehead and rubbed her cheek against the photograph of the daughter, who had died more than thirty years before; her whole body was shaking.

"Why did you have to leave me? Life has never been the same since. How I miss you!"

Minobé was deeply moved. Now at last he seemed to have discovered, beneath all the physical and moral ugliness with which age had marked old Umé, a human heart that felt and suffered. Bowing his head he left the room. He did not want to intrude on her terrible grief.

As soon as he closed the door, the sound of sobbing appeared suddenly to stop. He stood listening in the passage. There seemed to him something ominous about this silence following directly on the old lady's desperate weeping. Opening the door quietly, Minobé looked in. With an air of rapt concentration, Umé was removing the rubber band from her great-grandson's pants. The photograph lay discarded upon a heap of tattered cloth.

下
町

林芙美子

DOWNTOWN
BY Hayashi Fumiko

TRANSLATED BY Ivan Morris

    Hayashi Fumiko, born in 1904, was the daughter of an impecunious peddler and from her early childhood she moved from one part of the country to another with her parents. As soon as she had finished school, she launched out on her own in a desperate effort to support herself. She tried innumerable ways of making a living—as a maid, a clerk in a stockbroker's office, a worker in a celluloid factory, an assistant in a maternity hospital, a waitress in a German café, a street-stall vendor, to name only a few of her occupations. She was in constant poverty and often on the verge of starving or of taking to the streets; on at least one occasion she attempted suicide. All these experiences are realistically described in her first well-known work, "A Roving Record" (Hōrōki, 1922–27).

Hayashi Fumiko's devotion to literature started at an early age and continued during the course of her unsettled and esurient life. In her brief spare time she wrote poems, short stories, and children's tales, and gradually these began to attract attention. She went through a period of left-wing writing, but in describing poverty and social injustice her approach was always very different from that of the tough-minded authors of the proletarian school.

It was not until after the war that Hayashi Fumiko's literary reputation became established. By the time of her death in 1951 she was undoubtedly the most popular woman writer in Japan.

In her stories and novels Hayashi Fumiko portrays with realism and compassion the hardships of the Tokyo lower classes, with which she was so intimately acquainted from her own youth. She shows us a world of degeneration, humiliation, and instability in which men tyrannize over women and women themselves are, all too often, merely apathetic. Yet, tough as this world is,

Miss Hayashi suggests that there is a surprising degree of cheerfulness and hope in the lives of the members of the lower stratum that she describes. Her principal women characters are of the humble, yet undaunted, type. As in the present story, their impulses of despair are almost always balanced by a strong will to live and a faith in the future. Given its dominant subject and approach, it is inevitable that Hayashi Fumiko's writing should frequently verge on the sentimental; yet there is a simple, poetic quality about her language and a directness about her telling method that save her work from ever becoming maudlin.

"Downtown" (Shitamachi) was first published in 1948, when the author was forty-four.

IT WAS a bitter, windy afternoon. As Ryō hurried down the street with her rucksack, she kept to the side where the pale sun shone over the roofs of the office buildings. Every now and then she looked about curiously—at a building, at a parked car, at one of those innumerable bombsites scattered through downtown Tokyo.

Glancing over a board fence, Ryō saw a huge pile of rusty iron and, next to it, a cabin with a glass door. A fire was burning within and she could hear the warm sound of the crackling wood. In front of the cabin stood a man in overalls with a red kerchief about his head. There was something pleasant about this tall fellow and Ryō screwed up her courage to call out.

"Tea for sale! Would you like some tea, please?"

"Tea?" said the man.

"Yes," said Ryō with a nervous smile. "It's Shizuoka tea."

She stepped in through an opening in the board fence and, unfastening the straps of her rucksack, put it down by the cabin. Inside she could see a fire burning in an iron stove; from a bar above hung a brass kettle with a wisp of steam rising from the spout.

"Excuse me," said Ryō, "but would you mind if I came in and warmed myself by your stove a few minutes? It's freezing outside, and I've been walking for miles."

"Of course you can come in," said the man. "Close the door and get warm."

He pointed toward the stool, which was his only article of furniture, and sat down on a packing case in the corner. Ryō hesitated a moment.

Then she dragged her rucksack into the cabin and, crouching by the stove, held up her hands to the fire.

"You'll be more comfortable on that stool," said the man, glancing at her attractive face, flushed in the sudden warmth, and at her shabby attire.

"Surely this isn't what you usually do—peddle tea from door to door?"

"Oh yes, it's how I make my living," Ryō said. "I was told that this was a good neighborhood, but I've been walking around here since early morning and have managed to sell only one packet of tea. I'm about ready to go home now, but I thought I'd have my lunch somewhere on the way."

"Well, you're perfectly welcome to stay here and eat your lunch," said the man. "And don't worry about not having sold your tea," he added, smiling. "It's all in the luck of the draw, you know. You'll probably have a good day tomorrow."

The kettle came to a boil with a whistling sound. As he unhooked it from the bar, Ryō had a chance to look about her. She took in the boarded ceiling, black with soot; the blackboard by the window; the shelf for family gods, on which stood a potted *sakaki* tree.* The man picked up a limp-looking packet from the table and, unwrapping it, disclosed a piece of cod. A few minutes later the smell of baking fish permeated the cabin.

"Come on," said the man, "sit down and have something to eat."

Ryō took her lunch box out of the rucksack and seated herself on the stool.

"Selling things is never much fun, is it?" remarked the man, turning the cod over on the grill. "Tell me, how much do you get for a pound of that tea?"

"I should get about a hundred and fifty or sixty yen a pound, but then there's a lot of trash in it, and if the price is too high, it just won't sell."

In Ryō's lunch box were two small fish covered with some boiled barley and a few bean-paste pickles. She began eating.

"Where do you live?" the man asked her.

* *Leyera ochnacea,* the sacred tree of Shinto which decorates shrines and other holy places.

"In Shitaya. Actually I don't know one part of Tokyo from another. I've been here only a few weeks and a friend's putting me up until I find something better."

The cod was ready now. The man cut it in two and gave Ryō half, adding potatoes and rice from a platter. Ryō smiled and bowed slightly in thanks, then took out a bag of tea from her rucksack and poured some into a paper handkerchief.

"Put this into the kettle," she said, holding it out to him.

He shook his head and smiled, showing his white teeth.

"Oh, never! It's far too expensive."

Ryō removed the lid and poured the tea in before he could stop her. Laughing, the man went to fetch a teacup and a mug from the shelf.

"What about your husband?" he asked, while ranging them on the packing case. "You're married, aren't you?"

"Oh yes, I am. My husband's still in Siberia. That's why I have to work like this."

Ryō's thoughts flew to her husband, from whom she had not heard for six years; by now he had come to seem so remote that it required an effort to remember his looks, or the once-familiar sound of his voice. She woke up each morning with a feeling of emptiness and desolation. At times it seemed to Ryō that her husband had frozen into a ghost in that subarctic Siberia—a ghost, or a thin white pillar, or just a breath of frosty air. People no longer mentioned the war and she was almost embarrassed to have it known that her husband was still a prisoner.

"It's funny," the man said. "The fact is, I was in Siberia myself. I spent three years chopping wood near the Amur River—I managed to get sent home only last year. Well, it's all in the luck of the draw. It's tough on your husband. But it's just as tough on you."

"So you've really been repatriated from Siberia! You don't seem any the worse for it," Ryō said.

"I don't know about that," the man shrugged his shoulders. "Anyway, as you see, I'm still alive."

Ryō was studying him as she closed her lunch box. There was a simplicity and directness about this man that made her want to talk openly in a way that she found difficult with more educated people.

"Got any kids?" he said.

"Yes, a boy of six. He should be at school, but I've had difficulty getting him registered here in Tokyo. The government officials certainly know how to make life complicated for people!"

The man untied his kerchief, wiped the cup and the mug with it, and poured out the steaming tea.

"It's good stuff, this," he said, sipping noisily.

"Do you like it? It's not the best quality, you know: only a hundred yen a pound wholesale. Still, you're right—it's quite good."

The wind had grown stronger while they were talking; it whistled over the tin roof of the cabin. Ryō glanced out of the window, steeling herself for her long walk home.

"I'll have some of your tea—a pound and a half," the man told her, extracting three crumpled hundred-yen notes from the pocket of his overalls.

"Don't be silly," said Ryō. "You can have it for nothing."

"Oh no, that won't do. Business is business." He forced the money into her hand. "Well, if you're ever in this part of the world again, come in and have another chat."

"I'd like to," said Ryō, glancing around the tiny cabin. "But you don't live here, do you?"

"Oh yes I do. I look after that iron out there and help load the trucks. I'm here most of the day."

He opened a door under the shelf, disclosing a sort of cubbyhole with a bed neatly made up. Ryō noticed a colored postcard of the actress Yamada Isuzu tacked to the back of the door.

"My, you've fixed it up nicely," she said smiling. "You're really quite snug here, aren't you?"

She wondered how old he could be.

*　　　*　　　*

From that day on, Ryō came regularly to the Yotsugi district to sell tea; each time she visited the cabin on the bombsite. She learned that the man's name was Tsuruishi Yoshio. Almost invariably he had some small delicacy waiting for her to put in her lunch box—a pickled plum, a piece of beef, a sardine. Her business began to improve and she acquired a few regular customers in the nighborhood.

A week after their first meeting, she brought along her boy, Ryūkichi. Tsuruishi chatted with the child for a while and then took him out for a walk. When they returned, Ryūkichi was carrying a large caramel cake.

"He's got a good appetite, this youngster of yours," said Tsuruishi, patting the boy's close-cropped head.

Ryō wondered vaguely whether her new friend was married; in fact she found herself wondering about various aspects of his life. She was now twenty-eight, and she realized with a start that this was the first time she had been seriously interested in any man but her husband. Tsuruishi's easy, carefree temperament somehow appealed to her, though she took great care not to let him guess it.

A little later Tsuruishi suggested taking Ryō and Ryūkichi to see Asakusa* on his next free day. They met in front of the information booth in Ueno Station, Tsuruishi wearing an ancient gray suit that was far too tight, Ryō clad in a blue dress of kimono material and a light-brown coat. In spite of her cheap clothes, she had about her something youthful and elegant as she stood there in the crowded station. Beside the tall, heavy Tsuruishi, she looked like a schoolgirl off on a holiday. In her shopping bag was their lunch: bread, oranges, and rice wrapped with seaweed.

"Well, let's hope it doesn't rain," said Tsuruishi, putting his arm lightly around Ryō's waist as he steered her through the crowd.

They took the train to Asakusa Station, then walked from the Matsu-ya Department Store to the Niten Gate, past hundreds of tiny stalls. The Asakusa district was quite different from what Ryō had imagined. She was disappointed when Tsuruishi pointed to a small red-lacquered temple and told her that this was the home of the famous Asakusa Goddess of Mercy. Although Tsuruishi explained that, until the air raids, it had been a towering pavilion, it was hard for Ryō to visualize a huge temple. All she could see were the hundreds of people thronging about the little red shrine from all four directions. In the distance she could hear the plaintive wail of trumpet and saxophone emerging from some loud-speaker, mingling strangely with the sound of the wind whistling through the branches of the ancient trees.

They made their way through the old-clothes market and came to

* Asakusa in downtown *(shitamachi)* Tokyo has become an amusement district roughly corresponding to Montmartre. It has an ancient Buddhist temple dedicated to Kannon, the Goddess of Mercy.

a row of food stalls squeezed tightly against each other beside the Asakusa Pond; here the air smelled of burning oil. Tsuruishi went to one of the stalls and bought Ryūkichi a stick of yellow cotton candy. The boy nibbled at it as the three of them walked down a narrow street plastered with American-style billboards advertising restaurants, films, revues. It was less than a fortnight since Ryō had first noticed Tsuruishi by his cabin, yet she felt as much at ease with him as if she had known him all her life.

"Well, it's started raining after all," he said, holding out his hand. Ryō looked up, to see scattered drops of rain falling from the gray sky. So their precious excursion would be ruined, she thought.

"We'd better go in there," said Tsuruishi, pointing to one of the shops, outside which hung a garish lantern with characters announcing the "Merry Teahouse." They took seats at a table underneath a ceiling decorated with artificial cherry blossoms. The place had a strangely uncozy atmosphere, but they were determined to make the best of it and ordered a pot of tea; Ryō distributed her stuffed seaweed, bread, and oranges. It was not long before the meal was finished and by then it had started raining in earnest.

"We'd better wait till it lets up a bit," suggested Tsuruishi. "Then I'll take you home."

Ryō wondered if he was referring to her place or his. She was staying in the cramped apartment of a friend from her home town and did not even have a room to call her own; rather than go there, she would have preferred returning to Tsuruishi's cabin, but that too was scarcely large enough to hold three people. Taking out her purse, she counted her money under the table. The seven hundred yen should be enough to get shelter for a few hours at an inn.

"D'you know what I'd really like?" she said. "I'd like us to go to a film and then find some inn and have something to eat before we say goodbye. But I suppose that's all rather expensive."

"Yes, I suppose it is," said Tsuruishi, laughing. "Come on. We'll do it all the same."

Taking his overcoat from the peg, he threw it over Ryūkichi's head and they ran through the downpour to a cinema. Of course there were no seats. As they stood watching the film, the little boy fell sound asleep, leaning against Tsuruishi. The air seemed to get thicker and hotter every moment; on the roof they could hear the rain beating down.

It was getting dark as they left the theater and hurried through the rain, which pelted down with the swishing sound of banana-tree leaves in a high wind. At last they found a small inn where the landlord led them to a carpeted room at the end of a drafty passage. Ryō took off her wet socks. The boy sat down in a corner and promptly went back to sleep.

"Here, he can use this as a pillow," said Tsuruishi, picking up an old cushion from a chair and putting it under Ryūkichi's head.

From an overflowing gutter above the window the water poured down in a steady stream into the courtyard. It sounded like a waterfall in some faraway mountain village.

Tsuruishi took out a handkerchief and began wiping Ryō's wet hair. A feeling of happiness coursed through her as she looked up at him. It was as if the rain had begun to wash away all the loneliness that had been gathering within her year after year.

She went to see if they could get some food, and in the corridor met a maid in Western clothes carrying a teatray. After Ryō had ordered two bowls of noodles, she and Tsuruishi sat down to drink their tea, facing each other across an empty brazier. Later Tsuruishi came and sat on the floor beside her. Leaning their backs against the wall, they gazed out at the darkening, rainy sky.

"How old are you, Ryō?" Tsuruishi asked her. "I should guess twenty-five."

Ryō laughed. "I'm afraid not, Tsuru, I'm already an old woman. I'm twenty-eight."

"A year older than me."

"Goodness, you're young." said Ryō. "I thought you must be at least thirty."

She looked straight at him, into his dark, gentle eyes with their bushy brows. He seemed to be blushing slightly. Then he bent forward and took off his wet socks.

The rain continued unabated. Presently the maid came with some cold noodles and soup. Ryō woke the boy and gave him a plate of soup; he was half asleep as he sipped it.

"Look, Ryō," Tsuruishi said, "we might as well all spend the night at this inn. You can't go home in this rain, can you?"

"No," said Ryō. "No, I suppose not."

Tsuruishi left the room and returned with a load of quilted bedrolls which he spread on the floor. The whole room seemed to be full of bedding. Ryō tucked her son in one of the rolls, the boy sleeping soundly as she did so. Then she turned out the light, undressed, and lay down. She could hear Tsuruishi settling down at the other end of the room.

"I suppose the people in this inn think we're married," said Tsuruishi after a while.

"Yes, I suppose so. It's not very nice of us to fool them."

She spoke in jest, but now that she lay undressed in her bedroll, she felt for the first time vaguely disturbed and guilty. Her husband for some reason seemed much closer than he had for years. But of course she was here only because of the rain, she reminded herself. And gradually her thoughts began to wander pleasantly afield, and she dozed off.

When she awoke it was still dark. She could hear Tsuruishi whispering her name from his corner, and she sat up with a start.

"Ryō, Ryō, can I come and talk to you for a while?"

"No, Tsuru," she said, "I don't think you should."

On the roof the rain was still pattering down, but the force of the storm was over; only a trickle was dropping from the gutter into the yard. Under the sound of the rain she thought she could hear Tsuruishi sigh softly.

"Look, Tsuru," she said after a pause. "I've never asked you before, but are you married?"

"No. Not now," Tsuruishi said.

"You used to be?"

"Yes. I used to be. When I got back from the army, I found that my wife was living with another man."

"Were you—angry?"

"Angry? Yes, I suppose I was. But there wasn't much I could do about it. She'd left me, and that was that."

They were silent again.

"What shall we talk about?" Ryō asked.

Tsuruishi laughed. "Well, there really doesn't seem to be anything special to talk about. Those noodles weren't very good, were they?"

"No, you certainly couldn't call them good. And they charged us a hundred yen each."

"It would be nice if you and Ryūkichi had your own room to live in, wouldn't it?" Tsuruishi remarked.

"Oh yes, it would be marvelous! You don't think we might find a room near you? I'd really like to live near you, Tsuru, you know."

"It's pretty hard to find rooms these days, especially downtown. But I'll keep a lookout and let you know. . . . You're a wonderful person, Ryō."

"Me?" said Ryō laughing. "Don't be silly!"

"Yes, yes, you're wonderful . . . really wonderful!"

Ryō lay back on the floor. Suddenly she wanted to throw her arms around Tsuruishi, to feel his body close to hers. She did not dare speak for fear that her voice might betray her; her breath came almost painfully; her whole body tingled. Outside the window an early-morning lorry clattered past.

"Where are your parents, Tsuru?" she asked after a while.

"In the country near Fukuoka."

"But you have a sister in Tokyo?"

"Yes. She's all alone, like you, with two kids to take care of. She's got a sewing machine and makes clothes. Her husband was killed several years ago—in the war in China."

Outside the window Ryō could make out the first glimmer of dawn. So their night together was almost over, she thought unhappily. In a way she wished that Tsuruishi hadn't given up so easily, and yet she was convinced that it was best like this. If he had been a man she hardly knew, or for whom she felt nothing, she might have given herself to him with no afterthought. With Tsuruishi it would have been different —quite different.

"Ryō, I can't get to sleep." His voice reached her again. "I'm wide awake. I suppose I'm not used to this sort of thing."

"What sort of thing?"

"Why—sleeping in the same room with a girl."

"Oh, Tsuru, don't tell me that you don't have girl friends occasionally!"

"Only professional girl friends."

Ryō laughed. "Men have it easy. In some ways, at least. . . ."

She heard Tsuruishi moving about. Suddenly he was beside her, bending over her. Ryō did not move, not even when she felt his arms

round her, his face against hers. In the dark her eyes were wide open, and before them bright lights seemed to be flashing. His hot lips were pressed to her cheek.

"Ryō . . . Ryō."

"It's wrong you know, wrong to my husband . . ." she murmured.

But almost at once she regretted the words. As Tsuruishi bent over her, she could make out the silhouette of his face against the lightening sky. Bowed forward, he seemed to be offering obeisance to some god. Ryō hesitated for a moment. Then she threw her warm arms about his neck.

*   *   *

Two days later Ryō set out happily with her boy to visit Tsuruishi. When she reached the bombsite, she was surprised not to see him before his cabin, the red kerchief tied about his head. Ryūkichi ran ahead to find out if he was home and came back in a moment.

"There are strangers there, Mummy."

Seized with panic, Ryō hurried over to the cabin and peered in. Two workmen were busy piling up Tsuruishi's effects in a corner.

"What is it, ma'am?" one of them said, turning his head.

"I'm looking for Tsuruishi."

"Oh, didn't you know? Tsuruishi died yesterday."

"Died?" she said. She wanted to say something more, but no words would come.

She had noticed a small candle burning on the shelf for family gods, and now she was aware of its somber meaning.

"Yes," went on the man, "he was killed about eight o'clock last night. He went in a truck with one of his mates to deliver some iron bars in Ōmiya, and on their way back the truck turned over on a narrow bridge. He and the driver were both killed. His sister went to Ōmiya today with one of the company officials to see about the cremation."

Ryō stared vacantly before her. Vacantly she watched the two men piling up Tsuruishi's belongings. Beside the candle on the shelf she caught sight of the two bags of tea he had bought from her that first day—could it be only two weeks ago? One of them was folded halfway over; the other was still unopened.

"You were a friend of his, ma'am, I imagine? He was a fine fellow, Tsuru! Funny to think that he needn't have gone to Ōmiya at all. The driver wasn't feeling well and Tsuru said he'd go along to Ōmiya to help him unload. Crazy, isn't it—after getting through the war and Siberia and all the rest of it, to be killed like that."

One of the men took down the postcard of Yamada Isuzu and blew the dust from it. Ryō stood looking at Tsuruishi's belongings piled on the floor—the kettle, the frying pan, the rubber boots. When her eyes reached the blackboard, she noticed for the first time a message scratched awkwardly in red chalk: "Ryō—I waited for you till two o'clock. Back this evening."

Automatically she bowed to the two men and swung the rucksack to her back. She felt numb as she left the cabin, holding Ryūkichi by the hand, but as they passed the bombsite the burning tears welled into her eyes.

"Did that man die, Mummy?"

"Yes, he died," Ryō said.

"Why did he die?"

"He fell into a river."

The tears were running down her cheeks now; they poured out uncontrollably as she hurried through the downtown streets. She came to an arched bridge over the Sumida River, crossed it, and walked north along the bank in the direction of Shirahigé.

"Don't worry if you get pregnant," Tsuruishi had told her that morning in Asakusa, "I'll look after you whatever happens, Ryō." And later on, just before they parted, he had said: "I haven't got much money, but you must let me help you a little. I can give you two thousand yen a month out of my salary." He had taken Ryūkichi to a shop that specialized in foreign goods and bought him a baseball cap with his name written on it. Then the three of them had walked gaily along the tram lines, skirting the enormous puddles left by the rain. When they came to a milk bar, Tsuruishi had taken them in and ordered them each a big glass of milk. . . .

An icy wind seemed to have blown up from the dark river. A flock of water fowl stood on the opposite bank looking frozen and miserable. Barges moved slowly up and down the river.

, I want a sketchbook. You said I could have a sketch-

"Mur

book answered Ryō. "I'll get you one later."

immy, we just passed a shop with hundreds of sketchbooks.

, Mummy. Can't we have something to eat?"

A little later."

were passing a long row of barrack-like buildings. They must ... house, she thought. The people who lived there probably ... had rooms of their own. From one of the windows a bedroll had been hung out to air and through the window a woman could be seen tidying the room.

"Tea for sale!" called Ryō softly. "Best quality Shizuoka tea!"

There was no reply and Ryō repeated her call a little louder.

"I don't want any" said the woman. She pulled in the bedroll and shut the window with a bang.

Ryō went from house to house down the row, calling her ware, but nobody wanted any tea. Ryūkichi followed behind, muttering that he was hungry and tired. Ryō's rucksack dug painfully into her shoulders, and occasionally she had to stop to adjust the straps. Yet in a way she almost welcomed the physical pain.

*   *   *

The next day she went downtown by herself, leaving Ryūkichi at home. When she came to the bombsite she noticed that a fire was burning inside the cabin. She ran to the door and walked in. By Tsuruishi's stove sat an old man in a short workman's overcoat, feeding the flames with firewood. The room was full of smoke and it was billowing out of the window.

"What do you want?" said the old man, looking around.

"I've come to sell Shizuoka tea."

"Shizuoka tea? I've got plenty of good tea right here."

Ryō turned without a word and hurried off. She had thought of going to the address of Tsuruishi's sister and of burning a stick of incense in his memory, but suddenly this seemed quite pointless. She walked back to the river, which reflected the late afternoon sun, and sat down by a pile of broken concrete. The body of a dead kitten was lying on its back a few yards away. As her thoughts turned to Tsuru-

ishi, she wondered vaguely whether it would have been bet~
have met him. No, no, certainly not that! She could never reg~
ing him, nor anything that had happened with him. Nor did sh~
having come to Tokyo. When she had arrived, a month or so ~
she had planned to return to the country if her business was unsu~
ful, but now she knew that she would be staying on here in Toky~
yes, probably right here in downtown Tokyo where Tsuruishi ha~
lived.

She got up, swung the rucksack on her back, and walked away from
the river. As she strolled along a side street, she noticed a hut which
seemed to be made of old boards nailed haphazardly together. Going to
the door, she called out: "Tea for sale! Would anyone like some tea?"
The door opened and in the entrance appeared a woman dressed far
more poorly than Ryō herself.

"How much does it cost?" asked the woman. And then, seeing the
rucksack, she added: "Come in and rest a while, if you like. I'll see how
much money we've got left. We may have enough for some tea."

Ryō went in and put down her rucksack. In the small room four
sewing-women were sitting on the floor around an oil stove, working
on a mass of shirts and socks. They were women like herself, thought
Ryō, as she watched their busy needles moving in and out of the material. A feeling of warmth came over her.

A MAN'S LIFE
BY Hirabayashi Taiko

TRANSLATED BY George Saitō

The fact that Hirabayashi Taiko was born in Nagano Prefecture is of considerable significance to her literary career. The family into which she was born, in 1905, soon fell on hard times, and thus from early childhood Mrs. Hirabayashi knew the uncertainty of life. Nagano Prefecture, in the mountainous region of central Japan, is noted for its scenic beauty and its independence, as well as for being the birthplace of a number of educational and literary leaders of modern Japan.

In her prewar works Mrs. Hirabayashi seems to close her eyes to the beautiful and tranquil aspects of her native home, probably because of bitter memories.

Her grandfather ran a silk mill and led an active life as a conservative politician. He dissipated practically all his property, however, and was reduced to the position of a small farmer. Although her brothers and sisters were graduated only from primary school, Taiko went on to high school by taking the entrance examination without her parents' permission. She passed the examination and placed first on the list. Because of this her parents were persuaded to let her receive higher education. During her high-school days she devoted herself to reading the works of Russian authors and works by socialist writers and thinkers. After graduating from high school, she went to Tokyo, where she worked for a brief time as a telephone operator. Thereafter she worked at various jobs; she was a waitress for a time and also a maid. During this period she joined a group of anarchists.

From her youth she had set her heart on writing and she early earned her livelihood by writing fairy tales and detective stories. Her novel, "To Mock," won a prize in a contest sponsored by the Osaka Asahi Shimbun in 1927, and the publication of an autobiographical story, "In the Charity Hospital," also in 1927, established her fame as a proletarian writer. It was based upon experiences in Manchuria.

The decline of leftist literature which followed, and the outbreak of the Sino-Japanese Incident in 1937, left her in straitened circumstances. After a critical illness while in prison, she spent eight years in bed. With the end of the war, however, Mrs. Hirabayashi started writing again, this time transcending class consciousness and moving toward humanism. In "Song of the Underworld," dealing with the life of gamblers, she showed a mature skill and a broadened vision.

The present story (Hito no Inochi in Japanese) was first published in 1950, when the author was forty-five. It is representative of Mrs. Hirabayashi's postwar work.

"I WONDER if conversion is a word that anyone can use. If it doesn't sound too funny for a fellow like me to be using it . . . well, I suppose I've experienced a sort of conversion too."

We'd been talking about something else when Sei, an ex-gangster, said this to me.

"What?"

Noting my bewilderment, Sei hesitatingly began to tell me his story, one which he apparently had kept to himself for a long time, and one which in its telling seemed most natural.

*   *   *

Now let me tell it in my own way. Because if you don't understand what kind of fellow I am, the story won't make much sense.

It was when things were beginning to turn bad for Japan in the Pacific War and people's lives were being increasingly upset by conscription and forced labor. As for me, for about a year I'd been a prisoner at Sugamo—a convicted murderer.

In the spring of the year before I'd knifed a fellow named Shida. He ran a little hotel in Togoshi-Ginza. In my own mind, there were two motives for the killing. But even today I don't know which of the two provided the decisive strength to drive me to murder.

Both the police and the public procurator's office were convinced that I did away with Shida to eliminate his influence in the Ebara district and thus strengthen the power of the Kawanaka gang.

As you probably know, my boss, Kawanaka, was an old man of eighty. Taking this fact into consideration, it seemed only natural that I, who was the real power in the Kawanaka gang, should kill Shida to expand my own influence. The assumption wasn't far wrong.

To tell the truth, however, there was one thing else. Working in that hotel run by Shida there was a woman I'd fallen in love with. Her name was Machiko. She had a face likely to draw attention, and she had a gentle disposition. When I had to make duty calls on Shida for my boss, it was she who would attend to me and pour the wine.

Without quite realizing it, I'd become attracted to this woman and I found myself speaking to her affectionately. But I never laid a hand on her, nor asked her to marry me. Maybe I'm not the passionate type—the kind that falls blindly in love.

Then by chance I learned that Machiko was Shida's woman. With the feeling of having been betrayed by a woman, a livid anger surged in me against Shida . . . whom, of course, I had no reason to resent.

It was on a dark night not very long after I'd learned about Machiko that I called Shida outside the kitchen, where I was hiding behind a large trash bin, and killed him with a single knife thrust.

As was our standard practice, I turned myself in and exaggerated Shida's supposed breach of faith into an unpardonable betrayal. Where gang wars are concerned, even in case of a killing one can usually expect to get off with a sentence of five or six years at the most.

But the times were bad; my attempts to escape the draft came to light; and a previous police record didn't help either.

At the first trial they handed down a heavy sentence of eleven years at hard labor. Naturally I appealed, but because of the indifferent efforts of my lawyer, the verdict of the higher court was little better—ten years.

Ordinarily another appeal to a still higher court would have been made. But, besides being short-tempered, I found the whole thing unbearably tiresome and, out of spitefulness toward the fellow Kawanaka had provided to defend me, I decided, in a moment of youthful folly, to accept the verdict.

It was the day after the sentence. Breakfast over, my attention was vaguely directed to things going on outside—beyond the door of my cell. Morning at the prison begins with a guard's crying: "Sick call, breakfast; sick call, breakfast." Different voices can be heard passing by. It takes at least two months of cell life to distinguish the words "sick call" and "breakfast" from what at first seems an unintelligible mumbling. And it takes at least that long to realize that the affable, white-robed person who shouts "Sweets! Magazines!" and appears to be a peddler as he walks beside a trusty with a pushcart is, in fact, also a guard.

This one must have been working on a percentage basis, for he was quite good in his high-pressure salesmanship. The Prison Association, which at that time was still putting out a prison paper called *Man*, apparently had thought up this business for the guards to implement their meager pay.

Occasionally the cry "Rub that beard!" could be heard. After an application of ice-cold water from the spigot, beards would be vigorously massaged. Soon the turn for a shave would come. The process was swift and simple. It required only three or four strokes with a blunt-edged instrument called a razor, once down each side of the face, under the nose, and beneath the chin. It goes without saying that the whole operation was little short of torture.

On that particular morning, my ears were tuned for a sound I was waiting for with something more than ordinary expectation. Sure enough, the guard's footsteps came to a halt outside my cell door.

"No. 178! Ready for cell change!"

"Yes, sir! Ready, sir!"

The answer came out with a youthful bounce as I gave a glance at the cloth-bound bundle containing my personal belongings. Custom had it that those sentenced by courts of second instance, unless for ideological offenses, would be transferred from solitary confinement to a general cell. It is hard to imagine what this change of cells can mean to a young and gregarious fellow like me who has suffered from the loneliness of solitary confinement.

Already bundled in an arabesque-patterned green cloth were my earthly belongings, all bought since I had come here—a mirror, a bar of soap, toothpaste, a toothbrush, some underwear, a two-volume life of Hideyoshi, and three letters from Machiko. Snatching the bundle up, I stepped outside as the heavy door swung open. Now that I was leaving the place where I'd lived for a whole year, recollections flashed through my head of all the anguish, remorse, and irritation which had been breathed into the air of this cell. With an uncommon consciousness of human vanity, I'd been laughing at my own case; but as a matter of fact, I'd been awakened by the guard on many a night in the throes of a terrible nightmare.

Padding along in my straw sandals, I walked from my solitary cell on the second floor of Block Six to a general cell in Block Five. Block Five was an extension of Block Six, and the general cell was also on the second floor. The guard opened the door of the large cell.

"New man."

To these words I entered the cell. So from today I'd be with the inmates of this cell. It measured about twelve by fifteen feet. On either side of the two-foot-wide planked walk which ran from the door to the end of the room there were four mats, a total of eight for the room.

At the end of the walk, up against the wall, there was a box for personal effects; beside that, a glass-enclosed toilet; and above the latter, a window looking out over the shrubbery in the courtyard. On each of the mats on the two sides of the passage was a man, squatting on his mat in his own particular fashion.

This not being the first time I'd been in such a place, I knew immediately that the fiftyish-looking man squatting closest to the door was the cell boss. I lost no time in giving him the customary greeting of respect.

The fellow let out a grunt that was hardly audible and turned his ashen face aside. His airs annoyed me. I can see now how stupid I was, but at the time I was cut to the bone by a sudden feeling of resentment toward this old man who, I presumed, was nothing more than a petty criminal and who apparently didn't think much of me.

In the angry stare I shot at the old man, my thoughts were apparent: "Better make no mistake about the fellow you see in front of you," I was saying. "He's in here for murder. He's a little different from the sneak thieves you've got here, and you'd better not try to make a fool of him!"

But the old man apparently took no notice of the stripling in his twenties with the bright look in his eyes. His parched and restless glance shot here and there into the void. A shudder passed through me as I watched those eyes. They seemed starved, hungering for a spot on which to fix themselves. My random thoughts, however, did not pursue that impression to any great extent. It was for only one brief instant that I thought; "What queer people there are in this world."

Speaking of queer people, there was another one in that cell. He was about thirty-five, and he seemed well-bred and intellectual. Ever since I had entered the cell—and it was now close to the noon meal, for the meal cart could be heard in the distance as it moved along on its rails—this fellow had kept polishing the lid of his utensil box with a dirty rag. He had not stopped for an instant. The cloth made a queer, squeaking noise as it rubbed against the lid.

Until the war, these boxes for holding one's food utensils had been painted brown. Now, however, with the war situation so grave, they were made of just plain, unpainted wood. Without pause and without a glance elsewhere, the intellectual kept polishing the lid of his box, now old and gray from having been soaked in water so many times. The lid already had a brilliant sheen, yet with the same regular motion he continued his polishing. Soon, louder noises could be heard from the nearby cells as the trusty passed out the noon meal. Lightheartedly the men began arranging their boxes on the planked walk and taking out bowls and plates.

When I had been in here before, these bowls and plates had all been of aluminum, but the metal utensils had been turned in for use by the armed forces, and now we ate from chinaware, unmatched bowls and plates, large and small, which inmates had once bought as personal belongings from the prison sales stand. Of course, this stand no longer had such things to sell. The utensils that were being used were therefore quite old, left behind by previous inmates who had had full use of them. So there were all kinds, some chipped and some cracked, large ones and small ones. It was a little pathetic to note that even here one could see evidence of the hard times onto which the government had fallen.

When the curd soup was ladled out, those with small bowls naturally were at a disadvantage. Those who had foresight would offer whole lunches to some inmate due to leave soon, with the understanding that the large bowl he had been using would be left behind. But those who could not bear to part with an entire lunch had to be content with a small bowl, thereby incurring a loss with each meal.

As the cell door was opened from the outside, the cell boss turned and growled:

"Lid!"

"Here," someone answered and held out the lid of his box.

"Filthy! It's filthy!"

I turned at the sound of this different voice and its scathing comment. I saw the intellectual holding out his own shiny lid. The cell boss took it without a word. Using the lid as a tray, he placed each man's bowl on it in turn and held it out. The trusty scooped the rice from a bucket with a round, wooden implement resembling a ladle. After leveling the rice with the palm of his hand, he dumped it into the bowl. The rice was mixed with barley and soy beans.

I noticed that the guard who accompanied the trusty had suddenly moved a couple of yards away and looked off in another direction, apparently feigning ignorance. During this brief time, three lunches more than the number of inmates came into the cell.

" Well, this cell boss has a little pull."

With this thought I took a second look at the fellow. Beside him, the intellectual, with a satisfied look on his face, was now busily engaged in scraping into one corner of his box lid the grains of rice that had fallen on it. One at a time, he conveyed the grains to his mouth.

How well I understood now! To make these few dozen grains of rice his own—that was why he worked to polish his utensil box so much shinier than the others. But this was not particularly comical; nor was it particularly serious. It was quite ordinary here, and it impressed me little more than the touch of air.

While my thoughts thus wandered, the trusty at the entrance to the cell was handing in the last lunch. It was mine.

"No. 178—that you?"

The guard glanced at his notebook, peered into the darkness of the cell, and pointed at me with his chin.

"Yes, sir, sorry to trouble you, sir."

After getting my thumb print as a receipt, the guard shut the heavy door and followed the trusty to the next cell.

The cell boss, who had received my lunch from the guard, sat for some time with the lunch on his lap, apparently enjoying the whiteness of the grains of rice. His parched eyes darted hither and thither.

"Looks good. Think I'll keep this lunch for myself."

He'd no sooner mumbled these words than he got up to put the lunch with his personal effects.

"Hey, you! What d'ya think you're trying to do! Who d'ya think I am!"

I began hurling out the usual invective, but remembering that the fellow had quite a bit of influence, I immediately changed my tone:

"Course, if I was getting out of here in six months or a year, I wouldn't mind giving an old fellow like you something good to eat, but since I've got to stay in this hole for ten years . . ."

It was almost as if I were talking to myself. My words seemed to carry a note of sympathy, but in reality they were designed to let the men know that I was the possessor of a considerable criminal record.

There was every likelihood that by noting my number—the low number 178—people who knew the place would see that I was in for murder. But I hadn't been able to discern even the slightest suggestion of awe. Prodded on by a certain desire for distinction, I'd seen the need for intimidating this old man from the very beginning. I'd been deeply conscious of every word I'd spoken and every move I'd made, down to the motions of my eyes.

Though I raved and ranted, it had made little impression on this man. He went right on and put my lunch with his personal effects.

"Damn you! You still don't understand what I'm trying to tell you!"

In a fit of rage, I knocked the cell boss down from behind. His scrawny back felt like a piece of lumber through his dirty jacket, the only upper garment he wore.

Because of this commotion, I was the last to have lunch. Just as I finished, the cell boss was called outside for exercise.

"Queer fellow! What's he in for anyway?" I lost no time in asking a fortyish-looking fellow nearby.

"Sentenced to death." Two men spoke in unison. Their faces were thrust forward, alight with a sort of pride for having revealed something which would surprise me.

"So—sentenced to death." I acknowledged the information with a slight nod. But it set me to thinking, and my face no doubt paled a little.

"What did he do?"

"A long list: robbery, rape, murder, public indecency." The fortyish-looking fellow deliberately enunciated each word. His precise mode of expression was indicative of the intense respect the men with light sentences had for the older prisoner.

"Is it final?"

"Yes, it's been some time now since his appeal was turned down, and any day now, it's—this! You see, it's supposed to be carried out within a hundred days after it becomes final."

I felt myself in a strange vacuum and again fell silent.

Noting my youthful agitation, the fortyish one sidled up as if taking pity on me.

"Yes, you were hasty. You know, men condemned to death can get an extra lease on life, maybe three months or half a year—at least while the trial's going on—if they commit another murder. So you can never tell when they'll try it."

I knew that well enough. When I was in the station detention cell, my cell mate was a swindler. He had been imprisoned once with a fellow who'd killed his adopted child and been condemned to death. This child-killer also had a way of wanting other people's lunches. And when somebody would refuse, he'd take out his towel and twist it in his hands. "Since it's come to this, one or two more won't matter." As he mumbled the words, his sinister eyes would be directed at the throat of the man he was talking to. Everyone would contribute a part of his lunch.

Noticing my dejection, the intellectual, still polishing his utensil box, spoke from his place several mats away:

"Apologize. You've got to apologize."

"That's right! You've got to do it tactfully. Then there's—"

For some reason, the fortyish fellow cut himself short. Suddenly, a crafty light in his eyes, he gave me a sidelong glance.

"Long as a fellow sentenced to death is here, extra lunches come in. We won't lose anything by humoring him."

I realized that what these men were saying out of apparent kindness was certainly so. But knowing myself as I did, I was convinced it would hardly be possible for me to apologize to a man at whom I'd been shouting curses only a few moments before. In this perplexed state I passed the afternoon.

Presently, the boss was returned to the cell. The color had returned to his face, and he began to talk more freely.

Soon it was night. When the time came to go to sleep, I didn't know what to do. In the daytime, a sort of unwritten law prevailed within the cell. In accordance with their seniority, the men had places near the cell door: the cell boss at the door, the next oldest inmate beside him, and so on. At night, however, the prison regulations called for the prisoners to sleep according to their numbers.

This meant that the cell boss, No. 170, would be sleeping at the very end of the room, and that I, No. 178, would be next. I'd have to sleep next to him.

Sound sleep was out of the question that night. Whether he was sleeping or not, I never knew. He didn't twist or turn. He just lay there, his gaunt frame with its sallow, rough skin exposed to the glare of the electric light. His breathing was like air going in and out of a bellows.

I'd heard that there were two other men in Block Five who'd been condemned to death but whose sentences were not yet final. The sounds seemed to come from their direction, shrieks of men having nightmares. Each time they would be followed by the footsteps of the guards going to rouse the sleepers.

Morning came. We could stay in bed till the guard shouted "Get up! Get up!" but No. 170 next to me was already awake and sitting up.

I struggled awake. I took one glance at his face and was shocked into disbelief. So ashen was the face that the skin seemed transparent. It wasn't the face of a living person.

With the command to get up, the men began folding their thin bedding, sweeping the floor with short-handled brooms, and wiping the planked walk. But No. 170, the cell boss, remained motionless, squatting and facing the cell door.

"What's wrong with him anyway?" I whispered to the fortyish fellow with whom I'd become acquainted the day before.

"You never know when the order for execution will come. If it comes, it should be before the change of guards at nine o'clock. No wonder he's worried."

I muttered something as if I'd understood, but I felt myself paling and beginning to tremble.

In all likelihood, a single minute of this man's life now was equivalent to more than an entire year of the life he'd spent like water. The poor all look older than they really are, but he couldn't have been much over fifty. If he were to live out his normal lifetime, he'd still have another fifteen or twenty years. He was trying to live those fifteen or twenty years in the next hour.

Soon it was time for breakfast. Once again, the intellectual shoved aside the box lid offered by the man of the day before and handed the cell boss his own shiny one, as if this were his own personal prerogative. As had happened at supper the night before, this man and the intellectual engaged in a bit of rivalry. The intellectual again pushed aside that dirty cover, and I felt somehow that the fellow who would again and again offer his dirty cover, knowing it would be shoved aside, was a great deal greedier and more to be pitied than the intellectual who pushed it aside.

The trusty dished up the soup with a ladle. The ladle was big, the bowls small, and the soup spilled over onto the lid. By the time all the men had been served, there was a considerable amount of spilled soup in the lid.

After getting his lid back from the cell boss, who continued to sit in stony silence, the intellectual walked cautiously back to his own mat. He then tilted the cover and drank down the soup, his lips smacking with unutterable delight.

I turned to look at the cell boss. In front of him, lined up in a row, were his own meal and the two extra meals that had found their way into the cell. He made no move to take up his chopsticks and remained leaning against the door. I wondered whether he'd soon share his food with some of his favorites, but he didn't. In a little while he rose, took up the three meals, and placed them with his personal effects.

Time passed. It must have been after nine, for the voice of the day-shift guard could be heard down the corridor. Though we heard it each morning, the voice of the new guard always sounded as fresh as the chirping of sparrows.

"It's after nine," one of the men said, to let the cell boss know that the hour of danger had passed.

But the cell boss already knew. He didn't trouble to answer, but rose swiftly and took out the food he had put away only moments before.

To have to look at the hideous color and manner of the man was to have an enormous weight on top of one's head. We all wanted intensely to move away with him from that dangerous hour.

He began eating. Only a moment ago he had been unable to eat a single mouthful, and now he shoveled the food into his mouth with amazing relish. Quickly he disposed of one meal, and not many minutes later he'd finished the other two. His was indeed a formidable appetite. His spirits had recovered completely.

It began when somebody asked me: "And what're you in for?"

For some minutes, the talk was of my criminal record.

"Say, old man, today why don't you finally tell us the details of that rape, murder, and public indecency of yours?" Seeing the cell boss in a good humor, someone asked him this question. As a matter of fact, this was exactly the lurid account I too had been wanting to hear.

The beaming face of the cell boss suddenly turned grim.

"That's one thing I don't want to be asked."

His tone was heavy. For some time now I'd been darting glances in his direction, my face alight with a conscious youthfulness. I was giving him these meaningful little glances to let him know I'd be interested in making peace with him. For the life of me, I couldn't make myself say the words outright. So I'd taken this rather crafty way of making amends.

Soon he was taken out again for exercise.

" 'Robbery, rape, murder, public indecency.' What did he do anyway?" I asked the fortyish fellow. I'd memorized the list of crimes attributed to the cell boss though I'd heard it only once.

"Well, he seems bent on keeping that a secret if it's the last thing he does, but as a matter of fact, there's this."

He pulled a document from among the personal effects of the cell boss. It was the decision on a preliminary hearing.

The other men apparently had seen it already and I was the only one to extend my hand. It was couched in the stilted language of official documents, but as I read it, an image of the event formed itself, piece by piece, in my mind.

*   *   *

The season was spring; the scene, the lush pine woods of northern Kantō. Among the evergreens could be seen spring flowers, and to the nostrils came the strong odor of chestnut blossoms. From somewhere not far off sounded the song of a thrush. The time was just past noon and the air had the breath of late spring, almost like the soft touch of flesh.

For some time now the shrill voices of young girls had been coming from the other side of the woods. Soon, glimpses of school uniforms could be seen as the girls came filing down the hill through the straight-standing spruces.

"Looks like a picnic."

Two construction workers, on their way up the hill to where a power station was being built, were sitting on rocks by the road and smoking.

"There still must be snow at the top."

"No, not any more. The azaleas are in bloom."

The two fell silent. It was a meaningful silence.

Just then: "Go on. Go ahead. Don't look back. Don't."

Waving toward the group she'd just left, a schoolgirl of about eighteen ran behind some trees. Before the spot where the two workers were sitting there was a tangled thicket of withered pampas-like grass. The stems were graying and broken, but there were traces of green at the roots. The schoolgirl, worried only about whether she could be seen by her companions, pulled down her underpants and crouched down. Only the white calico showed clearly.

One of the workers whispered something to the other. Without replying, the latter rose and hurried off. The first jumped in front of the schoolgirl, who was still squatting down. The snapping of grass stems could be heard. In an instant she was overpowered. Her shrieks only echoed through the spruce branches. It was over in a matter of minutes. Then the other worker, who had been standing watch, came back and changed places with the first. It was No. 170, our cell boss.

The schoolgirl lay face upward, her soft hair wet from the oozing mire. The second worker did as the other had done. The schoolgirl had lost consciousness. The breath came from her dainty nostrils like a soft whisper.

With his big hands, the worker strangled her. And as he stood up, he saw the girl's tiny red purse lying a couple of feet away. It had so many bills in it that its clasp would not close. He picked it up and put it inside his waistband.

The two men dragged the body to soft ground and buried it. Cautiously, they left in different directions. Probably the other man hadn't thought of killing the girl.

* * *

When night begins to fall, there comes a moment when everyone becomes a bit emotional. I noticed the cell boss sitting perfectly still, facing the wall and murmuring a Buddhist prayer.

I slept little better that night. Occasionally, he'd roll over and kick me. I'd awake with a start, as if dashed with cold water. Even if he'd forgiven me, he hardly needed a pretext to commit another murder. It was I, close at hand, who had the greatest chance of becoming the victim.

But nothing unusual happened. With the morning there came again those terrible agonies we could hardly bear to watch. And yet at noon he'd be able to eat not only his own but other people's lunches too.

One day my chance came to make peace with him.

"Don't worry," I said. "We'll win this war soon, and then everyone will get a pardon."

It was nonsense. But if I was to say anything to him at all, what else could I say?

"Think so? But even if I should get out, I wouldn't have anything to wear."

"Oh, you don't have to worry about things to wear. A long time ago they had an amnesty when the Constitution was promulgated, and they say a market was set up outside the prison. I'll lend you a little money."

But one morning, at about eight o'clock:

"No. 178—visitor!"

Almost immediately the door opened. I'll never forget the look on No. 170's face as the guard said "one seventy . . ." and then added "eight." His face became chalk white, his eyes jerked upward, his whole body started to tremble. But it was just that one of the fellows in the Kawanaka gang had come to see me.

On the following morning, the same thing happened again. The shock was the same as it had been the day before. I could hardly stand to watch him.

Without saying why, I told the fellow from the Kawanaka gang not to visit me again. I'd begun to have a strange liking for the cell boss. You may laugh when I tell you the reason. You may not be able to understand. In a word, it was because he wasn't going to kill me.

I'd been thinking over and over again the frame of mind in which I'd killed Shida, and the frame of mind the cell boss must have been in when he'd killed the schoolgirl. They were deeds that couldn't be undone. But isn't it remarkable that this man would forego killing me, who slept beside him, and thus forego his chance to live longer? Isn't it wonderful that man is unable to kill without reason, even given his burning desire for life?

I asked that erudite fellow in his forties: "I've heard that men who've been sentenced to death think of killing someone else in prison. I wonder if anything like that has ever actually happened?"

"Well, it's something they often talk about, but I've never heard of an actual case."

I don't know why, but I thought happily: "Why, of course."

It was one morning some days later. An order was shouted by a guard to a man who had gone out to write a letter.

"Stop writing!"

I was the first to start up. When I was still in solitary, I had once heard that same order: "Stop writing!" I had wondered what it meant and later had asked one of the trusties.

"Yesterday, the janitor went in to sweep out the cellar room just under the gallows trap. That means there'll be a hanging today. Guess it'll be the German spy whose sentence was confirmed the other day."

As I recalled this, I thought: "Well, this is it!" I stole a glance at No. 170. In Cell Block Five there were three men sentenced to death, but it was only No. 170 whose sentence had been confirmed.

"Could be a news bulletin," someone was saying. Decidedly it couldn't be anything like that, however.

Soon there were footsteps and two guards stood at the entrance to our cell.

"No. 170. Visitor!"

The cell boss was ashen. He sat transfixed.

"Out, No. 170! Out! Visitor!"

The guards came inside without removing their shoes. They pulled No. 170 to his feet, supporting him from both sides. Swaying and staggering, No. 170 reached the cell door. One of the guards urged him to put on straw sandals, but his feet trembled so he couldn't keep them on.

He went off down the passage toward the women's cells. supported by two guards. The straw sandals lay on the concrete corridor where he had dropped them, a pace or so apart.

"Well, I wonder which guard will pull the rope today. He just has to pull that rope and he gets a whole bottle of saké, some eats, and the rest of the day off."

The fortyish fellow seemed quite proud of his store of knowledge. My face felt pale, I had an urge to slap him. But I fell silent, my head bowed.

THE IDIOT

BY Sakaguchi Ango

TRANSLATED BY George Saitō

Sakaguchi Ango was born in 1906 and graduated from the Department of Indian Philosophy, Tōyō University, in 1930. It was through his first two short stories, "Dr. Kaze" and "Kurotani Village," written soon after his graduation from the university for the group magazine of which he was one of the editors, that he first made his name in literary circles. He did not become widely known, however, until the publication after the war of a series of novels and essays.

His eccentricity, as reflected in the titles he chose ("Overcoat and Blue Sky," "Wind, Light, and I at Twenty," "A Woman Who Washes the Loincloth of a Blue Ogre," "Tale of Nippon—A History Begins with Sukiyaki," etc.), did not permit him to accept conventionality or established social institutions. His life was devoted to a search for a flowering utopia amid the chaos of worldly cares. In this respect he is reminiscent of Dazai Osamu. The yardstick that he used was himself. He therefore almost completely disregarded existing rhetorical mannerisms and created a unique style of his own. Practically none of the established moral or social values could escape his ridicule.

Just as in his writing Sakaguchi revolted against all accepted concepts, so his fate was that of a man who ruins himself in despair. This courageous man died in poverty in 1955, still making his heavy attacks on pseudo-authority and pseudo-ethics.

The present story (Hakuchi in Japanese) was first published in 1946, when the author was thirty-seven. Through its existentialist description of man living like trash under the gigantic force of war, the story results in focusing the reader's attention on the emptiness and corruption of wartime Japan. The *description of the hero's painful solitude as he wanders aimlessly in the desert of debris can be read as a realistic picture of the author's own plight.*

VARIOUS species lived in the house: human beings, a pig, a dog, a hen, a duck. But actually there was hardly any difference in their style of lodging or in the food they ate. It was a crooked building like a storehouse. The owner and his wife lived on the ground floor, while a mother and her daughter rented the attic. The daughter was pregnant, but no one knew who was responsible.

The room that Izawa rented was in a hut detached from the main house. It had formerly been occupied by the family's consumptive son, who had died. Even if it had been assigned to a consumptive pig, the hut could hardly have been considered extravagant. Nevertheless, it had drawers, shelves, and a lavatory.

The owner and his wife were tailors. They also gave sewing lessons to the neighbors, and this was the reason that the son had been placed in a separate hut. The owner was an official of the neighborhood association, in which the girl who lived in the attic had originally worked. It appeared that while she was living in the association's office, she had enjoyed sexual relations indiscriminately with all the officials of the association except the president and the tailor. She had thus had more than ten lovers and now she was with child by one of them. When this unfortunate fact became known, the officials collected a fund to take care of the child when it was born. In this world nothing goes to waste: among the officials was a bean-curd dealer who continued to visit the girl even after she had become pregnant and had taken refuge in the attic. In the end, the girl was virtually established as this man's mistress. When the other officials learned of the situation, they immediately withdrew their contributions and asserted that the bean-curd dealer ought to bear her living expenses. There were seven or eight of them who refused to pay, including the greengrocer, the watchmaker, and the landlord. Since they had been giving five yen each, the loss was considerable and there was no end to the girl's resentment.

She had a big mouth and two large eyes, yet she was fearfully thin. She disliked the duck and tried to give all the leftovers to the hen, but since the duck invariably butted in and snatched the food, she would chase it furiously round the room. The way she ran in a strangely erect posture, with her huge belly and her buttocks jutting out to the front and the rear, bore a striking resemblance to the duck's waddle.

At the entrance to the alley was a tobacconist, a thickly powdered woman of fifty-five. She had just got rid of her seventh or eighth lover, and rumor had it that she was now having trouble making up her mind about whether to choose in his stead a middle-aged Buddhist priest or a certain shopkeeper, also middle-aged. She was known to sell a couple of cigarettes (at the black-market price) to any young man who went to the back door of her shop. "Why don't you try buying some, sir?" the tailor had suggested to Izawa. Izawa, however, had no need to call on the old woman since he received a special ration at his office.

Behind the rice-supply office diagonally opposite the tobacconist's lived a widow who had accumulated some savings. She had two children: a son, who was a factory hand, and a younger daughter. Though really brother and sister, these two had lived as man and wife. The widow had connived at this, feeling that it would be cheaper in the long run. In the meantime, however, the son had acquired a mistress on the side. The need had therefore arisen to marry off the daughter, and it had been decided that she should become the bride of a man of fifty or sixty who was vaguely related. Thereupon the daughter had taken rat poison. After swallowing the poison, she had come to the tailor's (where Izawa lodged) for her sewing lesson. There she had begun to suffer the most atrocious agonies, and had finally died. The local doctor certified that she had died from a heart attack and this had been the end of the matter. "Eh?" Izawa had asked the tailor in surprise. "Where do you find doctors who'll issue such convenient certificates?" The tailor had been even more surprised. "D'you mean to say they don't do that sort of thing everywhere?" he said.

It was a neighborhood where tenements were clustered together. A considerable proportion of the rooms was occupied by kept women or prostitutes. Since these women had no children and since they were all inclined to keep their rooms neat, the caretakers of the buildings liked having them as tenants and did not mind about the disorderliness and immorality of their private lives. More than half of the apartments had become dormitories used by munition factories and were occupied by groups of women volunteer-workers. Among the tenants were pregnant volunteers who continued receiving their salaries even though they never went to work; the girl friend of Mr. So-and-So in such-and-such a section of the government; the "wartime wife" of the section chief (which meant that the real wife had been evacuated from Tokyo); the official mistress of a company director.

One of the women was reported to be a five-hundred-yen mistress and was the object of general envy. Next door to the soldier of fortune from Manchuria, who proudly boasted that his profession used to be murder (his younger sister studied sewing with the tailor), lived a manual therapist; next to him lived a man who, it was rumored, belonged to one of the traditional schools that practiced the fine art of picking pockets. Behind him lived a naval sub-lieutenant who ate fish, drank coffee, feasted on tinned food, and had saké every day. Because of the subterranean water which one found on digging a foot or so below the surface, it was almost impossible to construct air-raid shelters in this neighborhood; the sub-lieutenant, however, had somehow contrived to build a concrete shelter which was even finer than his actual apartment.

The department store, a wooden, two-story building on the route that Izawa took on his way to work, was closed because of the wartime lack of commodities; but on the upper floor gambling was being carried on every day. The boss of the gambling gang also controlled a number of "people's bars." He got dead drunk every day of the week and used to glare fiercely at the people who stood in queues waiting to enter his bars.

On graduating from university, Izawa had become a newspaper reporter; subsequently he had started working on educational films. This was his present job, but he was still an apprentice and had not yet directed anything independently. He was twenty-seven, an age at which one is likely to know something about the seamy side of society; and in fact he had managed to pick up a good deal of inside information about politicians, army officers, businessmen, geisha, and entertainers. Yet he had never imagined that life in a suburban shopping district surrounded by small factories and apartment buildings could be anything like this. It occurred to him that it might be due to the roughening effect of the war on people's characters, but when he asked the tailor about it one day, the man replied in a quiet, philosophical way: "No, to tell the truth, things have always been like this in our neighborhood."

But the outstanding character of them all was the man next door. This neighbor was mad. He was quite well off and one way in which his madness revealed itself was in an excessive fear of intrusion by burglars or other undesirable people. This had led him to choose for his house a place at the very end of the alley and to construct the entrance in such a way that one could not find it even if one went up to the house and past the gate. There was nothing to be seen from the front but a latticed window. The real entrance was at the opposite end of the house from the gate and one had to go around the entire building to reach it. The owner's plan was that an intruder would either give up and beat a hasty retreat, or else would be discovered as he roamed about the house looking for the elusive entrance. Izawa's mad neighbor had little liking for the common people of this floating world. His house was a two-story building with quite a large number of rooms, but even the well-informed tailor knew hardly anything about the interior design.

The madman was about thirty; he had a wife of about twenty-five, and a mother. People said that at least the mother should be classed as sane. She had an extremely hysterical nature, however, and was without doubt the most mettlesome woman in the neighborhood, so much so that when she was dissatisfied with her rationed allocations she would rush out of the house barefoot to complain instantly to the town block-association.

The man's wife was an idiot. One lucky year he had undergone a religious awakening, clad himself in white, and set out on a pilgrimage to Shikoku. In the course of the trip he had become friendly with a feeble-minded woman somewhere in Shikoku: he had brought her back as a sort of souvenir of his pilgrimage and had married her.

The madman was a handsome fellow. His feeble-minded wife had an elegance becoming a daughter of a good family; her narrow-eyed, oval face had the prettiness of an old-fashioned doll or of a Noh mask. Outwardly the two were not only good-looking but appeared to be a well-matched couple of considerable breeding. The madman was extremely shortsighted and wore strong spectacles. As a rule he had a pensive air, as though tired from reading innumerable books.

One day when an air-raid drill was being held in the alley and the housewives were all bustling about efficiently, the madman had stood there in his everyday kimono, giggling inanely as he observed the scene. Then he had suddenly left and reappeared wearing an air-raid uniform. Grabbing a bucket from someone, he had started to draw water and to throw it about the place, uttering various curious exclamations all the while. After that he placed a ladder against the wall, climbed to the top, and began shouting orders from the roof, ending in a stirring admonitory speech. This was the first time that Izawa had actually realized that the man was mad. He had, it is true, already noticed certain eccentricities in his neighbor. For instance, the man would occasionally break through the fence into the tailor's garden and empty a bucket of leftovers into the pigpen; after this he would suddenly throw a stone at the duck or, with an air of perfect nonchalance, start feeding the hen and then abruptly give her a kick. But on the whole Izawa had taken the man to be compos mentis and he used to exchange silent greetings with him when they happened to meet.

What was the real difference, he wondered, between the madman and normal people? The difference, if any, was that the madman was essentially more discreet. To be sure, he giggled when he wanted to, gave a speech when he felt like it, threw stones at the duck, and would spend a couple of hours poking a pig's head and rear if the spirit so moved him. Nevertheless, he was essentially far more apprehensive of public opinion than normal people and he took special care in trying to isolate the main part of his private life from others. This was another reason that he had placed the entrance to his house on exactly the opposite side from the gate. On the whole the madman's private life was devoid of noise, he did not go in for useless chatting, and he lived in a meditative way. On the opposite side of the alley was an apartment from which the sound of running water and of vulgar female voices constantly encroached upon Izawa's hut. The apartment was occupied by two sisters who were prostitutes. On nights when the elder sister had a customer, the younger one would pace the corridor; when the younger sister had a customer, the elder one would walk up and down deep into the night. And people considered the madman to be of a different race, thought Izawa, merely because he was in the habit of giggling.

The madman's feeble-minded wife was a remarkably quiet and gentle woman. Her speech consisted of a timid mumble; even when one could make out the words, her meaning was usually obscure. She did not know how to prepare a meal or boil rice. She might have been able to cook if she had had to, but as soon as she made a mistake and was scolded, she became so nervous that she began to spill and drop everything. Even when she went to get rations she could do nothing herself; she merely stood there and let the neighbors manage for her. People said that since she was the wife of a madman it was quite appropriate that she should be an idiot and that the man's family could hardly expect anything better. The mother, however, was greatly dissatisfied and was constantly complaining about the misfortune of having a daughter-in-law who could not even boil rice. As a rule she was a modest and refined old woman, but owing to her hysteria she could become even fiercer than her mad son once she had been aroused. Among the three unbalanced occupants of the house it was the old mother who uttered the loudest screams. The idiot wife was so intimidated by this that she was in a perpetual state of nerves, even on peaceful days when nothing had gone wrong. The mere sound of footsteps would fill her with alarm. When Izawa greeted her on the street, she would stand there petrified, with a vacant look on her face.

The wife, too, occasionally came to the tailor's pigpen. Whereas the husband broke in openly, as if the house belonged to him, and threw stones at the duck or poked the pig's jowls, the feeble-minded woman slipped in silently like a shadow and hid behind the pigpen. In a way this had become her sanctuary. After she had been there for a while, the old woman's croaking voice would usually come from the next door, shouting "Osayo, Osayo!" and the idiot's body would react to each call by crouching further in the corner or by bending over. Before reluctantly emerging from her hiding place, the wife would time after time repeat her impotent, worm-like movements of resistance.

Izawa's occupations of newspaper reporter and educational-film director were the meanest of the mean. The only thing such people seemed to understand was the current fashion, and their lives consisted of a constant effort not to be left behind by the times. In this world there was no room for personality, or the pursuit of the ego, or originality. Like office workers, civil servants, or school teachers, their daily conversation abounded with such words as ego, mankind, personality, originality. But all this was mere verbiage. What they meant by "human suffering" was some such nonsense as the discomfort of a hangover after a drunken night during which one has spent all one's money trying to seduce a woman. They absorbed themselves in making films or writing fanciful pieces of colored prose which had neither spiritual value nor any element of real feeling but made ample use of such clichés as "ah, how inspiring the sight of the Rising Sun flag!"; "all our thanks to you, brave soldiers!"; "despite oneself the hot tears well up"; "the thud-thud of bombs"; "frantically one hurls oneself to the ground"; "the chattering of machine-gun fire"; and they firmly believed that with this kind of drivel they were actually portraying war.

Some said they could not write because of military censorship, but the fact was that, war or no war, they had not the slightest idea how to write honestly on any subject. Truth or real feeling in writing has nothing to do with censorship. In whatever period these gentry had happened to live, their personalities would surely have displayed the same emptiness. They changed in accordance with the prevailing fashion, and took for their models expressions culled from popular novels of the day.

To be sure, the period itself was both crude and senseless. What relationship could there be between human honesty and the cataclysm of war and defeat in which Japan's two-thousand-year-old history was being submerged? The entire fate of the nation was being decided by the will of those men who had the feeblest power of introspection, and by the blind action of the ignorant mob that followed them. If you spoke about personality and originality in front of the city editor or the president, he would turn away as if to say that you were a fool. After all, a newspaper reporter was merely a machine whose function it was to spout forth "all our thanks to you, brave soldiers!"; "ah, how inspiring the sight of the Rising Sun flag!"; "despite oneself the hot tears well up." And so, indeed, was the entire period—it was all a mere machine. If you asked whether it was really necessary to give a full report of the speech by the divisional commander to his men, or whether you had to record every word of the weird Shinto prayer that the factory workers were obliged to recite each morning, the city editor would look away and click his tongue with annoyance; then he would suddenly turn round, crush his precious cigarette in the ash tray, and, glaring at you, shout: "Look here, what does beauty mean at a time like this? Art is powerless! Only news is real."

The directors, the members of the planning department, and the other groups had banded together to constitute their own private cabals, rather like the professional gambling societies of the Tokugawa period. Everything was based on group comradeship, and the individual talents of the members were used on a rotational basis with special emphasis on the traditional precepts of "duty" and "human feeling." The entire organization became more bureaucratic than the bureaucracy itself. Thus they managed to protect their respective mediocrities and to form a sort of mutual-aid relief organization founded on a hopeless dearth of talent. Any attempt to work one's way up by means of artistic individuality was regarded as a wicked violation of union rules. Internally the groups were relief organizations for the dearth of talent, but in their relations to the outside world they were alcohol-acquiring gangs whose members occupied the "people's bars" and argued drunkenly about art as they swilled their bottles of beer. Their berets, their long hair, their ties, and their blouses were those of artists; but in their souls they were more bureaucratic than the bureaucrats. Since Izawa believed in artistic creativeness and in individuality, he found it hard to breathe in the atmosphere of these cabals; their mediocrity, their vulgar and sordid spirit, were sheer anathema. He became an outcast: no one returned his greetings and some people in the office even glared at him when he made his appearance.

One day he strode resolutely into the president's office and asked whether there was any inevitable, logical link between the war and the current poverty of artistic output. Or was this poverty, he asked, the deliberate aim of the military, who insisted that all one needed to portray reality was a camera and a couple of fingers? Surely, said Izawa, the special duty of us artists is to decide on the particular angle from which we should portray reality so as to produce a work of art. While Izawa was still talking, the president turned aside and puffed at his cigarette with a look of disgust. Then he smiled sardonically as if to say "Why don't you leave our company if you don't like it here? Is it because you're afraid of being drafted for hard labor?" Gradually his expression changed to one of annoyance. "Why can't you fit in with our way of working?" he seemed to say. "Just do your daily stint like the other men and you'll collect your salary all the same! And stop thinking about what doesn't concern you. Damned impertinence!" Without a

Izawa made up two sets of bedding on the floor and told the woman to lie down. Then he switched off the light. A couple of minutes later he heard her crawling out of bed. She went to the corner of the room and crouched down. If it had not been the middle of winter, Izawa would probably have gone to sleep without troubling about her. But it was a bitterly cold night—so cold that he could not stop shivering. Since he had sacrificed one half of his bedding to his guest, the icy air seemed to impinge directly on his skin. He got up and turned on the light. The woman was crouching by the door, holding the front of her dress tightly about her body. Her eyes were those of a creature who has lost its hiding place and is driven to bay.

"What's the matter?" he said. "Go to bed."

The woman nodded—almost too readily—and crawled back into the bed. Izawa turned out the light. A moment later he heard her getting up as before. When he took the woman back to her bed this time, he tried to reassure her. "Don't worry," he said. "I'm not going to touch you." With a startled expression the woman muttered something that sounded vaguely like an excuse. The third time that he turned out the light, she got up without a moment's delay, opened the closet door, stepped inside, and shut herself in.

The woman's persistence had begun to annoy Izawa. He opened the closet roughly. "I don't know what you think you're doing," he said crossly, "but you seem to have got the wrong idea about me. Why on earth do you have to hide in the closet like that when I've told you I don't have the slightest intention of touching you? It's damned insulting. If you can't trust me, why come here in the first place? You've humiliated me, made a fool of me. What right have you to act as if you were being victimized in this place? I've had quite enough of your nonsense for one night."

Then it occurred to him that the woman could not possibly understand a word he was saying. What could be more futile than to remonstrate with a half-wit? Probably the best thing would be to give her a good slap on the cheek and then go to sleep without bothering any more about her. He noticed that the woman was muttering away with an inscrutable look on her face. Apparently she was stuttering out something to the effect that she wanted to go home and that it would have been better if she had never come.

"But now I have nowhere to go home to," she added.

Izawa could not help being touched. "Then why not spend the night here quietly?" he said. "There's really nothing to worry about, you know. The only reason I got a bit angry just now is that you started setting yourself up in the role of a victim when I didn't have the slightest intention of harming you. Now then, stay out of that closet and get into bed and have a good night's sleep!"

The woman stared at Izawa and launched into some more rapid mumbling.

"What?" he asked.

Then Izawa had the shock of his life. For out of her confused mumblings he clearly caught the words "I see you don't like me."

"Eh?" said Izawa, gazing at her with open-eyed amazement. "What's that you said?"

With a dejected expression, the woman began to explain herself, repeating over and over: "I shouldn't have come"; "You don't really like me"; "I thought you liked me, but you don't." Finally she lapsed into silence and gazed vacantly at a spot in the air.

Now Izawa understood for the first time. The woman had not been afraid of him. The situation was exactly the reverse. The woman had not come just because she had been scolded at home and didn't have anywhere else to hide. She had been counting on Izawa's imagined love for her. But what on earth could have made the woman believe that Izawa loved her? He had only exchanged the briefest possible greetings with her a few times near the pigpen or in the alley or on the road. The situation could hardly have been more absurd. Here he was being coerced by an idiot's will, by an idiot's susceptibility—forces that must be completely different from those of normal people. It was not clear to Izawa whether what had happened to the woman that evening was, in her idiot mind, a truly painful experience. Having lain in bed for a few minutes without Izawa's so much as touching her, the woman had come to the conclusion that she was unloved; this had filled her with shame and she had got out of bed. Finally she had shut herself in the closet. How could one interpret this peculiar action? As an expression of an idiot's shame and self-abasement? The trouble was that in the language of normal people there did not even exist the proper words in which to phrase a conclusion. In such a situation the only way was to lower oneself to the same level as the idiot's mentality. And after all, thought Izawa, what need was there for normal human wisdom? Would it be all that shameful if he himself adopted the frank simplicity of an idiot's mind? Perhaps that was what he needed more than anything else—the childlike, candid mind of an idiot. He had mislaid it somewhere, and in the meantime he had become bedraggled with thoughts of the workaday people who surrounded him; he had pursued false shadows and had nothing to show for it all but exhaustion.

He tucked the woman in bed and, sitting by the pillow, stroked her forelocks as if he were stroking a little girl—his own child perhaps—and trying to put her to sleep. Her eyes stayed open with a vacant look. There was an innocence about her, exactly like that of a little child's.

"I do not dislike you," Izawa began solemnly. "There are other ways, you know, of expressing love than by simple physical contact. The ultimate abode for us human beings is our birthplace, and in a strange way you seem to be living permanently in such a birthplace."

Of course there was no possibility of her understanding what he said. But what, after all, were words? What real value did they have? And where did reality reside? There was no evidence that it could be found even in human love. Where, if anywhere, could there be anything so real that it warranted a man's devoting his entire passion to it? Everything was merely a false shadow. But as he stroked the woman's hair, he felt like bursting into tears. He was overcome by the heartrending idea that this small, elusive, utterly uncertain love was the very haven of his life, that involuntarily he was stroking the hair of his own fate.

How was the war going to turn out? No doubt Japan would be defeated, the Americans would land on the mainland, and the greater part of the Japanese people would be annihilated. But all this could be conceived only as part of a supernatural destiny—the decree of Heaven, so to speak. What really bothered Izawa was a far more trivial problem—a surprisingly trivial problem, yet one that always flickered exigently before his eyes. It was the question of the two-hundred-yen wage he received every month from his company. How long would he continue to receive this salary? He never knew from one day to another when he would be dismissed and reduced to utter destitution.

Each time he went to collect his salary he was terrified that he would also be given his dismissal notice. And when he actually held his pay envelope in his hand he was invariably overcome by intense joy at having survived for another month. He always felt like crying at the thought of how trivial it all was. Here he was—a man who dreamed about the great ideals of art—yet a wage of two hundred yen, which in the presence of art was less than the smallest speck of dust, could become a source of such agony that it penetrated to his marrow and shook the entire foundation of his existence. It was not merely his external life that was circumscribed by the two hundred yen; his very mind and soul were absorbed by it. And the fact that he could gaze calmly, steadily, at this triviality and retain his sanity made him even more wretched.

The editor's loud, stupid voice, shouting "What does beauty mean at a time like this? Art is powerless!" filled Izawa's mind with a completely different sort of reality and ate into him with a great, biting force. Ah yes, he thought, Japan would lose. His countrymen would fall one after another like so many clay dolls, innumerable legs and heads and arms would fly skyward mixed with the debris of bricks and concrete, and the land would become a flat graveyard devoid of trees, buildings, everything. Where would he seek refuge? Which hole would he be driven into? Where would he be when finally he was blown up, hole and all?

Yet sometimes he dreamed of how things would be if, by some peculiar chance, he survived. What he felt chiefly at such moments was curiosity—curiosity about life in an unpredictable new world, life in rubble-buried fields, curiosity also about the regeneration that would come. It was bound to happen, in six months or perhaps a year; yet he could only imagine it as some remote fancy, like a world of dreams. Meanwhile the decisive force of a mere two hundred yen blocked off everything else and swept away all hope from his life; even in his dreams it choked and haunted him; it bleached every emotion of his youth, so that although he was still only twenty-seven years old, he already found himself wandering aimlessly over a dark moorland.

Izawa wanted a woman; this was what he longed for most of all. Yet life with any woman would ineluctably be limited by the two hundred yen. His saucepan, his cooking pot, his bean paste, his rice—

everything bore this curse. When his child was born, it too would be haunted by the curse, and the woman herself would turn into a demon obsessed by the same curse and would be grumbling from morning until night. His enthusiasm and his art and the light of his hopes were all dead; his very life was being trampled on like horse dung by the wayside, drying up and being blown away by the wind to disappear without a trace, without so much as the slightest nail mark. Such a curse it was that would cling to the woman's back.

His way of living was unbearably trivial and he himself lacked the power to resolve this triviality. War—this vast destructive force in which everyone was being judged with fantastic impartiality, in which all Japan was becoming a rubble-covered wasteland and the people were collapsing like clay dolls—what a heart-rending, what a gigantic love it represented on the part of nothingness! Izawa felt a desire to sleep soundly in the arms of the god of destruction. This resignation to the force of nothingness had the effect of making him rather more active than before, and when the air-raid alarm sounded he would briskly put on his leggings. The only thing that made life worth living each day was to toy with the uneasiness of life. When the all clear sounded, he would be thoroughly dispirited and once more would be overcome by the despair of having lost all emotion.

This feeble-minded woman did not know how to boil rice or to make bean-paste soup. She had trouble in expressing the simplest thought and the most she could do was to stand in line to get the rations. Like a thin sheet of glass, she reacted to the slightest suggestion of joy or anger; between the furrows of her fear and her abstractedness she simply received the will of others and passed it on. Even the evil spirit of the two hundred yen could not haunt such a soul. This woman, thought Izawa, was a forlorn puppet made for him. In his mind's eye he pictured an endless journey in which he would roam over the dark moorland with this woman in his arms and the wind blowing about him.

Yet he felt that there was something rather fantastic and ludicrous about the whole idea. This was probably because his external triviality had by now begun to erode his very heart in such a way that the frank feeling of love that was gushing up within him seemed entirely false. But why should it be false? Was there some intrinsic rule which said that the prostitutes in their apartments and the society ladies in their houses were more human than this feeble-minded woman? Yes, absurdly enough, it looked as if there really was such a rule.

What am I afraid of? It all comes from the evil spirit of those two hundred yen. Yes, now when I am on the point of freeing myself from the evil spirit by means of this woman, I find that I am still bound by its curse. The only thing I am really afraid of is worldly appearances. And what I mean by "world" is merely the collection of women who live here in the apartments—the prostitutes and the kept women and the pregnant volunteer-workers and the housewives who cackle away in their nasal voices like so many geese. I know that there is no other world. Yet, indisputable as this fact is, I am completely unable to *believe* it. For I live in fear of some strange rule.

It was a surprisingly short (yet at the same time an endlessly long) night. Dawn broke before he knew it and the chill of daybreak numbed his body into an unfeeling block of stone. All night long he had simply stayed by the woman's pillow, stroking her hair.

* * *

From that day a new life began for Izawa.

Yet, aside from the fact that a woman's body had been added to a house, there was nothing peculiar or even different. Unbelievable though it might seem, not a single new bud appeared to sprout forth round him or within him. His reason perceived what an extraordinary event it was; but apart from that, there was not the slightest alteration in his life—not so much as the position of his desk was changed. He went to work each morning, and while he was out a feeble-minded woman stayed in the closet awaiting his return. Once he had stepped outside, he forgot entirely about the woman, and if he thought at all about the event, it seemed like something that had happened in the indefinite past, ten or even twenty years before.

War produced a strangely wholesome kind of amnesia. Its fantastic destructive power caused a century of change to take place in a single day, made last week's events seem as if they had happened several years before and submerged the events of the previous year at the very bottom of one's memory. It was only recently that the buildings surrounding the factories near where Izawa lived had been torn down in a frenzy of "planned evacuation," which had turned the entire neighborhood into a whirling mass of dust; yet, though the debris had still not been cleared away, the demolition had already receded into the past as if it were something that had taken place over a year before. Immense changes that completely transformed the city were taken for granted when one saw them for the second time.

The feeble-minded woman too had become one of the multifarious blurred fragments belonging to this wholesome amnesia. Her face lay among the various other fragments: among the sticks and splinters on the site of the evacuated "people's bar" in front of the railway station where, until a couple of days before, people had been waiting in queues, among the holes in the nearby building that had been wrecked by a bomb, among the fire-ravaged ruins of the city.

Every day the siren rang out. Sometimes it was an air-raid warning. At its sound Izawa would be plunged into deep disquiet. What worried him was that there might be an air raid near where he lived and that even now, while he sat in his office, some unknown change might be taking place at home. If there was an air raid, the feeble-minded woman might well become excited and rush out of the house, thus exposing their secret to the entire neighborhood. Fear about an unknown change concerned Izawa more than anything else and made it impossible for him to return home while it was still light. Many were the times that he vainly struggled against this pitiful condition in which he was dominated by vulgar worries. If nothing else, he would have liked to be able to confide everything to the tailor; but this struck him as a hopelessly mean action, for it would simply have meant getting rid of his worries by the least damaging possible form of confession. So he remained silent and angrily cursed himself for being no better in his true nature than the common run of men whom he despised.

For Izawa the feeble-minded woman had two unforgettable faces. When turning a street corner, when walking up the stairs in his office building, when detaching himself from the crowd of people in front of a tram—at these and other unexpected moments he would suddenly recall the two faces. His thoughts would freeze up and he would be congealed in a momentary frenzy.

One face was that which he had seen when he first touched her body. The occurrence itself had on the very next day receded into the memories of a year before; only the face would come back to him, detached from the surrounding events.

From that day the feeble-minded woman had been no more than a waiting body with no other life, with not so much as a scrap of thought. She was always waiting. Merely from the fact that Izawa's hands had touched a part of her body, the woman's entire consciousness was absorbed by the sexual act; her body, her face, were simply waiting for it. Even in the middle of the night, if Izawa's hand happened to touch her, the woman's sleep-drugged body would show exactly the same reaction. Her body alone was alive, always waiting. Yes, even while asleep.

When it came to the question of what the woman was thinking about when awake, Izawa realized that her mind was a void. A coma of the mind combined with a vitality of the flesh—that was the sum and total of this woman. Even when she was awake, her mind slept; and even when she was asleep, her body was awake. Nothing existed in her but a sort of unconscious lust. The woman's body was constantly awake and reacted to outer stimuli by a tireless, worm-like wriggling.

But she had another face as well. There happened to be a daytime air-raid on Izawa's day off and for two solid hours the bombers had concentrated on a nearby part of the city. Since Izawa had no air-raid shelter, he hid in the closet with the woman, barricading their bodies with the thick bedding. The center of the bombing was about five hundred yards away, but the houses in Izawa's neighborhood trembled as the earth shook; with each great thud of the bombs Izawa's breath and thoughts stood still.

Although both incendiary and demolition bombs were dropped alike from the planes, they had all the difference in degree of horror that exists between a common grass snake and a viper. Incendiary bombs were equipped with a mechanism that produced a ghastly, rattling sound, but they did not explode on reaching the ground and the noise fizzled out above one's head. "A dragon's head and a serpent's tail,"* people used to say. In fact there was no tail at all, serpentine or otherwise, and one was spared the culminating terror. In the case of TNT bombs, however, the sound as they fell was like the subdued swishing of rain, but this ended in a fabulous explosion that seemed to shatter the very axis of the earth. The horror of the rain-like warning, the hopeless

* Proverbial expression, roughly corresponding to "Up like a rocket and down like a stick."

terror as the thud of the explosions approached, made one feel more dead than alive. Worse still, since the American planes flew at a high altitude, the sound of their passage overhead was extremely faint, and they gave the impression of being totally unconcerned with what was happening below. Accordingly, when the bombs fell, it was exactly like being struck by a huge axe wielded by a monster who is looking the other way. Because one could have no idea what the enemy planes were going to do, the strange buzzing of their motors in the distance filled one with a peculiar sense of uneasiness; then on top of this would come the swish of the falling bomb. The terror one felt while waiting for the explosion was really enough to stop every word and breath and thought. The only thing in one's mind was the despair that flashed through one, icy like impending madness—despair at the idea that this was assuredly one's final moment on earth.

Izawa's hut was fortunately surrounded on all sides by two-story buildings (apartments, the madman's house, the tailor's house) and it alone escaped without so much as a cracked windowpane, whereas the windows in the neighboring houses were shattered and, in some cases, the roofs badly damaged. The only untoward incident was that a blood-drenched hood, of the type people wore in air raids, fell on the field in front of the pigpen. In the darkness of the closet Izawa's eyes glittered. Then he saw it—he saw the idiot's face and its writhing agony of despair.

Ah yes, he thought, most people have intellect and even at the worst of times they retain control and resistance. How appalling it was to see someone who was entirely bereft of intellect and restraint and resistance! To the woman's face and body, as she gazed into the window of death, nothing adhered but anguish. Her anguish moved, it writhed, it shed a tear. If a dog's eyes were to shed tears, it would probably be infinitely ugly, just as if he were to laugh. Izawa was shocked to see how ugly tears could be when there was no trace of intellect behind them. Strangely enough, children of five or six rarely cry in the middle of a bombing. Their hearts beat like hammers, they become speechless, and they stare ahead with wide-open eyes. Only their eyes are alive; but apparently they are just kept wide open and they fail to show any direct or dramatic fear. The fact is that children calmly subdue their emotions to the extent that they appear more intelligent than under normal circumstances. At the instant of danger, they are the equal of adults. One might even say that they are superior, for adults plainly manifest their fears of death. Yes, children actually appear more intelligent at such times than adults.

But the idiot's anguish did not bear the slightest resemblance to the wide-eyed reaction that children show at times of danger. It was merely an instinctive fear of death, a single ugly movement. Her reaction was not that of a human being or even of an insect. If it could be said to resemble anything, it was like the writhings of a small three-inch caterpillar that has swollen to about six feet—and that has a teardrop in its eye.

There were no words, no screams, no groans; nor was there any expression. She was not even aware of Izawa's existence. If she were human, she would be incapable of such solitude. It was impossible that a man and a woman could be together in a closet with one of them entirely forgetting about the other. People talk of absolute solitude, but absolute solitude can exist only by one's being aware of the existence of others. Absolute solitude could never be such a blind and unconscious thing as what Izawa was now witnessing. This woman's solitude was like a caterpillar's—the ultimate in wretchedness. How unbearable it was— this anguish entirely devoid of any thought!

The bombing ended. Izawa raised the crouching woman in his arms. As a rule she reacted amorously if Izawa's finger so much as brushed against her breast, but now she appeared to have lost even her sense of lust. He was falling through space with a corpse in his arms. Nothing existed but the dark, dark, endless fall.

Immediately after the bombing Izawa took a walk past the houses that had just been mowed down. In the ruins he saw a woman's leg that had been torn from her body, a woman's trunk with the intestines protruding, and a woman's severed head.

Among the ruins of the great air raid of March tenth, Izawa had also wandered aimlessly through the still rising smoke. On all sides people lay dead like so many roast fowl. They lay dead in great clusters. Yes, they were exactly like roast fowl. They were neither gruesome nor dirty. Some of the corpses lay next to the bodies of dogs and were burned in exactly the same manner, as if to emphasize how utterly useless their deaths had been. Yet these bodies lacked even the pathos implied in the expression "a dog's death."* It was a case, not of people's having died like dogs, but of dogs lying there in the ruins next to other objects, as though they were all pieces of roast fowl neatly arranged on a platter. Those four-legged things were not really dogs; still less were those two-legged objects human beings.

If the idiot woman should be burned to death, would it not simply mean that a clay doll had returned to the earth whence it came? Izawa imagined the night that might come at any time when incendiary bombs would rain down on his street, and he could not help being conscious of his own form, his face, his eyes, as he lay there strangely calm, sunk in thought. I am calm, he thought. And I am waiting for an air raid. That's all right. He smiled scornfully. It's merely that I dislike ugly things. Is it not natural that a body which has no mind should burn and die? I shan't kill the woman. I am a cowardly and vulgar man. I don't have the courage for that. But the war will probably kill her. All that is necessary is to grasp the first opportunity to direct the unfeeling hand of war toward this woman's head. I shall not really be concerned. It will probably be a matter of having everything automatically settled by some crucial instant. Very calmly, Izawa awaited the next air raid.

*   *   *

It was April fifteenth. Two days before, on the thirteenth, the second great night-bombing had taken place, inflicting immense damage on Ikebukuro, Sugamo, and other residential districts in Tokyo. As a result of that raid, Izawa had managed to obtain a calamity certificate. This enabled him to take a train to Saitama Prefecture and to return with some rice in his rucksack. The air-raid alarm had started the moment he reached home.

By examining the areas of Tokyo that still remained unburned, anyone could surmise that the next raid would be directed at Izawa's neighborhood. Izawa knew that the fatal moment was near; at the earliest it would come on the following day, at the latest within a month. The reason Izawa thought it would not happen before the following day was that the tempo of raids until then indicated that at least another twenty-four hours would be necessary to complete preparations for a night

---

* To "die like a dog" (inujini suru) means to die in vain.

attack. It never occurred to him that this might be the day of doom. That is why he had gone food-hunting. The main purpose of his trip, however, was not to buy food. Since his school days he had had connections with a certain farm in Saitama, and his principal objective in going to the country had been to deposit his belongings, which he had packed in a couple of trunks and a rucksack.

Izawa was tired out. He had made the trip in his air-raid uniform and when he reached his room he lay down as he was, using his rucksack as a pillow. When the crucial moment came, he had actually dozed off. He awoke to the blaring of radios. At that moment the front of the attacking squadron was approaching the southern tip of Izu Peninsula. A moment later, the bombers were over the mainland and the sirens started to shriek out their warning. Instinctively Izawa knew that the final day for his neighborhood had come. He put the feeble-minded woman in the closet and went outside to the well with a towel in his hand and a toothbrush in his mouth. A few days before, Izawa had managed to obtain a tube of Lion toothpaste and he had been enjoying the astringent taste that had been denied him for such a long time. When it dawned on him that the fatal moment had come, he was for some reason inspired to brush his teeth and wash his face. But first it took him a while—it seemed like ages—to find the tube, which had been moved a small distance from where he remembered having put it; then he had trouble finding the soap (it was a perfumed cake of a type that was no longer obtainable in the shops) because it too had been slightly misplaced. "I'm getting rattled," he told himself. "Calm down, Izawa, calm down!" Thereupon he struck his head against the closet and stumbled over the desk.

For a while he tried to gather his wits by suspending all movement and thought; but his entire body was flustered and refused to respond to orderly control.

Finally he found the soap and went to the well. The tailor and his wife were throwing their belongings into the shelter that they had dug in the corner of the field, and the duck-like girl from the attic was bustling about with a suitcase in her hand. Izawa congratulated himself for his persistence in having found the toothpaste and the soap, and wondered what fate really had in store for him that night.

While he was still wiping his face, the anti-aircraft guns started banging away. When he looked up, he saw that a dozen or more searchlights were already crisscrossing overhead. In the very center of their beams an American plane showed up clearly. Then another plane and yet another. When he happened to glance in the direction of the station, he saw that the whole area was a sea of flames.

The time had finally come. Now that the situation was clear, Izawa calmed down. He put on his air-raid hood and covered himself in his bedding. Standing outside his hut, he counted up to twenty-four planes. They all flew overhead, clearly exposed in the beams of the searchlights.

The anti-aircraft guns boomed crazily, but there was still no sound of bombing. When he had counted the twenty-fifth plane, he heard the familiar rattling sound of incendiary bombs, like a freight train crossing a bridge. Apparently the planes were passing over Izawa's head and concentrating their attack on the factory area behind. Since he could not see from where he was standing, he went to the pigpen and looked back. The factory area was bathed in flames, and to his amazement Izawa saw that, apart from the bombers which had just passed overhead, planes were approaching in quick succession from the exact opposite direction and were bombing the entire area to the rear. Then the radios stopped. The whole sky was hidden by a thick, red curtain of smoke, which blotted out the American planes and the beams of the searchlights.

The tailor and his wife were a prudent couple. Some time before, they had made the shelter for their belongings and had even provided mud to seal up the entrance. Now they briskly stored everything in the shelter as planned, sealed it, and covered it with earth from the rice field.

"With a fire like this," said the tailor, "it's absolutely hopeless." He stood there in his old fireman's clothes, with his arms folded, and gazed at the flames. "It's all very well their telling us to put it out," he continued, "but when the fire gets as bad as this there's nothing to be done. I'm going to run for it. What's the use of staying here and being choked to death by the smoke?"

The tailor heaped his remaining belongings onto a bicycle-drawn cart. "Why don't you come along with me, sir?" he said to Izawa.

Izawa was seized with a complex form of terror. His body was on the verge of running away with the tailor, but he was checked by a strong internal resistance. As he stood there immobile, he felt that a splitting shriek was rising in his heart: because of this moment's delay I'm going to be burned to death! His terror almost benumbed his mind, yet somehow he managed to withstand the urgings of his body as it staggered into the motions of flight.

"I'll stay a little longer," he said. "I've got a job to do, you see. After all, I'm an entertainer and when I have an opportunity to study myself in the face of death I've got to carry on to the very end. I'd like to escape, but I can't. I can't miss this opportunity. You'd better run for it now. Hurry, hurry! In a minute it'll all be too late."

Hurry, hurry! In a minute it'll all be too late. In saying "all," Izawa was, of course, referring to his own life. "Hurry, hurry" was not aimed at urging the tailor to escape, but came from his own desire to get away as soon as possible. For him to get away, it was essential that everyone in the neighborhood should leave ahead of him. If not, people might find out about his feeble-minded woman.

"Very well, then," said the tailor, "but be careful." He started to pull his cart. But he too was thoroughly flustered and as he hurried along the alley he kept bumping into things. That was Izawa's last picture of his neighbors as they fled from their dwellings.

A ghastly rustling continued without pause or modulation. It sounded like the roaring of waves as they beat against the rocks, or like the endless pattering on rooftops of splinters from anti-aircraft guns; but it was the footsteps of a mass of evacuees scurrying along the main road. The sound of the anti-aircraft guns now seemed out of place, and the flow of footsteps had a strange vitality. Who in the world could possibly have imagined that the endless flow of this uncanny sound—this sound without pause or modulation—was produced by human footsteps? The sky and the earth were filled with countless sounds: the whirring of American planes, the anti-aircraft guns, the downpour, the roar of explosions, the sound of feet, the splinters striking the roofs. But the area immediately surrounding Izawa formed a quiet little realm of darkness in the midst of the red sky and earth. The walls of a strange silence, the walls of a maddening solitude, surrounded Izawa on all sides.

"Wait another thirty seconds. . . . Now just ten more." He did

and he was filled with immeasurable pride about that human being.

The two of them rushed through the wild flames. When they emerged from under the mass of hot air, both sides of the road were still a sea of flame; but the houses had already collapsed in the fire and as a result the force of the conflagration had decreased and the heat was less intense. Here again there was a ditch full of water. Izawa doused the woman from head to toe, soaked the bedding, and covered her and himself with it once again. Burned belongings and bedding lay strewn on the road, and two dead bodies also lay there. They were a middle-aged man and woman.

Izawa again put his arm around the woman and the two dashed through the flames. At last they reached the stream. The factories on both sides were sending up furious jets of flame. Retreat and advance were equally impossible, nor could they stay where they were. Looking around, Izawa noticed a ladder leading down to the stream. He covered the woman with the bedding and had her walk down, while he himself jumped for it.

People were walking along by the stream in little groups. Now and then the woman dipped herself in the water of her own accord. The situation was such that even a dog would have had to do so, but Izawa was wide-eyed at the sight of the birth of a new and lovable woman, and he watched her figure greedily as she immersed herself.

The stream emerged from beneath the flames and flowed beneath the darkness. It was not really dark because of the glow of the fire that covered the sky; but this semi-darkness, which he could see once again inasmuch as he was still alive, filled Izawa with a sense of vacancy— vacancy that came from a vast, ineffable weariness, from a boundless feeling of nothingness. At the bottom of it all lay a small sense of relief, but that struck him as strangely insignificant and absurd. He felt that everything was absurd.

Upstream they came to the wheat field. It was a large field enclosed on three sides by hills; a highway ran across the middle, cutting through the hills. The houses on the hills were all burning; and the buildings around the field—the Buddhist temple, the factory, the bathhouse— were also burning. The flames of each fire were a different color—white, red, orange, blue. A sudden wind sprang up and filled the air with a great roar, while minute, misty drops of water showered all around.

The crowd was still meandering down the highway. There were only a few hundred people resting in the wheat field—nothing in comparison with the crowds that stretched along the road. Next to the field was a little thicket-covered hill. There were hardly any people in this grove. Izawa and the woman spread their bedding under a tree and lay down. At the side of the field below the hill a farmhouse was burning. A few people could be seen throwing water on the flames. At the rear was a well where a man was working the pump handle and was drinking water. Seeing this, about twenty men and women rushed toward the well from all directions. They took turns in working the pump handle and drinking. Then they crowded about the burning house and stretched their hands toward the flames to warm themselves. As burning fragments fell from the house they sprang back and turned away from the smoke. Then they went on talking. Nobody lent a hand to try to put out the fire.

The woman said that she was sleepy. She also muttered that her feet ached, that her eyes smarted; but her main complaint was that she was sleepy.

"All right, then," said Izawa, "sleep for a while." He wrapped her in the bedding and lit a cigarette for himself. When he had smoked a number of cigarettes and was about to light another, the all-clear signal sounded in the distance and several policemen came running through the wheat field to announce that the alarm had been lifted. Their voices were hoarse, not like the voices of human beings at all.

"The raid is over," they shouted. "Everyone living in the area of the Kamata Police Station is to assemble at the Yaguchi Elementary School. The school building is still standing."

The people rose from the ridges in the field and walked down to the highway. But Izawa did not move. A policeman came up to him.

"What's the matter with that woman? Is she hurt?"

"No," said Izawa, "she's tired and sleeping."

"Do you know the Yaguchi Elementary School?"

"Yes. We'll have a rest here for a while and then we'll come along."

"Brace up, man! You mustn't let a little raid get you down."

The policeman's voice trailed off as he disappeared down the hill. Only two people were left in the grove. Two people? But wasn't the woman in fact a mere lump of flesh? Now she lay there sound asleep.

Everyone else was walking through the smoke of the fire-ravaged ruins. They had all lost their homes and they were all walking. Certainly none of them was thinking about sleep. The only ones who could sleep now were the dead and this woman. The dead would never wake again, but this woman would eventually wake up. Yet even when she awoke nothing would be added to this sleeping lump of flesh.

She was snoring faintly. It was the first time that he had heard her snore. It sounded like the grunting of a little pig. Yes, thought Izawa, everything about her is porcine. And abruptly a fragmentary memory from his childhood came back to him. A group of about a dozen urchins had been chasing a baby pig at the command of their gang leader. When they cornered the animal, the leader took out his jackknife and sliced a piece of flesh off its thigh. Izawa recalled that the pig's face had showed no sign of pain and that it had not even squealed very loudly. It simply ran away, evidently unaware that some flesh had been sliced off its thigh.

Now Izawa's mind conjured up a picture of himself and the woman as they would run away, stumbling among the clouds of dust, the crumbled buildings, the gaping holes. The American forces would have landed; the heavy artillery shells would be roaring on all sides, huge concrete buildings would be blown sky-high, enemy planes would be diving and spraying them with machine-gun fire. Behind a pile of rubble a woman would be held down by a man; he would overpower her and, while indulging in the sexual act, would be tearing off the flesh from her buttocks and devouring it. The flesh on the woman's buttocks would gradually diminish, but the woman would be so preoccupied with her carnal enjoyment that she would not even notice the depredations from behind.

As dawn approached, it began to grow cold. Izawa was wearing his winter overcoat and also had on a thick jacket, yet the cold was quite unbearable. The field below was still burning in places. Izawa wanted to go and warm himself, but he was unable to move because he was afraid of waking the woman. Somehow the thought of the woman waking up seemed intolerable.

He wanted to go away and leave her as she slept, but even that seemed too much trouble. When a person discards something, even a piece of waste paper, it means that he still possesses the necessary initiative and fastidiousness. But Izawa did not even have enough initiative or fastidiousness left to abandon this woman of his. He did not have the slightest affection for her now, not the slightest lingering attachment; yet neither did he have sufficient incentive to discard her. For he was devoid of any hopes for the future. Even if he were to get rid of the woman without delay, where would there be any hope for him? What was there to lean on in life? He did not even know where he would find a house to live in, a hole to sleep in. The Americans would land, and there would be all kinds of destruction in the heavens and on earth; and the gigantic love extended by the destructiveness of war would pass impartial judgment upon everything. There was no longer any need even to think.

Izawa decided that at daybreak he would wake the woman and that, without even a glance in the direction of the devastated area, they would set out for the most distant possible railway station in search of a roost. He wondered whether the trams and trains would be running. He wondered whether there would be a clear sky and whether the sun would pour down on his back and on the back of the pig that lay beside him. For it was a very cold morning.

猟
銃

井
上
靖

SHOTGUN

BY Inoué Yasushi

TRANSLATED BY George Saitō

Inoué Yasushi was born in Hokkaidō in 1907, the son of an army surgeon. From his early days in primary school until his graduation from the university he lived away from his parents. In 1932 he left Kyūshū Imperial University and entered Kyoto Imperial University. Upon graduation he was hired by the Mainichi newspaper and assigned to the Osaka office. In the following year he was drafted into the army. He served on the North China front for one year. In 1948 he was transferred to the Tokyo office of the Mainichi. It was in this year that he showed the manuscript of "Shotgun" (Ryōjū) to Satō Haruo, who gave him enthusiastic encouragement. The story appeared in the October issue of Bungakkai ("Literary World"). In 1950 Inoué was awarded the Akutagawa Prize for "Bullfight." In 1951 he resigned from the Mainichi and began writing full time.

His work is characterized by a poetic quality, and in fact he published many poems early in his career. Probably because of his experience as a newspaper reporter, he is careful in his study of material and historical facts. He is a most prolific writer. Almost all his heroes are solitary figures, like Uncle Jōsuké in "Shotgun."

Inoué is a great admirer of Mori Ōgai and says that he had aimed at producing works similar to Ōgai's. Recently he has taken to writing historical novels.

I RECENTLY contributed a poem called "Shotgun" to *Fellow Hunters*, a small magazine which is the organ of the Japan Hunters' Club.

People may take me for a man with some interest in hunting. The

416

fact is, however, that I was brought up by a mother who had an inborn hatred for killing, and I have never touched so much as an air rifle. It so happened that an old high-school classmate, the editor of *Fellow Hunters,* asked me to write a poem—noting that even at my age I was still writing poems after my fashion for obscure poetry magazines. He probably asked me in a mood of fancy and out of courtesy after a long lapse in our association. Ordinarily I would have declined such a proposal, since I had no interest in the magazine and his request was that I write about hunting. It happened, however, that I had thought of some day writing a poem about the hunting rifle and man's solitude. This would be exactly the right outlet.

I sat down at my desk one night toward the end of November, when one starts to feel the night chill. Working till after midnight, I wrote a prose poem of sorts and the next morning sent it to the editor of *Fellow Hunters.*

As my poem is tenuously connected with the story, I should like to quote it here:

"A man with a big seaman's pipe in his mouth went up the path slowly, weaving through the bushes on Mt. Amagi in early winter, walking a setter before him and treading the frost needles under his boots. What manner of man was this who armed himself with a double-barreled Churchill and a twenty-five bullet belt? What manner of man was this who took life with an instrument so glittering and white? For some reason I was attracted to this tall hunter who walked past, showing me his back. Since then I have recalled him fleetingly—at a railway station in a large city, in bustling places late at night. It is then that I should like to walk like that hunter. Slowly and quietly and coldly. I do not imagine the hunter against the cold landscape of Amagi in early winter. Rather, he is in a lonely white river bed. And the polished glittering gun radiates an exquisite, bloody beauty—never perceived when the gun is aimed at a creature—weighing heavily on the solitary spirit and the body of a middle-aged man."

*   *   *

It was only upon turning the pages of the magazine that I discovered the entirely too conspicuous contrast that my poem, for all its appropriate title, made with words like "hunting," "sportsmanship," and "healthy taste" which were scattered through the other articles. It was stupid of me to have realized this only after seeing my poem printed on a page that seemed isolated from the rest of the magazine. What I introduced into this poem was nonetheless the essential quality of a shotgun, as my poetic intuition had grasped it, or at least something I had aimed at and something for which I need not apologize. If it had been published in a different sort of magazine, there would have been no problem But this magazine, as the organ of the Japan Hunters' Club, was presenting hunting as the healthiest and most benign of hobbies. My sentiments were, therefore, somewhat heretical. I was able to imagine the awkward position in which my friend had found himself upon receiving the manuscript of my poem. Most probably he had hesitated for quite some time over it.

When I thought of his generosity, my heart ached. I thought I might receive a letter or two of protest from members of the club, but my fears turned out to be groundless. I did not receive so much as a postcard. For good or bad, my poem was disregarded by hunters throughout the country. Indeed it may not have been read at all. About two months later, when I had forgotten about the incident, I received a sealed letter from one Misugi Jōsuké, a complete stranger to me.

I remember a remark made by a historian to the effect that the characters carved on one of the ancient stone monuments of T'ai Shan were like the white glitter of the sun after a cold autumn wind has passed. Even though those characters have long since disappeared, without so much as a rubbing left to tell us of their grace and power, it nevertheless seemed to me that Misugi's handwriting on the large white envelope of Japanese paper must bear a remarkable resemblance to them. Certainly the handwriting, almost covering the face of the envelope, was magnificent. Yet something made me feel an emptiness coming from each of the characters, and it was this quality that reminded me of the historian's remarks about the T'ai Shan inscription. The address seemed to have been written rapidly with a single filling of the ink-soaked brush. The flow of the brush, however, suggested a strangely cold blankness, an indifference, to be distinguished from what one might call practiced indifference. In other words, I felt in the freeness of the style the egocentricity of a modern mind, though I noticed none of the vulgarity to be perceived in an ordinary hand.

At any rate, the magnificence of the writing seemed somehow out of place when I found it in my plain wooden mailbox. Upon opening the envelope, I found a six-foot-long roll of Chinese paper covered with lines of five or six large characters, all in the same free style.

"My hobby is hunting," the letter began. "Recently I happened to read your poem 'Shotgun' in *Fellow Hunters*. I am inarticulate and know nothing about poetry. To be honest with you, it was the very first time in my life that I had read a poem. I must confess too that this was the first time I ever heard your name. I must tell you, however, that I was immensely impressed."

As I started reading the letter, I recalled my half-forgotten prose poem. I was upset for a moment, taking it for the long-awaited letter of protest, perhaps from a distinguished hunter. As I went on reading, however, I saw that the letter was entirely different from what I had feared.

Politely and with assurance, Misugi Jōsuké said: "Am I mistaken in imagining the character to be myself? I gather that you caught sight of my tall figure somewhere in a village below Mt. Amagi when I was hunting in the early part of November. I was very proud of my black and white setter, specially trained for pheasant hunting; of the Churchill gun, which was a gift from my teacher when I was in London; and even of my favorite pipe, which you describe. I am further honored to have my state of mind, which is far from enlightened, become a subject for poetry. I am ashamed of it, and cannot help admiring your unusually keen poet's insight."

I tried to visualize once again the hunter whom I had come across, on a lane through cedar woods, one morning about five months before. I had been staying at a small hot-spring inn at the foot of Mt. Amagi, in Izu. I could recall nothing clearly except the peculiarly lonely aspect of the hunter as he walked away with his back to me. I remembered only that he was a tall, middle-aged gentleman.

The fact is that I had not studied the man very carefully. With a hunting gun hung across his shoulders and a pipe in his mouth, he somehow had a contemplative air about him, rather unusual in hunters, and he looked extraordinarily clean in the cold air of that early winter morning. That was the only reason that I turned back and looked at him after we had passed. He turned into a path from the lane I was on, climbing up among the thickets. I watched him for a while as he went slowly up the steep path. He seemed worried about slipping, and for reasons I could not understand, he gave me the impression of being very lonely. So I described him in my poem. Although I could see that his dog was a good one, how could I, who knew practically nothing about hunting, tell what kind of gun he was carrying? When I started preparing for my poem I learned that the best guns were the Richard and the Churchill. I took the liberty of giving my character a good British gun. Quite by accident the gun owned by the actual Misugi was a Churchill. Misugi Jōsuké remained a stranger to me.

His letter continued: "You may think it strange of me to mention that I have three letters. I meant to burn them. On reading your poem, however, it occurred to me that I might ask you to read them. I am very sorry to bother you, but may I ask you, at your leisure, to look at the three letters I am sending under separate cover? I would like to have you understand what you called the 'white river bed.' Man is a foolish creature who wants above all to have someone else know about him. I myself had never harbored such a desire until I learned that you had shown a special interest in me. Then I felt that I wanted you to know all about me. You are perfectly welcome to destroy the three letters after you have read them. Incidentally, it seems to have been just after I received the letters that you caught sight of me in Izu. The fact is that I had been interested in hunting for several years. It had been a rather peaceful period in both my private life and my public life, a contrast to the lonely life I lead now. Already by the time you saw me the shotgun had become everything to me."

Two days later I received an envelope on which was the sender's name, Misugi Jōsuké, followed by the words, "at a hotel in Izu." It contained three letters. They were all addressed to Misugi, and each was from a different woman. I shall not give my impressions. Instead, I shall quote the three letters. I must add that Misugi seemed to be a man of considerable social standing, and I therefore consulted various directories for his name. I was unable to find it. Most probably he was using a pseudonym. In presenting the letters here, I shall insert the name Misugi Jōsuké where the real name had apparently been blotted out. The names of other characters are all fictitious.

SHŌKO'S LETTER

Dear Uncle, my dear Uncle Jōsuké:

It is already three weeks since Mother died. We have had no sympathy calls since yesterday and the house has suddenly become quiet again. The sense that Mother is no longer alive has become acute and piercing. You must be awfully tired, Uncle. You did everything about the funeral, including sending announcements to the relatives and preparing food for the guests at the wake. Because of the nature of her death you visited the police station again and again on my behalf. Indeed, you left nothing undone. You departed for Tokyo on business immediately afterward. I sincerely hope that you have not tired yourself excessively.

According to your schedule, you should by now be gazing at the beautiful woods in Izu, bright but somehow subdued, like a design on chinaware. I have taken up my pen so that I might have you read my letter during your stay in Izu. Much as I wish that I could write it so that, after reading it, you would feel like giving yourself up to the wind, a pipe in your hand, I cannot do it. I have already wasted many sheets and find it impossible to go ahead. I did not expect this when I started. I wanted to tell you quietly what I had in mind and to ask you to understand it. I thought about the proper order again and again as I rehearsed this letter. Now that I have started writing it, however, what I want to tell you overwhelms me all at once. No, that is not exactly so. The truth is that grief surges on me from all directions, like the white waves of Ashiya on a windy day. I shall go on writing, though.

Shall I venture to tell you, Uncle? I know about it—about Mother and you. I knew everything on the day previous to her death. I had read her diary.

How hard it would be to speak these words directly to you! No matter how hard I tried, it would be impossible for me to utter a single sentence. I can express myself only because I write. It is not that I am afraid. It is only that I am sad. Sadness ties my tongue. I am not sad over you, over Mother, or over myself. Everything, everything, the blue sky, the light of the October sun, the bark of the crape myrtle, the bamboo leaves waving in the wind, the water, the stones, the soil, yes, all that exists in nature, becomes sad the moment I open my mouth. After the day I read Mother's diary I knew that nature around me could take on a sad color two and three times, even five and six times a day, much as the sun clouds over. A chance thought of you and Mother suddenly makes the world entirely different. Do you know that there is a sad color which one can clearly see, besides all the ordinary colors?

Through the affair between you and Mother I knew that there was a love blessed by no one and asking to be blessed by no one. The love between you was something only you knew about. Aunt Midori does not know about it, nor do I, nor does any one of our relatives. Neither our neighbors nor our closest friends know or should know about it. Since Mother's death only you have known about it. And after your death no one on the earth will imagine that such a love existed. Until now I believed that love was something bright and cheerful like the sun, something to be blessed eternally by God and man alike. I firmly believed that love was like a pure brook that glitters in the sun and ripples in the wind, and is tenderly watched by the grass, trees, and flowers on the banks, playing exquisite music as it grows. How could I imagine a love like a subterranean stream, with no sunshine and no one to know where the water comes from and goes?

Mother deceived me for thirteen years. She died at last deceiving me still. Not once did I dream that there could be a secret between Mother and myself. Mother used to tell me from time to time that the two of us, parent and child, were alone in the world. On the matter of how she parted with Father she said only that I would not be able to understand until I was ready for marriage. I wanted to grow up more quickly, not because I wanted to know about Mother and Father, but because I thought how difficult it must be for Mother to keep the secret. Mother seemed to suffer very much. To think that she was also able to keep another secret from me!

When I was a little girl, Mother used to tell me a story of a wolf that deceived a rabbit and was turned into stone for the misdeed. Mother deceived me, Aunt Midori, and the whole world. How could she? What terrible thing bewitched her? Yes, I remember she used the word "evil" in her diary. "Both Misugi and I are evil. We should like to be wholly evil." Why did she not write that she had been bewitched? Mother is far more unfortunate than the wolf that deceived the rabbit!

But that dear Mother and my dearest Uncle Jōsuké should have chosen to be bad—the most completely bad persons on the earth! What a sad love it is which requires that one become bad! I remember how on a festival day someone bought me a round paperweight of glass in which were set red artificial flower petals. I was only a child. I held it in my hand and I burst into tears. I must have puzzled everyone. I saw how the flower petals were frozen, as it were, inside cold glass; the flower petals remained still, whether spring or autumn came; the flower petals were being sacrificed. As I thought of the petals, sadness came to me all of a sudden. The same sadness is coming back to me now. The love between you and Mother, like those sad petals!

My dear Uncle, Uncle Jōsuké:

You must be angry with me for reading Mother's diary. Something told me on the day before Mother's death that she was unlikely to recover. I had this premonition. As you remember, nothing was noticeably wrong with her except a slight fever. Her appetite was good. Her cheeks were bright and even seemed rosier than usual. However, I could not help feeling depressed. The sight of her from the back—especially that line from the shoulders to the arms—was almost repellent. On the eve of her death, when Aunt Midori came to inquire after her, I entered Mother's room to let her know of the visit. As I opened the sliding door, I was taken aback. She was sitting on the bed with her back turned toward me. She had on a purple-gray kimono cloak boldly decorated with thistles which she had kept in a chest and rarely taken out. She would give to me, she had said, since it was becoming too loud for her.

"What's the matter?" She seemed unable to understand why I was startled.

"But you . . ."

I was unable to go on. I myself could not understand why I had been startled. A ridiculous lump rose in my throat. After all it was not surprising for Mother, who delighted in kimono, to take out a kimono cloak from her youth and put it on. Since she had taken ill it had become almost her daily practice to put on a kimono she had not worn in many years. Probably she wanted to divert her mind. Later, however, I knew why I had been surprised. Mother looked so beautiful that it

this line lay snarling like an ogre, glaring from the page as if to jump upon me.

I closed the diary. A terrible moment! In the silence I could hear the beating of my heart. I rose from my chair and made sure once again that the door and the windows were secured. Coming back to the desk, I fearfully opened the diary again. Then I read it from beginning to end, skipping nothing and feeling like a monster. Nothing could be found referring to Father. There, in frank language, was the affair between Mother and you, an affair of which I had never dreamed. I read how Mother had suffered at one time, rejoiced at another, prayed, despaired, and sometimes even wanted to commit suicide. Yes, she was determined to kill herself in the event that her affair was detected by Aunt Midori. Ah! Mother, who was always talking with Aunt Midori so pleasantly, was afraid of her!

Mother's diary shows that she lived with death those thirteen years. Sometimes she made entries for four or five days running, sometimes she laid it aside for two or three years. On every page of her diary she was facing death.

"I have to die. Death will solve everything." What made her write such things? "Why should you have anything to fear, now that you are determined to die? Be brave, Ayako!" What made my gentle mother cry this way? Was it love? The beautiful and glittering thing called love? You once gave me as a birthday gift a book describing a proud, naked woman who stood by a spring with her long hair coiled over her shoulders and her hands supporting her breasts, pressing them upward like buds. How different the love of Mother and you from the love described in that book!

From the moment I read Mother's diary, Aunt Midori became the most horrible person in the world. Mother's agony became mine. Ah, Aunt Midori, kissing my cheek with pursed lips! My loving Aunt Midori whom I could not tell from Mother! It was she who, when I entered primary school in Ashiya, gave me a book satchel decorated with large roses; and it was she who gave me a large pneumatic float shaped like a sea gull when I left for summer camp. On a class day when I was in the second grade I won applause for telling a story by the brothers Grimm. It was the same Aunt Midori who encouraged me to rehearse every evening and rewarded me for my perseverance. Aunt Midori, who was a cousin of Mother's and very close to her. Although she only dances now, Aunt Midori was once good at mahjong, golf, swimming, and skiing. It was Aunt Midori who baked pies bigger than my face and who startled Mother and me by bringing a group of dancing girls from Takarazuka to our home. Why had she come into our life so pleasantly, like a rose?

If I ever had a premonition concerning you and Mother, it was just once. That was about a year ago. I was on my way to school with a friend. When we arrived at Shukugawa Station, it occurred to me that I had forgotten my English reader. I asked my friend to wait at the station and hurried home. For reasons I could not understand I could not bring myself to open the gate. Our maid was on an errand and only Mother was at home. I felt somehow uneasy at her being at home alone. I was afraid. I stood at the gate wondering whether I should enter or not. I looked at the azaleas. Finally I gave up and went back to the railroad station in a strange state of mind which I myself could not understand. I felt that from the moment I left home for school, a special time for Mother began. I felt that if I entered the gate it would annoy her. In indescribable loneliness I went back to the station, kicking at stones on the road along the Ashiya River. Then I found myself leaning on a wooden bench in the waiting room, listening absently to my friend.

That was the first and last such experience. Now it seems unbearably frightful. What detestable qualities man posseses! How could I tell that Aunt Midori had not at times had the same premonition? Aunt Midori who, when she plays cards, is proud of her capacity to read her partner's mind. Just to think of it is a horror! Maybe it is stupid to worry, since all has ended and the secret was kept. No, Mama died to keep the secret. This I believe.

On that sad day just before her brief but violent agony started, Mother called me, saying with a strangely smooth, almost wooden expression: "I have just taken poison. I am tired, tired of living. . . ."

Her voice sounded like heavenly music, strangely clear, at if she were addressing God through me. I could hear the word "sin," piled up like the Eiffel Tower, crash down into my ears. The layers of sin that she had supported for thirteen years were now going to crush her weary being and wash it away. It was anger that overwhelmed me, like the blast of an autumn wind from a valley, as I sat in front of Mama and followed those eyes that gazed vacantly into the distance. Looking at Mother's sad face, I only answered "Oh?" as if this had nothing to do with me. Then my heart became cold as if doused by water. In a quiet state of mind, so quiet that I was surprised at myself, I went along the passage, instead of through the adjoining room, walking as though on water (it was at this moment that I heard Mother's cry as she was about to be swallowed by death). I went into the telephone alcove at the end of the passage and called you. It was not you, however, but Aunt Midori who, five minutes later, rushed into the house. Mother died, clasping hands with Aunt Midori, the nearest and the most feared. And those same hands laid a white cloth over Mother's face, now free from cares and sadness.

My dear Uncle Jōsuké:

The first night of the wake was a quiet one—unbelievably quiet. The crowds of visitors during the day, the policemen, the doctors, and the neighbors had all left. Only we sat before her coffin—you, Aunt Midori, and myself. No one spoke. It was as if we were listening to the faint lap of water on some shore. When the incense sticks burned out, we rose in turn and replaced them, and perhaps opened the windows for fresh air. You seemed the saddest. When you rose to light new incense sticks, you gazed so gently at Mother's picture. On your sad face there was a faint smile, so faint that one could hardly notice it. How many times that night I thought that Mother must have been happy after all.

About nine o'clock, when I was sitting by the window, I suddenly burst into tears. You rose and laid your hand quietly on my shoulder and stood so for some time. Then you went back to your chair without saying a word. It was not because I felt a pang of sorrow for Mother that I was crying. I thought of the fact that Mother said nothing about you in her last moments, and I wondered why it was not you but Aunt Midori who rushed to my side when I telephoned. My heart was wrenched. Your love and Mother's had to be hidden through the very moment of death. It seemed as pitiful as the flower petals crucified in the glass paperweight. So I rose and opened the window, gazing into the cold, starry sky and bearing a sorrow that was on the verge of finding voice. But then it came to me that Mother's love was ascending to heaven in that starry sky, fleeting among the stars, unknown to any of us. It seemed to me that sorrow for the death of an individual called "Mother" was trivial compared with the sorrow for a love that was ascending into heaven.

When I sat down to our midnight meal, I burst into tears again. Aunt Midori spoke to me in a gentle voice. "You must be brave. It breaks my heart to think that I can do nothing."

Wiping my tears and raising my head, I saw Aunt Midori looking at me. There were tears in her eyes too. I shook my head. Probably she did not mind. The truth is that I suddenly felt sorry for her. I watched her prepare four plates, for you and her and myself and Mother, and I suddenly felt that she was the saddest person there. That is why I wept.

I wept a third time that night. It was after you both had told me to go to bed. You said that the next day would be a hard one. Exhausted, I fell asleep in an adjoining room. I awoke bathed in sweat. I found that about an hour had passed. It was quiet in the next room, except for the click of the lighter you were using from time to time. Half an hour later I heard a brief exchange between you and Aunt Midori.

"How about having a rest, Midori? I'll stay up."

"No thanks. You go rest."

That was all, and the quietness returned. I sobbed perhaps three times. This time my sobbing went unheard by you. Everything seemed lonely and horrible. Three of you—Mother, who had already joined all the others, and you two—were in the same room. Each of you was there with different thoughts. The world of adults seemed to me unbearably lonely and horrible.

My dear Uncle, Uncle Jōsuké:

I have rambled on. I have tried to express my feelings as best I could so that you might understand the request I am going to make.

My request is only this: I do not want to see you or Aunt Midori again. I can no longer play the child the way I did before I read Mother's diary. I should like to escape the tangle of "sin" that finally crushed Mother. I have no courage to write further.

I am asking Uncle Tsumura to see to disposing of this house. Then I am going back to Akashi for a while. I am thinking of opening a small dressmaking shop. In her will, Mother suggested that I consult you. She would not have done so if she had known me as I am now.

I burned Mother's diary in the garden today. The notebook was reduced to a handful of ashes. A whirlwind carried them away with dead leaves while I was hunting a bucket for water.

Under separate cover I am sending a letter to you from Mother. I found it in her desk the day after you left for Tokyo.

MIDORI'S LETTER

My dear Mr. Misugi:

I address you thus formally, and my heart throbs as if I were writing a love letter. I seem too old for love letters (although I am but thirty-three). During these last ten years I have written dozens of love letters, sometimes secretly and sometimes openly. But why, I wonder, have none of them been addressed to you? I hardly know.

Some time ago Mrs. Takagi, whom you know (remember?—she looks like a fox when she makes up), was commenting on important people living between Osaka and Kobe. She said that you were an uninteresting man to women, a man who did not understand the intricacies of women's psychology, a man who could love women but never be loved by them. This was of course a careless remark. She was slightly intoxicated, and you need not mind. At the same time, however, you do have something of the quality she described. You do not know solitude, you have nothing of the lonely man about you. You sometimes look bored, but never lonely. You have a peculiarly clear point of view, and you depend entirely upon your own judgment. It makes me want to shake you. In short, you are a man who is unbearable to women, who commands no interest as a man, and whom it would be a waste of time to love.

Such being the case, it would be unreasonable to try to have you understand my feelings about the fact that not one of the dozens of love letters I have written has been addressed to you. Still it all seems very strange. A letter or two could just as well have gone to you. Although none did, there would have been little difference had I written them as if addressing you. I am shy and naive in spite of my years. I could not write a sweet letter to my husband but I could write to other men one after another. Maybe I was born under an unlucky star, your unlucky star too.

> If I could but know you,
> Then might your lofty tranquillity collapse.

I wrote this poem last autumn when I thought about you sitting in your study. It was a poem into which I poured the feelings of a poor wife who was trying not to disturb the tranquillity with which you might have been contemplating perhaps a piece of ancient Korean ceramics; or rather, perhaps it was the sentiment of one who did not know how to disturb your contemplations. (What a formidable and well-guarded fort you are!)

"Don't talk nonsense!" you will say. But even when I spend the entire night playing mahjong, I do still have the consideration to think of you in your study at times. I secretly put the poem on Mr. Tagami's desk—Mr. Tagami is the young philosopher who was promoted to be assistant professor last spring. My act resulted in disturbing the lofty serenity of the young professor. A gossip columnist wrote about it and caused you some trouble. I have said that I wanted to shake you. I wonder if this little incident shook you just a bit.

Since you will not enjoy reading this, I'll come to the main point.

Our ostensible relationship as man and wife has lasted a long time. Don't you want to put an end to it? It must be difficult for you too. If you have no objection, suppose we find a way for both of us to be free.

I think this is the time to end our unnatural relations, especially since you are retiring. (I never expected to find your name on the list of purged businessmen!) Let me be brief. If I may have the house at Takarazuka and the house at Yasé, I shall be satisfied. The house at Yasé is a reasonable size, and the environment is congenial to me. I can live there. The house at Takarazuka I shall sell for about two million yen, on which sum I can live the rest of my life. I've been making my own plans. This is the last time I shall ask to have my way, and the first time I am presuming upon your affections.

Though I am making this sudden request, I do not have a lover at present. You do not have to worry about my being robbed. I regret to tell you that I have never had a lover worthy of being called such. Very few men satisfy even my two basic requirements: a well-groomed neck, as fresh as a section of lemon, and a curve of the loin clean and strong as an antelope. I regret again that this feature which first drew me, a bride, to my husband is still a strong attraction after ten years. Speaking of antelopes, I remember reading a newspaper article about a naked boy who had been living with antelopes in the Syrian desert. What a beautiful picture! The coldness of his profile under that unkempt hair, and the charm of his long legs which, it seemed, could carry him at fifty miles an hour! Even now I feel my blood tingle for that boy. His intellectual face and his wild figure.

For the eye that has seen that boy, all other men are vulgar and boring. If a suspicion of inconstancy ever flickered in your wife's heart, it was only when she was attracted by the antelope-boy. When I imagine his tense skin wet with the night dew of the desert, when I think of his serenity, I become excited even now.

About two years ago I became enthusiastic over Matsushiro of the Shin Seisaku school of modern painting. But you are not to believe the rumors.

You looked at me then with eyes that had a strangely sad gleam, as of pity. There was nothing, really, to be pitied. Nonetheless, I was somehow attracted by your eyes. They couldn't be compared with those of the antelope-boy, but they were splendid. Why did you never before turn your eyes, your splendid eyes, even a little on me? Strength alone is not enough. Those are not eyes for appreciating pottery. I became cold, like old Kutani ware, and I desperately wanted to sit down quietly somewhere. That is why I visited Matsushiro's chilly studio and posed for him. Besides, I like the way he looks at buildings. Although he rather imitates Utrillo, I think he is unique in Japan in that he can paint a common building and yet put into it a modern melancholy (very faintly). But as a man he is no good. If I were to score you one hundred, he would rate only sixty-five. He does have talent, but it is somehow degenerate. He has a handsome face, but he lacks elegance. When he holds a pipe, he even looks funny, like a second-rate artist whose works have sucked all the good out of him.

It was around early summer of last year that I took up Tsumura, the jockey who won the Minister's Cup. Your eyes gleamed with cold contempt. At first I thought it was the green leaves outside that made your eyes look so when we passed each other on the veranda. Later, I discovered that I was wrong. It was most rash of me. Had I known, I could have had my own way of looking back at you. But my senses were numbed by the beauty of speed. Your fusty, medieval way of expressing yourself was beyond my understanding. You should have seen Tsumura as he passed a dozen horses in the stretch, one after another, on the back of that superb horse. Even you would have been struck if you had looked through the binoculars at that intense and lovable creature (I mean Tsumura, not the horse).

A twenty-two-year-old boy, little more than a hooligan, he broke his own record twice because he knew I was watching. It was my first experience of such passion. He wanted my admiration, and he became the incarnation of speed, forgetting me as he rode his brown mare. Life was worthwhile in those days. My love (maybe it can be called love) in the grandstand was stirred by his passion, clear as water, there on the long oval track. I never felt the loss of those three diamonds. They had survived the war and they were his reward. It was only when he was on horseback that he was amiable. Once his feet touched ground, he became a child, a primitive child who hardly understood the taste of coffee. With his fighting spirit on horseback, however, he was better than Seo the novelist or the ex-leftist Mitani. In the end, I acted as go-between when he married his eighteen-year-old dancer. She had pouting lips, and she too had been one of my pets.

I have wandered from the subject. Of course I am still much too young to live like a retired person even if I settle in Yasé. I have no intention of behaving like a saint, either. You may go ahead and build a kiln and make teacups and so on, but I think I shall be doing such things as growing flowers—one can make quite a profit by selling them in Kyoto, I am told. I shall be able to grow a couple of hundred carnations with the help of the two maids and two other young girl friends of mine. I should like to stay away from men for the time being. I am tired of men. I really mean it. I am making my plans so that I can find real happiness, starting all over again.

You may be surprised at my sudden proposal to leave you. No, it may be even more surprising that I did not propose it earlier. A thousand emotions are crowding my mind as I look back over our ten-odd years together. I do not see how we managed. I was labeled a loose woman, and it is likely that we gave others the impression of being an unusual couple. Yet we lived together as best we could, without causing much scandal, and sometimes we even went so far as to arrange marriages for others. I think I am entitled to your praise. What do you think?

What a difficult thing it is to write a farewell letter! How I hate to be maudlin! I do not like to be too outspoken, either. I would like to make my proposal gracefully, so that neither of us would be hurt, but an awkwardness comes out in what I am writing. After all, a letter of parting cannot be a beautiful letter, no matter who writes it. Let me, then, write in the direct and cold manner that becomes such a letter. You will not like what I have to say and it will make you even more indifferent to me.

It was in February, 1934, around nine o'clock in the morning. When I saw you from my upstairs room in the Atami Hotel, you had on a gray suit and were walking along the shore below. This is what happened on a day growing dim as in a half-forgotten dream. Listen to me calmly. Remember the kimono cloak with its thistles against the purple-gray background, worn by the tall, beautiful woman following you? I had never thought that my suspicious would prove so precisely accurate. I had come to Atami by night train to confirm these suspicions. I had not slept. To coin a phrase, I had hoped I was dreaming. I was twenty years old (the age Shōko is now). It was somewhat too strong a medicine for a newly married wife. I called the boy, paid the bill, and left the place as if pursued. The boy stared after me. Standing on the pavement in front of the hotel, I wondered whether I should go down to the shore or up to the railroad station. I started down the road to the shore, but stopped before I had walked fifty yards. I stood there gazing at a point where the sea shone in the mid-winter sun, a sea of Prussian blue rubbed on, as it were, from a tube of concentrated color. Then I took the road to the railroad station. Now I know that what began there is still going on. If I had gone down the road leading to the beach where you were, I should find myself a different person today. Whether for good or for bad, I went to the station. That was perhaps the turning point in my life.

Why didn't I go on down the road to the beach? It was because I could not help thinking that I was unequal to the beautiful Ayako, who was five or six years older than I—unequal to her in experience, knowledge, ability, beauty, gentleness of heart, deftness at holding a teacup, talking about literature, appreciating music, arranging a hairdo, everything. The meekness of a twenty-year-old bride which could be expressed only in the lines of a painting! You probably know how you stay motionless when you jump into the cold sea of early autumn because the slightest motion would make you feel the cold even more intensely. I was afraid to move. It was a long time before I decided to deceive you as you were deceiving me.

Once Ayako and you were waiting for a train in Sannomiya Station. It was perhaps a year after the experience at the Atami Hotel. I stood wondering whether I should go into the waiting room; I was surrounded by girls off on a gay school excursion. And the memory of yet another night is also vividly with me. Insects were humming. Watching the soft light coming through the curtains upstairs, I stood for hours unable to decide whether to push the button at Ayako's gate, closed tight as a clam. It was at about the same time as the incident in Sannomiya Station. I wonder whether it was spring or autumn. My memory for the seasons fails me at such times. There were many other occasions also, but I did nothing. Even at the Atami Hotel, I did not go down to the sea. Even then. A glaring Prussian-blue sea tortured me, and I felt the searing pain at my heart recede.

It was a painful period, but time solved our problem. Hot iron cools, and I cooled as you did, you even more than I. It was a wonderfully cold home, cold enough to freeze the eyelashes. So it is now. Home? No, it is far from being anything so human. I believe you will agree with me that it might better be called a citadel. During all these years we have been deceiving each other in this citadel. (You started first.) What sad covenants people make! Our life has been founded entirely on the secrets we've kept for each other. You pretended to be ignorant of my numerous misdeeds, although sometimes you showed contempt, sometimes displeasure and sadness. Often I shouted at the maid, perhaps telling her to bring cigarettes from the bathroom. I would come home and, taking a film program from my handbag, fan my naked breast with it. I scattered face powder everywhere, in the drawing room and in the hall. When I hung up the telephone receiver, I would come away waltzing. I invited a group of dancing girls to dinner and had a picture taken with them. In déshabillé, I played mahjong. On my birthday I had the maids wear ribbons while I sported with student guests. I knew that these acts would be objectionable to you. Never once, however, did you rebuke me—nor were you able to. There was no dispute between us. Our citadel was quiet, and the air was raw, sandy, and cold, like the wind in a desert. Why could you not shoot at my heart, you who have shot pheasants and turtledoves so expertly? If you were going to deceive why did you not deceive me thoroughly? A woman can be elevated to godliness by a man's perfidy.

Now I know that there lurked in my heart the expectation, faint but persistent, that there would be an end to our compromise, that something would take place, something would happen, and so I suffered for more than ten years. I could think of but two ways in which that end would come. Some day I would either lean on your shoulder and close my eyes quietly, or stab at your chest with that Egyptian penknife you gave me.

In which form did I expect the end to come? I do not know myself.

Five years have passed. Do you remember? I think it was after you had come back from southern Asia. I had been away three days and had staggered home drunk in broad daylight. I found you there, though. I had thought you would still be away. You were cleaning your gun. I only said, "Hello," and sitting on the veranda sofa, I turned from you to cool myself in the breeze. The glass window facing the veranda reflected part of the room as in a mirror. Back-dropped by the canopy over the terrace, it reflected you as you wiped the gun with a white cloth. Nervous and yet languid after my dissipations, I absent-mindedly watched your actions. After wiping your gun thoroughly and setting the polished breechblock, you held the gun up several times and stood as if you were ready to shoot. Then I found that you were aiming with one eye half closed. The gun was pointed at my back.

I wondered whether you were going to fire at me and whether, even though the gun was not loaded, you wanted to kill me. I closed my eyes, and I waited for the moment the click of the trigger would break the stillness of the room, wondering whether you were aiming at my shoulder, or at the back of my head, or at my neck. There was no click, however long I waited. I was preparing to faint at the click, thinking it would make life worth living after the years of ennui.

I opened my eyes and found that you were still aiming at me. I remained in that position for some time, but suddenly it all seemed very silly. I moved myself, turning toward you—not toward the figure in the glass. At that moment you aimed at the rhododendron you had brought from Amagi. It had bloomed for the first time that year. Then at long last there was the click of the trigger. Why didn't you shoot your unfaithful wife? I deserved being shot. You intended to kill me, and yet you did not pull the trigger. If you had pulled the trigger, if you had not forgiven my unfaithfulness, if you had shot hatred into my heart—then I might have fallen quietly into your arms. Or maybe I would have shown you my own shooting skill. Since you did not, I turned my eyes away from the rhododendron that had been substituted for me and withdrew to my room, humming some foreign tune and staggering more than was necessary.

The years have passed without our having had a chance to put an end to such things. This summer the crape myrtle was a heavy red—red as it had never been before. I was in an agony of expectation—certain that something unusual was about to take place.

It was on the eve of her death that I last visited Ayako. After ten-odd years I saw again the cloak of purple-gray that had printed itself on my retina in the bright morning sun of Atami. The purple thistles floated up and hung heavily on the thin shoulders of your loved one, who, incidentally, had become a little thinner. The moment I sat down, I thought I would have my revenge by praising the beauty of the cloak. Then the thought of her wearing that cloak in my presence made my blood boil out of control. I knew that self-control was now impossible. The effrontery of the woman who had stolen another woman's husband and the meekness of the twenty-year-old bride had to have their confrontation some day. The moment seemed now to have come. I

estly. I am afraid to tell you: I do not think I have shown you my real self even once in my life. The one who writes this is my true self. Only she is my true self. My true self!

The maples of Tennōzan after the autumn rain still linger before my eyes. Why were they so beautiful? We sheltered ourselves from the rain under the closed gate of a famous tea cottage in front of the railroad station. Looking up at the mountain that stood like a titan before us, its steep slope rising from the station, we were astounded by its beauty. I wonder if it was because of the play of light at that particular time of day. It was November, and growing dark. Or was it because of the weather that particular autumn day, a succession of brief showers? The mountain was so lovely that we were almost afraid to climb it together. That was thirteen years ago. The almost painful beauty of the maples is still vivid before my eyes.

We were alone for the first time. Having been taken by you from one place to another in the suburbs of Kyoto from early that morning, I was exhausted in body and mind. You were tired too. Climbing the steep mountain, you were now saying foolish things. "Love is attachment. Is there anything wrong with my being attached to a rare teacup? Well, then, why shouldn't I be attached to you?" And: "It's only you and I that have seen such beautiful maples. Only two of us have seen them, and at the same time. There's no help for it." It was like the pouting of a spoiled child.

These fretful words made my heart crumble as if before a violent shove—my heart, which had desperately been trying to fly from you all day. Your threats and your boundless sadness crystallized like a flower the happiness of a woman who is loved.

What an easy thing for me to forgive my own inconstancy—when I had been unable to forgive my husband's!

It was at the Atami Hotel that you used the word "evil." You said that we would be evil persons. Do you remember?

It was a windy night. The wooden shutters facing the sea kept rattling. At midnight you opened the window to tighten them. I saw a small fishing boat in the offing, burning like a torch. Several souls were in danger of death, yet I felt no fear. Only the beauty of the fire caught my eyes. When the window was closed, however, I suddenly felt uneasy. I opened the window again, but could no longer see that spot of fire. Probably the boat had burned to the water. The dark surface of the sea spread heavy and quiet.

Until that night I had been struggling to leave you. After I saw the fire in the fishing boat, a strange fatalism came over my thoughts.

"Let's be evil, the two of us," you said. "Join me and we will deceive Midori all our lives."

I answered without hesitation: "Let's become completely evil, now that we are determined to become evil. Let's deceive everyone, not only Midori." That night I slept well for the first time since we had begun our secret meetings.

It was as if I had seen the helplessness of our love in that boat, devoured completely by fire. As I write, the fire against the shroud of night lingers before my eyes. What I saw on the sea that night must have been the agony of a woman's life, brief and real and trying.

It is no use, however, to indulge in such memories. Despite the sufferings of the past thirteen years, I know I was happier than anyone else. I was so happy, shaken by your expansive love, that I hardly knew how I could bear it.

I went through my diary today. There I saw too many words like "death" and "sin" and "love." I felt I had to make note once again of the dangerous situation we were in. The weight of the notebook on my palm was the weight of my happiness under the burden of sin. I faced death day after day, thinking that I would die when the secret was discovered by Midori. Yes, that I would have to compensate with my life. For this very reason my happiness was so intense that it was unbearable.

Who would imagine that there was another "I" besides the one described here? (I may sound affected, but I know of no other way to express it.) Yes, another "I" lived within me. The other "I" you do not know and you cannot imagine.

Once you told me that everyone has a serpent within him. It was when you visited Dr. Takeda of the Science Faculty at Kyoto University. While you were talking to him, I killed time by looking at the serpents in a case at the end of the long, gloomy passage. When you came out after about half an hour, I was somehow sick of serpents.

Looking into the specimen case, you said to me jokingly: "This is Ayako, this is Midori, and this is I. Every man has a serpent in him." Midori's was a little sepia snake from the South Seas. Mine was a small one from Australia with white specks all over it and a sharp, pointed head like a gimlet. I wonder what you meant. Although I never spoke to you about it again, your remark remained in my memory. Occasionally I asked myself about the serpent that each man has in him. I answered sometimes that it was egotism, sometimes that it was jealousy.

Even now I do not know. In any event, a serpent did indeed dwell within me. The other self, which I do not understand, can only be called a serpent.

It happened this afternoon. When Midori came into my room, I was wearing that cloak of purple-gray from the Yūki looms. You had it sent from Kumamoto and it was my favorite when I was young. The moment Midori stepped into the room and saw me, I knew that she was about to say something. She stopped as if in surprise and kept silent for a while. I thought she must be surprised at my somewhat unusual choice of cloaks. Half in fun, I too was silent.

Suddenly Midori turned her eyes, peculiarly cold eyes, toward me and said: "It's the cloak you were wearing when you were in Atami with Misugi. I saw you that day."

The words stabbed me like a dagger. Her face was resolute and pale.

For a moment I did not understand what she meant. When the seriousness of the meaning came to me, I brought my hand to my throat and drew myself up as if upon command.

She had known everything for such a long time!

I felt strangely quiet, like the tide rising on an evening sea. I even thought I should take her hand and say: "Oh, so you knew it. You knew everything." Although the moment which I had been so afraid of had come, I felt no fear. Between us there was only quiet, as of water lapping against a beach. The veil of thirteen years had now been stripped off, and there remained not the death I had been thinking about but peace, yes, and quiet rest. The dark and heavy burden which had lain on my shoulders for such a long time had been removed and replaced by a strangely appealing blankness. There were so many things I had to think about. I felt not fear but something remote and vacant and yet quiet and satisfying. I was indulging in a kind of rapture that might be called liberation. Looking into Midori's eyes (yet I was not seeing anything), I sat there vacantly. I did not catch what she was saying.

When I came to myself, I saw her staggering toward the hall.

"Midori!" I called after her. Why? I do not know.

Maybe I wanted to have her sit before me forever. I might have asked her bluntly, if she had come back: "May I have Misugi?"

Or I might have said something entirely different, yet with the same feeling: "The time has come when I must return Misugi to you." I really do not know which I would have chosen. Anyhow Midori did not come back.

What a ridiculous thought, dying because we were found out by Midori! Sin, sin. What a meaningless sense of guilt! Has the person who sells his soul to the devil no choice but to become a devil? Had I been deceiving myself and God for thirteen years?

I fell into a deep sleep. When Shōko woke me, I was aching all over, as if the fatigue of thirteen years had made itself felt all at once. Then I found my uncle from Akashi sitting at my bedside. He is a contractor whom you once met, and he stopped by to inquire about my illness on his way to Osaka. He left after a certain amount of small talk. Then, tying his shoes at the door, he said: "Kadota married again not long ago."

Kadota! How long since I had last heard that name? Of course he meant Kadota Reiichirō, my ex-husband. He spoke casually, but his words shook me.

"When?" I knew my voice was trembling.

"Last month. Maybe it was the month before last. They say he had a new house built near the hospital in Hyōgo."

"Is that so?" That is all I could say.

After my uncle had left, I pulled myself along the veranda step by step. Holding to a pillar, I felt as if I were sinking. Although it was windy outside and the trees were swaying, it seemed as if I were gazing at a still underwater world through the glass of an aquarium.

"Ah, it's all over!" I was not aware myself that I had spoken, but Shōko, whom I had not noticed, answered:

"What's over?"

"I don't know."

With a laugh, Shōko took me lightly from behind. "Don't be silly. Suppose you go back to bed."

Urged on by Shōko, I walked to my bedroom. As I sat up in bed, however, I felt everything come crumbling down around me. Propping myself up on one hand, I managed to control myself while Shōko was there. When she left for the kitchen, tears came streaming down my cheeks.

Why should the simple fact of Kadota's getting married be such a blow? What was this all about? I do not remember how much time passed. Through the window I saw Shōko burning leaves in the garden. The sun had already set. It was a quiet evening such as I had never seen before in my life.

"You are already burning leaves." I spoke softly, and, as if the whole thing had been previously arranged, I rose and took my diary from the bottom of the desk drawer. Shōko was burning leaves to burn my diary. How could it be otherwise? Going out to the veranda with the diary, I sat on the cane chair and turned over the pages. A diary with an array of words like "sin," "death," and "love." Confessions of a sinner. The words "sin," "death," and "love," inscribed in the course of thirteen years, had lost the fire which they bore until yesterday, and were ready to share the fate of the leaves that rose in purple smoke.

As I handed the diary to Shōko, I made up my mind to die. I thought the time had come for me to die. It might be more appropriate to say that I had lost the power to live.

Kadota had been living alone ever since we were divorced. He had missed chances to remarry because of his study abroad and his service in the South Seas during the war. At any rate, he had remained unmarried. It seems to me now that his being unmarried is what made life bearable for me. I would like to have you believe this much, however, that I never met him again nor wanted to meet him after I left him. Except for fragmentary gossip about him from my relatives in Akashi, years had passed during which I was completely unaware of his existence.

Night fell. After Shōko and the maid had retired to their rooms, I pulled out an album from the bookshelf. About two dozen pictures of Kadota and myself were pasted in it.

It was several years ago that Shōko had startled me by remarking:

"The pictures of Mother and Father are pasted so that their faces meet."

Shōko said it innocently, but I found that pictures taken at the time of our marriage happened to be pasted on opposite pages, so that our faces indeed met each other when the album was closed. I let it go that time. Her words, however, remained in my heart and once or twice a year emerged to consciousness. But for the time being I neither removed the pictures nor pasted them otherwise. Finally today I thought the time had come for me to strip them off. I would take Kadota's pictures from the album and paste them in Shōko's red album, so that she might keep them as images of her father as a young man.

My other self was such a person. The little serpent from Australia which you said was lurking in me made its appearance this morning, speckled white all over. I wonder if the little sepia serpent from the South Pacific, its red tongue like a filament, kept pretending for thirteen years not to know of our meeting at Atami.

What, after all, is the serpent that every man has? Is it something like karma, relentless, ready to swallow up all, egotism, jealousy, and destiny? It is a pity that I will have no more chance to learn of this from you. What a sad creature, the serpent each man has! I remember reading in a book about the "sadness of life." As I write this letter, I find my heart touching on something so sad and cold that it is beyond help. What does man have that is so unbearably hateful and so unbearably sad?

It occurs to me that I haven't presented you with my real self even yet. It seems that my first resolution has weakened and fled from the horror.

The other self that I am not aware of—what a good excuse! I told you that today I had discovered the little white serpent lurking in me. I told you that it had made its first appearance today.

A lie, a lie. I should have noticed it all along.

My heart breaks to think of the night of August sixth, when the area between Osaka and Kobe turned into a sea of flames. Shōko and I were hiding ourselves in the air-raid shelter you designed. As the waves of B-29's passed over, I was thrown into a loneliness that I was absolutely incapable of helping. It was such an intense loneliness that it was beyond description. I found it impossible to stay there any longer. I was about to leave the shelter when I saw you standing before me.

The entire sky was red. You had run to my house and you stood at the entrance to the shelter. Your neighborhood was already in flames. I went back into the shelter with you and burst into tears. Both Shōko and you seemed to take my hysteria for terror. I do not think I was able to explain then or afterwards. Forgive me. While I was wrapped in your generous, much too generous, love, I wished I could stand before the air-raid shelter of Kadota's hospital in Hyōgo, that hospital, white and clean, that I had seen only once from the train window. I wanted to stand there just as you stood at the entrance to my air-raid shelter. I was trembling with an unbearable longing and resisting it with tears.

But this was not the first time I had noticed. Several years before, I was transfixed when you told me that I had a little white serpent in me. Never before had I been so afraid of your eyes. Although you may not have meant to be serious, I felt as if my mind had been read and I shrank back with fear. My revulsion at actual snakes had gone. When I timidly looked into your face, I saw that you seemed to be looking into the distance with your unlit pipe in your mouth. You had never done that before. Perhaps it was my imagination, but you wore the most vacant face of all your faces that I knew. It was a matter of a moment. When you looked toward me, you had the usual gentle expression.

Until then I had never grasped my "other self" clearly. Since then I have seen it as a little white snake. That night I wrote about the white snake in my diary. Filling a page with the words "white snake," I imagined the little snake in my heart, coiling tightly into a cone, its gimlet head pointed straight to heaven. It brought me quiet to compare the most detestable part of myself to such a form, pure and somehow expressive of a woman's sorrow and honesty. God will regard it with mercy. I am selfish even now. I seemed to have become a still more evil person.

Yes, I shall write everything, now that I have written this much. Please do not be angry. This happened that windy night at the Atami Hotel thirteen years ago, the very night when you and I determined to become thoroughly evil and to deceive everyone while we nurtured our love.

That night, just after we had exchanged our oaths of love, I found that there was nothing more to say. I lay on the well-starched bed sheet, and I gazed up into the darkness in silence. I do not recall any more impressively quiet hour. Was it only five or six minutes? Or was it for half an hour or an hour that we were silent?

I was entirely alone. Forgetting that you were beside me, I seemed to be encompassing my own soul. Why did I fall into such a helpless solitude at a moment when the secret front, as it were, of our love was formed, when it gave promise of being exquisitely fruitful for both of us?

That night you determined to deceive everyone in the world. Could you dream of deceiving me? I never excepted you. I would deceive all the living creatures in the world, including you and even myself. That would be my life. The thought kept burning, flickering in the bottom of my solitary soul like an elfin flame.

I had to cut off my attachment to Kadota, which was not to be distinguished from love or hatred. I could never forgive Kadota's inconstancy, no matter what sort of weakness may have been the cause of it. I thought I could be anything, could do anything, in order to cut it off. It beset me. I was seeking with all my being that which would extinguish my suffering. And the result! Nothing has changed since that night thirteen years ago.

"To love" and "to be loved." What sad relationships! It was when I was in the second or third year of girls' school. Our teacher of English grammar gave us a test in the active and passive voices. Among such words as "to beat" and "to be beaten," "to see" and "to be seen," there were those dazzling words "to love" and "to be loved." As I got a grip on my pencil and prepared to answer, someone passed a note to me from behind. It consisted of two sentences:—"Do you want to love?" and "Do you want to be loved?"—and their respective answers. Underneath the sentence "I want to be loved" there were many circles in ink or blue or red pencil. Underneath the other sentence, "I want to love," there was nothing. I was no exception and put a small circle under "I want to be loved." Did we instinctively know the happiness of being loved even though we were only sixteen and could not know what it meant "to love" and "to be loved"?

Only the girl who sat next to me drew a large thick circle where there had been no mark. This she did with almost no hesitation. "I want to love." I still remember how I hated her uncompromising attitude and at the same time how vulnerable I felt. She did not do very well in school and she was an unattractive girl with a melancholy manner. I have no way of knowing what became of her, that lonely girl with her dusty hair. Even now, more than twenty years later, her lonely look comes before me for reasons I cannot understand.

I wonder to whom, at the end of the way, God will give rest, the woman who enjoyed the happiness of being loved or the one who declared that she wanted to love, even though she may not have been rewarded with much happiness. Can any woman declare in the presence of God that she *loved?* Yes, there must be such women. That girl with the dusty hair may have become one of the elect. With disheveled hair and wounded body and torn clothes, she will raise her head triumphantly and say that she loved.

Oh, I hate it. I want to fly from it. But I cannot keep it away—the girl's face that haunts me. What is this worry over my death, only a few hours ahead of me? It seems the proper reward for a woman who, to escape the pain of loving, sought the happiness of being loved.

I am sorry I have to write this to you after thirteen happy years.

The moment has come when the boat must burn to the water. The moment which I knew would come. I am too tired to live. I think I have finally told you what I really am—I have given the true picture of myself—as best I could. It is a life that lasts but fifteen or twenty minutes as you read my testament, but it is my real life, the life of your Ayako.

I would like to tell you only one thing more. Those thirteen years were like a dream. I was happy and wrapped in your expansive love, happier than anyone else in the world.

It was late at night when I finished reading the three letters to Misugi Jōsuké. Taking out Misugi's letter to me, I read it again. Several times I reread the suggestive passage toward the end: "The fact is that I had been interested in hunting for several years. It had been a rather peaceful period in both my private and my public life, a contrast to the lonely life I lead now. Already by the time you saw me, the shotgun had become everything to me." There was something unbearably sad in the neat array of letters. As Ayako had said, perhaps it was the serpent that lurked in the man Misugi.

I went to the north window of my study, where I looked out into the dark March night. Electric trains gave forth blue sparks in the distance. What were those three letters to Misugi? What did he learn from them? Was it not that he had learned nothing at all? That he was already aware of Midori's serpent, and of Ayako's serpent too?

With my face turned into the chilly night wind, I stood by the window, feeling slightly drunk. Putting my hands to the window frame, I looked into the wooded courtyard below, into Misugi's "white river bed."

山月記　中島敦

TIGER-POET

BY Nakajima Ton

TRANSLATED BY Ivan Morris

Nakajima Ton (his given name may also be read Atsushi), who died in 1942 at the age of thirty-three, came from a family of Chinese scholars, and he himself had a thorough knowledge of classical Chinese. He was also a student of English, French, and German literature. After graduating from the Japanese Literature Department of Tokyo Imperial University, he became an official in the South Sea Islands Government Office. His best-known work, "Light, Wind, and Dream," was published in the year of his death.

Nakajima's short stories, which made him famous despite his short career, are marked by a wide erudition and a very individual type of fantasy that often brings to mind the work of Akutagawa Ryūnosuké and occasionally, as in the present story, of Franz Kafka. It is for his sense of literary style, however, that Nakajima is most respected: there is a terseness and a clarity about his language which undoubtedly reflect the strong influence of Chinese classical style.

Many of Nakajima's best-known stories, including the present one, are set in the China of the distant past, with which he was so familiar from his reading.

"Tiger-Poet" (Sangetsuki) was published in 1942, the year of the author's death. It expresses in a rather original form the orthodox conception of karma, namely that an individual's present lot is determined by behavior in previous existences.

Li Chêng's poem is in the traditional Chinese style. It consists of eight lines of seven characters each, with the parts of speech in one line being roughly matched by the same parts of speech in the next line. The poem observes the *strict conventions of classical composition but is artistically rather jejune.*

That a civil servant should aspire to become a poet may seem strange to some Western readers. In China, however, where the training for the senior civil-service examinations consisted almost entirely of literary studies, such an ambition would by no means be abnormal; nor would the ability of another civil servant to discern his friend's poetic shortcomings.

LI CHÊNG was a man of great erudition. At an early age he passed the senior civil-service examinations with high distinction and his name was inscribed on the military list. Shortly thereafter he was made Captain of the Guards in the Lower Yangtze area.

He took up his appointment but, because of his proud and independent nature, soon began to chafe under the restrictions of his new post, which he scorned as unworthy of his talents. Since rapid promotion appeared unlikely, Li Chêng before long resigned from government service. He broke off relations with all his former friends and colleagues and retired with his family to his native town of Kuolüeh, resolved thenceforth to devote himself wholeheartedly to writing poetry. Rather than remain year after year as a subordinate official in the civil service, groveling before so-called superiors, would it not, he thought, be infinitely preferable to live the dignified, independent life of a man of letters and finally to bequeath his name to posterity as a great poet?

Alas, it requires more than determination to be a successful writer. Before long Li Chêng had exhausted his private means. Thereafter his days were a struggle with the exigencies of practical life. The handsome, round-cheeked youth who had so brilliantly passed the examinations into the senior civil service vanished utterly and in his place appeared an emaciated man of harsh demeanor, in whose eyes could be seen the piercing, impatient look of one whose goal is constantly receding.

After some years he could no longer bear the grinding poverty to which the pursuit of poetry condemned him; he realized that he must swallow his pride and take a job which would at least provide him and his family with food and clothing. He applied to the Civil Service Board and in due course received an appointment as Assistant District Officer in an eastern province. By this time most of his former colleagues had risen to high posts, so Li Chêng now found himself in the galling situation of having to take orders from men who had passed the examinations far below him on the list, most of whom he had despised as boors and blockheads. The constant humiliation of his new role, following on his hard years as a poet, made Li Chêng increasingly morose and bitter, to the extent that he sometimes appeared to be verging on insanity.

A year after his re-entry into the civil service, he was ordered to travel to the south on official business. On his way, he stayed at an inn by the River Ju and here it was that he suddenly went mad. In the middle of the night he was heard to emit an incomprehensible scream. With distorted face and glaring eyes he jumped out of the window and, before anyone could stop him, rushed headlong into the dark. A search party was sent out the following morning, but, though they scoured the hills and fields in all directions, they could find no trace of Li Chêng. He did not reappear, and even his family was never to learn the strange fate that had befallen him.

In the following year, Yüan Ts'an, a Supervising Censor on the provincial circuit, was proceeding to the south on imperial orders and stopped for the night at Shangyü near the River Ju. He was about to set out next morning before dawn when the landlord warned him that a man-eating tiger had been seen on the road directly to the south.

"Travelers have been told to avoid the road by night," said the landlord. "May I respectfully suggest that Your Honor wait until daybreak?"

"Thank you," said Yüan Ts'an, "but I have my brave men to guard me." Without further ado, he mounted his horse and left the inn, followed by his retinue.

Shortly thereafter, they were making their way by the light of the moon through a thick grove. Suddenly a huge tiger leaped out of a thicket near the road and, roaring savagely, rushed at Yüan Ts'an. The beast was about to spring upon him when abruptly it turned and bounded back into the thicket.

For a moment no one spoke. Then from inside the thicket came a peculiar voice: "Great Heavens! That was close!"

Shaken though Yüan Ts'an was, he instantly recognized the voice. "Surely that is the voice of my old friend Li Chêng, is it not?" he said.

Yüan Ts'an and Li Chêng had taken their final examinations in the capital at the same time and had been close friends for many years. Only a man of Yüan Ts'an's mild temperament could have tolerated the harsh, self-willed Li Chêng.

For a long time there was no answer from the thicket, only a strange sound as of stifled sobbing. At last a rasping voice said: "Yes, I am indeed Li Chêng of Kuolüeh, whom once you knew."

Forgetting all fear, Yüan Ts'an dismounted and walked up to the thicket. "Come out of there, my old friend," he said, "and let us converse for a while."

"Alas," answered the voice, "I am hideously transfigured! For very shame I cannot let you look at me again in my present form. I know that just to glance at me would fill you with horror and disgust. Yet now that we have met so strangely, I pray you to stay and talk, even though we are unable to see each other."

When Yüan Ts'an thought about it later, it all seemed impossibly weird but at the time he felt it to be almost normal, just as in one's dreams one can accept without question the most preposterous events. He ordered his retinue to wait and, stationing himself boldly next to the thicket, began to talk to his invisible friend.

First he told him the news from the capital, the latest gossip about their former colleagues, and the circumstances of his own brilliant career. In a dolorous tone the voice from the thicket congratulated him on his promotions. After this there was a painful pause. Finally Yüan Ts'an brought himself to ask: "And what has happened to *you?*"

From behind the tall shrubs, Li Chêng's voice related the following tale:

"About a year ago I was dispatched to the south on some paltry errand. On my way I spent the night by the River Ju. I retired early and went to sleep almost at once, but after what seemed a short time, I was awakened by a strange voice outside calling my name. I got up, opened the window, and looked out. From the darkness the unknown voice summoned me, and an irresistible impulse caused me to obey.

"Without hesitation, I jumped out of the window and rushed off into the night, running as if in a delirium, heedless of direction. Before I knew it, I was on a path entering the woodland. To my surprise, I found that I was running with both hands on the ground; I seemed to be able to move much faster in this manner. As I ran, I felt a strange strength filling my body, and I sprang lightly over rocks and tree trunks. Then I noticed that thick hair had grown around my fingers, my arms and shoulders, in fact all over me. By now I had quite forgotten about the voice, but still I hurried on—running for the sake of running, as it were.

"When dawn began to break, I stopped by a mountain stream and looked into the clear water. At once I saw that I had become a full-fledged tiger. After my first shock, I realized with relief that this must be a dream. You see, I had often had dreams, especially nightmares, in which I had been perfectly aware that I was dreaming. But as the hours passed and dawn turned into full daylight, I finally had to admit to myself that I was wide awake. Now for the first time I was aghast and horror-struck. Most frightening of all was my feeling that the normal rules of life had broken down—that from now on anything might occur, however horrible.

"I crouched in the thick grass near a boulder and tried to think things out as clearly as I could. Why had this happened? I asked myself, but no answer sprang to mind. Pondering there beside the rock, the thought came to me that no one could ever be sure why things did happen to him. Were not all men controlled throughout their lives by forces of which they understood little or nothing? Wisdom lay in accepting this ultimate ignorance and in not fighting constantly against one's fate, as I indeed had done. Now it was too late. My life as a human being had been a web of struggles and rebellions; enlightenment had come only when it could no longer be of use. I looked at my tiger-body and wished I could have died.

"Just then a hare ran past, a few yards from where I crouched. In a single instant all humanity left me. When human thoughts returned, I found that my mouth was stained with blood and that tufts of white fur were scattered round about. This was my first real experience as a tiger. The horrors and brutalities that I have committed every day since then I do not dare recount.

"Only for a few hours each day does the human spirit still return. At these times, I can speak as I am speaking to you now—can actually think out the most complicated thoughts. Yes, I can even recite to my-

self whole pages from the classics. Then also I remember the terrible things that I have done as a tiger; my ears echo with the screams of my victims and I am overcome with shame, fear, indignation at my animal nature.

"Yet as the weeks go by, these hours of human lucidity become fewer. Until recently I used to wonder how I could have turned into a tiger. Now the question that haunts me is a different one: how could I ever have been human? This is a terrible sign, is it not? Soon all memory of my past will have disappeared and such human spirit as still is left me will have vanished, like the foundations of some ancient palace finally covered over with earth and sand. Then I shall be nothing but a wild beast, the scourge of these forests, who, were he to meet you, Yüan Ts'an, would tear you limb from limb and devour you without the slightest compunction. . . ."

The voice dwindled off and for a while Yüan Ts'an could hear only the sound of heavy panting. Then the voice resumed, but in a more labored way:

"These days a certain thought keeps coming to me—not original, to be sure, yet never before fully understood by me. Were we not all of us—both animals and human beings—at one time something else? While young we may remember dimly our earlier existence, but as we grow accustomed to our present form, we fall under the illusion that we have always been as we are now.

"Well, be that as it may, such abstract notions will soon be foreign to my mind. In a way I shall no doubt be happier when my human side has disappeared, yet it is precisely this final disappearance of my humanity that I fear most. The prospect of becoming a wild beast with no recollection of my former self is excruciating beyond words. That is my fate, alas, and now there is no way to escape it. . . ."

Again the voice died away; for some time there was silence in the grove. Yüan Ts'an and his attendants stood with bated breath, awestruck by the incredible recital. Then at length the voice was heard once more:

"Before I leave the human realm for good, I have a request to make of you."

"Name it," said Yüan Ts'an. "It shall be fulfilled."

"My request is this. The ambition of my former days was to be recognized as a great poet, but before this could be realized I came to my present pass. Of the countless poems I composed, none, I expect, is still extant. Doubtless they have disappeared from human ken like smoke blown by the wind. The sole remaining vestige of my art is a dozen or so poems that I have committed to memory. Write these down, I beg you, and make sure that they do not follow their author into oblivion.

"Yet do not think, my friend, that on the strength of these few verses I now hope to set myself up as a great poet! My only thought is that I cannot bear to leave this world without knowing that at least some of the poems which cost me my career, my fortune, and at last my mind may be transmitted to posterity."

Yüan Ts'an ordered one of his attendants to take a brush and record the words of the being in the thicket. Quite clearly Li Chêng's voice recited thirty-odd poems of elegant style and admirable sentiment. Yet as Yüan Ts'an listened, the dismal truth dawned on him that his friend could never have achieved his literary ambition, however long he had lived. Though Li Chêng was a writer of skill and erudition, he clearly lacked the spark of genius that alone brings poetry to life.

When Li Chêng had finished reciting his poems, he paused for a while, then continued in the harsh, self-deprecatory tone which Yüan Ts'an remembered from their student days:

"It really is absurd, but often as I crouch in my cave at night, I dream of my collected poems, beautifully bound, lying on the desk of some scholar in the capital. He picks up the book with an air of respect and begins to read. . . . How idiotic! Go ahead and laugh! Laugh at the poor fool who aspired to be a poet and instead became a tiger!"

Yüan Ts'an was far from laughing as he listened to his friend's bitter voice. He recalled how in the past such an access of self-ridicule had almost always followed Li Chêng's flights of conceit.

"Yes, I'm a laughingstock," Li Chêng went on, almost spitting out the words. "And here's a final poem for you to remember me by. I've composed it on the spur of the moment . . . a poem about a poor fool like me."

Yüan Ts'an beckoned to his attendant to continue writing, and Li Chêng recited:

Misfortune followed misfortune
    Till at last my mind succumbed;
Raging illness of the spirit then
    Reduced me to this hideous form.

Now I dwell in murky caves
    While you in golden chariots ride.

Last night I stood upon yon mountain peak
    And faced the silver moon.
'Twas not the dreaded tiger's roar that
    Echoed o'er the hills,
But howls of abject misery.

Meanwhile the fading light of the moon, the dew on the grass, and a cool breeze announced the approach of dawn. Yüan Ts'an and his attendants had recovered from their first shock at Li Chêng's metamorphosis. They had come to feel pity rather than fear for the tiger-poet.

"Alas, how tragic a destiny!" they murmured. "With all his knowledge and gifts—to come to this."

Then Li Chêng's voice continued:

"Earlier I told you that I ignored the cause of my transformation. And so at first I did. In the past year I have, I think, come to perceive at least a glimmering of the truth.

"In my human days, I retired to my home town, as you know, and shunned the company of men. People thought my behavior arrogant and haughty, not realizing that in large part it sprang from diffidence. I shall not pretend to you that I, the reputed genius of the town, was entirely devoid of pride. But mine was a timid pride—the pride of a coward. Though I had resolved to be a poet, I declined to study under a master or to mix with fellow writers, and this because of cowardly diffidence—because unconsciously I feared that, if I were to associate with other poets, the jewel of genius within me might be revealed as paste.

"At the same time, I hoped and half believed that the jewel was real, and I disdained to mingle with vulgar people whose lives were not spent in literary pursuits. Thus, I cut myself off from the outside world and lived in isolation with my family. More and more I looked down on the common run of men, and financial difficulties only served to increase my scorn for the world of money-makers. But the whole time the fear grew that I was, in truth, far from being a poetic genius. Pride and diffidence—the two battened within me until they became almost my entire being.

"It is said, is it not, that all of us are by nature wild beasts and that our duty as human beings is to become like trainers who hold their animals in check, and even teach them to perform tasks alien to their bestiality. My diffident pride was that of a wild beast and, despite all my intelligence and culture, I was in the end unable to keep it under control. This pride it was that prevented me from becoming a great poet. Well I know that many men with far less talent than mine have achieved poetic fame by humble study of the works of others and by devoted application. Yes, my pride it was that made life for my family a misery and for myself a torment! That raging pride finally turned me into a wild beast in form as well as spirit.

"Now, alas, the time for repentance has run out. My human days are ended and the last vestiges of my humanity will gradually disappear. O the waste! O the pity! Often at night I stand alone on those rocks and howl into the deserted valleys below. Will no one who hears me understand my suffering? The smaller animals hear me and in their lairs they prostrate themselves with fear. The mountains and the trees, the moon and the dew, hear me and marvel at the ferocity of the tiger's roar. Leaping into the air and throwing myself on the ground, I howl into the night. But no one, nothing, understands the despair that seethes within me. And so indeed it was in my human days. . . ."

Now the darkness had almost lifted. From the distance came the plaintive sound of a hunter's horn.

"The time has come to part," said Li Chêng. "The witching hour is close at hand when I shall again become a tiger in mind as well as body. But first let me make one more request. When you return to the north, pray go to my family in Kuolüeh. Say nothing of this meeting, but tell them rather that in the course of your travels you heard of my death. And if they lack for food and shelter, take pity on them, I implore you."

When Li Chêng had finished speaking, there came the sound of wailing from within the thicket. Deeply moved, Yüan Ts'an answered that he would comply with his friend's wishes in every respect. Then Li Chêng's voice abruptly reverted to its previous hard, self-mocking tone:

"No doubt you are thinking that I should have made this second request before the first. You are quite right. It is precisely because I was the sort of man who was more concerned with having people notice his own feeble poems than with providing for his starving wife and children that I ended up as a wild beast. By the way, may I suggest that on your return trip you take some other road? By then I may well be beyond recognizing old friends and I hate to think that I might tear you to pieces and eat you. In case you might ever have any desire to renew our acquaintanceship, pray halt today when you reach the top of yonder hill and glance back. You can then look at me for the last time, and that will remove any wish to meet me again."

"I bid you farewell, my dear friend," said Yüan Ts'an courteously in the direction of the thicket. With solemn mien he mounted his horse and rode off, followed by his attendants. From behind the shrubs came the sound of harsh sobs.

When the party reached the top of the hill, Yüan Ts'an looked back at the grove whence they had just come. Suddenly a tiger leaped out of the dense grass onto the road. For a few moments it stood there motionless, then gazed up at the pale white moon and howled thrice. As the last wail echoed through the valley, the tiger jumped back into the underbrush and disappeared from sight.

親友交歓

太宰治

THE COURTESY CALL

BY Dazai Osamu

TRANSLATED BY Ivan Morris

Dazai Osamu was born in 1909 into a prosperous, well-established landowning family in the north of Japan. He killed himself at the age of thirty-nine by throwing himself into a river in the suburbs of Tokyo. His death caused little surprise. Not only was this his fourth attempt at suicide, but every aspect of his life and work seemed to lead inexorably to his dismal ending.

Dazai started to write in the early 1930's, but it was not until after the war that he made his name in literary circles. In his writing (as well as in his death) Dazai was greatly influenced by the pessimistic Weltanschauung of Akutagawa Ryūnosuké. Dazai's work, however, is far more circumscribed by the personal approach than Akutagawa's, and it occasionally tends towards a certain monotony as, in page after page, he pours out the agony of his distraught life. This life, as Mr. Seidensticker has written, was "almost a parody on desperate bohemianism: flirtations with communism, drunkenness, addiction to drugs, repeated attempts at suicide."

Dazai's masterpiece is generally considered to be the novel "Setting Sun" (1947), which in fine, sensitive prose describes the final disintegration of an aristocratic family in postwar Japan. Most of Dazai's work is marked by a thoroughgoing negative approach; he belonged to the so-called nihilistic school of writers much in vogue after the war at the same time that existentialism was making its mark in Japan. His later stories and novels provide a remarkable record of the spiritual climate in the early postwar years when all traditional values had been shattered and when much of Japan was, quite literally, a waste-

*land. He enjoyed enormous popularity, especially among the younger genera-
tion.*

*The profound pessimism that permeated Dazai's writing did not deprive
him of a certain sense of humor, and "The Courtesy Call" (Shinyū Kokan)
is typical of his more lighthearted stories. The story was first published in
1946, when the author was thirty-five, and is autobiographical, at least in
outline. Its interest lies as much in the picture that it reflects of the author himself as in the description of his "old friend." Beneath its somewhat flippant
surface, it is perhaps possible to detect Dazai's troubled state of mind, which
became intensified in the following years and which led to his suicide in 1948.
At the same time, it provides a rather refreshing contrast to the sentimental
approach that many Japanese writers tend to adopt when describing members of
the working class.*

UNTIL the day of my death I shall not forget the man
who came to my house that afternoon last September. Although on
the surface there may have been nothing very spectacular about his visit,
I am convinced that it was a momentous event in my life. For to me
this man foretold a new species of humanity. During my years in Tokyo,
I had frequented the lowest class of drinking house and mixed with
some quite appalling rogues. But this man was in a category all his own:
he was far and away the most disagreeable, the most loathsome, person
I had ever met; there was not a jot of goodness in him.

After my house in Tokyo was bombed, I moved with my family to
a cottage in a remote country district where I had lived as a child and
where my brother had recently stood for election. Here it was after
lunch one day, as I sat smoking dreamily by myself in the living room,
that a tall, corpulent man appeared, dressed in a farmer's smock.

"I'll be damned," he said, when I opened the door. "If it isn't old
Osamu himself!"

I looked at him blankly.

"Come, come," he said, laughing and showing a set of sharp, white
teeth, "don't say you've forgotten me! I'm Hirata, your old friend from
primary school."

From the dim recesses of my memory there emerged some vague

recollection of the face. We may indeed have known each other in school, but as for being old friends, I was not so sure.

"Of course I remember you," I said with a great show of urbanity. "Do come in, Mr. Hirata."

He removed his clogs and strode into the living room.

"Well, well," he said loudly, "it's been a long time, hasn't it?"

"Yes, years and years."

"Years?" he shouted. "Decades, you mean! It must be over twenty years since I saw you. I heard some time ago that you'd moved to our village but I've been far too busy on the farm to call. By the way, they tell me you've become quite a tippler. Spend most of your time at the bottle, eh? Ha, ha, ha!"

I forced a smile and puffed at my cigarette.

"D'you remember how we used to fight at school?" he said, starting on a new tack. "We were always fighting, you and me."

"Were we really?"

"Were we really, indeed!" he said, mimicking my intonation. "Of course we were! I've got a scar here on the back of my hand to remind me. You gave me this scar."

He held out his hand for me to examine, but I could see nothing that even vaguely resembled a scar.

"And what about that one on your left shin? You remember where I hit you with a stone. I bet you've still got a nasty scar to show for it."

I did not have the slightest mark on either of my shins. I smiled vaguely and looked at his large face with its shrewd eyes and fleshy lips.

"Well, so much for all that," he said. "Now I'll tell you why I've come. I want you and me to organize a class reunion. I'll get together about twenty of the lads and we'll have ten gallons of saké. It'll be a real drinking bout. Not such a bad idea, eh?"

"No," I said dubiously. "But isn't ten gallons rather a lot?"

"Of course not," he said. "To have a good time, you want at least eight pints a head."

"Where are you going to buy ten gallons of saké these days?" I said. "One's lucky to find a single bottle."

"Don't worry about that," he said. "I know where I can lay my hands on the stuff. But it's expensive, you know, even here in the country. That's where I want you to help out."

I stood up with a knowing smile. So it was as simple as all that, I thought almost with relief. I went to the back room and returned with a couple of bank notes.

"Here you are," I said.

"Oh no," he said, "I didn't come here today to get money. I came to discuss the class reunion. I wanted to hear your ideas. Besides, I wanted to see my old pal again after all these years. . . . Anyhow that won't be nearly enough. We'll need at least a thousand yen. You can put those notes away."

"Really?" I said, replacing the money in my wallet.

"What about something to drink?" he said all of a sudden.

I looked at him coldly, but he stood his ground.

"Come on," he said, "you needn't look as if you'd never heard of the stuff! They tell me you've always got a good supply put away. Let's have a little drink together! Call the missus! She can pour for us."

"All right," I said, standing up, "come with me." From that moment I was lost.

I led him to the back room, which I used as my study.

"I'm afraid it's in a bit of a mess," I said.

"It doesn't matter," he answered tolerantly. "Scholars' rooms are always like pigsties. I used to know quite a few of you bookworms in my Tokyo days."

I glanced at him suspiciously; his "Tokyo days" were, without doubt, another figment of his imagination.

"It's not a bad little room, all the same," he said. "You've got a nice view of the garden, haven't you? Ah, I see you have some *hiiragi* holly trees out there. Now tell me: do you know what the word *hiiragi* comes from?"

"No," I replied.

"Ha, ha! You're a fine scholar, aren't you?" he said. "Don't you really know? Well, I'll give you a hint. The whole word has a universal meaning and part of the word means something that you bookworms use for your scribbling."

He seemed to be talking gibberish and I began to wonder if he was not mentally deficient. By the end of the afternoon I was to realize how far from deficient he really was.

"Well, have you figured it out?"

"No, I'm afraid not," I said. "I give up. What's the answer?"

"I'll tell you some other time," he said, smiling self-importantly.

I went to the cupboard and took out a bottle of good whisky, which was about half full.

"I don't have any saké," I said. "I hope you won't mind some whisky."

"It'll do," he said. "But I want your little woman to pour the stuff."

"I'm sorry but my wife isn't at home," I said.

In fact she was in the bedroom, but I was determined to spare her this ordeal. Besides, I felt sure that the farmer would be disappointed in her. He would no doubt expect a smart, sophisticated woman from the city and, although my wife was born and bred in Tokyo, she had about her something rustic, almost gauche.

But the deception did not escape my visitor.

"Of course she's at home," he said. "Tell her to come and do the pouring."

I decided simply to ignore his request and, filling a teacup with whisky, handed it to him.

"I'm afraid it's not quite up to prewar quality," I said.

He tossed it off at a single draught, smacked his lips loudly and said: "It's pretty cheap stuff, isn't it?"

"I'm sorry, but it's the best I can get. . . . I wouldn't drink it down too quickly if I were you," I added.

"Ha, ha!" he said, putting the cup to his lips. "I can see you don't know who you're dealing with. I used to polish off two bottles an evening just by myself. And that was real Suntory whisky, not this watered-down stuff. I shouldn't think this is more than sixty percent, is it?"

"I really don't know."

He took the bottle and poured a cup for me. Then he filled his own cup to the brim.

"The bottle's almost empty," he announced.

"Oh, really?" I said, assuming a nonchalance that I was far from feeling. I took another bottle out of the cupboard.

The man continued drinking and as the level of the whisky in the second bottle began to sink, I finally felt anger rise within me. It was not that I was usually jealous about my property. Far from it. Having lost almost all my possessions in the bombings, what was left meant hardly anything to me. But this whisky was an exception. I had obtained it some time before at immense difficulty and expense, and had rationed myself severely, only now and then sipping a small glass after dinner. At the beginning of that afternoon two and a half bottles remained, and I had looked forward to offering some to my friend Mr. Ibusé Masuji when he came to visit, for I knew that he was partial to an occasional glass. When this terrible farmer appeared after lunch, I brought out the whisky, never for a moment dreaming that he would take more than one cup. Now as I watched in impotent fury while he gulped the contents of the second bottle, I almost felt that the whisky was my lifeblood being poured down his insensitive gullet.

"I hear you got into plenty of trouble over women in Tokyo," he said, filling his cup once more. "Well, to tell you the truth, I got into trouble myself during my Tokyo period. But I got myself out of it all right. Yes, it takes more than a woman to hold me. Of course, once they've set their hearts on you, they don't let go easy. Mine still writes me every now and then. Why, only the other day she sent me a packet of rice cakes. Women are fools, aren't they, damned fools! When they're in love with you, they don't care about your looks or even about how much money you've got. All they think about is feelings and heart and all that claptrap." He laughed raucously. "Yes, I had quite a wild time in my Tokyo period. Come to think of it, I must have been in Tokyo about the same time that you were there, breaking the hearts of your geisha girls. You made quite a name for yourself, didn't you? Ha, ha! Funny we never bumped into each other. Where did you hang out in those days?"

I had no idea to which days he was referring, nor did I remember breaking the hearts of any geisha. To be sure, I had had various emotional complications when I lived in Tokyo. For this I had been amply abused by my literary acquaintances and even by so-called friends, until their criticisms had now ceased utterly to affect me. Yet something about this man's tone made me feel, for the first time in years, that I had to defend myself from the charge of being a callous libertine.

"You know," I said, looking straight at him, "I've never set myself up as a lady-killer. And I don't get any pleasure from going round seducing women indiscriminately."

"I know all about you," he said, looking at me with a snigger, and I realized that he did not believe a word I had said. An unpleasant feeling of cheapness came over me. This man with his ugly mind seemed to see right through me—into the ugliest recesses of my being.

I suddenly wanted to ask him to leave. Yet the fact was that I did not dare to. Our position in this village was far from secure and I could not risk offending someone who appeared to be an old and well-established inhabitant. Besides, I was afraid that if I asked him to go, he might think that I looked down on him for being an uneducated farmer. I went into the living room and came back with a plate of fruit.

"Have a pear," I said. "It'll do you good."

I was terrified that the man would soon become roaring drunk and it occurred to me that some fruit might avert this calamity. He looked blankly at the plate and reached for his cup of whisky.

"I hate politics," he said abruptly. "In fact we farmers all hate politics. What good have those politicians ever done us? If they helped us in any way, we'd support them. We're grateful folk, you know, us country people, and we always return favors. But all those politicians can do is jabber away, while we get on with the real work. Socialists, Progressives, Liberals—bah! They're all the same to us!"

For a moment I wondered where this new line was leading.

"Your brother was campaigning in the last elections, wasn't he?" continued the farmer.

"Yes," I said, "this was his district. He lost."

"I suppose you did quite a bit of campaigning yourself?"

"No, I didn't even bother to vote. I stayed at home and worked."

"Nonsense," he said, "of course you campaigned for your own brother! It's just a simple matter of humanity. I may not be a great scholar like you, but at least I know what humanity is. That's one thing we farmers understand. I hate politics, but when I heard that the brother of my old school pal was a candidate, I went right out and voted for him without even waiting for anyone to ask me. That's humanity for you! As long as we don't lose that quality, we farmers are going to be all right."

His object was now transparent: his vote—if, indeed, he had ever cast it—was to be a passport for an indefinite amount of whisky.

"It was very good of you to support my brother," I said with a sardonic smile.

"Don't get me wrong," he said. "I did it out of common humanity —not because I thought he was any good. Your family may have got ahead in the world now, but a couple of generations ago they were just common oil-sellers. Did you know that? I've been doing a bit of research. Your family used to sell cans of oil and if anyone bought half a pint or more, they gave him a piece of toffee as a premium. That's how they made their money. It's the same with almost all the so-called 'good' families. Take the Ōiké family, for instance, who own half the land around here and go about lording it over us all. It's not so long ago that their ancestors were putting buckets by the roadside for the passersby to piss in. As soon as the buckets were full, they sold them to the farmers to mix with their fertilizer. That's how they started their fortune. You can't fool me!"

"I'm sure I can't," I said, wondering whether he was inventing all this on the spur of the moment or whether he had come fully prepared.

"I myself come from a really old family, though," he continued. "My ancestors moved to this village hundreds of years ago from Kyoto."

"Really? In that case, I expect you are of noble lineage."

"You may not be far wrong," he said with a nasal laugh. "Of course, you wouldn't think it to see me in these clothes. But both my brothers went to university. The older one's made quite a name for himself in the government. You've probably seen his name in the papers."

"Yes, of course," I said.

"Well, I didn't bother to go to university myself. I decided to stay in the country and do some really useful work. And now, of course, I'm the one who's got ahead and they have to come begging me for rice and all the things they can't get in Tokyo. Not that I begrudge them anything. And look here," he said, sticking his finger almost into my face, "if you're ever short of food, you can come to my farm too and I'll give you whatever you need. I'm not the sort of fellow who'd drink a man's liquor for nothing. I'll repay you—down to the last penny. We farmers are grateful folk."

He examined his empty cup pensively and then all of a sudden shouted: "Call in the little woman! I won't drink another drop unless she pours it for me herself. Not another drop, d'you hear?" He staggered to his feet. "Where is the little woman, anyway? In the bedroom, I expect, snug in bed, eh? D'you know who I am? I'm Hirata, I'm a lord among farmers! Haven't you heard of the great Hirata family?"

My worst fears were being realized and I saw that there was nothing for it but to fetch my wife.

"Do sit down, Mr. Hirata," I said calmly. "I'll call her right away, if it means all that much to you."

I went into the bedroom, where my wife was busy darning some socks.

"Would you mind coming in for a minute?" I asked her casually. "An old schoolfriend has come to see me." I said no more, as I did not want my wife to be prejudiced in advance against the visitor. In particular I did not want her to think that I considered him in any way inferior to us. She nodded and followed me into the back room.

"Let me introduce Mr. Hirata," I said, "my old friend from primary school. We were always fighting when we were kids. He's got a mark on the back of his hand where I scratched him. Today he's come to get his revenge."

"How terrifying!" she said, laughing. "Anyhow, I'm glad to meet you." She bowed in his direction.

Our visitor seemed to relish these courtesies.

"Glad to meet you, Madam," he said. "But you needn't stand on ceremony with me. By the way, I'd very much appreciate it if you'd pour me some whisky."

I noticed that he was sober enough to address my wife politely, although a few moments before he had been referring to her as "the little woman."

"You know, Madam," he said, when my wife had filled his cup, "I was just telling Osamu here that if you ever need any food, be sure to come round to my place. I've got plenty of everything: potatoes, vegetables, rice, eggs, chickens. What about some horse meat? Would you like a nice hunk of horse meat? I'm a great expert at stripping horsehides, you know. Come along tomorrow and I'll give you a whole horse's leg to take home. Do you like pheasant? Of course you do! Well, I'm the

most famous shot in these parts. Just tell me what you want and I'll shoot it. Maybe Madam would fancy some nice wild duck. Right, I'll go out tomorrow morning and shoot a dozen for you. That's nothing —a dozen. I've shot five dozen before breakfast in my day. If you don't believe me, ask anyone round here. I'm the greatest marksman in the district. The young people are all scared stiff of me. That's right—they know I can show them a thing or two. Hey, you there, bookworm!" he shouted at me. "Why don't you come along to the Shinto gate one of these evenings? There's usually a good fight going on down there— a lot of rowdy youngsters slogging at each other. Well, as soon as I get there, I throw myself right into the middle of them all and make them stop fighting. Of course, I'm risking my life every time I go there, but what does that matter? I've got a bit of money put aside for my wife and little ones. They'll be all right even when I'm gone."

For a moment his tone was maudlin. Then, suddenly turning to me again, he shouted almost ferociously: "Hey you, Mr. Bookworm! I'll call for you tomorrow evening and we'll go down to the gate together. I'll show you what life is really like. You won't be able to write anyth ng good just sitting here on your backside all day long. What you need is a little experience. What sort of books do you write anyway? Books about geisha girls, I suppose. Ha, ha, ha! The trouble is, you don't know what life's all about. Now take me. I've had three wives already. But I always like the present one best. How many wives have you had? Two? Three? What about it, Madam? Does he know how to make love to you right?"

"Please go and fetch some cakes," I said to my wife, with a sigh.

"I imagine you're going back to Tokyo pretty soon," said Mr. Hirata, as my wife left the room. "You'll be playing around with those girls again. Ha, ha! Where do you live in Tokyo?"

"I lost my house in the war."

"So you were bombed out, were you? That's the first I've heard of it. Well, in that case you must have got that special allocation of a blanket that they gave each family of evacuees. Would you mind letting me have it?"

I looked at him with renewed amazement.

"That's right," he said, calmly refilling his cup, "give me the blanket. It's meant to be quite good wool. My wife can make me a jumper with it. . . . I suppose you think it's funny of me to ask you for the blanket like this. But that's the way I do things. If I want something, I just ask for it. And when you come to my place, you can do the same. I'll give you whatever you like. What's the use of standing on ceremony with each other? Well, what about it? Are you going to let me have that blanket?"

I still stared at him blankly. This wool blanket, which we had been given as a sort of consolation prize, seemed to be my wife's most treasured possession. When our house was bombed and we moved to the country with our children, like a family of crabs whose shells have been smashed and who crawl naked and helpless across a hostile beach, she had kept the blanket constantly in sight, as though it were some sort of talisman. The man who now faced me could never know how a family felt who had lost their house in the war, or how close to committing mass suicide such families often were.

"I'm afraid you'll have to forget about the blanket," I said firmly.

"You stingy devil!" he said. "Why can't I have it?"

At this moment I was delighted to see my wife reappear with a tray of cakes. As I expected, our visitor instantly forgot about the blanket.

"Good gracious, Madam," he said, "you shouldn't have gone to all that trouble. I don't want anything to eat. I came here to drink. But I want you to do the pouring from now on. This husband of yours is too damned stingy for my liking." He glared at me. "What about it, Madam? Shall I give him a good beating? I used to be quite a fighter in my Tokyo days. I know a bit of jujitsu too. He'll be an easy match, even though he may be a few years younger than me. Well, Madam, if he ever gives you any trouble, just tell me and I'll let him have a thrashing he won't forget in a hurry. You see, I've known him since we were boys together at school and he doesn't dare put on any of his airs with me."

It was then that the various stories which I had read years ago in text-books on moral training came back to me—stories about great men like Kimura Shigenari, Kanzaki Yogorō, and Kanshin, who, on being abused by unmannerly rogues like this, did not answer in kind, but instead displayed their true moral superiority, as well as their fathomless contempt for these ruffians, by forthrightly asking them for forgiveness, when by all rights it was they who deserved apology. I remembered how, in the case of Kanzaki Yogorō, his assailant, who was a pack-horse driver, had been so impressed by the great man's humility and forbearance that he had spent days trying to compose an adequate letter of apology and had thereafter fallen into a decline and taken to drink. Until now, rather than admire the much-vaunted patience of these men, I had always tended to despise it as concealing an arrogant sense of superiority; my sympathy had, in fact, been on the side of the so-called rogues, whose behavior was at least natural and unpretentious. But now unexpectedly I found myself in the role of Kimura, Kanzaki, and Kanshin. All of a sudden I knew the sense of isolation which they too must have felt when being attacked. It occurred to me that these didactic stories should be classified, not under the usual headings of "Forbearance" or "Great Men and Little Men," but, rather, under "Loneliness." At the same time I perceived that forbearance really had very little to do with the matter. It was simply that these "great men" were weaker than their assailants and knew that they would not stand a chance if it came to a fight.

"Always fly a wild horse!"—that simple maxim explained their conduct, as well as my own behavior in face of this "old friend." I had a horrible vision of our visitor suddenly running amuck and smashing the screens, sliding doors, and furniture. Since none of the property belonged to me, I lived in a constant state of apprehension that the children might scribble on the walls or push the doors too roughly; the idea of the terrible ravages that this farmer might now perpetrate made cold shivers run down my spine. At all cost, I thought in my lonely cowardice, I must avoid offending him.

Suddenly I heard him roaring at the top of his lungs; "Ho, ho!" I looked up aghast. "Good Lord, I'm drunk!" he shouted. "Yes, damn it, I'm drunk!"

Then he gave a groan, closed his eyes tightly, and planting both elbows on his knees, sat there with a look of complete concentration, as if desperately fighting his drunkenness. The perspiration glistened on his forehead and his face was almost purple. He looked like some great struggling behemoth. He certainly must have been drunk: he had finished over half of the second bottle of whisky. My wife and I looked at each other uneasily. Then, to our amazement, he opened his eyes and said calmly, as if nothing whatever had happened: "When all's said and done, I like an occasional nip of whisky. It makes me feel good. Come over here, Madam, and pour me another cup. Don't worry, us farmers can drink as much as we like without getting tipsy."

Seeing that my wife made no move, he reached for the bottle himself, filled his cup, and drained it at a single draught.

"Well, you've both been very civil," he said, smacking his lips. "Next time you must be my guests. The trouble is, though, I really don't know what I'd give you if you did come to my place. I have a few birds, of course, but I'm keeping them for the cockfights in November. You'll have to wait till November. I suppose I could let you have a couple of pickled radishes. . . ." His words trailed off into a murmur and for a while he was silent.

"I've really got nothing in my place," he continued, "nothing at all. That's why I came here today for a drink. Of course, I could try to shoot a wild duck. We'd eat it together—just the three of us—and Osamu here would provide the whisky. But I'll do it only on one condition: while you're eating it you've got to keep saying: 'How delicious! What a splendid duck!' If you don't, I'll be furious. In fact I'll never forgive you. Ha, ha, ha! Yes, Madam, that's the way we farmers are. Treat us right and there's nothing in the world we won't do for you. But if you're snooty and standoffish, we won't give you as much as a piece of string. No use putting on airs with me, Madam. You look pretty cool and haughty right now, don't you, but I bet when you're in bed you let yourself go—just like other women."

My wife laughed good-naturedly and stood up. "I'm afraid I'll have to leave you," she said. "I hear the baby crying."

"She's no good!" he shouted, as soon as my wife had left the room. "Your missus is no damned good, I tell you! Now take my old woman, for instance. There's a real wife for you! We've got six lovely kids and we're as happy a family as you'll find anywhere in these parts. Ask anyone in the village if you don't believe me." He glared at me defiantly. "Your missus thinks she can make a fool of me by walking out like that. Well, I'm going to bring her right back to say she's sorry. Where is she? In the bedroom, I expect. I'll go and drag her out of her bedroom."

He staggered to his feet. I immediately got up and took him by the hand.

"Forget about her." I said. "Sit down and have another drink." He flopped heavily into the chair. I tried to smile, but my face was frozen.

"I knew it all along," he said. "You're having trouble with your wife. You're unhappily married, aren't you? I felt it right away."

I did not bother to contradict him.

"Well, it's none of my business," he said, filling his cup. "What about a poem to make you forget your troubles? Shall I recite you a poem?"

This was a welcome departure. Not only would it take his mind off my wife and her imagined insult, but to hear him recite a poem—perhaps some ancient melancholy verses handed down from generation to generation in this remote little village—might mitigate the picture of unrelieved loathsomeness that I had by now formed of my "old friend," a picture that I feared would pursue me to the end of my days.

"Yes, do let me hear your poem," I said warmly. For the first time that afternoon, I was sincere.

He took a drink, hiccoughed loudly, and started to recite:

> O'er mountains, rivers, plants, and trees
> The dreary air of desolation grows.
> Mile after mile stretches the fearful battlefield
> Reeking of new-spilled blood.

He hiccoughed again. "I've forgotten the second verse," he said. "It's something I read in a magazine."

"I see."

"Well, I'm off," he said, getting slowly to his feet. "Your missus has left and I don't enjoy drinking the whisky when you pour it."

I did not try to detain him.

"We'll discuss the class reunion when I have more time," he said. "I'll have to leave most of the arrangements to you. In the meantime you can let me have a little of your whisky to take home."

I was prepared for this and immediately started to pour the whisky that remained in his cup into the bottle, which was still about a quarter full.

"You can have this bottle," I said, handing it to him.

"Hey, hey," he said, "none of that!" I've had enough of your stinginess for one day. You've still got another full bottle stored away in that cupboard, haven't you? Let me have it!"

Mishima's writing, however, has gone far beyond the limited scope pro-vided by such specialized themes and has already covered an amazingly wide range. "The Thirst for Love" (1951) is focused on the life of a sensitive, depressed, and highly emotional woman who attempts to find the warmth of love in the aridity of a morally sordid household and who ends by committing murder; "The Sound of Waves" (1954) tells the fairy-like love story of a young fisherman and a girl on a little island off Japan; "The Temple of the Golden Pavilion" (1956) is a penetrating account of the unbalanced young acolyte whose entire life becomes absorbed by the beauty of the temple, to which he finally sets fire as an act of supreme defiance and liberation.

Mishima's talent and energy have enabled him to produce an amazing volume of work. No less striking is the versatility of his writing. He has already published a dozen novels and more than fifty volumes of short stories and poetry, as well as articles and newspaper sketches by the gross; he has written Kabuki plays which have been produced in various parts of the country; six of his modern plays have been staged in Tokyo; finally, his modern-version Noh plays have been produced with great success. With such an immense output, a writer is inevitably in danger of developing literary mannerisms and even of becoming mechanical or stereotyped in his form of expression. These are dangers that Mishima has so far avoided, on the whole, mainly because he has con-stantly set himself the task of seeking fresh ideas and new modes of expression. At the same time, prolific writers are prone to be extremely uneven. Even Mishima's keenest admirers admit that there is a considerable proportion of his published work that does not add to his literary reputation.

The style of Mishima's stories and novels is in most cases ornate and rather obscure; often it verges on the precious. This type of writing, difficult as it is for the translator, appears to have a great appeal for the younger generation in Japan.

Another reason for Mishima's literary success is the extremely effective way he has succeeded in describing the manners and thoughts of the "lost genera-tion" of postwar Japan. His stories and novels vividly evoke the despair, confusion, and sense of void that have been prevalent among many young Japanese since the war.

Although Mishima is best known for his portrayal of postwar youth, he frequently turns to Japanese classical literature for his material. He has a far greater interest in his country's cultural traditions than most young writers of *the postwar period. This interest is revealed in his work on Kabuki, in his modern-style Noh plays, and in stories like the present one, where he applies a modern psychological approach to the motivation of characters from an ancient Japanese chronicle.*

"The Priest and His Love" (Shigadera Shōnin no Koi) was first published in 1954, when the author was twenty-nine. It is based on a brief account contained in Volume 37 of the fourteenth-century war chronicle which (rather inaptly) is entitled "Chronicles of the Peaceful Reign." Mr. Mishima's interest lies in the motivation of his two protagonists, rather than in the events themselves, which he uses simply as a springboard. He is particularly concerned with the inner conflict between wordly love and religious faith—a conflict which, he points out, has been a common theme in the West, but which is relatively rare in Japanese literature. The religious belief with which both the main characters are imbued is that of Jōdo, or Pure Land, Buddhism, a doctrine of salvation by faith founded by Hōnen Shōnin in the twelfth century and based on the worship of Amitābha Buddha, the Lord of Boundless Light. "Jōdo Buddhism," writes Mr. Mishima in an introductory section, "was not so much a creed as the discovery of a conceptual world. . . . The love story between the Priest and the Imperial Concubine was enacted at the crucial point where the ideal world structure that they had both envisaged was balanced between collapse and survival."

The great precursor of the Jōdo Sect was Eshin (Genshin) who lived from 942 to 1017, and whose Ōjō Yōshū ("Essentials of Salvation") sets forth the main themes that were later to be incorporated into the doctrines of the Jōdo Sect. According to Eshin, enlightenment can be attained only by simple faith expressed in the invocation of the name of Amitābha Buddha, by means of which the believer will be reborn into the Western Paradise or Pure Land. Ōjō Yōshū is especially noted for its vivid depiction of Heaven and Hell. From the middle of the Heian period it exerted an enormous popular appeal, and it is believed to have been one of the first printed books in Japan.

The interview behind the blind toward the end of the story may require a few words of explanation. As readers of "The Tale of Genji" will recall, it was customary in the Heian period for noblewomen to be hidden by a ceremonial screen or blind when receiving male visitors. To invite a man behind the screen normally meant that a woman was prepared to accept his advances.

ACCORDING to Eshin's "Essentials of Salvation," the Ten Pleasures are but a drop in the ocean when compared to the joys of the Pure Land. In that land the earth is made of emerald and the roads that lead across it are lined by cordons of gold rope. The surface is endlessly level and there are no boundaries. Within each of the sacred precincts are fifty thousand million halls and towers wrought of gold, silver, lapis lazuli, crystal, coral, agate, and pearls; and wondrous garments are spread out on all the jeweled daises. Within the halls and above the towers a multitude of angels is forever playing sacred music and singing paeans of praise to the Tathagata Buddha. In the gardens that surround the halls and the towers and the cloisters are great gold and emerald ponds where the faithful may perform their ablutions; the gold ponds are lined with silver sand, and the emerald ponds are lined with crystal sand. The ponds are covered with lotus plants which sparkle in variegated colors and, as the breeze wafts over the surface of the water, magnificent lights crisscross in all directions. Both day and night the air is filled with the songs of cranes, geese, mandarin ducks, peacocks, parrots, and sweet-voiced Kalavinkas, who have the faces of beautiful women. All these and the myriad other hundred-jeweled birds are raising their melodious voices in praise of the Buddha. (However sweet their voices may sound, so immense a collection of birds must be extremely noisy.)

The borders of the ponds and the banks of the rivers are lined with groves of sacred treasure trees. These trees have golden stems and silver branches and coral blossoms, and their beauty is mirrored in the waters. The air is full of jeweled cords, and from these cords hang the myriad treasure bells which forever ring out the Supreme Law of Buddha; and strange musical instruments, which play by themselves without ever being touched, also stretch far into the pellucid sky.

If one feels like having something to eat, there automatically appears before one's eyes a seven-jeweled table on whose shining surface rest seven-jeweled bowls heaped high with the choicest delicacies. But there is no need to pick up these viands and put them in one's mouth. All that is necessary is to look at their inviting colors and to enjoy their aroma; thereby the stomach is filled and the body nourished, while one remains oneself spiritually and physically pure. When one has thus finished one's meal without any eating, the bowls and the table are instantly wafted off.

Likewise, one's body is automatically arrayed in clothes, without any need for sewing, laundering, dyeing, or repairing. Lamps, too, are unnecessary, for the sky is illumined by an omnipresent light. Furthermore, the Pure Land enjoys a moderate temperature all year round, so that neither heating nor cooling is required. A hundred thousand subtle scents perfume the air, and lotus petals rain down constantly.

In the chapter on the Inspection Gate we are told that, since uninitiated sightseers cannot hope to penetrate deep into the Pure Land, they must concentrate, first, on awakening their powers of "external imagination" and, thereafter, on steadily expanding these powers. Imaginative power can provide a short cut for escaping from the trammels of our mundane life and for seeing the Buddha. If we are endowed with a rich, turbulent imagination, we can focus our attention on a single lotus flower and from there can spread out to infinite horizons.

By means of microscopic observation and astronomical projection the lotus flower can become the foundation for an entire theory of the universe and an agent whereby we may perceive Truth. And first we must know that each of the petals has eighty-four thousand veins and that each vein gives off eighty-four thousand lights. Furthermore, the smallest of these flowers has a diameter of two hundred and fifty *yojana*. Thus, assuming that the *yojana* of which we read in the Holy Writings correspond to seventy-five miles each, we may conclude that a lotus flower with a diameter of nineteen thousand miles is on the small side.

Now such a flower has eighty-four thousand petals and between each of the petals there are one million jewels, each emitting one thousand lights. Above the beautifully adorned calyx of the flower rise four bejeweled pillars and each of these pillars is one hundred billion times as great as Mount Sumeru, which towers in the center of the Buddhist universe. From the pillars hang great draperies and each drapery is adorned with fifty thousand million jewels, and each jewel emits eighty-four thousand lights, and each light is composed of eighty-four thousand different golden colors, and each of those golden colors in its turn is variously transmogrified.

To concentrate on such images is known as "thinking of the Lotus Seat on which Lord Buddha sits"; and the conceptual world that hovers in the background of our story is a world imagined on such a scale.

*   *   *

The Great Priest of Shiga Temple was a man of the most eminent virtue. His eyebrows were white, and it was as much as he could do to move his old bones along as he hobbled on his stick from one part of the temple to another.

In the eyes of this learned ascetic, the world was a mere pile of rubbish. He had lived away from it for many a long year, and the little pine sapling that he had planted with his own hands on moving into his present cell had grown into a great tree whose branches swelled in the wind. A monk who had succeeded in abandoning the Floating World for so long a time must feel secure about his afterlife.

When the Great Priest saw the rich and the noble, he smiled with compassion and wondered how it was that these people did not recognize their pleasures for the empty dreams that they were. When he noticed beautiful women, his only reaction was to be moved with pity for men who still inhabited the world of delusion and who were tossed about on the waves of carnal pleasure.

From the moment that a man no longer responds in the slightest to the motives that regulate the material world, that world appears to be at complete repose. In the eyes of the Great Priest the world showed only repose; it had become a mere picture drawn on a piece of paper, a map of some foreign land. When one has attained a state of mind from which the evil passions of the present world have been so utterly winnowed, fear too is forgotten. Thus it was that the priest no longer could understand why Hell should exist. He knew beyond all peradventure that the present world no longer had any power left over him; but, as he was completely devoid of conceit, it did not occur to him that this was the effect of his own eminent virtue.

So far as his body was concerned, one might say that the priest had well nigh been deserted by his own flesh. On such occasions as he observed it—when taking a bath, for instance—he would rejoice to see how his protruding bones were precariously covered by his withered skin. Now that his body had reached this stage, he felt that he could come to terms with it, as if it belonged to someone else. Such a body, it seemed, was already more suited for the nourishment of the Pure Land than for terrestrial food and drink.

In his dreams he lived nightly in the Pure Land, and when he awoke he knew that to subsist in the present world was to be tied to a sad and evanescent dream.

In the flower-viewing season large numbers of people came from the Capital to visit the village of Shiga. This did not trouble the priest in the slightest, for he had long since transcended that state in which the clamors of the world can irritate the mind. One spring evening he left his cell, leaning on his stick, and walked down to the lake. It was the hour when dusky shadows slowly begin to thrust their way into the bright light of the afternoon. There was not the slightest ripple to disturb the surface of the water. The priest stood by himself at the edge of the lake and began to perform the holy rite of Water Contemplation.

At that moment an ox-drawn carriage, clearly belonging to a person of high rank, came round the lake and stopped close to where the priest was standing. The owner was a court lady from the Kyōgoku district of the Capital who held the exalted title of Great Imperial Concubine. This lady had come to view the springtime scenery in Shiga and now on her return she stopped the carriage and raised the blind in order to have a final look at the lake.

Unwittingly the Great Priest glanced in her direction and at once he was overwhelmed by her beauty. His eyes met hers and, as he did nothing to avert his gaze, she did not take it upon herself to turn away. It was not that her liberality of spirit was such as to allow men to gaze on her with brazen looks; but the motives of this austere old ascetic could hardly, she felt, be those of ordinary men.

After a few moments the lady pulled down the blind. Her carriage started to move and, having gone through the Shiga Pass, rolled slowly down the road that led to the Capital. Night fell and the carriage made its way toward the city along the Road of the Silver Temple. Until the carriage had become a pinprick that disappeared between the distant trees, the Great Priest stood rooted to the spot.

In the twinkling of an eye the present world had wreaked its revenge with terrible force on the priest. What he had imagined to be completely safe had collapsed in ruins.

He returned to the temple, faced the main image of Buddha, and invoked the Sacred Name. But impure thoughts now cast their opaque shadows about him. A woman's beauty, he told himself, was but a fleeting apparition, a temporary phenomenon composed of flesh——of flesh that was soon to be destroyed. Yet, try as he might to ward it off, the ineffable beauty which had overpowered him at that instant by the lake now pressed on his heart with the force of something that has come from an infinite distance. The Great Priest was not young enough, either spiritually or physically, to believe that this new feeling was simply a trick that his flesh had played on him. A man's flesh, he knew full well, could not alter so rapidly. Rather, he seemed to have been immersed in some swift, subtle poison which had abruptly transmuted his spirit.

The Great Priest had never broken his vow of chastity. The inner fight that he had waged in his youth against the demands of the flesh had made him think of women as mere carnal beings. The only real flesh was the flesh that existed in his imagination. Since, therefore, he regarded the flesh as an ideal abstraction rather than as a physical fact, he had relied on his spiritual strength to subjugate it. In this effort the priest had achieved success—success, indeed, that no one who knew him could possibly doubt.

Yet the face of the woman who had raised the carriage blind and gazed across the lake was too harmonious, too refulgent, to be designated as a mere object of flesh, and the priest did not know what name to give it. He could only think that, in order to bring about that wondrous moment, something which had for a long time lurked deceptively within him had finally revealed itself. That thing was nothing other than the present world, which until then had been at repose, but which had now suddenly lifted itself out of the darkness and begun to stir.

It was as if he had been standing by the highway that led to the Capital, with his hands firmly covering both ears, and had watched two great ox-carts rumble past each other. All of a sudden he had removed his hands and the noise from outside had surged all about him.

To perceive the ebb and flow of passing phenomena, to have their noise roaring in one's ears, was to enter into the circle of the present world. For a man like the Great Priest who had severed his relations with all outside things, this was to place himself once again into a state of relationship.

Even as he read the sutras he would time after time hear himself heaving great sighs of anguish. Perhaps nature, he thought, might serve to distract his spirit, and he gazed out the window of his cell at the mountains that towered in the distance under the evening sky. Yet his thoughts, instead of concentrating on the beauty, broke up like tufts of cloud and drifted away. He fixed his gaze on the moon, but his thoughts continued to wander as before; and when once again he went and stood before the main image in a desperate effort to regain his purity of mind, the countenance of the Buddha was transformed and looked like the face of the lady in the carriage. His universe had been imprisoned within the confines of a small circle: at one point was the Great Priest and opposite him was the Great Imperial Concubine.

*　　　*　　　*

The Great Imperial Concubine of Kyōgoku had soon forgotten about the old priest whom she had noticed gazing so intently at her by the lake at Shiga. After some time, however, a rumor came to her ears and she was reminded of the incident. One of the villagers happened to have caught sight of the Great Priest as he had stood watching the lady's carriage disappear into the distance. He had mentioned the matter to a Court gentleman who had come to Shiga for flower-viewing, and had added that since that day the priest had behaved like one crazed.

The Imperial Concubine pretended to disbelieve the rumor. The virtue of this particular priest, however, was noted throughout the Capital, and the incident was bound to feed the lady's vanity.

For she was utterly weary of the love that she received from the men of this world. The Imperial Concubine was fully aware of her own beauty, and she tended to be attracted by any force, such as religion, that treated her beauty and her high rank as things of no value. Being exceedingly bored with the present world, she believed in the Pure Land. It was inevitable that Jōdo Buddhism, which rejected all the beauty and brilliance of the visual world as being mere filth and defilement, should have a particular appeal for someone like the Imperial Concubine who was thoroughly disillusioned with the super-ficial elegance of court life—an elegance that seemed unmistakably to bespeak the Latter Days of the Law and their degeneracy.

Among those whose special interest was love, the Great Imperial Concubine was held in honor as the very personification of courtly refinement. The fact that she was known never to have given her love to any man added to this reputation. Though she performed her duties toward the Emperor with the most perfect decorum, no one for a moment believed that she loved him from her heart. The Great Imperial Concubine dreamed of a passion that lay on the boundary of the im-possible.

The Great Priest of Shiga Temple was famous for his virtue, and everyone in the Capital knew how this aged prelate had totally aban-doned the present world. All the more startling, then, was the rumor that he had been dazzled by the charms of the Imperial Concubine and that for her sake he had sacrificed the future world. To give up the joys of the Pure Land which were so close at hand—there could be no greater sacrifice than this, no greater gift.

The Great Imperial Concubine was utterly indifferent to the charms of the young rakes who flocked about the court and of the handsome noblemen who came her way. The physical attributes of men no longer meant anything to her. Her only concern was to find a man who could give her the strongest and deepest possible love. A woman with such aspirations is a truly terrifying creature. If she is a mere courtesan, she will no doubt be satisfied with wordly wealth. The Great Imperial Concubine, however, already enjoyed all those things that the wealth of the world can provide. The man whom she awaited must offer her the wealth of the future world.

The rumors of the Great Priest's infatuation spread throughout the court. In the end the story was even told half-jokingly to the Emperor himself. The Great Concubine took no pleasure in this bantering gossip and preserved a cool, indifferent mien. As she was well aware, there were two reasons that the people of the court could joke freely about a matter which would normally have been forbidden: first, by referring to the Great Priest's love they were paying a compliment to the beauty of the woman who could inspire even an ecclesiastic of such great virtue to forsake his meditations; secondly, everyone fully realized that the old man's love for the noblewoman could never possibly be requited.

The Great Imperial Concubine called to mind the face of the old priest whom she had seen through her carriage window. It did not bear the remotest resemblance to the face of any of the men who had loved her until then. Strange it was that love should spring up in the heart of a man who did not have the slightest qualification for being loved. The lady recalled such phrases as "my love forlorn and without hope" that were widely used by poetasters in the palace when they wished to awaken some sympathy in the hearts of their indifferent paramours. Compared to the hopeless situation in which the Great Priest now found himself, the state of the least fortunate of these elegant lovers was almost enviable, and their poetic tags struck her now as mere trappings of wordly dalliance, inspired by vanity and utterly devoid of pathos.

At this point it will be clear to the reader that the Great Imperial Concubine was not, as was so widely believed, the personification of courtly elegance, but, rather, a person who found the real relish of life in the knowledge of being loved. Despite her high rank, she was first of all a woman; and all the power and authority in the world seemed to her empty things if they were bereft of this knowledge. The men about her might devote themselves to struggles for political power; but she dreamed of subduing the world by different means, by purely feminine means. Many of the women whom she had known had taken the tonsure and retired from the world. Such women struck her as laughable. For, whatever a woman may say about abandoning the world, it is almost impossible for her to give up the things that she possesses. Only men are really capable of giving up what they possess.

That old priest by the lake had at a certain stage in his life given up the Floating World and all its pleasures. In the eyes of the Imperial Concubine he was far more of a man than all the nobles whom she knew the lotus flowers, she had become vaster than Mount Sumeru, vaster than an entire realm.

The more the Great Priest turned his love into something impossible, the more deeply was he betraying the Buddha. For the impossibility of this love had become bound up with the impossibility of attaining enlightenment. The more he thought of his love as hopeless, the firmer grew the fantasy that supported it and the deeper rooted became his impure thoughts. So long as he regarded his love as being even remotely feasible, it was paradoxically possible for him to resign himself; but now that the Great Concubine had grown into a fabulous and utterly unattainable creature, the priest's love became motionless like a great, stagnant lake which firmly, obdurately, covers the earth's surface.

He hoped that somehow he might see the lady's face once more, yet he feared that when he met her that figure, which had now become like a giant lotus, would crumble away without a trace. If that were to happen, he would without doubt be saved. Yes, this time he was bound to attain enlightenment. And the very prospect filled the Great Priest with fear and awe.

The priest's lonely love had begun to devise strange, self-deceiving guiles, and when at length he reached the decision to go and see the lady, he was under the delusion that he had almost recovered from the illness that was searing his body. The bemused priest even mistook the joy that accompanied his decision for relief at having finally escaped from the trammels of his love.

*　　　*　　　*

None of the Great Concubine's people found anything especially strange in the sight of an old priest standing silently in the corner of the garden, leaning on a stick and gazing somberly at the residence. Ascetics and beggars frequently stood outside the great houses of the Capital and waited for alms. One of the ladies in attendance mentioned the matter to her mistress. The Great Imperial Concubine casually glanced through the blind that separated her from the garden. There in the shadow of the fresh green foliage stood a withered old priest with faded black robes and bowed head. For some time the lady looked at him. When she realized that this was without any question the priest whom she had seen by the lake at Shiga, her pale face turned paler still.

After a few moments of indecision, she gave orders that the priest's presence in her garden should be ignored. Her attendants bowed and withdrew.

Now for the first time the lady fell prey to uneasiness. In her lifetime she had seen many people who had abandoned the world, but never before had she laid eyes on someone who had abandoned the future world. The sight was ominous and inexpressibly fearful. All the pleasure that her imagination had conjured up from the idea of the priest's love disappeared in a flash. Much as he might have surrendered the future world on her behalf, that world, she now realized, would never pass into her own hands.

The Great Imperial Concubine looked down at her elegant clothes and at her beautiful hands, and then she looked across the garden at the uncomely features of the old priest and at his shabby robes. There was a horrible fascination in the fact that a connection should exist between them.

How different it all was from the splendid vision! The Great Priest seemed now like a person who had hobbled out of Hell itself. Nothing remained of that man of virtuous presence who had trailed the brightness of the Pure Land behind him. The brilliance which had resided within him and which had called to mind the glory of the Pure Land had vanished utterly. Though this was certainly the man who had stood by Shiga Lake, it was at the same time a totally different person.

Like most people of the court, the Great Imperial Concubine tended to be on her guard against her own emotions, especially when she was confronted with something that could be expected to affect her deeply. Now on seeing this evidence of the Great Priest's love, she felt disheartened at the thought that the consummate passion of which she had dreamed during all these years should assume so colorless a form.

When the priest had finally limped into the Capital leaning on his stick, he had almost forgotten his exhaustion. Secretly he made his way into the grounds of the Great Imperial Concubine's residence at Kyōgoku and looked across the garden. Behind those blinds, he thought, was sitting none other than the lady whom he loved.

future world. Though he saw the figure of the maid approaching from the residence into the dusky garden, it did not occur to him that what he had been awaiting was finally at hand.

The maid delivered her mistress' message. When she had finished, the priest uttered a dreadful, almost inhuman, cry. The maid tried to lead him by the hand, but he pulled away and walked by himself toward the house with fantastically swift, firm steps.

It was dark on the other side of the blind and from outside it was impossible to see the lady's form. The priest knelt down and, covering his face with his hands, he wept. For a long time he stayed there without a word and his body shook convulsively.

Then in the dawn darkness a white hand gently emerged from behind the lowered blind. The priest of the Shiga Temple took it in his own hands and pressed it to his forehead and cheek.

The Great Imperial Concubine of Kyōgoku felt a strange, cold hand touching her hand. At the same time she was aware of a warm moisture. Her hand was being bedewed by someone else's tears. Yet when the pallid shafts of morning light began to reach her through the blind, the lady's fervent faith imbued her with a wonderful inspiration: she became convinced that the unknown hand which touched hers belonged to none other than the Buddha.

Then the great vision sprang up anew in the lady's heart: the emerald earth of the Pure Land, the millions of seven-jeweled towers, the angels playing music, the golden ponds strewn with silver sand, the resplendent lotus, and the sweet voices of the Kalavinkas—all this was born afresh. If this was the Pure Land that she was to inherit—and so she now believed—why should she not accept the Great Priest's love?

She waited for the man with the hands of Buddha to ask her to raise the blind that separated her from him. Presently he would ask her; and then she would remove the barrier and her incomparably beautiful body would appear before him as it had on that day by the edge of the lake at Shiga; and she would invite him to come in.

The Great Imperial Concubine waited.

But the priest of Shiga Temple did not utter a word. He asked her for nothing. After a while his old hands relaxed their grip and the lady's snow-white hand was left alone in the dawn light. The priest departed. The heart of the Great Imperial Concubine turned cold.

A few days later a rumor reached the Court that the Great Priest's spirit had achieved its final liberation in his cell at Shiga. At this news the lady of Kyōgoku set to copying the sutras in roll after roll of beautiful writing.

SELECTED BIBLIOGRAPHY

GIVEN HERE is a listing of selected translations into English of works by the authors included in the present anthology. Unless otherwise indicated, all the works are short stories. The authors are arranged alphabetically, with the works of each listed in the order of the first Japanese publication. Note that the stories in the present anthology have not been included. The following abbreviations of frequently cited works have been used:

EACJ—*Eminent Authors of Contemporary Japan: One-Act Plays and Short Stories*, ed. Eric S. Bell and Ukai Eiji. Kaitakusha, Tokyo, 1930–31 (2 vols.)

"Hell Screen"—*Hell Screen and Other Stores*, ed. W.H.H. Norman.
Hokuseidō, Tokyo, 1948

JQ—*Japan Quarterly*.   Asahi Shimbun-sha, Tokyo, since 1954

MJL—*Modern Japanese Literature: Anthology from 1868 to the Present*, ed. Donald Keene.   Grove Press, New York, 1956

"Paulownia"—*Paulownia: Seven Stories from Contemporary Japanese Writers*, ed. Takemoto Torao.   Duffield, New York, 1918

"Rashomon"—*Rashomon and Other Stories*, ed. Kojima Takashi.
Charles E. Tuttle Co., Tokyo, 1952, and Liveright, New York, 1952

RTJ—*Representative Tales of Japan*, ed. Miyamori Asatarō.
Sankō Shoten, Tokyo, 1914 (2 vols.)

SMJW—*Selections from Modern Japanese Writers*, ed. Arthur L. Sadler.
Australasian Medical Publishing Co., Sydney, 1943

SJSS—*The Heart Is Alone: A Selection of 20th-Century Japanese Short Stories*, ed. Richard N. McKinnon.   Hokuseidō, Tokyo, 1957

"Tales Grotesque"—*Tales Grotesque and Curious*, ed. Glenn W. Shaw.
Hokuseidō, Tokyo, 1930

"Three Treasures"—*The Three Treasures and Other Stories for Children*, ed. Sasaki Takamasa.   Hokuseidō, Tokyo, 1944

503

WIE—*The Writing of Idiomatic English,* ed. S. G. Brickley.   Tokyo, 1951
"Young Forever"—*Young Forever and Five Other Novelettes by Contemporary Japanese Authors,* ed. Japan Writers' Society.   Hokuseidō, Tokyo, 1941.

AKUTAGAWA RYŪNOSUKÉ

RASHOMON (*Rashōmon,* 1915), tr. Kojima—"Rashomon"
LICE (*Shirami,* 1916), tr. Shaw—"Tales Grotesque"
MENSURA ZOILI (*Mensura Zoili,* 1916), tr. W. Norman—"Hell Screen"
SENNIN (*Sennin,* 1916), tr. Sasaki—"Three Treasures"
THE HANDKERCHIEF (*Hankechi,* 1916), tr. Shaw—"Tales Grotesque"
THE NOSE (*Hana,* 1916), tr. Ivan Morris—JQ, II, 4
THE PIPE (*Kiseru,* 1916), tr. Shaw—"Tales Grotesque"
THE WINE WORM (*Sakamushi,* 1916), tr. Shaw—"Tales Grotesque"
YAM GRUEL (*Imogayu,* 1916), tr. Kojima—"Rashomon"
TOBACCO AND THE DEVEL (*Tabako to Akuma,* 1917), tr. Shaw—
                                                            "Tales Grotesque"
HELL SCREEN (*Jigokuhen,* 1918), tr. W.H.H. Norman—MJL
JASHUMON (*Jashūmon,* 1918), tr. Norman—"Hell Screen"
KESA AND MORITO (*Kesa to Moritō,* 1918), tr. Howard Hibbett—MJL
STORY OF YONOSUKE (*Yonosuke no Hanashi,* 1918), tr. Kojima Takashi.
                                            Pacific Spectator, no. 2, 1955
THE MARTYR (*Hōkyōnin no Shi,* 1918), tr. Kojima—"Rashomon"
THE SPIDER'S THREAD (*Kumo no Ito,* 1918), tr. Shaw—"Tales Grotesque"
THE STORY OF A FALLEN HEAD (*Kubi ga Ochita Hanashi,* 1918), tr. Bell and Ukai
                                                            —EACJ
MORI SENSEI (*Mōri Sensei,* 1919), tr. Shaw—"Tales Grotesque"
THE DRAGON (*Tatsu,* 1919), tr. Kojima—"Rashomon"
THE MANDARIN ORANGES (*Mikan,* 1919), tr. T. Yuasa.
                                    Contemporary Japan, March, 1938
MAGIC (*Majutsu,* 1920), tr. Sasaki—"Three Treasures"
THE AUTUMN (*Aki,* 1920), tr. Bell and Ukai—EACJ
THE BALL (*Butōkai,* 1920), tr. Shaw—"Tales Grotesque"
TU TSUCHUN (*To Shishun,* 1920), tr. Bell and Ukai—EACJ
THE GOD OF AGNI (*Aguni no Kami,* 1921), tr. Sasaki—"Three Treasures"
FLATCAR (*Torokko,* 1922), tr. McKinnon—SJSS
IN A GROVE (*Yabu no Naka,* 1922), tr. Kojima—"Rashomon"
KAPPA (*Kappa,* novel, 1922), tr. Shiojiri Seiichi.   Akitaya, Osaka, 1947
OTOMI'S VIRTUE (*Otomi no Teishō,* 1922), tr. Nishida Kazuo.
                                            Asia Scene, I, 2, 1955
THE THREE TREASURES (*Mitsu no Takara,* 1923), tr. Sasaki—"Three Treasures"
WHITIE THE DOG (*Shiro,* 1923), tr. Sasaki—"Three Treasures"
A CLOD OF EARTH (*Ikkai no Tsuchi,* 1924), tr. McKinnon—SJSS

SAN SEBASTIEN: A SCENARIO (*Yūwaku*, 1927), tr. Arthur Waley.
Horizon, September, 1949
THE BADGER (*Jujina*, 1928), tr. Shaw—"Tales Grotesque"

DAZAI OSAMU

OF WOMEN (*Mesu ni tsuite*, 1936), tr. Edward Seidensticker.
Encounter I, 1 (1953)
I ACCUSE (*Kakemoni Uttae*, 1940), tr. Katayama Tadao. *The Reeds*, IV, 1958
THE CRIMINAL (*Hannin*, 1940), tr. Kojima Takashi.
English and American Literature, no. 2, Meiji University, Tokyo, 1956
OSAN (*Osan*, 1947), Edward Seidensticker—JQ, IV
THE SETTING SUN (*Shayō*, novel, 1947), tr. Donald Keene.
New Directions, New York, 1956
VILLON'S WIFE (*Villon no Tsuma*, 1947), tr. Keene—MJL
CHERRIES (*Ōtō*, 1948), Edward Seidensticker. *Encounter* I, 1 (1953)
NO LONGER HUMAN (*Ningen Shikkaku*, novel, 1948), tr. Donald Keene.
New Directions, New York, 1958

HAYASHI FUMIKO

LATE CHRYSANTHEMUM (*Bangiku*, 1948), tr. John Bester—JQ, III, 4
FLOATING CLOUD (*Ukigumo*, novel, 1951), tr. Koitabashi Yoshiyuki.
Information Publishing, Tokyo, 1958

HIRABAYASHI TAIKO

THE GODDESS OF CHILDREN (*Kishimojin*, 1946) tr. Murayama Ken.
Pacific Spectator, Autumn, 1952

IBUSÉ MASUJI

THE SALAMANDER (*Sanshō-uo*, 1923), tr. Katayama Tatsuo. *The Reeds*, II
JOHN MANJIRO: THE CAST-AWAY, HIS LIFE AND ADVENTURES (*Manjirō Hyōryū Ki*, novel, 1938), tr. Kaneko Hisakazu. Hokuseidō, Tokyo, 1940
A FAR-WORSHIPPING COMMANDER (*Yōhai Taichō*, 1950), tr. Glenn W. Shaw—
JQ, I, 1
THE CRAZY IRIS (*Kakitsubata*, 1951), tr. Ivan Morris. *Encounter*, May, 1956
SWAN SONG (*Hakuchō no Uta*, 1954), tr. Geoffrey Sargent.
The Rising Generation, Vol. 102 (9–12), 1956
NO CONSULATIONS TODAY (*Honjitsu Kyūshin*, 1955), tr. Edward Seidensticker—
JQ, VIII, 1

INOUÉ YASUSHI

THE HUNTING GUN (*Ryōjū*, 1949), tr. Yokoö Sadamichi and Sanford Goldstein. Tuttle; Rutland, Vermont, and Tokyo, Japan, 1961
THE AZALEAS OF HIRA (*Hira no Shakunage*, 1954), tr. Edward Seidenticker— JQ, II, 3

KAWABATA YASUNARI

THE IZU DANCER (*Izu no Odoriko*, 1925), tr. Edward Seidensticker.
Perspective of Japan, New York, 1954
SNOW COUNTRY (*Yukiguni*, novel, 1935, 1947), tr. Edward Seidensticker.
Knopf, New York, 1955
THE MOLE (*Hokuro no Nikki*, 1940), tr. Edward Seidensticker—MJL
THOUSAND CRANES (*Sembazuru*, novel, 1955), tr. Edward Seidensticker.
Knopf, New York, 1959

KIKUCHI KAN

THE MADMAN ON THE ROOF (*Okujō no Kyōjin*, one-act play, 1916), tr. Iwasaki Yozan and Glenn Hughes—MJL
LAUGHING AT THE DEAD (*Shisha wo Warau*, 1918), tr. Michael Y. Matsudaira—SJSS
THE SUPREME REALM BEYOND THE PASSION (*Onshū no Kanatani*, 1919), tr. Andō Kanichi.
Kenkyūsha, Tokyo, 1922
TOJURO'S LOVE AND FOUR OTHER PLAYS (*Tōjurō no Koi*, etc.), tr. Glenn W. Shaw.
Hokuseidō, Tokyo, 1925
LAUGHTER (*Warai*, 1920), tr. Frank Daniels.
Adam, no. 261, 1957
THE LOVE MATCH (*Renai Kekkon*, 1926), tr. Yonezawa Naoto.
Contemporary Japan, March, 1933
VICTORY OR DEFEAT (*Shōhai*, novel, 1931), tr. Nishi Kiichi.
Kairyūdō, Tokyo, 1934

MISHIMA YUKIO

CONFESSIONS OF A MASK (*Kamen no Kokuhaku*, novel, 1949), tr. Meredith Weatherby.
New Directions, New York, 1956
DEATH IN MIDSUMMER (*Manatsu no Shi*, 1952), tr. Edward Seidensticker—
JQ, III, 3
TWILIGHT SUNFLOWER (*Yoru no Himawari*, play, 1953), tr. Shinozaki Shigehō and Virgil A. Warren.
Hokuseidō, Tokyo, 1958
FIVE MODERN MODERN NO PLAYS (*Kindai Nōgakushū*, 1950–55), tr. Donald Keene.
Knopf, New York, 1957

REVENGE (*Fukushū*, 1954), tr. Grace Suzuki.
Ukiyo: Eleven Short Stories of Post-War Japan, Tokyo, 1954
THE SOUND OF WAVES (*Shiosai*, novel, 1954), tr. Meredith Weatherby.
Knopf, New York, 1956
THE TEMPLE OF THE GOLDEN PAVILION (*Kinkakuji*, novel, 1956), tr. Ivan Morris.
Knopf, New York, 1959

MORI ŌGAI

CUPS (*Sakazuki*, 1910), tr. Miyamori—RTJ
HANAKO (*Hanako*, 1910), tr. Takemoto—"Paulownia"
THE PIER (*Sambashi*, 1910), tr. Takemoto—"Paulownia"
THE WILD GEESE (*Gan*, novel, 1911–13), tr. Ochiai Kingo and Sanford Goldstein.
Tuttle; Rutland, Vermont, and Tokyo, 1959
THE WILD GOOSE (*Gan*, extract from novel, 1911–13), tr. Burton Watson—
MJL
AS IF (*Kano yō ni*, 1912), tr. Gregg Sinclair and Suita Kazo.
Tokyo People, Keibunkan, Tokyo, 1925
SANSHŌ-DAYŪ (*Sanshō Dayū*, novel, 1915), tr. Fukuda Tsutomu.
Hokuseidō, Tokyo, 1952
TAKASEBUNE (*Takasebune*, 1916), tr. Garland W. Paschall—SJSS

NAGAI KAFŪ

THE FOX (*Kitsune*, 1909), tr. Miyamori—RTJ
THE RIVER SUMIDA (*Sumidagawa*, extract from novel, 1909), tr. Keene—
MJL
THE BILL COLLECTING (*Kaketori*, 1912), tr. Taketomo—"Paulownia"
THE TWO WIVES (*Futarizuma*, 1922), tr. Brickley—WIE
A STRANGE TALE FROM EAST OF THE RIVER (*Bokutō Kidan*, extract from novel, 1937), tr. Edward Seidensticker—JQ, V, 2

NAGAI TATSUO

THE WHITE FENCE (*Shiroi Saku*, 1952), tr. William L. Clark.
Various Kinds of Bugs, Kenkyūsha, Tokyo, 1958

NAKAJIMA TON

THE EXPERT (*Meijinden*, 1942), tr. Ivan Morris.
Encounter, May, 1958, and *Harper's Bazaar*, August, 1958

NIWA FUMIO

A TOUCH OF SHYNESS (*Shūchi*, 1951), tr. Edward Seidensticker—JQ, II, 1

OGAWA MIMEI

A WINTER'S NIGHT'S EPISODE IN ECHIGO (*Echigo no Fuyu*, 1910), tr. Miyamori—
RTJ
ROSE WITCH AND OTHER STORIES, tr. Myrtle B. McKinney and Seison N.
Yoshioka.   Overland Publishing Co., California, 1925
THE TIPSY STAR AND OTHER TALES, tr. Akiyama Yoshiko.
Hokuseidō, Tokyo, 1957

SHIGA NAOYA

THE RAZOR (*Kamisori*, 1910), tr. M. J. Mathy.
Monumenta Nipponica, XIII (3–4), Tokyo, 1957
AN OLD MAN (*Rōjin*, 1911), tr. Sadler—SMJW
FUSUMA (*Fusuma*, 1911), tr. A. L. Sadler.   *The Far East*, XX, 452
HAN'S CRIME (*Han no Hanzai*, 1913), tr. Ivan Morris—MJL
AKANISHI KAKITA (*Akanishi Kakita*, 1917), tr. Haneda Saburō.
The Reeds, Vol. II
ARAGINU (*Araginu*, 1917), tr. Bell and Ukai—EACJ
AT KINOSAKI (*Kinosaki nite*, 1917), tr. Edward Seidensticker—MJL
DEATH OF A HERMIT CRAB (*Yadokari no Shi*, 1917), tr. Brickley—WIE
THE CASE OF SASAKI (*Sasaki no Baai*, 1917), tr. A. L. Sadler.
The Far East, XXIV, 503
THE PATRON SAINT (*Kozō no Kamisama*, 1920), tr. Michael Y. Matsudaira—
SJSS
A GRAY MOON (*Haiiro no Tsuki*, 1946), tr. Haneda Saburō.
The Reeds, Vol. II

TANIZAKI JUNICHIRŌ

A SPRING-TIME CASE (*Otsuya-goroshi*, novel, 1915), tr. Iwado Zenichi.
Tokyo, 1927
THE HOUSE WHERE I WAS BORN (*Umareta Ie*, 1921), tr. Brickley—WIE
THE WHITE FOX (*Shirogitsune no Yu*, one-act play, 1923), tr. Bell and Ukai—
EACJ
SOME PREFER NETTLES (*Tade Kuu Mushi*, novel, 1928), tr. Edward Seidensticker.
Knopf, New York, 1955
ASHIKARI AND THE STORY OF SHUNKIN (*Ashikari, Shunkinshō*, 2 short novels,
1932, 1933), tr. Roy Humpherson and Okita Hajime.
Hokuseidō, Tokyo, 1936

IN PRAISE OF SHADOWS (*Inei Raisan,* essay, 1934), tr. Edward Seidensticker.
Atlantic Monthly, January, 1955

THE MAKIOKA SISTERS (*Sasameyuki,* novel, 1942–48), tr. Edward Seidensticker.
Knopf, New York, 1957

THE MOTHER OF CAPTAIN SHIGEMOTO (*Shōshō Shigemoto no Haha,* extract from novel, 1950), tr. Edward Seidensticker—MJL

THE KEY (*Kagi,* novel, 1956), tr. Howard Hibbett.   Knopf, New York, 1961

TOKUDA SHŪSEI

THE SHOIAGE (*Shoiage,* 1908), tr. Miyamori—RTJ

YOKOMITSU RIICHI

SPRING CAME ON A HORSE-DRAWN CART (*Haru wa Basha ni Notte,* 1926), tr.
Mary M. Suzuki—SJSS

TIME (*Jikan,* 1931), tr. Keene—MJL

YOUNG FOREVER (*Seishu,* 1937), tr. Japan Writers' Society—"Young Forever"

INDEX OF AUTHORS
SHOWING STORY TITLES AND DATES

Akutagawa Ryūnosuké (1892–1927): "Autumn Mountain"
(Shūzanzu, 1921), page 173

Dazai Osamu (1909–48): "The Courtesy Call" *(Shinyū Kōkan, 1946), 464*

Hayama Yoshiki (1894–1945): "Letter Found in a Cement-Barrel"
(Sementodaru no Naka no Tegami, 1926), 204

Hayashi Fumiko (1904–51), "Downtown" *(Shitamachi, 1948), 349*

Hirabayashi Taiko (b. 1905): "A Man's Life" *(Hito no Inochi, 1950), 365*

Ibusé Masuji (b. 1898): "The Charcoal Bus" *(Noriai Jidōsha, 1952), 211*

Inoué Yasushi (b. 1907): "Shotgun" *(Ryōjū, 1949), 416*

Itō Einosuké (b. 1903): "Nightingale" *(Uguisu, 1938), 258*

Kawabata Yasunari or Kōsei (b. 1899): "The Moon on the Water"
(Suigetsu, 1953), 245

Kikuchi Kan or Hiroshi (1888–1948): "On the Conduct of Lord Tadanao"
(Tadanao-kyō Gyōjōki, 1918), 101

Mishima Yukio (b. 1925): "The Priest and His Love"
(Shigadera Shōnin no Koi, 1954), 481

Mori Ōgai (1862–1922): "Under Reconstruction" *(Fushinchū, 1910), 35*

Murō Saisei (b. 1889): "Brother and Sister" *(Ani Imōto, 1934), 144*

Nagai Kafū (1879–1959): "Hydrangea" *(Ajisai, 1931), 65*

Nagai Tatsuo (b. 1904): "Morning Mist" *(Asagiri, 1950), 302*

Nakajima Ton or Atsushi (1909–42): "Tiger-Poet" *(Sangetsuki, 1942), 452*

Niwa Fumio (b. 1904): "The Hateful Age" *(Iyagarase no Nenrei, 1947), 320*

Ogawa Mimei (b. 1892): "The Handstand" *(Kūchū no Geitō, 1920), 185*

Sakaguchi Ango (1906–54): "The Idiot" *(Hakuchi, 1946), 383*

Satō Haruo (b. 1892): "The House of a Spanish Dog"
(Supein-inu no Ie, 1916), 162

Satomi Ton (b. 1888): "The Camellia" *(Tsubaki, 1923), 138*

Shiga Naoya (b. 1883): "Seibei's Gourds" *(Seibei to Hyōtan, 1913), 81*

Tanizaki Junichirō (b. 1886): "Tattoo" *(Irezumi, 1910), 90*

Tokuda Shūsei (1870–1943): "Order of the White Paulownia"
(Kunshō, 1935), 45

Yokomitsu Riichi (1898–1947): "Machine" *(Kikai, 1930), 223*

INDEX OF TRANSLATORS
SHOWING STORIES TRANSLATED

MORRIS, IVAN—Doctorate in classical Japanese literature from the School of Oriental Studies, London University, 1951. Author of *Nationalism and the Right Wing in Japan,* 1960, and translator of several works of Japanese literature. Presently lecturing on Japanese history and literature at Columbia University.—

Akutagawa Ryūnosuké: "Autumn Mountain," *page 173*
Dazai Osamu: "The Courtesy Call," *464*
Hayama Yoshiki: "Letter Found in a Cement-Barrel," *204*
Hayashi Fumiko: "Downtown," *349*
Ibusé Masuji: "The Charcoal Bus," *211*
Mishima Yukio: "The Priest and His Love," *481*
Mori Ōgai: "Under Reconstruction," *35*
Nakajima Ton: "Tiger-Poet," *452*
Niwa Fumio: "The Hateful Age," *320*
Ogawa Mimei: "The Handstand," *185*
Shiga Naoya: "Seibei's Gourds," *81*
Tanizaki Junichirō: "Tattoo," *90*
Tokuda Shūsei: "Order of the White Paulownia," *45*

SAITŌ, GEORGE—Graduate of Kyoto Imperial University, 1943. Translator of numerous works from European languages into Japanese and from Japanese into English. Presently Cultural Adviser at the American Embassy, Tokyo.

Hirabayashi Taiko: "A Man's Life," *365*
Inoué Yasushi: "Shotgun," *416*
Kawabata Yasunari: "The Moon on the Water," *245*
Sakaguchi Ango: "The Idiot," *383*
Satō Haruo: "The House of a Spanish Dog," *162*

SARGENT, GEOFFREY—Doctorate in Japanese studies from Cambridge University. Taught in Japan 1951–58. Presently teaching Japanese literature at the University of Sydney, Australia.—

Itō Einosuké· "Nightingale," *258*
Kikuchi Kan: "On the Conduct of Lord Tadanao," *101*

SEIDENSTICKER, EDWARD—Well-known American critic and writer on the Far East, resident in Japan. Translator of numerous works of Japanese literature, both classic and modern. Author of the Japan volume in the *Time-Life* series.—

Murō Saisei: "Brother and Sister," *144*
Nagai Kafū: "Hydrangea," *65*
Nagai Tatsuo: "Morning Mist," *302*
Satomi Ton: "The Camellia," *138*
Yokomitsu Riichi: "Machine," *223*